Moral Problems

Moral Problems

A Collection of Philosophical Essays

Third Edition

Edited by

James Rachels

University of Alabama in Birmingham

Harper & Row, Publishers

New York   Hagerstown   Philadelphia
San Francisco   London

Sponsoring Editors: Ann Ludwig and Sharmon Hilfinger
Project Editor: Julie Segedy
Production Manager: Marian Hartsough
Designers: Thomas E. Dorsaneo & Robert Devoluy
Cover Artist: Robert Devoluy
Compositor: Typesetting Services of California
Printer & Binder: Halliday Lithograph

MORAL PROBLEMS: A Collection of Philosophical Essays,
Third Edition

Library of Congress Cataloging in Publication Data

Rachels, James, 1941–   comp.
  Moral problems.

  Includes bibliographies.
  1. Social ethics. I. Title.
HM216.R24   1979   170'.8   78-23885
ISBN 0-06-387100-9

Contents

Preface

Ten years ago, moral philosophy was still concerned with the analysis of language and the merits of general ethical theories. College courses in ethics were often limited to this arena, or to the thoughts of the great philosophers of the past. A few philosophers, however, began to write on more contemporary moral issues, such as abortion, war, and racial prejudice. While these essays were few and far between—hardly noticeable amid more traditional writings—they were brought together in the first edition of *Moral Problems*

A great deal has changed since then. Today it is not at all unusual for moral philosophers to concentrate their writing on current issues of controversy, and it is the rule—not the exception—for college courses in ethics to include such discussions.

The third edition of *Moral Problems* continues to explore contemporary moral issues, each of which must be critically analyzed to discover what reasons there are for accepting one conclusion over another. For example, is it *right* to have an economic system that allows some people to become rich while others remain poor? Are we *justified* in spending money for luxuries while others are starving? What are our *duties* to other people? What *principles* should we follow? The readings in this text offer alternative answers to these questions, arguing for and against various possible views. Because each unit is independent, beginning with an introduction to identify the main philosophical questions involved and concluding with some suggestions for further readings, they may be read in any order.

The choice of topics for inclusion in any anthology is not easy. This revised and updated edition of *Moral Problems* contains materials on several topics not covered in earlier editions—such as fetal research, hunger and poverty, and euthanasia. As ever, I have sought essays in which the consideration of practical moral problems leads to more abstract issues in ethical theory. The authors of these essays have not avoided the hard questions of theory. Indeed, that is what makes the essays philosophical, while the practical issues give the essays their focus and point. Of course the choice of topics is further dictated by the availability of readings: In the unit on "Prejudice and Discrimination," for example, I could find no appropriate selection treating discrimination against homosexuals.

Many people have made helpful suggestions about the contents of this volume, but two deserve special recognition: George Graham and Cora Diamond each called my attention to an essay that is included, which I otherwise might not have seen.

James Rachels
April 1978

Part I
Prejudice and Discrimination

The American civil rights movement began in Montgomery, Alabama, in 1955, when Dr. Martin Luther King, Jr., a local minister, led a boycott aimed at desegregating public buses. At that time virtually all public facilities in the South were segregated by race. In addition, blacks were unofficially barred from voting, and were denied decent jobs, housing, and medical care. The income of black families was but a small fraction of that of white families. The same pattern of racial discrimination was repeated elsewhere in the country, but was most prominent in the South because of the cultural heritage of slavery and the large numbers of black people who lived there. Following the Montgomery bus boycott, there were other challenges to segregation in the South: massive protest demonstrations, sit-ins at segregated facilities, voter registration drives, economic boycotts, and the famous "Freedom Rides" on integrated interstate buses. Many victories were won, but there were also many civil rights workers, and many black citizens, who were terrorized, beaten, and killed.

In the early 1960s Richard Wasserstrom, now a Professor of Law and Philosophy at the University of California, Los Angeles, worked at the Tuskegee Institute in Alabama and was active in the civil rights movement in that state. In 1964 he was invited to address the American Philosophical Association on the subject of human rights and racial discrimination. The paper that Wasserstrom wrote for the occasion is the first selection in this unit. In it he develops the idea that human rights are rights that all people have simply by virtue of being human: freedom and well-being are conspicuous examples. Racial discrimination, he argues, typically involves the denial that members of one race have such rights. This, in turn, leads to the attitude that, although perhaps "we" ought to treat "them" decently, they have no right to decent treatment—what they get is due to our generosity rather than their rights. This sort of malignant pater-

nalism, Wasserstrom notes, ultimately leads to the implicit denial that members of the oppressed race are even human.

The success of the civil rights movement gave a fresh impetus to other liberation movements, the most notable of which was the women's movement. A number of feminist leaders began to suggest that the treatment of women in American society was comparable in many ways to the treatment of blacks. Women, like blacks, were denied jobs and educational opportunities simply because they were women, even though they could do the jobs as well as men, and when women did hold the same jobs as men, they were not paid as much. In general, women were under-represented in every part of American life, except perhaps as school teachers, secretaries, and nurses. This, it was urged, was due to "sexist" prejudice which was analogous to, and ran at least as deep as, racial prejudice in our society. What was needed was thought to be not merely the piecemeal correction of certain injustices against women, but the thorough reorganization of perceptions and attitudes so that no one would be cast into a role on the basis of his or her sex, making it impossible to have a satisfying life of one's own devising.

Two selections in this chapter treat aspects of the controversy over sexism. In "Women's Liberation" Betty Roszak recounts the ways that women are discriminated against; in her analysis, the evils of sexism are at least as great as the evils of racism and, in order to deal with them, a fundamental change in society's thinking patterns is required. However, Ann Dummett, a British writer, argues that the comparison of sexism with racism is a "false analogy." Although Dummett agrees that women are often treated unjustly, and that the correction of these injustices is an important social problem, she rejects much of the ideology commonly associated with the women's movement.

One of the most controversial issues emerging from

3

these two movements is the question of "reverse discrimination." Granted that blacks and women have been discriminated against—and are still being discriminated against—what is to be done about it? Some people believe it is enough that the discrimination simply be stopped; others argue that this is not enough, that in order to combat the effects of past discrimination, we should temporarily discriminate in favor of blacks and women. For example, because of past discrimination against blacks, there are relatively few black physicians. It is argued that we ought now to give black medical school applicants special consideration. Similarly, if the result of past prejudice is that a police department has no black officers above a certain rank, it ought specifically to promote some black officers to those ranks.

A number of arguments can be given in favor of such policies. For one thing, black policemen and doctors are likely to serve black citizens more effectively because they can better understand the problems of black citizens. Therefore it is desirable to get more blacks into those roles as quickly as possible. Another reason is that it is necessary to have visibly successful blacks and women in previously inaccessible positions to serve as "role models" for younger blacks and women, who may aspire to such positions.

Programs of reverse discrimination are, in fact, now fairly common in the United States. Because the words "reverse discrimination" have unfavorable connotations, however, these programs are usually called by other names, such as "equal opportunity" or "affirmative action." The justice of these programs is challenged on the grounds that the white males who are disadvantaged by them are treated unfairly. For example, a student named Allan Bakke was denied admission to the University of California Medical School at Davis, even though several less qualified black students were admitted. Bakke brought suit against the school, arguing that his rights had been violated, for, he contended, he had been discriminated against solely because of his race; if he had been a minority member, he contended, he would have been admitted. Why isn't this equally as reprehensible as denying admission to someone because they are black? In 1978 the U.S. Supreme Court ruled (by a vote of 5–4) that Bakke had indeed been unfairly discriminated against. However, the Court carefully refrained from condemning all "affirmative action" programs; so there are many legal issues here still undecided.

The moral question, however, is this: is it really unjust to give preferential treatment to members of disadvantaged groups, as a way of rectifying past injustices? In his paper on "Justifying Reverse Discrimination in Employment," George Sher takes up this issue. Sher argues that reverse discrimination need not be unjust, if it serves to neutralize the competitive disadvantages which blacks have as the result of past privations. His argument is reminiscent of Lyndon Johnson's famous defense of affirmative action, in his commencement speech at Howard University in 1965. Johnson said, "You do not take a person who, for years, has been hobbled by chains and liberate him, bring him up to the starting line of a race and then say, 'You are free to compete with all the others' and still justly believe that you have been completely fair." The point is that if such a person were given a head start, it would make the race more, not less, fair. Similarly, if a person has been made less able to compete for jobs or educational opportunities by past privations, it does not make the competition less fair if he is given a sufficient edge to compensate for the extra advantages others have enjoyed. Although Sher agrees with this in the abstract, he is sceptical about whether we can apply it fairly in actual practice.

One principle which emerges from the discussions of racism and sexism is that we ought not to treat individuals differently unless there is a relevant difference between them. Racism and sexism involve making distinctions between people on the basis of morally irrelevant characteristics. Sexism, for example, may mean that a woman is paid less for her work simply because she is a woman—but that is irrelevant to the question of what she should be paid; the only relevant matter is how well she does the work. Similarly, race is not a relevant factor in determining the kind of medical care or housing a person merits. It seems an important moral principle, then, to not treat individuals or groups differently unless there are real and important differences between them that justify the differences in treatment.

There is, however, one enormous group that we do treat differently without regard to relevant differences: namely, nonhuman animals. In 1973 a young philosopher from Australia, Peter Singer, published an article in **The New York Review of Books** in which he argued that "speciesism" is an evil comparable to racism and sexism. We use animals in experiments, we kill them, eat them, take their skins for ornamental clothing and rugs, subject them to cruel treatment in zoos, circuses, and rodeos, and use them for the manufacture of perfume and other frivolous products. In all this the animals suffer terribly. The question is, can it be justified? Singer argues that it cannot, and that our treatment of nonhuman animals is a form of discrimination against another class of beings which is a moral disgrace. His article, "Animal Liberation," had led to a broad reconsideration among philosophers of the ethics of our treatment of nonhumans.

Rights, Human Rights, and Racial Discrimination

Richard Wasserstrom

The subject of natural, or human, rights is one that has recently come to enjoy a new-found intellectual and philosophical respectability. This has come about in part, I think, because of a change in philosophical mood—in philosophical attitudes and opinions toward topics in moral and political theory. And this change in mood has been reflected in a renewed interest in the whole subject of rights and duties. In addition, though, this renaissance has been influenced, I believe, by certain events of recent history—notably the horrors of Nazi Germany and the increasingly obvious injustices of racial discrimination in both the United States and Africa. For in each case one of the things that was or is involved is a denial of certain human rights.

This concern over the subject of natural rights, whatever the causes may be, is, however, in the nature of a reinstatement. Certainly there was, just a relatively few years ago, fairly general agreement that the doctrine of natural rights had been thoroughly and irretrievably discredited. Indeed, this was sometimes looked upon as the

From the *Journal of Philosophy*, vol. 61 (1964). Reprinted by permission of the author and the *Journal of Philosophy*.

paradigm case of the manner in which a moral and political doctrine could be both rhetorically influential and intellectually inadequate and unacceptable. A number of objections, each deemed absolutely dispositive, had been put
forward: the vagueness of almost every formulation of a
set of natural rights, the failure of persons to agree upon
what one's natural rights are, the ease with which almost
everyone would acknowledge the desirability of overriding
or disregarding any proffered natural rights in any one of a
variety of readily familiar circumstances, the lack of any
ground or argument for any doctrine of natural rights.

Typical is the following statement from J. B. Mabbott's
little book, *The State and the Citizens.*[1]

> [T]he niceties of the theory [of natural rights] need not de-
> tain us if we can attack it at its roots, and there it is most
> clearly vulnerable. Natural rights must be self-evident and
> they must be absolute if they are to be rights at all. For if a
> right is derivative from a more fundamental right, then it is
> not natural in the sense intended; and if a right is to be
> explained or defended by reference to the good of the com-
> munity or of the individual concerned, then these "goods"
> are the ultimate values in the case, and their pursuit may
> obviously infringe or destroy the "rights" in question. Now
> the only way in which to demonstrate the absurdity of a
> theory which claims self-evidence for every article of its
> creed is to make a list of the articles. . . .
>
> Not only are the lists indeterminate and capricious in
> extent, they are also confused in content. . . . [T]here is no
> single "natural right" which is, in fact, regarded even by its
> own supporters as sacrosanct. Every one of them is con-
> stantly invaded in the public interest with universal ap-
> proval (57–58).

Mabbott's approach to the problem is instructive both as
an example of the ease with which the subject has been
taken up and dismissed, and more importantly, as a reminder of the fact that the theory of natural rights has not

---

[1]London: Arrow, 1958.

been a single coherent doctrine. Instead, it has served, and doubtless may still serve, as a quite indiscriminate collection of a number of logically independent propositions. It is, therefore, at least as necessary here as in many other situations that we achieve considerable precision in defining and describing the specific subject of inquiry.

This paper is an attempt to delineate schematically the form of one set of arguments for natural, or human rights.[2] I do this in the following fashion. First, I consider several important and distinctive features and functions of rights in general. Next, I describe and define certain characteristics of human rights and certain specific functions and attributes that they have. Then, I delineate and evaluate one kind of argument for human rights, as so described and defined. And finally, I analyze one particular case of a denial of human rights—that produced by the system of racial discrimination as it exists in the South today.

I

If there are any such things as human rights, they have certain important characteristics and functions just because rights themselves are valuable and distinctive moral "commodities." This is, I think, a point that is all too often overlooked whenever the concept of a right is treated as a largely uninteresting, derivative notion—one that can be taken into account in wholly satisfactory fashion through an explication of the concepts of duty and obligation.[3]

Now, it is not my intention to argue that there can be rights for which there are no correlative duties, nor that there can be duties for which there are no correlative rights—although I think that there are, e.g., the duty to be kind to animals or the duty to be charitable. Instead, what I want to show is that there are important differences be-

---

[2]Because the phrase "natural rights" is so encrusted with certain special meanings, I shall often use the more neutral phrase "human rights." For my purposes there are no differences in meaning between the two expressions.

[3]See, for example, S. I. Benn and R. S. Peters, *Social Principles and the Democratic State*, p. 89: "Right and duty are different names for the same normative relation, according to the point of view from which it is regarded."

tween rights and duties, and, in particular, that rights fulfill certain functions that neither duties (even correlative duties) nor any other moral or legal concepts can fulfill.

Perhaps the most obvious thing to be said about rights is that they are constitutive of the domain of entitlements. They help to define and serve to protect those things concerning which one can make a very special kind of claim—a claim of right. To claim or to acquire anything as a matter of right is crucially different from seeking or obtaining it as through the grant of a privilege, the receipt of a favor, or the presence of a permission. To have a right to something is, typically, to be entitled to receive or possess or enjoy it now,[4] and to do so without securing the consent of another. As long as one has a right to anything, it is beyond the reach of another properly to withhold or deny it. In addition, to have a right is to be absolved from the obligation to weigh a variety of what would in other contexts be relevant considerations; it is to be entitled to the object of the right—at least *prima facie*—without any more ado. To have a right to anything is, in short, to have a very strong moral or legal claim upon it. It is the strongest kind of claim that there is.

Because this is so, it is apparent, as well, that the things to which one is entitled as a matter of right are not usually trivial or insignificant. The objects of rights are things that matter.

Another way to make what are perhaps some of the same points is to observe that rights provide special kinds of grounds or reasons for making moral judgments of at least two kinds. First, if a person has a right to something, he can properly cite that right as the *justification* for having acted in accordance with or in the exercise of that right. If a person has acted so as to exercise his right, he has, without more ado, acted rightly—at least *prima facie*. To exercise one's right is to act in a way that gives appreciable assurance of immunity from criticism. Such immun-

---

[4]There are some rights as to which the possession of the object of the right can be claimed only at a future time, e.g., the right (founded upon a promise) to be repaid next week.

ity is far less assured when one leaves the areas of rights and goes, say, to the realm of the permitted or the non-prohibited.

And second, just as exercising or standing upon one's rights by itself needs no defense, so invading or interfering with or denying another's rights is by itself appropriate ground for serious censure and rebuke. Here there is a difference in emphasis and import between the breach or neglect of a duty and the invasion of or interference with a right. For to focus upon duties and their breaches is to concentrate necessarily upon the person who has the duty; it is to invoke criteria by which to make moral assessments of his conduct. Rights, on the other hand, call attention to the injury inflicted; to the fact that the possessor of the right was adversely affected by the action. Furthermore, the invasion of a right constitutes, as such, a special and independent injury, whereas this is not the case with less stringent claims.

Finally, just because rights are those moral commodities which delineate the areas of entitlement, they have an additional important function: that of defining the respects in which one can reasonably entertain certain kinds of expectations. To live in a society in which there are rights and in which rights are generally respected is to live in a society in which the social environment has been made appreciably more predictable and secure. It is to be able to count on receiving and enjoying objects of value. Rights have, therefore, an obvious psychological, as well as moral, dimension and significance.

II

If the above are some of the characteristics and characteristic functions of rights in general, what then can we say about human rights? More specifically, what is it for a right to be a human right, and what special role might human rights play?

Probably the simplest thing that might be said of a human right is that it is a right possessed by human beings. To talk about human rights would be to distinguish those rights which humans have from those which nonhuman entities, e.g., animals or corporations, might have.

It is certain that this is not what is generally meant by human rights. Rather than constituting the genus of all particular rights that humans have, human rights have almost always been deemed to be one species of these rights. If nothing else about the subject is clear, it is evident that one's particular legal rights, as well as some of one's moral rights, are not among one's human rights. If any right is a *human* right, it must, I believe, have at least four very general characteristics. First, it must be possessed by all human beings, as well as only by human beings. Second, because it is the same right that all human beings possess, it must be possessed equally by all human beings. Third, because human rights are possessed by all human beings, we can rule out as possible candidates any of those rights which one might have in virtue of occupying any particular status or relationship, such as that of parent, president, or promisee. And fourth, if there are any human rights, they have the additional characteristic of being assertable, in a manner of speaking, "against the whole world." That is to say, because they are rights that are not possessed in virtue of any contingent status or relationship, they are rights that can be claimed equally against any and every other human being.

Furthermore, to repeat, if there are any human *rights*, they also have certain characteristics as rights. Thus, if there are any human rights, these constitute the strongest of all moral claims that all men can assert. They serve to define and protect those things which all men are entitled to have and enjoy. They indicate those objects toward which and those areas within which every human being is entitled to act without securing further permission or assent. They function so as to put certain matters beyond the power of anyone else to grant or to deny. They provide every human being with a ready justification for acting in certain ways, and they provide each person with ready grounds upon which to condemn any interference or invasion. And they operate, as well, to induce well-founded confidence that the values or objects protected by them will be readily and predictably obtainable. If there are any human rights, they are powerful moral commodities.

Finally, it is, perhaps, desirable to observe that there are certain characteristics I have not ascribed to these rights. In particular, I have not said that human rights need have either of two features: absoluteness and self-evidence, which Mabbott found to be most suspect. I have not said that human rights are absolute in the sense that there are no conditions under which they can properly be overridden, although I have asserted—what is quite different— that they are absolute in the sense that they are possessed equally without any special, additional qualification by all human beings.[5]

Neither have I said (nor do I want to assert) that human rights are self-evident in any sense. Indeed, I want explicitly to deny that a special manner of knowing or a specific epistemology is needed for the development of a theory of human rights. I want to assert that there is much that can be said in defense or support of the claim that a particular right is a human right. And I want to insist, as well, that to adduce reasons for human rights is consistent with their character as human, or natural, rights. Nothing that I have said about human rights entails a contrary conclusion.

III

To ask whether there are any human, or natural, rights is to pose a potentially misleading question. Rights of any kind, and particularly natural rights, are not like chairs or trees. One cannot simply look and see whether they are there. There are, though, at least two senses in which rights of all kinds can be said to exist. There is first the sense in which we can ask and answer the empirical question of whether in a given society there is intellectual or conceptual acknowledgment of the fact that persons or other entities have rights at all. We can ask, that is, whether the persons in that society "have" the concept of

---

[5]For the purposes of this paper and the points I wish here to make, I am not concerned with whether human rights are *prima facie* or absolute. I do not think that anything I say depends significantly upon this distinction. Without analyzing the notion, I will assume, though, that they are *prima facie* rights in the sense that there may be cases in which overriding a human right would be less undesirable than protecting it.

a right (or a human right), and whether they regard that concept as meaningfully applicable to persons or other entities in that society. And there is, secondly, the sense in which we can ask the question, to what extent, in a society that acknowledges the existence of rights, is there general respect for, protection of, or noninterference with the exercise of those rights.[6]

These are not, though, the only two questions that can be asked. For we can also seek to establish whether any rights, and particularly human rights, ought to be both acknowledged and respected. I want now to begin to do this by considering the way in which an argument for human rights might be developed.

It is evident, I think, that almost any argument for the acknowledgment of any rights as human rights starts with the factual assertion that there are certain respects in which all persons are alike or equal. The argument moves typically from that assertion to the conclusion that there are certain human rights. What often remains unclear, however, is the precise way in which the truth of any proposition about the respects in which persons are alike advances an argument for the acknowledgment of human rights. And what must be supplied, therefore, are the plausible intermediate premises that connect the initial premise with the conclusion.

One of the most careful and complete illustrations of an argument that does indicate some of these intermediate steps is that provided by Gregory Vlastos in an article entitled, "Justice and Equality."[7] Our morality, he says, puts an equal intrinsic value on each person's well-being and freedom. In detail, the argument goes like this:

There is, Vlastos asserts, a wide variety of cases in which all persons are capable of experiencing the same values.

---

[6]This is an important distinction. Incontinence in respect to rights is a fairly common occurrence. In the South, for example, many persons might acknowledge that Negroes have certain rights while at the same time neglecting or refusing (out of timidity, cowardice, or general self-interest) to do what is necessary to permit these rights to be exercised.

[7]In Richard B. Brandt, ed., *Social Justice* (Englewood Cliffs, N.J.: Prentice-Hall, 1962), pp. 31–72.

Thus, to take a perfectly clear case, no matter how A and B might differ in taste and style of life, they would both crave relief from acute physical pain. In that case we would put the same value on giving this to either of them, regardless of the fact that A might be a talented, brilliantly successful person, B "a mere nobody." . . . [I]n all cases where human beings are capable of enjoying the same goods, we feel that the intrinsic value of their enjoyment is the same. In just this sense we hold that (1) *one man's well-being is as valuable as any other's.* . . . [Similarly] we feel that choosing for oneself what one will do, believe, approve, say, read, worship, has its own intrinsic value, the same for all persons, and quite independently of the value of the things they happen to choose. Naturally we hope that all of them will make the best possible use of their freedom of choice. But we value their exercise of the freedom, regardless of the outcome and we value it equally for all. For us (2) *one man's freedom is as valuable as any other's.* . . . [Thus], since we do believe in equal value as to human well-being and freedom, we should also believe in the *prima facie* equality of men's *right* to well-being and to freedom (51–52).

As it is stated, I am not certain that this argument answers certain kinds of attack. In particular, there are three questions that merit further attention. First, why should anyone have a right to the enjoyment of any goods at all, and, more specifically, well-being and freedom? Second, for what reasons might we be warranted in believing that the intrinsic value of the enjoyment of such goods is the same for all persons? And third, even if someone ought to have a right to well-being and freedom and even if the intrinsic value of each person's enjoyment of these things is equal, why should all men have the equal right—and hence the human right—to secure, obtain, or enjoy these goods?

I think that the third question is the simplest of the three to answer. If anyone has a right to well-being and freedom and if the intrinsic value of any person's enjoyment of these goods is equal to that of any other's, then all men do have an equal right—and hence a human right—to secure, obtain, or enjoy these goods, just because it would be irrational to distinguish among persons as to the possession of these rights. That is to say, the principle that no person should be treated differently from any or all other persons unless there is some general and relevant reason that justifies this difference in treatment is a fundamental principle of morality, if not of rationality itself. Indeed, although I am not certain how one might argue for this, I think it could well be said that all men do have a "second-order" human right—that is, an absolute right— to expect all persons to adhere to this principle.

This principle, or this right, does not by itself establish that there are any specific human rights. But either the principle or the right does seem to establish that well-being and freedom are human rights if they are rights at all and if the intrinsic value of each person's enjoyment is the same. For, given these premises, it does appear to follow that there is no relevant and general reason to differentiate among persons as to the possession of this right.

I say "seem to" and "appear to" because this general principle of morality may not be strong enough. What has been said so far does not in any obvious fashion rule out the possibility that there is some general and relevant principle of differentiation. It only, apparently, rules out possible variations in intrinsic value as a reason for making differentiations.

The requirement of *relevance* does, I think, seem to make the argument secure. For, if *the reason* for acknowledging in a person a right to freedom and well-being is the intrinsic value of his enjoyment of these goods, then the nature of the intrinsic value of any other person's enjoyment is the only relevant reason for making exceptions or for differentiating among persons as to the possession of these rights.[8]

---

[8]See, e.g., Bernard Williams, "The Idea of Equality," in P. Laslett and W. G. Runciman, eds., *Philosophy, Politics and Society,* II (Oxford: Basil Blackwell, 1962), pp. 111–113.

Professor Vlastos imposes a somewhat different requirement which, I think, comes to about the same thing: "An equalitarian concept of justice may admit just inequalities without inconsistency if, and only if, it provides grounds for equal human rights *which are also grounds for unequal rights of other sorts"* (Vlastos, op. cit., p. 40; italics in text).

As to the first question, that of whether a person has a right to well-being and freedom, I am not certain what kind of answer is most satisfactory. If Vlastos is correct in asserting that these enjoyments are *values*, then that is, perhaps, answer enough. That is to say, if enjoying well-being is something *valuable*—and especially if it is intrinsically valuable—then it seems to follow that this is the kind of thing to which one ought to have a right. For if anything ought to be given the kind of protection afforded by a right, it ought surely be that which is valuable. Perhaps, too, there is nothing more that need be said other than to point out that we simply do properly value well-being and freedom.

I think that another, more general answer is also possible. Here I would revert more specifically to my earlier discussion of some of the characteristics and functions of rights. There are two points to be made. First, if we are asked, why ought anyone have a right to anything? or why not have a system in which there are not rights at all? the answer is that such a system would be a morally impoverished one. It would prevent persons from asserting those kinds of claims, it would preclude persons from having those types of expectations, and it would prohibit persons from making those kinds of judgments which a system of rights makes possible.

Thus, if we can answer the question of why have rights at all, we can then ask and answer the question of what things—among others—ought to be protected by *rights*. And the answer, I take it, is that one ought to be able to claim as entitlements those minimal things without which it is impossible to develop one's capabilities and to live a life as a human being. Hence, to take one thing that is a precondition of well-being, the relief from acute physical pain, this is the kind of enjoyment that ought to be protected as a right of some kind just because without such relief there is precious little that one can effectively do or become. And similarly for the opportunity to make choices, examine beliefs, and the like.

To recapitulate. The discussion so far has indicated two things: (1) the conditions under which any specific right would be a human right, and (2) some possible grounds for

arguing that certain values or enjoyments ought to be regarded as matters of right. The final question that remains
is whether there are any specific rights that satisfy the
conditions necessary to make them human rights. Or,
more specifically, whether it is plausible to believe that
there are no general and relevant principles that justify
making distinctions among persons in respect to their
rights to well-being and freedom.

Vlastos has it that the rights to well-being and freedom
do satisfy these conditions, since he asserts that we, at
least, do regard each person's well-being and freedom as
having equal intrinsic value. If this is correct, if each person's well-being and freedom does have *equal* intrinsic
value, then there is no general and relevant principle for
differentiating among persons as to these values and,
hence, as to their rights to secure these values. But this
does not seem wholly satisfactory. It does not give us any
reason for supposing that it is plausible to ascribe equal
intrinsic value to each person's well-being and freedom.

The crucial question, then, is the plausibility of ascribing intrinsic value to each person's well-being and freedom. There are, I think, at least three different answers
that might be given.

First, it might be asserted that this ascription simply
constitutes another feature of our morality. The only
things that can be done are to point out that this is an
assumption that we do make and to ask persons whether
they would not prefer to live in a society in which such an
assumption is made.

While perhaps correct and persuasive, this does not
seem to me to be all that can be done. In particular, these
are, I think, two further arguments that may be made.

The first is that there are cases in which all human beings *equally* are capable of enjoying the same goods, e.g.,
relief from acute physical pain,[9] or that they are capable of

---

[9]See, Williams, op. cit., p. 112: "These respects [in which men are alike] are
notably the capacity to feel pain, both from immediate physical causes and from
various situations represented in perception and in thought; and the capacity to
feel affection for others, and the consequences of this, connected with the frustration of this affection, loss of its objects, etc."

deriving equal enjoyment from the same goods. If this is true, then if anyone has a right to this enjoyment, that right is a human right just because there is no rational ground for preferring one man's enjoyment to another's. For, if all persons do have equal capacities of these sorts and if the existence of these capacities is the reason for ascribing these rights to anyone, then all persons ought to have the right to claim equality of treatment in respect to the possession and exercise of these rights.

The difficulty inherent in this argument is at the same time the strength of the next one. The difficulty is simply that it does seem extraordinarily difficult to know how one would show that all men are equally capable of enjoying any of the same goods, or even how one might attempt to gather or evaluate relevant evidence in this matter. In a real sense, interpersonal comparisons of such a thing as the ability to bear pain seems to be logically as well as empirically unobtainable. Even more unobtainable, no doubt, is a measure of the comparative enjoyments derivable from choosing for oneself.[10] These are simply enjoyments the comparative worths of which, as different persons, there is no way to assess. If this is so, then this fact gives rise to an alternative argument.

We do know, through inspection of human history as well as of our own lives, that the denial of the opportunity to experience the enjoyment of these goods makes it impossible to live either a full or a satisfying life. In a real sense, the enjoyment of these goods differentiates human from nonhuman entities. And therefore, even if we have no meaningful or reliable criteria for comparing and weighing capabilities for enjoyment or for measuring their quantity or quality, we probably know all we need to know to justify our refusal to attempt to grade the value of the enjoyment of these goods. Hence, the dual grounds for treating their intrinsic values as equal for all persons: either these values are equal for all persons, or, if there are

---

[10]At times, Vlastos seems to adopt this view as well as the preceding one. See, e.g., Vlastos, op. cit., p. 49: "So understood a person's well-being and freedom are aspects of his individual existence as unique and unrepeatable as is that existence itself. . . ."

differences, they are not in principle discoverable or measurable. Hence, the argument, or an argument, for the human rights to well-being and freedom.

Because the foregoing discussion has been quite general and abstract, I want finally to consider briefly one illustration of a denial of human rights and to delineate both the several ways in which such a denial can occur and some of the different consequences of that denial. My example is that of the way in which Negro persons are regarded and treated by many whites in the South.

The first thing that is obvious is that many white Southerners would or might be willing to accept all that has been said so far and yet seek to justify their attitudes and behavior toward Negroes.

They might agree, for example, that all persons do have a right to be accorded equal treatment unless there is a general and relevant principle of differentiation. They would also surely acknowledge that some persons do have rights to many different things, including most certainly well-being and freedom. But they would insist, nonetheless, that there exists a general and relevant principle of differentiation, namely, that some persons are Negroes and others are not.

Now, those who do bother to concern themselves with arguments and with the need to give reasons would not, typically, assert that the mere fact of color difference does constitute a general and relevant reason. Rather, they would argue that this color difference is correlated with certain other characteristics and attitudes that are relevant.[11] In so doing, they invariably commit certain logical and moral mistakes.

First, the purported differentiating characteristic is usually not relevant to the differentiation sought to be made; e.g., none of the characteristics that supposedly differentiate Negroes from whites has any relevance to the capacity to bear acute physical pain or to the strength of the desire to be free from it. Indeed, almost all arguments neg-

---

[11]See, Williams, op. cit., p. 113.

lect the fact that the capacities to enjoy those things which are constitutive of well-being and freedom are either incommensurable among persons or alike in all persons.

Second, the invocation of these differentiating characteristics always violates the requirement of relevance in another sense. For, given the typical definition of a Negro (in Alabama the legal definition is any person with "a drop of Negro blood"), it is apparent that there could not—under any plausible scientific theory—be good grounds for making any differentiations between Negroes and whites.[12]

Third, and related to the above, any argument that makes distinctions as to the possession of human rights in virtue of the truth of certain empirical generalizations invariably produces some unjust denials of those rights. That is to say, even if some of the generalizations about Negroes are correct, they are correct only in the sense that the distinguishing characteristics ascribed to Negroes are possessed by some or many Negroes but not by all Negroes. Yet, before any reason for differentiating among persons as to the possession of human rights can be a relevant reason, that reason must be relevant in respect to *each person* so affected or distinguished. To argue otherwise is to neglect the fact, among other things, that human rights are personal and of at least *prima facie* equal importance to each possessor of those rights.

A different reaction or argument of white Southeners in respect to recent events in the South is bewilderment. Rather than (or in addition) arguing for the existence of principles of differentiation, the white Southerner will say that he simply cannot understand the Negro's dissatisfaction with his lot. This is so because he, the white Southerner, has always treated his Negroes very well. With appreciable sincerity, he will assert that he has real affection for many Negroes. He would never needlessly inflict pain or suffering upon them. Indeed, he has often assumed spe-

---

[12]This is to say nothing, of course, of the speciousness of any principle of differentiation that builds upon inequalities that are themselves produced by the unequal and unjust distribution of *opportunities*.

cial obligations to make certain that their lives were free from hunger, pain, and disease.

Now of course, this description of the facts is seldom accurate at all. Negroes have almost always been made to endure needless and extremely severe suffering in all too many obvious ways for all too many obviously wrong reasons. But I want to assume for my purposes the accuracy of the white Southerner's assertions. For these assertions are instructive just because they reveal some of the less obvious effects of a denial of human rights.

What is wholly missing from this description of the situation is the ability and inclination to conceptualize the Negro—any Negro—as the possible possessor of rights of any kind, and *a fortiori* of any human rights. And this has certain especially obnoxious consequences.

In the first place, the white Southerner's moral universe illustrates both the fact that it is possible to conceive of duties without conceiving of their correlative rights and the fact that the mistakes thereby committed are not chiefly mistakes of logic and definition. The mistakes matter morally. For what this way of conceiving most denies to any Negro is the opportunity to assert claims as a matter of right. It denies him the standing to protest against the way he is treated. If the white Southerner fails to do this duty, that is simply a matter between him and his conscience.

In the second place, it requires of any Negro that *he* make out his case for the enjoyment of any goods. It reduces all of *his* claims to the level of requests, privileges, and favors. But there are simply certain things, certain goods, that nobody ought to have to request of another. There are certain things that no one else ought to have the power to decide to refuse or to grant. To observe what happens to any person who is required to adopt habits of obsequious, deferential behavior in order to minimize the likelihood of physical abuse, arbitrary treatment, or economic destitution is to see most graphically how important human rights are and what their denial can mean. To witness what happens to a person's own attitudes, aspirations, and conceptions of himself[13] when he must request or petition for the opportunity to voice an opinion, to consult with a public official, or to secure the protection of the law is to be given dramatic and convincing assurance of the moral necessity of a conception of human rights.

And there is one final point. In a real sense, a society that simply lacks any conception of human rights is less offensive than one which has such a conception but denies that some persons have these rights. This is so not just because of the inequality and unfairness involved in differentiating for the wrong reasons among persons. Rather, a society based on such denial is especially offensive because it implicitly, if not explicitly, entails that there are some persons who do not and would not desire or need or enjoy those minimal goods which all men do need and desire and enjoy. It is to read certain persons, all of whom are most certainly human beings, out of the human race. This is surely among the greatest of all moral wrongs.

I know of no better example of the magnitude of this evil than that provided by a lengthy account in a Southern newspaper about the high school band program in a certain city. The article described fully the magnificence of the program and emphasized especially the fact that it was a program in which *all high school students* in the city participated.

Negro children neither were nor could be participants in the program. The article, however, saw no need to point this out. I submit that it neglected to do so not because everyone knew the fact, but because in a real sense the writer and the newspaper do not regard Negro high school students as children—persons, human beings—at all.

What is the Negro parent who reads this article to say to

---

[13]Vlastos puts what I take to be the same point this way: "Any practice which tends to so weaken and confuse the personal esteem of a group of persons— slavery, serfdom or, in our own time racial segregation—may be morally condemned on this one ground, even if there were no other for indicting it" (Vlastos, op. cit., p. 71).

his children? What are his children supposed to think? How does a Negro parent even begin to demonstrate to the world that his children are really children, too? These are burdens no civilized society ought ever to impose. These are among the burdens that an established and acknowledged system of human rights helps to eliminate.

Women's Liberation

Betty Roszak

Recent years have seen a resurgence of feminism that has taken mainstream America by surprise. It began with the discontent of lonely middle-class suburban housewives, whose malady was given a name by Betty Friedan in her immensely influential book, *The Feminine Mystique*. But it didn't become what we know as a "women's liberation movement" until the growth of the New Left from the civil rights and peace movements of the early 1960s. It wasn't until then that hundreds of young women, many of whom were seasoned veterans of antiwar and antisegregationist activities, began to realize the anomaly of their situation. Here they were, radical women involved in a struggle for human equality and an end to oppression, willing to dedicate years of effort to effecting political change, and what were they being allowed to do? Typing, mimeographing, addressing envelopes, sweeping, providing coffee and sexual diversion for the vigorous young men who were making all the decisions. Far from going forward together to change the world, men and women were once more stuck (and this time with a vengeance) with their time-honored roles: the men to think and act; the women to serve and drudge. The last equality—that between women and men—was never even mentioned. In fact, movement

From Betty Roszak, "The Human Continuum," in *Masculine/Feminine*, ed. Betty Roszak and Theodore Roszak (New York: Harper & Row, 1969), pp. 297–306. Copyright © 1969 by Betty Roszak and Theodore Roszak. Reprinted by permission of Harper & Row, Publishers, Inc.

women found that they were even worse off than apolitical women, because they were aware of and extremely sensitive to the hypocrisies of their male colleagues who talked idealistically of equality, but who acted scornful of women in their everyday lives. The rhetoric of equality was directed at black, brown, and Third World *men* only. The New Left of the late sixties had begun to take on a tough, aggressively male tone, born of the idolization of Ché Guevara, guerrilla warfare, and admiration for the exaggerated, overcompensating manliness of the Black Panthers. As nonviolence, exemplified by Martin Luther King, Jr., became discredited by revolutionary and black militancy, so the tough style became a political requirement. In deference to this new brutalism men found it easy to take the necessary traditional he-man attitude toward women, the attitude of dominance and power. This left women in a bewildering dilemma. Were they to remain in a movement which allowed them to exist only as lackeys and silently submissive bedmates, or would they refuse to accept a subordinate status?

As this dilemma is being resolved today, there sounds in the background the laughter of contemptuous radical men: "Crazy feminist bitches!" The words merely echo a shared male ridicule that knows no class lines. Women find themselves of necessity beginning to re-examine the traditions of misogyny that even radical men have unknowingly inherited.

In our cultural past "Woman" was the symbol of sex; and sex, though necessary, was at the same time known to be an abhorrent evil, a degrading passion. In the Middle Ages, the masculine world view of the church dared not make light of women. Church authorities of the fifteenth century, ever on the alert for the malevolence of the devil, used a popular handbook on the identification and treatment of witches, the *Malleus Maleficarum*, in searching out evil in the form of women. "What else is woman," says this medieval antisubversive activities manual, "but a foe to friendship, an unescapable punishment, a necessary evil, a natural temptation, a desirable calamity, a domestic danger, a delectable detriment, an evil of nature painted with fair colors?" By the eighteenth century, Rousseau, one of France's most prolific proponents of democratic equality, could write with impunity, "Women have in general no love of any art; they have no proper knowledge of any; and they have no genius," thus curtly dismissing half of humanity to a status of hopeless inferiority. By mid-nineteenth century, the "evil of nature" had turned into an object of scorn, and Schopenhauer's indictment of women as "that undersized, narrow-shouldered, broad-hipped, and short-legged race," denied women even their beauty, their "fair colors," along with their intellectual capacity.

Today's predominantly male society no longer sees women as evil, at least on the surface. The ambivalent fear and attraction of the Middle Ages has changed along with the prevailing attitude toward sex. Now that sexuality has lost its mystery, the once dangerous and seductive female can be safely ignored and denied her power. The fear has turned to ridicule. One cannot ignore evil, but one can pretend that the ridiculous does not exist. Men irritably ask the rhetorical question (echoing Freud), "What do women want?" meaning, of course, that anything women want is absurd. The question is asked not of individual women but of the world, and in an exasperated tone, as if women were dumb and couldn't answer. The false barrier continues to be built: "We" cannot understand "Them." Why are "They" so restive? Further communication between the sexes seems useless. Always it is men talking to men about women.

The fact of ridicule is constantly with us. When it was proposed in 1969 in the British House of Commons that attention be paid to developing a contraceptive pill for men, "the idea provoked hearty laughter," according to Paul Vaughan in the London *Observer*. Moreover, he tells us, the British government has rejected outright any allocation of funds for research on a pill for men. When the question was under discussion in the House of Lords, one Labour peer advised the government to ignore "'these do-gooders who take all the fun out of life' (laughter)." Researchers explain their reluctance to tamper with the male germ cells. Yet the same researchers have not hesitated to tamper with the female germ cells in developing the pill for women. Nor have unpleasant side effects or hazards to women's health deterred them, while they quickly stopped research on a substance being tested on men because it was noted that when men drank alcohol while taking it, their eyes became reddened! Doctors have been known to laugh at the mention of labor pains during childbirth and in the not too distant past have been willing to stand by, calmly withholding anesthetics while women underwent great agonies in labor. So, too, male legislators have laughed at the idea of the legalization of abortion, hinting at unprecedented promiscuity (on the part of women, not men) if such a thing were allowed. Meanwhile, thousands of desperate women die each year as the direct result of male laws making abortion illegal.

Women are learning the meaning of this male laughter and indifference in the face of the most hazardous and serious biological enterprise women undertake, willingly or not. And in cultural enterprises, whenever women attempt to enter any of the male-dominated professions (who ever heard of a woman chairman of the board, a women orchestra conductor, a woman Chief Justice, a woman President or a woman getting equal pay for equal work?), we again hear the familiar laughter of male ridicule. If we look at the image of woman men present to us in novels, drama, or advertising, we see a scatter-brained, helpless flunky, or a comical sex-pot, or a dumb beast of burden. Is this what they mean when they exhort us in popular song to "enjoy being a girl"? But women are beginning to relearn the old lesson: in this male-dominated world, it is a misfortune to be born female.

From the very moment of birth a higher value is placed by his society on the male infant, a value which accumulates and accelerates into his adult life. By the time the female infant has grown into adulthood, however, if she has learned society's lessons well, she will have come to acquiesce in her second-class status—to accept unconsciously the burden of her inferiority. No matter what honors she wins, what her exploits, what her achievements or talents, she will always be considered a women first, and thus inferior to the least honored, talented and worthy male of that society—foremost a sexual being, still fair game for his aggressive sexual fantasies. As Albert Memmi puts it," . . . every man, no matter how low he may be, holds women in contempt and judges masculinity to be an inestimable good."

Male society's disparagement of women has all the force of an unconscious conspiracy. It is even more subtle than the racist and colonial oppressions to which it is so closely allied, because it is softened and hidden by the silken padding of eroticism. We women grow to think that because we are wanted as lover, wives, and mothers, it might be because we are wanted as human beings. But if by chance or natural inclination we attempt to move outside these male-defined and male-dependent roles, we find that they are, in reality, barriers.

For many women this is the first inkling of the fact of oppression. Pressed from birth into the mold of an exclusively sexual being, the growing girl soon develops what Sartre calls the "phantom personality"; she comes to feel that she is what "they" tell her she is. This other self envelopes her like a second skin. When she begins to experience a natural sense of constriction (which is growth), her real feelings clash with what "they" say she should feel. The more forceful and vital she is, the more she will have to repress her real feelings, because girls are to be passive and manipulatable. She becomes frightened, suspicious, anxious about herself. A sense of malaise overcomes her. She must obey the social prohibitions which force her back into the mold of the sexual being. She is not to desire or act, but to *be* desired and acted upon. Many women give up the struggle right there and dully force themselves to remain stunted human beings. The butterfly must not be allowed to come forth from its chrysalis: her vitality is only allowed guilty expression in certain private moments or is turned into sullen resentment which smolders during all her unfulfilled life.

Family and home, which look like a refuge and a sanctuary, turn out to be the same kind of trap. Beyond the marriage ghetto there is outright rejection and exclusion. In the work world there are lower wages, union and employer discrimination, the prohibitive cost of child care. In the professions mere tokenism takes the place of acceptance and equality. The same is true in government and political activity. The single woman knows only too well the psychological exclusionism practiced by male society. She is suspect, or comic, if over a certain age. All men assume she would be married if she could—there must be something psychologically wrong with her if she isn't. And single women have the added burden of not being socially acceptable without an "escort"—a man, any man.

Further, women are the nonexistent people in the very life of the nation itself—now more so even than the blacks who have at last forced themselves into the nation's consciousness. The invisible man has become the invisible *woman*. William James called it a "fiendish punishment" that "one should be turned loose on society and remain absolutely unnoticed by all the members thereof." Yet that is the treatment male society metes out to those women who wish to escape from the male-defined erotic roles. Left out of the history books, not credited with a past worth mentioning in the masculine chronicles of state, women of today remain ignorant of women's movements of the past and the important role individual women have played in the history of the human race. Male historical scholarship sees the suffragists and feminists of the nineteenth century as figures of fun, worthy of only a paragraph here and there, as footnotes on the by-ways of social customs, far from the main roads of masculine endeavor: the wars, political intrigues, and diplomatic maneuverings which make up the history of power.

With the blacks and other oppressed minorities, women can say, "How can we hope to shape the future without some knowledge of our past?" If the historic heroines of feminism are ignored or treated trivially, today's women are hindered from dealing with their own repression. This undermining of self-confidence is common to all oppressed peoples, along with the doubts of the reality of one's own perceptions. Women's self-rejection as worthwhile human beings thus becomes an inevitable extension of the cycle of oppression.

But radical women have begun to rebel against the false, exclusively sexual image men have created for them. And in rebelling, many women are seeing the need for bypassing the marriage ghetto altogether. They are recognizing the true nature of the institution of marriage as an economic bargain glossed over by misty sentimentalizing. Wash off the romantic love ideal, and underneath we see the true face of the marriage contract. It is grimly epitomized by the immortal slogan found chalked on innumerable honeymoon getaway cars: "She got him today; he'll get her tonight." Or, as put more sophisticatedly by Robert Briffault, "Whether she aims at freedom or a home a woman is thrown back on the defense of her own interests; she must defend herself against man's attempt to bind her, or sell herself to advantage. Woman is to man a sexual prey; man is to woman an economic prey." And this kind of oppression cuts across all economic class lines, even though there may be social differences between streetwalker Jane X, housewife Joan Y, and debutante Jacqueline Z. One may sell her body for a few dollars to the likeliest passerby; one for a four-bedroomed house in the suburbs; and one for rubies and yachts. But all must sell their bodies in order to participate in the bargain. Yet if women were to refuse to enter into the sexual bargain, they not only would refute the masculine idea of women as property, but they also would make it possible to free men from the equally self-destructive role of sole breadwinner. Thus there would be a chance to break the predatory cycle.

Beyond marriage and the old, outmoded roles, radical women are seeking new ways of dealing with the oppressive institutions of society. No longer will they acquiesce in the pattern of dominance and submission. They are beginning to take control of their own lives, building new relationships, developing new modes of work, political activity, child rearing and education. Rejection of male exploitation must start with psychic as well as economic independence. The new female consciousness is going to develop cooperative forms of child care; women's centers as sanctuaries for talk, planning, and action; all-female communes where women can escape for a while from the all-pervading male influence; the sharing of domestic drudgery with men in cooperative living arrangements; the building up of competence and self-confidence in such previously male-dependent endeavors as general mechanical repair work, carpentry, and construction.

By rejecting the false self for so long imposed upon us and in which we have participated unwittingly, we women can forge the self-respect necessary in order to discover our own true values. Only when we refuse to be made use of by those who despise and ridicule us, can we throw off our heavy burden of resentment. We must take our lives in our own hands. This is what liberation means. Out of a common oppression women can break the stereotypes of masculine-feminine and enter once more into the freedom of the human continuum.

Women's liberation will thus inevitably bring with it, as a concomitant, men's liberation. Men, no less than women, are imprisoned by the heavy carapace of their sexual stereotype. The fact that they gain more advantages and privileges from women's oppression has blinded them to their own bondage which is the bondage of an artificial duality. This is the male problem: the positing of a difference, the establishment of a dichotomy emphasizing oppositeness. Men are to behave in this way; women in that; women do this; men do the other. And it just so happens that the way men behave and act is important and valuable, while what women do is unimportant and trivial. Instead of identifying both the sexes as part of humanity, there is a false separation which is to the advantage of men. Masculine society has insisted on seeing in sexuality that same sense of conflict and competition that it has imposed upon its relation to the planet as a whole. From the bedroom to the board room to the international conference table, separateness, differentiation, opposition, exclusion, antithesis have been the cause and goal of the male politics of power. Human characteristics belonging to the entire species have been crystallized out of the living flow of human experience and made into either/or categories. This male habit of setting up boundary lines between imagined polarities has been the impetus for untold hatred and destruction. Masculine/feminine is just one of such polarities among many, including body/mind, organism/environment, plant/animal, good/evil, black/

white, feeling/intellect, passive/active, sane/insane, living/
dead. Such language hardens what is in reality a continuum and a unity into separate mental images always in
opposition to one another.

If we think of ourselves as "a woman" or "a man," we
are already participating in a fantasy of language. People
become preoccupied with images of one another—surely
the deepest and most desperate alienation there is. The
very process of conceptualization warps our primary, uni-
tary feelings of what we are. Mental images take the place
of the primary stimuli of sex which involve the entire organism. Instead of a sense of identification, we have por-
nographic sex with its restrictive emphasis on genital
stimulation. This "short circuiting between genital and
cortex" as William E. Galt calls it (in a brilliant article,
"The Male-Female Dichotomy," in *Psychiatry*, 1943) is a
peculiarly modern distortion of the original, instinctual
nature of sex. We are suffering from D. H. Lawrence's "sex
in the head." In childhood we know sexuality as a
generalized body response; the body is an erotic organ of
sensation. To this Freud gave the nasty name of
polymorphous perversity. But it is actually the restriction
to localized genitality of the so-called "normal" adult that
is perverted, in the sense of a twisting away from the original and primary body eroticism. Biological evidence indicates that the sex response is a primitive, gross sensory
stimulation—diffused and nonlocalizable. Phallic man,
however, wishes to assert the primacy of his aggressive organ. The ego of phallic man divides him off from the rest
of the world, and in this symbolic division he maintains
the deep-seated tradition of man *against* woman, wresting
his sexual pleasure *from* her, like the spoils of war. The
total body response must be repressed in order to satisfy
the sharpness of his genital cravings.

But in the primary sexual response of the body, there is
no differentiation between man or woman; there is no
"man," there is no "woman" (mental images), just a
shared organism responding to touch, smell, taste, sound.
The sexual response can then be seen as one part of the
species' total response to and participation in, the environment. We sense the world with our sensitive bodies as

an ever-changing flow of relationships in which we move and partake. Phallic man sees the world as a collection of things from which he is sharply differentiated. If we consider the phenomenon of the orgasm in this light, we can see that its basic qualities are the same for male and female. There can be no real distinction between the feminine and masculine *self*-abandonment in a sexual climax. The self, or controlling power, simply vanishes. All talk of masculine or feminine orgasm misses this point entirely, because this is a surrender which goes beyond masculine or feminine. Yet how many men are there who are willing to see their own sexual vitality as exactly this self-surrender?

When men want desperately to preserve that which they deem masculine—the controlling power—then they insist on the necessity of the feminine as that which must be controlled and mastered. Men force themselves into the role of phallic man and seek always to be hard, to be tough, to be competitive, to assert their "manhood." Alan Watts wisely sees this masculine striving for rigidity as "nothing more than an emotional paralysis" which causes men to misunderstand the bisexuality of their own nature, to force a necessarily unsatisfactory sexual response, and to be exploitative in their relations with women and the world.

According to Plato's myth, the ancients thought of men and women as originally a single being cut asunder into male and female by an angry god. There is a good biological basis to this myth; although the sexes are externally differentiated, they are still structurally homologous. Psychologically, too, the speculations of George Groddeck are apt:

> Personal sex cuts right across the fundamental qualities of human nature; the very word suggests the violent splitting asunder of humanity into male and female. *Sexus* is derived from *secare*, to cut, from which we also get *segmentum*, a part cut from a circle. It conveys the idea that man and woman once formed a unity, that together they make a complete whole, the perfect circle of the individuum and that both sections share the properties of this individuum.

These suggestions are of course in harmony with the ancient Hebrew legend, which told how God first created a
human being who was both male and female, Adam-Lilith,
and later sawed this asunder.[1]

The dichotomizing of human qualities can thus be seen as
a basic error in men's understanding of nature. Biologically, both sexes are always present in each. Perhaps with
the overcoming of women's oppression, the woman in
man will be allowed to emerge. If, as Coleridge said, great
minds are androgynous, there can be no feminine or masculine ideal, but only as the poet realizes,

> . . . what is true is human,
> homosexuality, heterosexuality
> There is something more important:

> to be human
> in which kind
> is kind.[2]

---

[1]*The World of Man* (New York, Vision Press, 1951).
[2]Clayton Eshleman, from "Holding Duncan's Hand."

Racism and Sexism: A False Analogy

Ann Dummett

Anyone who cares about getting rid of racism in Britain is accustomed to massive difficulties. The disastrous immigration policies of governments of both parties since 1962, the institutionalised racial discrimination built into public and private organisations, the tragedy of human potential lost and destroyed in our educational system, the insensitivity and ignorance of many people in the news industry, racism in entertainment and cartoons, public indifference and private malice, are all too bitterly familiar. But the anti-racist, as if he had not trouble enough with enemies, needs more and more protection from his friends. Government money for 'community relations' has recently become more plentiful, but practised hands are holding the purse-strings and know just how and when to draw them tight. Job opportunities brighten a little for specialised social workers, charged with containing the discontents of the young and black: *their* job opportunities are less than ever. Various groups on the Left are eager to help in the racial struggle, but usually on their own terms. And now we have Women's Lib as well.

'Women's Lib' is a vague and disputed term; it is more usual to hear of 'the women's movement' now in this country. This includes some formal organisations, some informal groups and some individuals, all in some way or another concerned with women's rights. These groups and

Reprinted from *New Blackfriars*, November 1975, by permission of the author.

individuals vary in beliefs and in action. Some are old-established reforming organisations, some new community action groups, and so on; their work often overlaps, but there is a marked difference, all the same, between the new ideology of liberation and the old ideology of equal rights for women. The difference is in mood and style rather than in a set programme; the new mood and style can conveniently be called 'anti-sexism'. Anti-sexism is putting together the fight for more nursery schools and for getting men to look after the children, campaigning for easy abortion as well as for equal pay, asking for picture-books in which little girls play with trains and mothers are depicted following interesting professions like medicine and the law. Anti-sexism is also claiming that it is the same kind of fight as anti-racism. It is not.

Anti-sexism has in fact imitated much of the language of anti-racism, transferring it unadapted in some cases, for example, where women are referred to as a minority, which they observably are not. The word 'sexism' itself is a coinage struck from the mould of racism, and the word 'liberation' draws its power from association with the fight against colonialism, against economic imperialism, against disfranchisement, fought by non-Europeans in many parts of the world; it resounds with echoes of events in Vietnam and southern Africa. Anti-sexism has in short, cashed in on the turnover of the worldwide racial conflict. The style of its complaints and demands seeks to elevate women's escape from the domination of men to the same importance as the fight against racism. But this attempt has to ignore or distort contemporary world history. It has to point to women's sufferings alone in many countries where women's sufferings are either no worse than or not significantly different from men's, where menial work and degraded status are the lot of the poor of both sexes, or where to have the job of caring for children at home is a kind of blessing compared with toiling in mines or enduring permanent unemployment. It has either to show that the separate struggle of women as women is as significant in international politics and economics as the struggle of oppressed or despised racial groups, or else it has to imply that racism is no worse than sexism.

While the women's liberation movement itself of course insists on the worldwide importance of its own struggle, those who are committed to working against racism must surely be fearful of the debilitating effects of the comparison on their own strength. In the United States, the great Civil Rights movement of the early sixties, followed by the Black Power movement, black nationalism and a tremendous eruption of change in public debate and public attitudes on race *preceded* the new style of women's liberation, and provided a vocabulary and style that could be copied. In Britain, there has been no equivalent of the American transformation of the race picture during the Sixties; there has been far less publicity, too, for racial discrimination and its effects. An imitation here and now of the American women's movement appears in quite a different context from its original, and women's liberation gets much more press coverage here than racial issues. Anti-racist demands will often be seen here, therefore, against a background of women's demands, instead of the other way round. And where women's demands seem trivial or misdirected, it will be all too easy for anti-racists' demands of a superficially similar kind to be dismissed as trivial too. For example, the anti-racist protest against the presentation of black people in children's books as savages, cannibals or primitive idiots is a difficult enough protest to get taken seriously in Britain by educators and publishers. It will not be helped by the good offices of *soi-disant* allies in the women's movement who want to get rid of pictures of mothers ironing and little girls playing with dolls. If the two protests are taken to be of the same character and importance, we shall have all the longer to wait for improvement in any direction. Indeed, I fear we shall get pictures of father ironing and little girls playing with trains long before we shall get much accurate and rational presentation of African, Asian and Caribbean peoples in children's books.

Racism, arguably the most important political phenomenon of the twentieth century, is a denial in theory and practice of the equal humanity, equal capacities and equal rights of men, women and children categorised by physical appearance or by national descent. Sexism, anti-sexists would say, is exactly analogous: the denial of these same kinds of equality on the grounds of physical difference. But this apparent similarity breaks down as soon as we begin to examine the *results* of racism and sexism. Millions of people in this century have been killed because of their 'race': Jews systematically exterminated by gassing, American blacks lynched, shot, beaten to death, burnt. Many more have been enslaved, in practice if not always in name, because of their race; Slavs by the Nazis, worked to death in forced labour; Africans in South Africa, serving prison sentences for breaches of the pass laws which are explicitly racial, and working the land unpaid and unfree. Many more again have been reduced to utter poverty, degradation and powerlessness because of their race; many denied the right to be with their own wives or husbands or children because of their race: the victims of South African and Rhodesian land and labour laws, the victims of Britain's immigration laws.

It is impossible to understand racism, to evaluate its workings realistically, to assess the true nature and importance of any of its manifestations, even apparently minor ones, unless we look at it against this hideous backcloth of cruelty and death. Racism denies the right of certain people to be alive. It does not always deny them life itself; since it is often a matter of economic or political policy to keep them alive, but ultimately it regards the lives of certain human beings, racially categorised, as disposable. It may be expedient to give a few of them good jobs in certain circumstances, as a tactical manoeuvre, but in other circumstances it may be expedient to deport them, evict them, or leave them unpublicly to starve: always in the background is the shadow of death.

The doctrine of women's inferiority to men has no results comparable with these. It is true that in many countries women have fewer rights under the law than men. Concern for their difficulties was not the guide to shaping anti-sexist doctrine and policies. Their distress has been absorbed into the concerns of the women's movement at a later stage than the comparatively far less serious difficulties of well-to-do wives in the West who resent looking after babies, washing their husbands' shirts and being re-

garded as featherheads. Anti-sexist magazines in this
country devote more space to discussing abortion, les-
bianism and sexual self-stimulation than to injustice, or to
international political issues. And the fact is that sexism is
not, in the same sense as racism, an international political issue. It does not swing foreign policy decisions, guide
investment or affect the course of wars. Nor has it caused
mass exterminations. We have not seen millions of
women being put to death because they were women.
Women were shot down at Sharpeville, but because they
were black, not because they were female. Women in the
twentieth century have been killed, tortured and imprisoned, but not because they were hated or despised *as
women*, always for their race, their political opinions and
activities, their religion or some other cause for which
men have suffered at the same time.

This vital difference between sexism and racism is not
one of degree, but of kind. Racism postulates an essential
functional difference between one 'racial' group and
another, associating with skin colour or national descent
the possession of certain qualities and lack of others: e.g.:
'they' are less intelligent or more cunning; they are more
violent by nature or more cowardly; they are better adapted
to hard physical work, less apt at the arts, more feeble,
more avaricious, less technically adept, because of their
race. Thus their function in society must be marked off
separately; their history must be distorted to fit these assumptions. Male prejudice and discrimination against
women postulate similarly false theories: women are less
intelligent or more emotional and so on, but with the crucial difference that there *is* a functional physical difference
between the sexes, and a fundamentally important one,
whereas there is no analogous functional difference between racial groups, however defined. Women bear and
feed children: men do not. This fact has nothing to do
with women's intelligence or aptitudes, but it has a great
deal to do with their relationships towards the youngest
human beings. In most parts of the world now, as in all
parts of the world in the past, a baby needs a mother's (or a
nurse's) feeding for many months, perhaps years, in order
to survive; more obviously still, it needs a mother's

nourishment before birth and effort at birth to be born at all. These are functions that no man can perform. Anti-sexists would like to have a world where this functional difference was as illusory as the supposed functional differences between races that racists pretend exist: that is why abortion and deviant sexual behaviour are so important to anti-sexists.

Western technology and social organisation have taken away some of the functions of a mother with artificial feeding; they have attempted to take away more, by experimenting with rearing embryos outside the womb; they have given women the power to avoid conception or to have some choice over when it takes place by the use of oral contraceptives. In most of the world outside the rich countries (apart from the disastrous effects on infant health in parts of Africa of the commercial promotion of artificial feeding) these innovations have had little effect. Women in the richest countries have been greatly affected by the use of contraception and artificial feeding; most women have not. Some women in rich countries have taken these changes to be on a line of development towards complete abolition of sexual function, and are impatient to press on to the end of the line: a point at which men's and women's physiology are not essentially different from each other. (Germaine Greer says: 'Of forty-eight chromosomes, only one is different: on this difference we base a complete separation of male and female, pretending as it were that all forty-eight were different'. She also argues that body-hair varies racially rather than sexually and gives as an example—an example whose expression suggests that she is ready to swallow racial stereotypes if not sexual ones—'That most virile of creatures, the buck negro [sic], has very little body hair at all'.)

Anti-sexism's idea of women's equality is quite different from what might be called the political or reforming idea of equality; it depends not on accepting a functional sexual difference while demanding equal rights in education, employment, property and so on but on minimising sexual difference itself, sexually as well as socially and politically. An important part of anti-sexism is an attempt to find a new theory of human sexuality. Sometimes the

minimising of difference involves rejection of motherhood,
sometimes sexual admiration centred on the self rather
than on another person, sometimes a sexual attraction towards other women rather than towards men, sometimes a
relationship with men in which women can play the part
of aggressors. All these attempts represent a revolt against
conventions of Western cultures, but unhappily they do
more than this. They deny universal qualities and hap-
pinesses which American conventions in particular have
vulgarised: they vulgarise in their turn, and counter one
distorted theory of human sexuality with another.

The mood and style of anti-sexism have come to Britain
and elsewhere, but derive originally from the United
States, and reflect many aspects of culture, convention and
economic organisation which are peculiarly American.
Transplanting this mood, this style, to different cultures,
sometimes leads to absurdities. They are less immediately
obvious here, so heavily are we influenced by American
culture, than they would be in many places—in West
Africa, for instance, where women are traditionally in
charge of commerce, in a way that is quite alien to American culture, or among the nomadic peoples of central Asia
whose women do the creative artistic work of making
superb individual carpets while the men look after the
animals, or in the kind of Muslim society where it is
enormously practically important to have a son because
custom decrees that the eldest son is responsible for looking after his parents in their old age when they cannot
work to support themselves. The idea that a woman cannot be beautiful *and* intelligent would seem extraordinary
in many cultures; anti-sexism has rebelled against the idea
in the United States where it is particularly strong: indeed,
the dumb blonde is a specifically American creation, as is
the girl who gets her man by taking off her glasses and
forgetting her interest in books. The anti-sexists' objection
to beauty contests represents a reasonable and valid revulsion against what American culture has done to the idea of
what a woman is, but outside the United States a demonstration against beauty contests has a less deep significance. It finds fewer echoes, for instance, in the treatment of little girls; for a long time little American girls of

kindergarten age and above a certain income-level have endured elaborate hair-dos, nail-varnish and a different dress each day of the week as though they were miniature contestant sex-symbols; most of the world has mercifully been spared this phenomenon.

Anti-sexism has attempted to generalise from the situation of the discontented middle-class white woman in an American-style culture. This generalisation very rapidly becomes strained. First, it enlarges its own claims by asserting or implying that all kinds of misery suffered by women are due to sexism, to the denial of women's equal humanity with men. But in doing this it muddles a lot of issues, claiming as manifestations of sexism what are really manifestations of racism, of oppression of the poor, of the cruelty of the strong to the weak, sometimes too of the protection of the weak against the strong. Second, it creates a new theory of what a woman is, a theory in no way analogous to the anti-racist's theory of what a human being is, since it is an attempt to throw off responsibility towards babies, even if this means killing off the unborn ones, whereas the anti-racist argues responsibility towards other human beings. The anti-racist's human being is a personality worthy of life and respect, regardless of racial or national character; the anti-sexist's woman is defined in terms much narrower and more specific: a woman who does not accept that it is her job to look after children, a woman who goes out to work, a woman who does not want to look after a man; a woman whose rights over her own body include rights of life and death over her own unborn children (even if these are female). The style adopted by this new kind of woman is distinctive and recognisable: it is not the same as that of the 'New Woman' of the early twentieth century, confident in her own femaleness at the same time as being intellectual and independent-minded; rather it is ambiguous, disliking and yet imitating men at the same time, asserting the value of woman while resenting being one, and keener on karate than on either knitting or classical studies. The language used about sexuality by anti-sexists is crude, mechanical and often contemptuous. Whereas anti-racism has used as one of its slogans, 'Black is beautiful', anti-sexism abso-

lutely rejects, 'Woman is beautiful.' That would have to
be, in their book, a sexist concept, a way of implying
women are mere sex-objects. (It would also imply accepting that beauty in all its aspects is an important human
value; an idea that would fit very uneasily into the style of
most anti-sexist propaganda.)

Yet the liberated woman represents a revolt against real
evils in the society from which it springs. If anti-sexists
hate the ideals and stereotypes of American womanhood,
who can blame them? The mindless fun-girl, Bunny or
topless waitress; the active and hygienic suburban pie-
maker and committee-runner; the career girl who comes
to understand in the end that all the time she has been
yearning really to put on an apron and start cooking and
that her career was just a freakish phase; the horny-handed
pioneering mother who raises ten children and a shotgun
with equal facility: none of these ideals is associated with
sensitivity, tenderness, wisdom, gentleness or subtlety,
qualities which other cultures, rightly or wrongly, have attributed in different ways to women. But nor is the
counter-ideal the anti-sexists have put up. The counter-
ideal, instead of building on all the real potential of real
American women themselves, has abandoned the
stereotypes of American womanhood in favour of some
equally unappealing stereotypes of American manhood:
toughness, go-getting, self-assertiveness—and preferring
karate to knitting or classical studies. Of course, in the
United States, rape is commonplace enough for it to make
very good sense for a woman to learn karate: she has a
powerful practical need to be able to defend herself which
is much more important than being able to produce
hand-made woollies or construe a passage of Greek. When,
however, an American style of women's liberation is imitated outside the United States, it is important to remember that such a style has a different significance in
different kinds of culture: what may express, in one place,
a practical need for self-defense, may in another signify
only a readiness to be aggressive. In countries where a
woman is well protected from random violence, she may
also suffer restriction on her freedom of movement. The
restriction that guarantees security may often be excessive; it may lead to real oppression, but it originates not in

contempt for women but in a desire to give them more security than men. There are other ways in which a status for women that is different from men's offers advantages as well as disadvantages: the poorer and less technologically advanced a country is, the more disruptive of a practicable pattern of life will be the attempt to transplant a Western idea of the liberated woman.

Male prejudice against women is often combined with respect for women. In this way male prejudice is very different from racism. The denial of women's rights to work and live as they individually choose is often associated with contempt for women's intelligence and capacity, but at the same time with a desire to protect those who have the main responsibility for perpetuating human life. The slogan, 'Women and children first,' invoked in shipwreck or other disaster, is not an expression of contempt or hostility but of a belief in the special *importance* of women and children in the crucial moments when the choice of who among many are to deserve survival is a real one. The racist would not be crying 'Jews and blacks first'; on the contrary, racially despised groups would be the expendable ones.

Anti-sexism is concerned with many genuinely good causes: the protection of women against rape and of wives against extreme physical violence from their husbands; the right to work in all kinds of employment and to receive an equal rate of pay with men for so doing; the provision of day nurseries for small children; legal help against heartless bureaucracy; help for widows; decent housing. All these causes, however, can be and have been fought for without the necessary accompaniment of anti-sexism's characteristic style, and without being listed alongside abortion on demand and sterilisation or with the suggestion that if women want an amelioration of their condition they must refuse to marry, bring to an end the patriarchal family and stop buying cosmetics. Anti-sexists tend to sneer at old-style women reformers; here again they borrow terms from quite a different kind of political battle in demanding revolution, not reform. But their desired revolution is in sexuality, not in the workings of justice throughout a society: pubic events, rather than public events, are their chief concern.

Western societies have for some time been socially very unstable. The centres of rapid change and new development have shifted away, in the twentieth century, from Europe and from the European culture that countries dominated by white people have inherited. Anyone who seriously wants to imagine how the world will look in two centuries' time (assuming it is still there) would be foolish to study the West now in search of answers; Asia and Africa are going to determine the patterns of change. Even before the West's self-confidence in its own assured economic progress and supremacy was badly shaken by the oil-price crisis, its instability had become evident in many ways: the rate of destruction of natural resources, the disruptive social consequences of wars, a loss of confidence in progress, a tendency to heavily bureaucratic form of organisation, forced movements of population (from refugees to the victims of large-scale property development and municipal housing policies). In societies whose normal condition is one of flux and uncertainty, it is natural for a constant search to be going on for new definitions and new images that will make sense of the confusion. Women's liberation is one of the attempted new definitions, and its protagonists want to claim that it is the only possible definition of woman and her relationship to the rest of society that makes sense. Anti-sexism places itself on the Left, alongside anti-colonialism, anti-capitalism, anti-pollution, and so pitches its appeal to radicals and revolutionaries.

Those who are already convinced of the validity of other causes generally labelled leftish or radical find it very hard to dissociate themselves from any revolutionary appeal. They have an understandable reluctance, for example, if they happen to believe that abortion is a particularly abominable killing of the innocent, to find themselves sneered at by anti-sexists and cheered on by the defenders of South African apartheid; if they find commercial pornography repellent, they may keep quiet about it rather than find themselves on the same side as Mrs. Mary Whitehouse, and the opposite one from women whose names are associated with legal aid for the poor. But each cause must be examined for itself, not for its associations, and when we examine the anti-sexist cause, we find that despite its claims to be revolutionary it does not belong with those causes that are concerned with justice and a respect for human life. Far from being revolutionary, it has, I think, many of the reactionary characteristics of the rich capitalist culture from which it springs: aggressive egoism, ignorance of or arrogance towards the cultures of others, admiration for the strong self-willed individual.

Anti-racism, on the contrary, insists on a historical view of humankind wider than that taken by the contemporary West, and favours human variety and interdependence. I do not want to say that racism and anti-sexism are exactly analogous: rather, that the issue between racism and anti-racism is a completely different kind of issue, and a far bigger one, than the issue between sexism and anti-sexism. Attempts to pretend that these issues are, as a member of a conference I attended recently put it, 'two sides of the same coin,' can only result in muddled thinking and false conclusions. Practical harm as well as theoretical difficulty can result from such superficial comparison of sexism and racism. The theoretical harm I have attempted to indicate briefly in some of its aspects. The practical harm is two fold: the devaluation of work against racism in this country, by false analogy with women's liberation, and the setting up of an ideal of what a woman should be which is grotesque, denatured and self-absorbed. A women's movement which really cared about human beings would be nothing like anti-sexism; it would be one that drew on all the strengths and capacities of women, including their special capacity to care for the youngest and most helpless humans, which respected the intricate balance between personal relationships and social organisation that exist in many different kinds of society, that was more concerned with helping people to be together than to be apart, and which honoured the need of men and women to care for each other—in a manner summed up by the phrase we used to hear when the Labour Party in this country was something like a Socialist Party instead of a Conservative one: 'from each according to his capacity, to each according to his need'.

Justifying Reverse Discrimination in Employment

George Sher

A currently favored way of compensating for past discrimination is to afford preferential treatment to the members of those groups which have been discriminated against in the past. I propose to examine the rationale behind this practice when it is applied in the area of employment. I want to ask whether, and if so under what conditions, past acts of discrimination against members of a particular group justify the current hiring of a member of that group who is less than the best qualified applicant for a given job. Since I am mainly concerned about exploring the relations between past discrimination and present claims to employment, I shall make the assumption that each applicant is at least minimally competent to perform the job he seeks; this will eliminate the need to consider the claims of those who are to receive the services in question. Whether it is ever justifiable to discriminate in favor of an incompetent applicant, or a less than best qualified applicant for a job such as teaching, in which almost any increase in employee competence brings a real increase in services rendered, will be left to be decided elsewhere.

I am grateful to Michael Levin, Edward Erwin, and my wife Emily Gordon Sher for helpful discussion of this topic.

Such questions, which turn on balancing the claim of the less than best qualified applicant against the competing claims of those of who are to receive his services, are not as basic as the question of whether the less than best qualified applicant ever *has* a claim to employment.[1]

I

It is sometimes argued, when members of a particular group have been barred from employment of a certain kind, that since this group has in the past received *less* than its fair share of the employment in question, it now deserves to receive *more* by way of compensation.[2] This argument, if sound, has the virtue of showing clearly why preferential treatment should be extended even to those current group members who have not themselves been denied employment: if the point of reverse discrimination is to compensate a wronged *group*, it will presumably hardly matter if those who are preferentially hired were not among the original victims of discrimination. However, the argument's basic presupposition, that groups as opposed to their individual members are the sorts of entities that can be wronged and deserve redress, is itself problematic.[3] Thus the defense of reverse discrimination

---

[1] In what follows I will have nothing to say about utilitarian justifications of reverse discrimination. There are two reasons for this. First, the winds of utilitarian argumentation blow in too many directions. It is certainly socially beneficial to avoid the desperate actions to which festering resentments may lead—but so too is it socially useful to confirm the validity of qualifications of the traditional sort, to assure those who have amassed such qualifications that "the rules of the game have not been changed in the middle," that accomplishment has not been downgraded in society's eyes. How could these conflicting utilities possibly be measured against one another?

Second and even more important, to rest a defense of reverse discrimination upon utilitarian considerations would be to ignore what is surely the guiding intuition of its proponents, that this treatment is *deserved* where discrimination has been practiced in the past. It is the intuition that reverse discrimination is a matter not (only) of social good but of right which I want to try to elucidate.

[2] This argument, as well as the others I shall consider, presupposes that jobs are (among other things) *goods*, and so ought to be distributed as fairly as possible. This presupposition seems to be amply supported by the sheer economic necessity of earning a living, as well as by the fact that some jobs carry more prestige and are more interesting and pay better than others.

[3] As Robert Simon has pointed out in "Preferential Hiring: A Reply to Judith Jarvis Thomson," *Philosophy & Public Affairs* 3, no. 3 (Spring 1974): 312–320, it is also far from clear that the preferential hiring of its individual members could be a proper form of compensation for any wronged group that *did* exist.

would only be convincing if it were backed by a further argument showing that groups can indeed be wronged and have deserts of the relevant sort. No one, as far as I know, has yet produced a powerful argument to this effect, and I am not hopeful about the possibilities. Therefore I shall not try to develop a defense of reverse discrimination along these lines.

Another possible way of connecting past acts of discrimination in hiring with the claims of current group members is to argue that even if these current group members have not (yet) been denied *employment*, their membership in the group makes it very likely that they have been discriminatorily deprived of *other* sorts of goods. It is a commonplace, after all, that people who are forced to do menial and low-paying jobs must often endure corresponding privations in housing, diet, and other areas. These privations are apt to be distributed among young and old alike, and so to afflict even those group members who are still too young to have had their qualifications for employment bypassed. It is, moreover, generally acknowledged by both common sense and law that a person who has been deprived of a certain amount of one sort of good may sometimes reasonably be compensated by an equivalent amount of a good of another sort. (It is this principle, surely, that underlies the legal practice of awarding sums of money to compensate for pain incurred in accidents, damaged reputations, etc.) Given these facts and this principle, it appears that the preferential hiring of current members of discriminated-against groups may be justified as compensation for the *other* sorts of discrimination these individuals are apt to have suffered.[4]

But, although this argument seems more promising than one presupposing group deserts, it surely cannot be accepted as it stands. For one thing, insofar as the point is simply to compensate individuals for the various sorts of privations they have suffered, there is no special reason to use reverse discrimination rather than some other

---

[4]A version of this argument is advanced by Judith Jarvis Thomson in "Preferential Hiring," *Philosophy & Public Affairs* 2, no. 4 (Simmer 1973): 364–384.

mechanism to effect compensation. There are, moreover, certain other mechanisms of redress which seem prima facie preferable. It seems, for instance, that it would be most appropriate to compensate for past privations simply by making preferentially available to the discriminated-against individuals equivalent amounts of the very same sorts of goods of which they have been deprived; simple cash settlements would allow a far greater precision in the adjustment of compensation to privation than reverse discriminatory hiring ever could. Insofar as it does not provide any reason to adopt reverse discrimination rather than these *prima facie* preferable mechanisms of redress, the suggested defense of reverse discrimination is at least incomplete.

Moreover, and even more important, if reverse discrimination is viewed simply as a form of compensation for past privations, there are serious questions about its fairness. Certainly the privations to be compensated for are not the sole responsibility of those individuals whose superior qualifications will have to be bypassed in the reverse discriminatory process. These individuals, if responsible for those privations at all, will at least be no more responsible than others with relevantly similar histories. Yet reverse discrimination will compensate for the privations in question at the expense of these individuals alone. It will have no effect at all upon those other, equally responsible persons whose qualifications are inferior to begin with, who are already entrenched in their jobs, or whose vocations are noncompetitive in nature. Surely it is unfair to distribute the burden of compensation so unequally.[5]

These considerations show, I think, that reverse discriminatory hiring of members of groups that have been denied jobs in the past cannot be justified simply by the fact that each group member has been discriminated against in other areas. If this fact is to enter into the justification of reverse discrimination at all, it must be in some more complicated way.

---

[5]Cf. Simon, "Preferential Hiring," sec. III.

II

Consider again the sorts of privations that are apt to be distributed among the members of those groups restricted in large part to menial and low-paying jobs. These individuals, we said, are apt to live in substandard homes, to subsist on improper and imbalanced diets, and to receive inadequate educations. Now, it is certainly true that adequate housing, food, and education are goods in and of themselves; a life without them is certainly less pleasant and less full than one with them. But, and crucially, they are also goods in a different sense entirely. It is an obvious and well-documented fact that (at least) the sorts of nourishment and education a person receives as a child will causally affect the sorts of skills and capacities he will have as an adult—including, of course, the very skills which are needed if he is to compete on equal terms for jobs and other goods. Since this is so, a child who is deprived of adequate food and education may lose not only the immediate enjoyments which a comfortable and stimulating environment bring but also the subsequent ability to compete equally for other things of intrinsic value. But to lose this ability to compete is, in essence, to lose one's access to the goods that are being competed for; and this, surely, is itself a privation to be compensated for if possible. It is, I think, the key to an adequate justification of reverse discrimination to see that practice, not as the redressing of *past* privations, but rather as a way of neutralizing the *present* competitive disadvantage *caused* by those past privations and thus as a way of restoring equal access to those goods which society distributes competitively.[6] When reverse discrimination is justified in this

---

[6]A similar justification of reverse discrimination is suggested, but not ultimately endorsed, by Thomas Nagel in "Equal Treatment and Compensatory Discrimination," *Philosophy & Public Affairs* 2, no. 4 (Summer 1973): 348–363. Nagel rejects this justification on the grounds that a system distributing goods solely on the basis of performance determined by native ability would itself be unjust, even if not *as* unjust as one distributing goods on a racial or sexual basis. I shall not comment on this, except to remark that our moral intuitions surely run the other way: the average person would certainly find the latter system of distribution *far* more unjust than the former, if, indeed, he found the former unjust at all. Because of this, the burden is on Nagel to show exactly why a purely meritocratic system of distribution would be unjust.

way, many of the difficulties besetting the simpler justification of it disappear.

For whenever someone has been irrevocably deprived of
a certain good and there are several alternative ways of
providing him with an equivalent amount of another good,
it will ceteris paribus be preferable to choose whichever
substitute comes closest to actually replacing the lost
good. It is this principle that makes preferential access to
decent housing, food, and education especially desirable as
a way of compensating for the experiential impoverish-
ment of a deprived childhood. If, however, we are concerned to compensate not for the experiential poverty, but
for the effects of childhood deprivations, then this principle tells just as heavily for reverse discrimination as the
proper form of compensation. If the lost good is just the
ability to compete on equal terms for first-level goods like
desirable jobs, then surely the most appropriate (and so
preferable) way of substituting for what has been lost is
just to remove the *necessity* of competing on equal terms
for these goods—which, of course, is precisely what reverse discrimination does.

When reverse discrimination is viewed as compensation
for lost ability to compete on equal terms, a reasonable
case can also be made for its fairness. Our doubts about its
fairness arose because it seemed to place the entire burden
of redress upon those individuals whose superior qualifications are bypassed in the reverse discriminatory process.
This seemed wrong because these individuals are, of
course, not apt to be any more responsible for past discrimination than others with relevantly similar histories.
But, as we are now in a position to see, this objection
misses the point. The crucial fact about these individuals
is that not that they are more *responsible* for past discrimination than others with relevantly similar histories (in fact,
the dirty work may well have been done before any of their
generation attained the age of responsibility), but rather
that unless reverse discrimination is practiced, they will
benefit more than the others from its effects on their competitors. They will benefit more because unless they are
restrained, they, but not the others, will use their competitive edge to claim jobs which their competitors would

otherwise have gotten. Thus, it is only because they stand to *gain* the most from the relevant effects of the *original* discrimination, that the bypassed individuals stand to *lose* the most from *reverse* discrimination.[7] This is surely a valid reply to the charge that reverse discrimination does not distribute the burden of compensation equally.

III

So far, the argument has been that reverse discrimination is justified insofar as it neutralizes competitive disadvantages caused by past privations. This may be correct, but it is also oversimplified. In actuality, there are many ways in which a person's environment may affect his ability to compete; and there may well be logical differences among these ways which affect the degree to which reverse discrimination is called for. Consider, for example, the following cases:

1. An inadequate education prevents someone from acquiring the degree of a certain skill that he would have been able to acquire with a better education.
2. An inadequate diet, lack of early intellectual stimulation, etc., lower an individual's ability, and thus pre-

---

[7]It is tempting, but I think largely irrelevant, to object here that many who are now entrenched in their jobs (tenured professors, for example) have already benefited from the effects of past discrimination at least as much as the currently best qualified applicant will if reverse discrimination is not practiced. While many such individuals have undoubtedly benefited from the effects of discrimination upon *their original* competitors, few if any are likely to have benefited from a reduction in the abilities of the *currently best qualified applicant's* competitor. As long as none of them have so benefited, the best qualified applicant in question will still stand to gain the most from that *particular* effect of past discrimination, and so reverse discrimination against him will remain fair. Of course, there will also be cases in which an entrenched person *has* previously benefited from the reduced abilities of the currently best qualified applicant's competitor. In these cases, the best qualified applicant will *not* be the single main beneficiary of his rival's handicap, and so reverse discrimination against him will *not* be entirely fair. I am inclined to think there may be a case for reverse discrimination even here, however; for if it is truly impossible to dislodge the entrenched previous beneficiary of his rival's handicap, reverse discrimination against the best qualified applicant may at least be the fairest (or least unfair) of the practical alternatives.

vent him from acquiring the degree of competence in a skill that he would otherwise have been able to acquire.

3. The likelihood that he will not be able to use a certain skill because he belongs to a group which has been discriminated against in the past leads a person to decide, rationally, not even to try developing that skill.

4. Some aspect of his childhood environment renders an individual incapable of putting forth the sustained effort needed to improve his skills.

These are four different ways in which past privations might adversely affect a person's skills. Ignoring for analytical purposes the fact that privation often works in more than one of these ways at a time, shall we say that reverse discrimination is equally called for in each case?

It might seem that we should say it is, since in each case a difference in the individual's environment would have been accompanied by an increase in his mastery of a certain skill (and, hence, by an improvement in his competitive position with respect to jobs requiring that skill). But this blanket counterfactual formulation conceals several important distinctions. For one thing, it suggests (and our justification of reverse discrimination seems to require) the possibility of giving *just enough* preferential treatment to the disadvantaged individual in each case to restore to him the competitive position that he would have had, had he not suffered his initial disadvantage. But in fact, this does not seem to be equally possible in all cases. We can roughly calculate the difference that a certain improvement in education or intellectual stimulation would have made in the development of a person's skills if his efforts had been held constant (cases 1 and 2); for achievement is known to be a relatively straightforward compositional function of ability, environmental factors, and effort. We cannot, however, calculate in the same way the difference that improved prospects or environment would have made in degree of *effort* expended; for although effort is affected by environmental factors, it is not a known compositional function of them (or of anything else). Because of this, there would be no way for us to decide how much preferential treatment is just enough to make up for the efforts that a particular disadvantaged individual would have made under happier circumstances.

There is also another problem with (3) and (4). Even if there were a way to afford a disadvantaged person just enough preferential treatment to make up for the efforts he was prevented from making by his environment, it is not clear that he *ought* to be afforded that much preferential treatment. To allow this, after all, would be to concede that the effort he *would* have made under other conditions is worth just as much as the effort that his rival actually *did* make; and this, I think, is implausible. Surely a person who *actually has* labored long and hard to achieve a given degree of a certain skill is more deserving of a job requiring that skill than another who is equal in all other relevant respects, but who merely *would* have worked and achieved the same amount under different conditions. Because actual effort creates desert in a way that merely possible effort does not, reverse discrimination to restore precisely the competitive position that a person would have had if he had not been prevented from working harder would not be desirable even if it were possible.

There is perhaps also a further distinction to be made here. A person who is rationally persuaded by an absence of opportunities not to develop a certain skill (case 3) will typically not undergo any sort of character transformation in the process of making this decision. He will be the same person after his decision as before it, and, most often, the same person without his skill as with it. In cases such as (4), this is less clear. A person who is rendered incapable of effort by his environment does in a sense undergo a character transformation; to become truly incapable of sustained effort is to become a different (and less meritorious) person from the person one would otherwise have been. Because of this (and somewhat paradoxically, since his character change is itself apt to stem from factors beyond his control), such an individual may have less of a claim to reverse discrimination than one whose lack of effort does not flow from even an environmentally induced character fault, but rather from a justified rational decision.[8]

IV

When reverse discrimination is discussed in a nontheoretical context, it is usually assumed that the people most deserving of such treatment are blacks, members of other ethnic minorities, and women. In this last section, I shall bring the results of the foregoing discussion to bear on this assumption. Doubts will be raised both about the analogy between the claims of blacks and women to reverse discrimination and about the propriety, in absolute terms, of singling out either group as the proper recipient of such treatment.

For many people, the analogy between the claims of blacks and the claims of women to reverse discrimination rests simply upon the undoubted fact that both groups have been discriminatorily denied jobs in the past. But on the account just proposed, past discrimination justifies reverse discrimination only insofar as it has adversely affected the competitive position of present group members. When this standard is invoked, the analogy between the claims of blacks and those of women seems immediately to break down. The exclusion of blacks from good jobs in the past has been only one element in an interlocking pattern of exclusions and often has resulted in a poverty issuing in (and in turn reinforced by) such other privations as inadequate nourishment, housing, and health care, lack of time to provide adequate guidance and intellectual stimulation for the young, dependence on (often inadequate) public education, etc. It is this whole complex of privations that undermines the ability of the young to compete;

---

[8]A somewhat similar difference might seem to obtain between cases (1) and (2). One's ability to learn is more intimately a part of him than his actual degree of education; hence, someone whose ability to learn is lowered by his environment (case 2) is a changed person in a way in which a person who is merely denied education (case 1) is not. However, one's ability to learn is not a feature of *moral* character in the way ability to exert effort is, and so this difference between (1) and (2) will have little bearing on the degree to which reverse discrimination is called for in these cases.

and it is largely because of its central causal role in this complex that the past unavailability of good jobs for blacks justifies reverse discrimination in their favor now. In the case of women, past discrimination in employment simply has not played the same role. Because children commonly come equipped with both male *and* female parents, the inability of the female parent to get a good job need not, and usually does not, result in a poverty detracting from the quality of the nourishment, education, housing, health, or intellectual stimulation of the female child (and, of course, when such poverty does result, it affects male and female children indifferently). For this reason, the past inaccessibility of good jobs for women does not seem to create for them the same sort of claim on reverse discrimination that its counterpart does for blacks.

Many defenders of reverse discrimination in favor of women would reply at this point that although past discrimination in employment has of course not played the *same* causal role in the case of women which it has in the case of blacks, it has nevertheless played *a* causal role in both cases. In the case of women, the argument runs, that role has been mainly psychological: past discrimination in hiring has led to a scarcity of female "role-models" of suitably high achievement. This lack, together with a culture which in many other ways subtly inculcates the idea that women should not or cannot do the jobs that men do, has in turn made women psychologically less able to do these jobs. This argument is hard to assess fully, since it obviously rests on a complex and problematic psychological claim.[9] The following objections, however, are surely relevant. First, even if it is granted without question that cultural bias and absence of suitable role-models do have some direct and pervasive effect upon women, it is not clear that this effect must take the form of a reduction of women's *abilities* to do the jobs men do. A more likely outcome would seem to be a reduction of women's *inclinations* to do these jobs—a result whose proper compensa-

---

[9]The feminist movement has convincingly documented the ways in which sexual bias is built into the information received by the young; but it is one thing to show that such information is received, and quite another to show how, and to what extent, its reception is causally efficacious.

tion is not preferential treatment of those women who have sought the jobs in question, but rather the encouragement of others to seek those jobs as well. Of course, this disinclination to do these jobs may in turn lead some women not to develop the relevant skills; to the extent that this occurs, the competitive position of these women will indeed be affected, albeit indirectly, by the scarcity of female role-models. Even here, however, the resulting disadvantage will not be comparable to those commonly produced by the poverty syndrome. It will flow solely from lack of effort, and so will be of the sort (cases 3 and 4) that neither calls for nor admits of full equalization by reverse discrimination. Moreover, and conclusively, since there is surely the same dearth of role-models, etc., for blacks as for women, whatever psychological disadvantages accrue to women because of this will beset blacks as well. Since blacks, but not women, must also suffer the privations associated with poverty, it follows that they are the group more deserving of reverse discrimination.

Strictly speaking, however, the account offered here does not allow us to speak this way of *either* group. If the point of reverse discrimination is to compensate for competitive disadvantages caused by past discrimination, it will be justified in favor of only those group members whose abilities have actually been reduced; and it would be most implausible to suppose that *every* black (or *every* woman) has been affected in this way. Blacks from middle-class or affluent backgrounds will surely have escaped many, if not all, of the competitive handicaps besetting those raised under less fortunate circumstances; and if they have, our account provides no reason to practice reverse discrimination in their favor. Again, whites from impoverished backgrounds may suffer many, if not all, of the competitive handicaps besetting their black counterparts; and if they do, the account provides no reason *not* to practice reverse discrimination in their favor. Generally, the proposed account allows us to view racial (and sexual) boundaries only as roughly suggesting which individuals are likely to have been disadvantaged by past discrimination. Anyone who construes these boundaries as playing a different and more decisive role must show us that a different defense of reverse discrimination is plausible.

University of California v. Bakke (1978)

United States Supreme Court

Mr. Justice Powell announced the judgment of the Court.

The Medical School of the University of California at Davis opened in 1968 with an entering class of 50 students. In 1971, the size of the entering class was increased to 100 students, a level at which it remains. No admissions program for disadvantaged or minority students existed when the school opened, and the first class contained three Asians but no blacks, no Mexican-Americans, and no American Indians. Over the next two years, the faculty devised a special admissions program to increase the representation of "disadvantaged" students in each medical school class. The special program consisted of a separate admissions system operating in coordination with the regular admissions process.

Under the regular admissions procedure, a candidate could submit his application to the medical school beginning in July of the year preceding the academic year for which admission was sought. Because of the large number of applications, the admissions committee screened each one to select candidates for further consideration. Candidates whose overall undergraduate grade point averages fell below 2.5 on a scale of 4.0 were summarily rejected. About one out of six applicants was invited for a personal interview. Following the interviews, each candidate was rated on a scale of 1 to 100 by his interviewers and four other members of the admissions committee. The rating embraced the interviewers' summaries, the candidate's overall grade point average, grade point average in science courses, and scores on the Medical College Admissions Test (MCAT), letters of recommendation, extracurricular activities, and other biographical data. The ratings were added together to arrive at each candidate's "benchmark" score. Since five committee members rated each candidate in 1973, a perfect score was 500; in 1974, six members rated each candidate, so that a perfect score was 600. The full committee then reviewed the file and scores of each applicant and made offers of admission on a "rolling" basis. The chairman was responsible for placing names on the waiting list. They were not placed in strict numerical order; instead, the chairman had discretion to include persons with "special skills."

The special admissions program operated with a separate committee, a majority of whom were members of minority groups. On the 1973 application form, candidates were asked to indicate whether they wished to be considered as "economically and/or educationally disadvantaged" applicants; on the 1974 form the question was whether they wished to be considered as members of a "minority group," which the medical school apparently viewed as "Blacks," "Chicanos," "Asians," and "American Indians." If these questions were answered affirmatively, the application was forwarded to the special admissions committee. No formal definition of "disadvantage" was ever produced, but the chairman of the special committee screened each application to see whether it reflected economic or educational deprivation. Having passed this initial hurdle, the applications then were rated by the special committee in a fashion similar to that used by the general admissions committee, except that special candidates did not have to meet the 2.5 grade point average cut-off applied to regular applicants. About one-fifth of the total number of special applicants were invited for interviews in 1973 and 1974. Following each interview, the special committee assigned each special applicant a benchmark score. The special committee then presented its top choices to the general admissions committee. The latter did not rate or compare the special candidates against the general applicants, but could reject recommended special candidates for failure to meet course requirements or other specific deficiencies. The special committee continued to recommend special applicants until a number prescribed by faculty vote were admitted. While the overall class size was still 50, the prescribed number was eight; in 1973 and 1974, when the class size had doubled to 100, the prescribed number of special admissions also doubled, to 16.

From the year of the increase in class size—1971— through 1974, the special program resulted in the admission of 21 black students, 30 Mexican-Americans, and 12 Asians, for a total of 63 minority students. Over the same period, the regular admissions program produced one black, six Mexican-Americans, and 37 Asians, for a total of 44 minority students. Although disadvantaged whites applied to the special program in large numbers, none received an offer of admission through that process. Indeed, in 1974, at least, the special committee explicitly considered only "disadvantaged" special applicants who were members of one of the designated minority groups.

Allan Bakke is a white male who applied to the Davis Medical School in both 1973 and 1974. In both years Bakke's application was considered by the general admissions program, and he received an interview. His 1973 interview was with Dr. Theodore H. West, who considered Bakke "a very desirable applicant to [the] medical school." Despite a strong benchmark score of 468 out of 500, Bakke was rejected. His application had come late in the year, and no applicants in the general admissions process with scores below 470 were accepted after Bakke's application was completed. There were four special admissions slots unfilled at that time, however, for which Bakke was not considered. After his 1973 rejection, Bakke wrote to Dr. George H. Lowrey, Associate Dean and Chairman of the Admissions Committee, protesting that the special admissions program operated as a racial and ethnic quota.

Bakke's 1974 application was completed early in the year. His student interviewer gave him an overall rating of 94, finding him "friendly, well tempered, conscientious and delightful to speak with." His faculty interviewer was, by coincidence, the same Dr. Lowrey to whom he had written in protest of the special admissions program. Dr.

Lowrey found Bakke "rather limited in his approach" to the problems of the medical profession and found disturbing Bakke's "very definite opinions which were based more on his personal viewpoints than upon a study of the total problem." Dr. Lowrey gave Bakke the lowest of his six ratings, an 86; his total was 549 out of 600. Again, Bakke's application was rejected. In neither year did the chairman of the admissions committee, Dr. Lowrey, exercise his discretion to place Bakke on the waiting list. In both years, applicants were admitted under the special program with grade point averages, MCAT scores, and bench mark scores significantly lower than Bakke's.

After the second rejection, Bakke filed the instant suit in the Superior Court of California. He sought mandatory, injunctive, and declaratory relief compelling his admission to the Medical School. He alleged that the Medical School's special admissions program operated to exclude him from the school on the basis of his race, in violation of his rights under the Equal Protection Clause of the Fourteenth Amendment, Art. I, § 21 of the California Constitution, and § 601 of Title VI of the Civil Rights Act of 1964. The University cross-complained for a declaration that its special admissions program was lawful. The trial court found that the special program operated as a racial quota, because minority applicants in the special program were rated only against one another, and 16 places in the class of 100 were reserved for them. Declaring that the University could not take race into account in making admissions decisions, the trial court held the challenged program violative of the Federal Constitution, the state constitution and Title VI. The court refused to order Bakke's admission, however, holding that he had failed to carry his burden of proving that he would have been admitted but for the existence of the special program.

Bakke appealed from the portion of the trial court judgment denying him admission, and the University appealed from the decision that its special admissions program was unlawful and the order enjoining it from considering race in the processing of applications. The Supreme Court of California transferred the case directly from the trial court, "because of the importance of the issues involved." The

California court accepted the findings of the trial court with respect to the University's program. Because the special admissions program involved a racial classification, the supreme court held itself bound to apply strict scrutiny. It then turned to the goals the University presented as justifying the special program. Although the court agreed that the goals of integrating the medical profession and increasing the number of physicians willing to serve members of minority groups were compelling state interests, it concluded that the special admissions program was not the least intrusive means of achieving those goals. Without passing on the state constitutional or the federal statutory grounds cited in the trial court's judgment, the California court held that the Equal Protection Clause of the Fourteenth Amendment required that "no applicant may be rejected because of his race, in favor of another who is less qualified, as measured by standards applied without regard to race."

Turning to Bakke's appeal, the court ruled that since Bakke had established that the University had discriminated against him on the basis of his race, the burden of proof shifted to the University to demonstrate that he would not have been admitted even in the absence of the special admissions program. . . . The court initially ordered a remand for the purpose of determining whether, under the newly allocated burden of proof, Bakke would have been admitted to either the 1973 or the 1974 entering class in the absence of the special admissions program. In its petition for rehearing below, however, the University conceded its inability to carry that burden. The California court thereupon amended its opinion to direct that the trial court enter judgment ordering Bakke's admission to the medical school. That order was stayed pending review in this Court.

. . . . . .

Although many of the Framers of the Fourteenth Amendment conceived of its primary function as bridging the vast distance between members of the Negro race and the white "majority," the Amendment itself was framed in universal terms, without reference to color, ethnic origin, or condition of prior servitude. As this Court recently remarked in interpreting the 1866 Civil Rights Act to extend to claims of racial discrimination against white persons, "the 39th Congress was intent upon establishing in federal law a broader principle than would have been necessary to meet the particular and immediate plight of the newly freed Negro slaves." . . .

Over the past 30 years, this Court has embarked upon the crucial mission of interpreting the Equal Protection Clause with the view of assuring to all persons "the protection of equal laws," in a Nation confronting a legacy of slavery and racial discrimination. Because the landmark decisions in this area arose in response to the continued exclusion of Negroes from the mainstream of American society, they could be characterized as involving discrimination by the "majority" white race against the Negro minority. But they need not be read as depending upon that characterization for their results. It suffices to say that "[o]ver the years, this Court consistently repudiated '[d]istinctions between citizens solely because of their ancestry' as being 'odious to a free people whose institutions are founded upon the doctrine of equality.'"

Petitioner urges us to adopt for the first time a more restrictive view of the Equal Protection Clause and hold that discrimination against members of the white "majority" cannot be suspect if its purpose can be characterized as "benign." The clock of our liberties, however, cannot be turned back to 1868. It is far too late to argue that the guarantee of equal protection to *all* persons permits the recognition of special wards entitled to a degree of protection greater than that accorded others. "The Fourteenth Amendment is not directed solely against discrimination due to a 'two-class theory'—that is, based upon differences between 'white' and Negro."

Once the artificial line of a "two-class theory" of the Fourteenth Amendment is put aside, the difficulties entailed in varying the level of judicial review according to a perceived "preferred" status of a particular racial or ethnic minority are intractable. The concepts of "majority" and "minority" necessarily reflect temporary arrangements and political judgments. As observed above, the white "majority" itself is composed of various minority groups, most of which can lay claim to a history of prior discrimination at the hands of the state and private individuals. Not all of these groups can receive preferential treatment and corresponding judicial tolerance of distinctions drawn in terms of race and nationality, for then the only "majority" left would be a new minority of White Anglo-Saxon Protestants. There is no principled basis for deciding which groups would merit "heightened judicial solicitude" and which would not. Courts would be asked to evaluate the extent of the prejudice and consequent harm suffered by various minority groups. Those whose societal injury is thought to exceed some arbitrary level of tolerability then would be entitled to preferential classifications at the expense of individuals belonging to other groups. Those classifications would be free from exacting judicial scrutiny. As these preferences began to have their desired effect, and the consequences of past discrimination were undone, new judicial rankings would be necessary. The kind of variable sociological and political analysis necessary to produce such rankings simply does not lie within the judicial competence—even if they otherwise were politically feasible and socially desirable.

Moreover, there are serious problems of justice connected with the idea of preference itself. First, it may not always be clear that a so-called preference is in fact benign. Courts may be asked to validate burdens imposed upon individual members of particular groups in order to advance the group's general interest. Nothing in the Constitution supports the notion that individuals may be asked to suffer otherwise impermissible burdens in order to enhance the societal standing of their ethnic groups. Second, preferential programs may only reinforce common stereotypes holding that certain groups are unable to achieve success without special protection based on a factor having no relationship to individual worth. Third, there is a measure of inequity in forcing innocent persons in respondent's position to bear the burdens of redressing grievances not of their making.

By hitching the meaning of the Equal Protection Clause to these transitory considerations, we would be holding, as a constitutional principle, that judicial scrutiny of classifications touching on racial and ethnic background may vary with the ebb and flow of political forces. Disparate constitutional tolerance of such classifications well may serve to exacerbate racial and ethnic antagonisms rather than alleviate them. Also, the mutability of a constitutional principle, based upon shifting political and social judgments, undermines the chances for consistent application of the Constitution from one generation to the next, a critical feature of its coherent interpretation. In expounding the Constitution, the Court's role is to discern "principles sufficiently absolute to give them roots throughout the community and continuity over significant periods of time, and to lift them above the level of the pragmatic political judgments of a particular time and place."

If it is the individual who is entitled to judicial protection against classifications based upon his racial or ethnic background because such distinctions impinge upon personal rights, rather than the individual only because of his membership in a particular group, then constitutional standards may be applied consistently. Political judgments regarding the necessity for the particular classification may be weighed in the constitutional balance, but the standard of justification will remain constant. This is as it should be, since those political judgments are the product of rough compromise struck by contending groups within the democratic process. When they touch upon an individual's race or ethnic background, he is entitled to a judicial determination that the burden he is asked to bear on that basis is precisely tailored to serve a compelling governmental interest. The Constitution guarantees that right to every person regardless of his background.

. . . . . .

We have held that in "order to justify the use of a suspect classification, a State must show that its purpose or interest is both constitutionally permissible and substantial, and that its use of the classification is 'necessary . . . to the accomplishment' of its purpose or the safeguarding of its interest." The special admissions program purports to serve the purposes of: (i) "reducing the historic deficit of traditionally disfavored minorities in medical schools and

the medical profession," (ii) countering the effects of
societal discrimination; (iii) increasing the number of
physicians who will practice in communities currently
underserved; and (iv) obtaining the educational benefits
that flow from an ethnically diverse student body. It is
necessary to decide which, if any, of these purposes is substantial enough to support the use of a suspect classification.

(i) If petitioner's purpose is to assure within its student
body some specified percentage of a particular group
merely because of its race or ethnic origin, such a preferential purpose must be rejected not as insubstantial but as
facially invalid. Preferring members of any one group for
no reason other than race or ethnic origin is discrimination for its own sake. This the Constitution forbids.

(ii) The State certainly has a legitimate and substantial
interest in ameliorating, or eliminating where feasible, the
disabling effects of identified discrimination. The line of
school desegregation cases, commencing with *Brown,* at-
tests to the importance of this state goal and the commitment of the judiciary to affirm all lawful means towards
its attainment. In the school cases, the States were required by court order to redress the wrongs worked by
specific instances of racial discrimination. That goal was
far more focused than the remedying of the effects of
"societal discrimination," an amorphous concept of injury
that may be ageless in its reach into the past.

We have never approved a classification that aids persons perceived as members of relatively victimized groups
at the expense of other innocent individuals in the absence
of judicial, legislative, or administrative findings of constitutional or statutory violations. After such findings
have been made, the governmental interest in preferring
members of the injured groups at the expense of others is
substantial, since the legal rights of the victims must be
vindicated. In such a case, the extent of the injury and the
consequent remedy will have been judicially, legislatively,
or administratively defined. Also, the remedial action usually remains subject to continuing oversight to assure that

it will work the least harm possible to other innocent persons competing for the benefit. Without such findings of constitutional or statutory violations, it cannot be said that the government has any greater interest in helping one individual than in refraining from harming another. Thus, the government has no compelling justification for inflicting such harm.

Petitioner does not purport to have made, and is in no position to make, such findings. Its broad mission is education, not the formulation of any legislative policy or the adjudication of particular claims of illegality. For reasons similar to those (already) stated, isolated segments of our vast governmental structures are not competent to make those decisions, at least in the absence of legislative mandates and legislatively determined criteria. Before relying upon these sorts of findings in establishing a racial classification, a governmental body must have the authority and capability to establish, in the record, that the classification is responsive to identified discrimination. Lacking this capability, petitioner has not carried its burden of justification on this issue.

Hence, the purpose of helping certain groups whom the faculty of the Davis Medical School perceived as victims of "societal discrimination" does not justify a classification that imposes disadvantages upon persons like respondent, who bear no responsibility for whatever harm the beneficiaries of the special admissions program are thought to have suffered. To hold otherwise would be to convert a remedy heretofore reserved for violations of legal rights into a privilege that all institutions throughout the Nation could grant at their pleasure to whatever groups are perceived as victims of societal discrimination. That is a step we have never approved.

(iii) Petitioner identifies, as another purpose of its program, improving the delivery of health care services to communities currently underserved. It may be assumed that in some situations a State's interest in facilitating the health care of its citizens is sufficiently compelling to support the use of a suspect classification. But there is virtually no evidence in the record indicating that petitioner's special admissions program is either needed or geared to promote that goal. The court below addressed this failure of proof:

> "The University concedes it cannot assure that minority doctors who entered under the program, all of whom express an 'interest' in participating in a disadvantaged community, will actually do so. It may be correct to assume that some of them will carry out this intention, and that it is more likely they will practice in minority communities than the average white doctor. Nevertheless, there are more precise and reliable ways to identify applicants who are genuinely interested in the medical problems of minorities than by race. An applicant of whatever race who has demonstrated his concern for disadvantaged minorities in the past and who declares that practice in such a community is his primary professional goal would be more likely to contribute to alleviation of the medical shortage than one who is chosen entirely on the basis of race and disadvantage. In short, there is [sic] no empirical data to demonstrate that any one race is more selflessly socially oriented or by contrast that another is more selfishly acquisitive."

Petitioner simply has not carried its burden of demonstrating that it must prefer members of particular ethnic groups over all other individuals in order to promote better health care delivery to deprived citizens. Indeed, petitioner has not shown that its preferential classification is likely to have any significant effect on the problem.

(iv) The fourth goal asserted by petitioner is the attainment of a diverse student body. This clearly is a constitutionally permissible goal for an institution of higher education. Academic freedom, though not a specifically enumerated constitutional right, long has been viewed as a special concern of the First Amendment. The freedom of a university to make its own judgments as to education includes the selection of its student body. Mr. Justice Frankfurter summarized the "four essential freedoms" that comprise academic freedom:

"'. . . . It is the business of a university to provide that atmosphere which is most conducive to speculation, experiment and creation. It is an atmosphere in which there prevail 'the four essential freedoms' of a university—to determine for itself on academic grounds who may teach, what may be taught, how it shall be taught, and who may be admitted to study.'"

. . . . . .

The atmosphere of "speculation, experiment and creation"—so essential to the quality of higher education—is widely believed to be promoted by a diverse student body. As the Court noted in *Keyishian*, it is not too much to say that the "nation's future depends upon leaders trained through wide exposure" to the ideas and mores of students as diverse as this Nation of many peoples.

Thus, in arguing that its universities must be accorded the right to select those students who will contribute the most to the "robust exchange of ideas," petitioner invokes a countervailing constitutional interest, that of the First Amendment. In this light, petitioner must be viewed as seeking to achieve a goal that is of paramount importance in the fulfillment of its mission.

It may be argued that there is greater force to these views at the undergraduate level than in a medical school where the training is centered primarily on professional competency. But even at the graduate level, our tradition and experience lend support to the view that the contribution of diversity is substantial. In *Sweatt* v. *Painter*, the Court made a similar point with specific reference to legal education:

> "The law school, the proving ground for legal learning and practice, cannot be effective in isolation from the individuals and institutions with which the law interacts. Few students and no one who has practiced law would choose to study in an academic vacuum, removed from the interplay of ideas and the exchange of views with which the law is concerned."

Physicians serve a heterogenous population. An otherwise qualified medical student with a particular background—whether it be ethnic, geographic, culturally advantaged or disadvantaged—may bring to a professional school of medicine experiences, outlooks and ideas that enrich the training of its student body and better equip its graduates to render with understanding their vital service to humanity.

Ethnic diversity, however, is only one element in a range of factors a university properly may consider in attaining the goal of a heterogeneous student body. Although a university must have wide discretion in making the sensitive judgments as to who should be admitted, constitutional limitations protecting individual rights may not be disregarded. Respondent urges—and the courts below have held—that petitioner's dual admissions program is a racial classification that impermissibly infringes his rights under the Fourteenth Amendment. As the interest of diversity is compelling in the context of a university's admissions program, the question remains whether the program's racial classification is necessary to promote this interest.

It may be assumed that the reservation of a specified number of seats in each class for individuals from the preferred ethnic groups would contribute to the attainment of considerable ethnic diversity in the student body. But petitioner's argument that this is the only effective means of serving the interest of diversity is seriously flawed. In a most fundamental sense the argument misconceives the nature of the state interest that would justify consideration of race or ethnic background. It is not an interest in simple ethnic diversity, in which a specified percentage of the student body is in effect guaranteed to be members of selected ethnic groups, with the remaining percentage an undifferentiated aggregation of students. The diversity that furthers a compelling state interest encompasses a far broader array of qualifications and characteristics of which racial or ethnic origin is but a single though important element. Petitioner's special admissions program, focused *solely* on ethnic diversity, would hinder rather than further attainment of genuine diversity.

Nor would the state interest in genuine diversity be served by expanding petitioner's two-track system into a multitrack program with a prescribed number of seats set aside for each identifiable category of applicants. Indeed, it is inconceivable that a university would thus pursue the logic of petitioner's two-track program to the illogical end of insulating each category of applicants with certain desired qualifications from competition with all other applicants.

The experience of other university admissions programs, which take race into account in achieving the educational diversity valued by the First Amendment, demonstrates that the assignment of a fixed number of places to a minority group is not a necessary means toward that end. An illuminating example is found in the Harvard College program:

> "In recent years Harvard College has expanded the concept of diversity to include students from disadvantaged economic, racial and ethnic groups. Harvard College now recruits not only Californians or Louisianans but also blacks and Chicanos and other minority students.
>
> . . . . . .
>
> "In practice, this new definition of diversity has meant that race has been a factor in some admission decisions. When the Committee on Admissions reviews the large middle group of applicants who are 'admissible' and deemed capable of doing good work in their courses, the race of an applicant may tip the balance in his favor just as geographic origin or a life spent on a farm may tip the balance in other candidates' cases. A farm boy from Idaho can bring something to Harvard College that a Bostonian cannot offer. Similarly, a black student can usually bring something that a white person cannot offer."
>
> . . . . . .
>
> "In Harvard college admissions the Committee has not set target-quotas for the number of blacks, or of musicians, football players, physicists or Californians to be admitted

in a given years. . . . But that awareness [of the necessity of including more than a token number of black students] does not mean that the Committee sets the minimum number of blacks or of people from west of the Mississippi who are to be admitted. It means only that in choosing among thousands of applicants who are not only 'admissible' academically but have other strong qualities, the Committee, with a number of criteria in mind, pays some attention to distribution among many types and categories of students."

In such an admissions program, race or ethnic background may be deemed a "plus" in a particular applicant's file, yet it does not insulate the individual from comparison with all other candidates for the available seats. The file of a particular black applicant may be examined for his potential contribution to diversity without the factor of race being decisive when compared, for example, with that of an applicant identified as an Italian-American if the latter is thought to exhibit qualities more likely to promote beneficial educational pluralism. Such qualities could include exceptional personal talents, unique work or service experience, leadership potential, maturity, demonstrated compassion, a history of overcoming disadvantage, ability to communicate with the poor, or other qualifications deemed important. In short, an admissions program operated in this way is flexible enough to consider all pertinent elements of diversity in light of the particular qualifications of each applicant, and to place them on the same footing for consideration, although not necessarily according them the same weight. Indeed, the weight attributed to a particular quality may vary from year to year depending upon the "mix" both of the student body and the applicants for the incoming class.

This kind of program treats each applicant as an individual in the admissions process. The applicant who loses out on the last available seat to another candidate receiving a "plus" on the basis of ethnic background will not have been foreclosed from all consideration for that seat simply because he was not the right color or had the wrong surname. It would mean only that his combined qualifications, which may have included similar nonobjective factors, did not outweigh those of the other applicant. His qualifications would have been weighed fairly and competitively, and he would have no basis to complain of unequal treatment under the Fourteenth Amendment.

. . . . . .

In summary, it is evident that the Davis special admission program involves the use of an explicit racial classification never before countenanced by this Court. It tells applicants who are not Negro, Asian, or "Chicano" that they are totally excluded from a specific percentage of the seats in an entering class. No matter how strong their qualifications, quantitative and extracurricular, including their own potential for contribution to educational diversity, they are never afforded the chance to compete with applicants from the preferred groups for the special admission seats. At the same time, the preferred applicants have the opportunity to compete for every seat in the class.

The fatal flaw in petitioner's preferential program is its disregard of individual rights as guaranteed by the Fourteenth Amendment. Such rights are not absolute. But when a State's distribution of benefits or imposition of burdens hinges on the color of a person's skin or ancestry, that individual is entitled to a demonstration that the challenged classification is necessary to promote a substantial state interest. Petitioner has failed to carry this burden. For this reason, that portion of the California court's judgment holding petitioner's special admissions program invalid under the Fourteenth Amendment must be affirmed.

In enjoining petitioner from ever considering the race of any applicant, however, the courts below failed to recognize that the State has a substantial interest that legitimately may be served by a properly devised admissions program involving the competitive consideration of race and ethnic origin. For this reason, so much of the California court's judgment as enjoins petitioner from any consideration of the race of any applicant must be reversed.

With respect to respondent's entitlement to an injunction directing his admission to the Medical School, petitioner has conceded that it could not carry its burden of proving that, but for the existence of its unlawful special admissions program, respondent still would not have been admitted. Hence, respondent is entitled to the injunction, and that portion of the judgment must be affirmed.

Opinion of Mr. Justice Brennan, Mr. Justice White, Mr. Justice Marshall, and Mr. Justice Blackmun, concurring in the judgment in part and dissenting.

. . . . . .

Davis' articulated purpose of remedying the effects of past societal discrimination is, under our cases, sufficiently important to justify the use of race-conscious admissions programs where there is a sound basis for concluding that minority underrepresentation is substantial and chronic, and that the handicap of past discrimination is impeding access of minorities to the medical school.

. . . . A state government may adopt race-conscious programs if the purpose of such programs is to remove the disparate racial impact its actions might otherwise have and if there is reason to believe that the disparate impact is itself the product of past discrimination, whether its own or that of society at large. There is no question that Davis' program is valid under this test.

Certainly, on the basis of the undisputed factual submissions before this Court, Davis had a sound basis for believing that the problem of underrepresentation of minorities was substantial and chronic and that the problem was attributable to handicaps imposed on minority applicants by past and present racial discrimination. Until at least 1973, the practice of medicine in this country was, in fact, if not in law, largely the prerogative of whites. In 1950, for example, while Negroes comprised 10% of the total population, Negro physicians constituted only 2.2% of the total number of physicians. The overwhelming majority of these, moreover, were educated in two predominantly Negro medical schools, Howard and Meharry. By 1970, the gap between the proportion of Negroes in medicine and their proportion in the population had widened: The number of Negroes employed in medicine remained frozen at 2.2% while the Negro population had increased to 11.1%. The number of Negro admittees to predominantly white medical schools, moreover, had declined in absolute numbers during the years 1955 to 1964.

Moreover, Davis had very good reason to believe that the national pattern of underrepresentation of minorities in medicine would be perpetuated if it retained a single admissions standard. For example, the entering classes in 1968 and 1969, the years in which such a standard was used, included only one Chicano and two Negroes out of 100 admittees. Nor is there any relief from this pattern of underrepresentation in the statistics for the regular admissions program in later years.

Davis clearly could conclude that the serious and persistent underrepresentation of minorities in medicine depicted by these statistics is the result of handicaps under which minority applicants labor as a consequence of a background of delierate, purposeful discrimination against minorities in education and in society generally, as well as in the medical profession. From the inception of our national life, Negroes have been subjected to unique legal disabilities impairing access to equal educational opportunity. Under slavery, penal sanctions were imposed upon anyone attempting to educate Negroes. After enactment of the Fourteenth Amendment the States continued to deny Negroes equal educational opportunity, enforcing a strict policy of segregation that itself stamped Negroes as inferior, which relegated minorities to inferior educational institutions, and which denied them intercourse in the mainstream of professional life necessary to advancement. Segregation was not limited to public facilities, moreover, but was enforced by criminal penalties against private action as well. Thus, as late as 1908, this Court enforced a state criminal conviction against a private college for teaching Negroes together with whites.

Green v. *County School Board* gave explicit recognition to the fact that the habit of discrimination and the cultural tradition of race prejudice cultivated by centuries of legal slavery and segregation were not immediately dissipated when *Brown I* announced the constitutional principle that equal educational opportunity and participation in all aspects of American life could not be denied on the basis of race. Rather, massive official and private resistance prevented, and to a lesser extent still prevents, attainment of equal opportunity in education at all levels and in the professions. The generation of minority students applying to Davis Medical School since it opened in 1968 — most of whom were born before or about the time *Brown I* was decided — clearly have been victims of this discrimination. Judicial decrees recognizing discrimination in public education in California testify to the fact of widespread discrimination suffered by California-born minority applicants; many minority group members living in California, moreover, were born and reared in school districts in southern States segregated by law. Since separation of school children by race "generates a feeling of inferiority as to their status in the community that may affect their hearts and minds in a way unlikely ever to be undone," the conclusion is inescapable that applicants to medical school must be few indeed who endured the effects of *de jure* segregation, the resistance to *Brown I,* or the equally debilitating pervasive private discrimination fostered by our long history of official discrimination, and yet come to the starting line with an education equal to whites.

Moreover, we need not rest solely on our own conclusion that Davis had sound reason to believe that the effects of past discrimination were handicapping minority applicants to the Medical School, because the Department of Health, Education, and Welfare, the expert agency charged by Congress with promulgating regulations enforcing Title VI of the Civil Rights Act of 1964, has also reached the conclusion that race may be taken into account in situations where a failure to do so would limit participation by minorities in federally funded programs, and regulations promulgated by the Department expressly contemplate that appropriate race-conscious programs may be adopted by universities to remedy unequal access to university programs caused by their own or by past societal discrimination. It cannot be questioned that, in the absence of the special admissions program, access of minority students to the Medical School would be severely limited and, accordingly, race-conscious admissions would be deemed an appropriate response under these federal regulations. . . .

The second prong of our test—whether the Davis program stigmatizes any discrete group or individual and whether race is reasonably used in light of the program's objectives—is clearly satisfied by the Davis program.

It is not even claimed that Davis' program in any way operates to stigmatize or single out any discrete and insular, or even any identifiable, nonminority group. Nor will harm comparable to that imposed upon racial minorities by exclusion or separation on grounds of race be the likely result of the program. It does not, for example, establish an exclusive preserve for minority students apart from and exclusive of whites. Rather, its purpose is to overcome the effects of segregation by bringing the races together. True, whites are excluded from participation in the special admissions program, but this fact only operates to reduce the number of whites to be admitted in the regular admissions program in order to permit admission of a reasonable percentage—less than their proportion of the California population—of otherwise underrepresented qualified minority applicants.

Nor was Bakke in any sense stamped as inferior by the Medical School's rejection of him. Indeed, it is conceded by all that he satisfied those criteria regarded by the School as generally relevant to academic performance better than most of the minority members who were admitted. Moreover, there is absolutely no basis for concluding that Bakke's rejection as a result of Davis' use of racial preference will affect him throughout his life in the same way as the segregation of the Negro school children in *Brown I* would have affected them. Unlike discrimination against racial minorities, the use of racial preferences for remedial purposes does not inflict a pervasive injury upon individual whites in the sense that wherever they go or whatever they do there is a significant likelihood that they will be treated as second-class citizens because of their color. This distinction does not mean that the exclusion of a white resulting from the preferential use of race is not sufficiently serious to require justification; but it does mean that the injury inflicted by such a policy is not distinguishable from disadvantages caused by a wide range of government actions, none of which has ever been thought impermissible for that reason alone.

In addition, there is simply no evidence that the Davis program discriminates intentionally or unintentionally against any minority group which it purports to benefit. The program does not establish a quota in the invidious sense of a ceiling on the number of minority applicants to be admitted. Nor can the program reasonably be regarded as stigmatizing the program's beneficiaries or their race as inferior. The Davis program does not simply advance less qualified applicants; rather, it compensates applicants, whom it is uncontested are fully qualified to study medicine, for educational disadvantage which it was reasonable to conclude was a product of state-fostered discrimination. Once admitted, these students must satisfy the same degree requirements as regularly admitted students; they are taught by the same faculty in the same classes; and their performance is evaluated by the same standards by which regularly admitted students are judged. Under these circumstances, their performance and degrees must be regarded equally with the regularly admitted students with whom they compete for standing. Since minority graduates cannot justifiably be regarded as less well qualified than nonminority graduates by virtue of the special admissions program, there is no reasonable basis to conclude that minority graduates at schools using such programs would be stigmatized as inferior by the existence of such programs.

. . . . . .

Finally, Davis' special admissions program cannot be said to violate the Constitution simply because it has set aside a predetermined number of places for qualified minority applicants rather than using minority status as a positive factor to be considered in evaluating the applications of disadvantaged minority applicants. For purposes of constitutional adjudication, there is no difference between the two approaches. In any admissions program which accords special consideration to disadvantaged racial minorities, a determination of the degree of preference to be given is unavoidable, and any given preference that results in the exclusion of a white candidate is no more or less constitutionally acceptable than a program such as that at Davis. Furthermore, the extent of the preference inevitably depends on how many minority applicants the particular school is seeking to admit in any particular year so long as the number of qualified minority applicants exceeds that number. There is no sensible, and certainly no constitutional, distinction between, for example, adding a set number of points to the admissions rating of disadvantaged minority applicants as an expression of the preference with the expectation that this will result in the admission of an approximately determined number of qualified minority applicants and setting a fixed number of places for such applicants as was done here.

The "Harvard" program, as those employing it readily concede, openly and successfully employs a racial criterion for the purpose of ensuring that some of the scarce places in institutions of higher education are allocated to disadvantaged minority students. That the Harvard approach does not also make public the extent of the preference and the precise workings of the system while the Davis program employs a specific, openly stated number, does not condemn the latter plan for purposes of Fourteenth Amendment adjudication. It may be that the Harvard plan is more acceptable to the public than is the Davis "quota." If it is, any State, including California, is free to adopt it in preference to a less acceptable alternative, just as it is generally free, as far as the Constitution is concerned, to abjure granting any racial preferences in its admissions program. But there is no basis for preferring a particular preference program simply because in achieving the same goals that the Davis Medical School is pursuing, it proceeds in a manner that is not immediately apparent to the public.

Animal Liberation

Peter Singer

I

We are familiar with Black Liberation, Gay Liberation, and
a variety of other movements. With Women's Liberation
some thought we had come to the end of the road. Discrimination on the basis of sex, it has been said, is the last
form of discrimination that is universally accepted and
practiced without pretense, even in those liberal circles
which have long prided themselves on their freedom from
racial discrimination. But one should always be wary of
talking of "the last remaining form of discrimination." If
we have learned anything from the liberation movements,
we should have learned how difficult it is to be aware of
the ways in which we discriminate until they are force-
fully pointed out to us. A liberation movement demands
an expansion of our moral horizons, so that practices that
were previously regarded as natural and inevitable are now
seen as intolerable.

Animals, Men and Morals is a manifesto for an Animal
Liberation movement. The contributors to the book may
not all see the issue this way. They are a varied group.
Philosophers, ranging from professors to graduate students,
make up the largest contingent. There are five of them,
including the three editors, and there is also an extract
from the unjustly neglected German philosopher with an
English name, Leonard Nelson, who died in 1927. There

From *The New York Review of Books*, April 5, 1973. Reprinted by permission of
the author. This article originally appeared as a review of a book edited by Stanley and Roslind Godlovitch and John Harris, *Animals, Men and Morals* (London:
Taplinger, 1972). The "Postscript" has been added for this reprinting.

are essays by two novelist/critics, Brigid Brophy and Maureen Duffy, and another by Muriel the Lady Dowding, widow of Dowding of Battle of Britain fame and the founder of "Beauty Without Cruelty," a movement that campaigns against the use of animals for furs and cosmetics. The other pieces are by a pscyhologist, a botanist, a sociologist, and Ruth Harrison, who is probably best described as a professional campaigner for animal welfare.

Whether or not these people, as individuals, would all agree that they are launching a liberation movement for animals, the book as a whole amounts to no less. It is a demand for a complete change in our attitudes to nonhumans. It is a demand that we cease to regard the exploitation of other species as natural and inevitable, and that, instead, we see it as a continuing moral outrage. Patrick Corbett, Professor of Philosophy at Sussex University, captures the spirit of the book in his closing words:

> . . . We require now to extend the great principles of liberty, equality and fraternity over the lives of animals. Let animal slavery join human slavery in the graveyard of the past.

The reader is likely to be skeptical. "Animal Liberation" sounds more like a parody of liberation movements than a serious objective. The reader may think: We support the claims of blacks and women for equality because blacks and women really are equal to whites and males—equal in intelligence and in abilities, capacity for leadership, rationality, and so on. Humans and nonhumans obviously are not equal in these respects. Since justice demands only that we treat equals equally, unequal treatment of humans and nonhumans cannot be an injustice.

This is a tempting reply, but a dangerous one. It commits the non-racist and non-sexist to a dogmatic belief that blacks and women really are just as intelligent, able, etc., as whites and males—and no more. Quite possibly this happens to be the case. Certainly attempts to prove that racial or sexual differences in these respects have a genetic origin have not been conclusive. But do we really want to stake our demand for equality on the assumption that there are no genetic differences of this kind between the different races or sexes? Surely the appropriate response to those who claim to have found evidence for sure genetic differences is not to stick to the belief that there are no differences, whatever the evidence to the contrary; rather one should be clear that the claim to equality does not depend on IQ. Moral equality is distinct from factual equality. Otherwise it would be nonsense to talk of the equality of human beings, since humans, as individuals, obviously differ in intelligence and almost any ability one cares to name. If possessing greater intelligence does not entitle one human to exploit another, why should it entitle humans to exploit nonhumans?

Jeremy Bentham expressed the essential basis of equality in his famous formula: "Each to count for one and none for more than one." In other words, the interests of every being that has interests are to be taken into account and treated equally with the like interests of any other being. Other moral philosophers, before and after Bentham, have made the same point in different ways. Our concern for others must not depend on whether they possess certain characteristics, though just what that concern involves may, of course, vary according to such characteristics.

Bentham, incidentally, was well aware that the logic of the demand for racial equality did not stop at the equality of humans. He wrote:

> The day *may* come when the rest of the animal creation may acquire those rights which never could have been withholden from them but by the hand of tyranny. The French have already discovered that the blackness of the skin is no reason why a human being should be abandoned without redress to the caprice of a tormentor. It may one day come to be recognized that the number of the legs, the villosity of the skin, or the termination of the *os sacrum*, are reasons equally insufficient for abandoning a sensitive being to the same rate. What else is it that should trace the insuperable line? Is it the faculty of reason, or perhaps the faculty of discourse? But a full-grown horse or dog is beyond comparison a more rational, as well as a more conversable animal, than an infant of a day, or a week, or even

a month, old. But suppose they were otherwise, what would it avail? The question is not, Can they *reason*? nor Can they *talk*? but, Can they *suffer*?[1]

Surely Bentham was right. If a being suffers, there can be no moral justification for refusing to take that suffering into consideration, and, indeed, to count it equally with the like suffering (if rough comparisons can be made) of any other being.

So the only question is: Do animals other than man suffer? Most people agree unhesitatingly that animals like cats and dogs can and do suffer, and this seems also to be assumed by those laws that prohibit wanton cruelty to such animals. Personally, I have no doubt at all about this and find it hard to take seriously the doubts that a few people apparently do have. The editors and contributors of *Animals, Men and Morals* seem to feel the same way, for although the question is raised more than once, doubts are quickly dismissed each time. Nevertheless, because this is such a fundamental point, it is worth asking what grounds we have for attributing suffering to other animals.

It is best to begin by asking what grounds any individual human has for supposing that other humans feel pain. Since pain is a state of consciousness, a "mental event," it can never be directly observed. No observations, whether behavioral signs such as writhing or screaming or physiological or neurological recordings, are observations of pain itself. Pain is something one feels, and one can only infer that others are feeling it from various external indications. The fact that only philosophers are ever skeptical about whether other humans feel pain shows that we regard such inference as justifiable in the case of humans.

Is there any reason why the same inference should be unjustifiable for other animals? Nearly all the external signs which lead us to infer pain in other humans can be seen in other species, especially "higher" animals such as mammals and birds. Behavioral signs—writhing, yelping,

---

[1] *The Principles of Morals and Legislation*, ch. XVII, sec. 1, footnote to paragraph 4. (Italics in original.)

or other forms of calling, attempts to avoid the source of pain, and many others—are present. We know, too, that these animals are biologically similar in the relevant respects, having nervous systems like ours which can be observed to function as ours do.

So the grounds for inferring that these animals can feel pain are nearly as good as the grounds for inferring other humans do. Only nearly, for there is one behavioral sign that humans have but nonhumans, with the exception of one or two specially raised chimpanzees, do not have. This, of course, is a developed language. As the quotation from Bentham indicates, this has long been regarded as an important distinction between man and other animals. Other animals may communicate with each other, but not in the way we do. Following Chomsky, many people now mark this distinction by saying that only humans communicate in a form that is governed by rules of syntax. (For the purposes of this argument, linguists allow those chimpanzees who have learned a syntactic sign language to rank as honorary humans.) Nevertheless, as Bentham pointed out, this distinction is not relevant to the question of how animals ought to be treated, unless it can be linked to the issue of whether animals suffer.

This link may be attempted in two ways. First, there is a hazy line of philosophical thought, stemming perhaps from some doctrines associated with Wittgenstein, which maintains that we cannot meaningfully attribute states of consciousness to beings without language. I have not seen this argument made explicit in print, though I have come across it in conversation. This position seems to me very implausible, and I doubt that it would be held at all if it were not thought to be a consequence of a broader view of the significance of language. It may be that the use of a public, rule-governed language is a precondition of conceptual thought. It may even be, although personally I doubt it, that we cannot meaningfully speak of a creature having an intention unless that creature can use a language. But states like pain, surely, are more primitive than either of these, and seem to have nothing to do with language.

Indeed, as Jane Goodall points out in her study of chimpanzees, when it comes to the expression of feelings and emotions, humans tend to fall back on non-linguistic modes of communication which are often found among apes, such as a cheering pat on the back, an exuberant embrace, a clasp of hands, and so on.[2] Michael Peters makes a similar point in his contribution to *Animals, Men and Morals* when he notes that the basic signals we use to convey pain, fear, sexual arousal, and so on are not specific to our species. So there seems to be no reason at all to believe that a creature without language cannot suffer.

The second, and more easily appreciated way of linking language and the existence of pain is to say that the best evidence that we can have that another creature is in pain is when he tells us that he is. This is a distinct line of argument, for it is not being denied that a non-language-user conceivably could suffer, but only that we could know that he is suffering. Still, this line of argument seems to me to fail, and for reasons similar to those just given. "I am in pain" is not the best possible evidence that the speaker is in pain (he might be lying) and it is certainly not the only possible evidence. Behavioral signs and knowledge of the animal's biological similarity to ourselves together provide adequate evidence that animals do suffer. After all, we would not accept linguistic evidence if it contradicted the rest of the evidence. If a man was severely burned, and behaved as if he were in pain, writhing, groaning, being very careful not to let his burned skin touch anything, and so on, but later said he had not been in pain at all, we would be more likely to conclude that he was lying or suffering from amnesia than that he had not been in pain.

Even if there were stronger grounds for refusing to attribute pain to those who do not have a language, the consequences of this refusal might lead us to examine these grounds unusually critically. Human infants, as well as some adults, are unable to use language. Are we to deny that a year-old infant can suffer? If not, how can language be crucial? Of course, most parents can understand the re-

---

[2]Jane van Lawick-Goodall, *In the Shadow of Man* (Houghton Mifflin, 1971), p. 225.

sponses of even very young infants better than they understand the responses of other animals, and sometimes infant responses can be understood in the light of later development.

This, however, is just a fact about the relative knowledge we have of our own species and other species, and most of this knowledge is simply derived from closer contact. Those who have studied the behavior of other animals soon learn to understand their responses at least as well as we understand those of an infant. (I am not just referring to Jane Goodall's and other well-known studies of apes. Consider, for example, the degree of understanding achieved by Tinbergen from watching herring gulls.)[3] Just as we can understand infant human behavior in the light of adult human behavior, so we can understand the behavior of other species in the light of our own behavior (and sometimes we can understand our own behavior better in the light of the behavior of other species).

The grounds we have for believing that other mammals and birds suffer are, then, closely analogous to the grounds we have for believing that other humans suffer. It remains to consider how far down the evolutionary scale this analogy holds. Obviously it becomes poorer when we get further away from man. To be more precise would require a detailed examination of all that we know about other forms of life. With fish, reptiles, and other vertebrates the analogy still seems strong, with molluscs like oysters it is much weaker. Insects are more difficult, and it may be that in our present state of knowledge we must be agnostic about whether they are capable of suffering.

If there is no moral justification for ignoring suffering when it occurs, and it does occur in other species, what are we to say of our attitudes toward these other species? Richard Ryder, one of the contributors to *Animals, Men and Morals*, uses the term "speciesism" to describe the belief that we are entitled to treat members of other species in a way in which it would be wrong to treat members of our own species. The term is not euphonious,

---

[3]N. Tinbergen, *The Herring Gull's World* (Basic Books, 1961).

but it neatly makes the analogy with racism. The non-racist would do well to bear the analogy in mind when he is inclined to defend human behavior toward nonhumans. "Shouldn't we worry about improving the lot of our own species before we concern ourselves with other species?" he may ask. If we substitute "race" for "species" we shall see that the question is better not asked. "Is a vegetarian diet nutritionally adequate?" resembles the slaveowner's claim that he and the whole economy of the South would be ruined without slave labor. There is even a parallel with skeptical doubts about whether animals suffer, for some defenders of slavery professed to doubt whether blacks really suffer in the way that whites do.

I do not want to give the impression, however, that the case for Animal Liberation is based on the analogy with racism and no more. On the contrary, *Animals, Men and Morals* describes the various ways in which humans exploit nonhumans, and several contributors consider the defenses that have been offered, including the defense of meat-eating mentioned in the last paragraph. Sometimes the rebuttals are scornfully dismissive, rather than carefully designed to convince the detached critic. This may be a fault, but it is a fault that is inevitable, given the kind of book this is. The issue is not one on which one can remain detached. As the editors state in their Introduction:

> Once the full force of moral assessment has been made explicit there can be no rational excuse left for killing animals, be they killed for food, science, or sheer personal indulgence. We have not assembled this book to provide the reader with yet another manual on how to make brutalities less brutal. Compromise, in the traditional sense of the term, is simply unthinking weakness when one considers the actual reasons for our crude relationships with the other animals.

The point is that on this issue there are few critics who are genuinely detached. People who eat pieces of slaughtered nonhumans every day find it hard to believe that they are doing wrong; and they also find it hard to imagine what else they could eat. So for those who do not place nonhumans beyond the pale of morality, there comes a stage when further argument seems pointless, a stage at which one can only accuse one's opponent of hypocrisy and reach for the sort of sociological account of our practices and the way we defend them that is attempted by David Wood in his contribution to this book. On the other hand, to those unconvinced by the arguments, and unable to accept that they are merely rationalizing their dietary preferences and their fear of being thought peculiar, such sociological explanations can only seem insultingly arrogant.

II

The logic of speciesism is most apparent in the practice of experimenting on nonhumans in order to benefit humans. This is because the issue is rarely obscured by allegations that nonhumans are so different from humans that we cannot know anything about whether they suffer. The defender of vivisection cannot use this argument because he needs to stress the similarities between man and other animals in order to justify the usefulness to the former of experiments on the latter. The researcher who makes rats choose between starvation and electric shocks to see if they develop ulcers (they do) does so because he knows that the rat has a nervous system very similar to man's, and presumably feels an electric shock in a similar way.

Richard Ryder's restrained account of experiments on animals made me angrier with my fellow men than anything else in this book. Ryder, a clinical psychologist by profession, himself experimented on animals before he came to hold the view he puts forward in his essay. Experimenting on animals is now a large industry, both academic and commercial. In 1969, more than 5 million experiments were performed in Britain, the vast majority without anesthetic (though how many of these involved pain is not known). There are no accurate U.S. figures, since there is no federal law on the subject, and in many cases no state law either. Estimates vary from 20 million to 200 million. Ryder suggests that 80 million may be the best guess. We tend to think that this is all for vital medical research, but of course it is not. Huge numbers of animals are used in university departments from Forestry to Psychology, and even more are used for commercial purposes, to test whether cosmetics can cause skin damage, or shampoos eye damage, or to test food additives or laxatives or sleeping pills or anything else.

A standard test for foodstuffs is the "LD50." The object of this test is to find the dosage level at which 50 percent of the test animals will die. This means that nearly all of them will become very sick before finally succumbing or surviving. When the substance is a harmless one, it may be necessary to force huge doses down the animals, until in some cases sheer volume or concentration causes death.

Ryder gives a selection of experiments, taken from recent scientific journals. I will quote two, not for the sake of indulging in gory details, but in order to give an idea of what normal researchers think they may legitimately do to other species. The point is not that the individual researchers are cruel men, but that they are behaving in a way that is allowed by our speciesist attitudes. As Ryder points out, even if only 1 percent of the experiments involve severe pain, that is 50,000 experiments in Britain each year, or nearly 150 every day (and about fifteen times as many in the United States, if Ryder's guess is right). Here then are two experiments:

O. S. Ray and R. J. Barrett of Pittsburg gave electric shocks to the feet of 1,042 mice. They then caused convulsions by giving more intense shocks through cup-shaped electrodes applied to the animal's eyes or through pressure spring clips attached to their ears. Unfortunately some of the mice who "successfully completed Day One training were found sick or dead prior to testing on Day Two." [*Journal of Comparative and Physiological Psychology*, 1969, vol. 67, pp. 110–116]

At the National Institute for Medical Research, Mill Hill, London, W. Feldberg and S. L. Sherwood injected chemicals into the brains of cats—"with a number of widely different substances, recurrent patterns of reaction were obtained. Retching, vomiting, defaecation, increased salivation and greatly accelerated respiration leading to panting were common features." . . .

The injection into the brain of a large dose of Tubocuraine caused the cat to jump "from the table to the floor and then straight into its cage, where it started calling more and more noisily whilst moving about restlessly and jerkily . . . finally the cat fell with legs and neck flexed, jerking in rapid clonic movements, the condition being that of a major [epileptic] convulsion . . . within a few seconds the cat got up, ran for a few yards at high speed and fell in another fit. The whole process was repeated several times within the next ten minutes, during which the cat lost faeces and foamed at the mouth."

This animal finally died thirty-five minutes after the brain injection. [*Journal of Physiology*, 1954, vol. 123, pp. 148–167]

There is nothing secret about these experiments. One has only to open any recent volume of a learned journal, such as the *Journal of Comparative and Physiological Psychology*, to find full descriptions of experiments of this sort, together with the results obtained—results that are frequently trivial and obvious. The experiments are often supported by public funds.

It is a significant indication of the level of acceptability of these practices that, although these experiments are taking place at this moment on university campuses throughout the country, there has, so far as I know, not been the slightest protest from the student movement. Students have been rightly concerned that their universities should not discriminate on grounds of race or sex, and that they should not serve the purposes of the military or big business. Speciesism continues undisturbed, and many students participate in it. There may be a few qualms at first, but since everyone regards it as normal, and it may even be a required part of a course, the student soon becomes hardened and, dismissing his earlier feelings as "mere sentiment," comes to regard animals as statistics rather than sentient beings with interests that warrant consideration.

Argument about vivisection has often missed the point because it has been put in absolutist terms: Would the abolitionist be prepared to let thousands die if they could be saved by experimenting on a single animal? The way to reply to this purely hypothetical question is to pose another: Would the experimenter be prepared to experiment on a human orphan under six months old, if it were the only way to save many lives? (I say "orphan" to avoid the complication of parental feelings, although in doing so I am being overfair to the experimenter, since the nonhuman subjects of experiments are not orphans.) A negative answer to this question indicates that the experimenter's readiness to use nonhumans is simple discrimination, for adult apes, cats, mice, and other mammals are more conscious of what is happening to them, more self-directing, and, so far as we can tell, just as sensitive to pain as a human infant. There is no characteristic that human infants possess that adult mammals do not have to the same or a higher degree.

(It might be possible to hold that what makes it wrong to experiment on a human infant is that the infant will in time develop into more than the nonhuman, but one would then, to be consistent, have to oppose abortion, and perhaps contraception, too, for the fetus and the egg and sperm have the same potential as the infant. Moreover, one would still have no reason for experimenting on a nonhuman rather than a human with brain damage severe enough to make it impossible for him to rise above infant level.)

The experimenter, then, shows a bias for his own species whenever he carries out an experiment on a nonhuman for a purpose that he would not think justified him in using a human being at an equal or lower level of sentience, awareness, ability to be self-directing, etc. No one familiar with the kind of results yielded by these experiments can have the slightest doubt that if this bias were eliminated the number of experiments performed would be zero or very close to it.

III

If it is vivisection that shows the logic of speciesism most clearly, it is the use of other species for food that is at the heart of our attitudes toward them. Most of *Animals, Men and Morals* is an attack on meat-eating—an attack which is based solely on concern for nonhumans, without reference to arguments derived from considerations of ecology, macrobiotics, health, or religion.

The idea that nonhumans are utilities, means to our ends, pervades our thought. Even conservationists who are concerned about the slaughter of wild fowl but not about the vastly greater slaughter of chickens for our tables are thinking in this way—they are worried about what we would lose if there were less wildlife. Stanley Godlovitch, pursuing the Marxist idea that our thinking is formed by the activities we undertake in satisfying our needs, suggests that man's first classification of his environment was into Edibles and Inedibles. Most animals came into the first category, and there they have remained.

Man may always have killed other species for food, but he has never exploited them so ruthlessly as he does today. Farming has succumbed to business methods, the objective being to get the highest possible ratio of output (meat, eggs, milk) to input (fodder, labor costs, etc.). Ruth Harrison's essay "On Factory Farming" gives an account of some aspects of modern methods, and of the unsuccessful British campaign for effective controls, a campaign which was sparked off by her *Animal Machines* (Stuart: London, 1964).

Her article is in no way a substitute for her earlier book. This is a pity since, as she says, "Farm produce is still associated with mental pictures of animals browsing in the fields, . . . of hens having a last forage before going to roost. . . ." Yet neither in her article nor elsewhere in *Animals, Men and Morals* is this false image replaced by a clear idea of the nature and extent of factory farming. We learn of this only indirectly, when we hear of the code of reform proposed by an advisory committee set up by the British government.

Among the proposals, which the government refused to implement on the grounds that they were too idealistic, were: *"Any animal should at least have room to turn around freely."*

Factory farm animals need liberation in the most literal sense. Veal calves are kept in stalls five feet by two feet. They are usually slaughtered when about four months old, and have been too big to turn in their stalls for at least a month. Intensive beef herds, kept in stalls only proportionately larger for much longer periods, account for a growing percentage of beef production. Sows are often similarly confined when pregnant, which, because of artificial methods of increasing fertility, can be most of the time. Animals confined in this way do not waste food by exercising, nor do they develop unpalatable muscle.

"A dry bedded area should be provided for all stock." Intensively kept animals usually have to stand and sleep on slatted floors without straw, because this makes cleaning easier.

"Palatable roughage must be readily available to all calves after one week of age." In order to produce the pale veal housewives are said to prefer, calves are fed on an all-liquid diet until slaughter, even though they are long past the age at which they would normally eat grass. They develop a craving for roughage, evidenced by attempts to gnaw wood from their stalls. (For the same reason, their diet is deficient in iron.)

"Battery cages for poultry should be large enough for a bird to be able to stretch one wing at a time." Under current British practice, a cage for four or five laying hens has a floor area of twenty inches by eighteen inches, scarcely larger than a double page of the *New York Review of Books.* In this space, on a sloping wire floor (sloping so the eggs roll down, wire so the dung drops through) the birds live for a year or eighteen months while artificial lighting and temperature conditions combine with drugs in their food to squeeze the maximum number of eggs out of them. Table birds are also sometimes kept in cages. More often they are reared in sheds, no less crowded. Under these conditions all the birds' natural activities are frustrated, and they develop "vices" such as pecking each other to death. To prevent this, beaks are often cut off, and the sheds kept dark.

How many of those who support factory farming by buying its produce know anything about the way it is produced? How many have heard something about it, but are reluctant to check up for fear that it will make them uncomfortable? To non-speciesists, the typical consumer's mixture of ignorance, reluctance to find out the truth, and vague belief that nothing really bad could be allowed seems analogous to the attitudes of "decent Germans" to the death camps.

There are, of course, some defenders of factory farming. Their arguments are considered, though again rather sketchily, by John Harris. Among the most common: "Since they have never known anything else, they don't suffer." This argument will not be put by anyone who knows anything about animal behavior, since he will know that not all behavior has to be learned. Chickens attempt to stretch wings, walk around, scratch, and even dustbathe or build a nest, even though they have never lived under conditions that allowed these activities. Calves can suffer from maternal deprivation no matter at what age they were taken from their mothers. "We need these intensive methods to provide protein for a growing population." As ecologists and famine relief organizations know, we can produce far more protein per acre if we grow the right vegetable crop, soy beans for instance, than if we use the land to grow crops to be converted into protein by animals who use nearly 90 percent of the protein themselves, even when unable to exercise.

There will be many readers of this book who will agree that factory farming involves an unjustifiable degree of exploitation of sentient creatures, and yet will want to say that there is nothing wrong with rearing animals for food, provided it is done "humanely." These people are saying, in effect, that although we should not cause animals to suffer, there is nothing wrong with killing them.

There are two possible replies to this view. One is to attempt to show that this combination of attitudes is absurd. Roslind Godlovitch takes this course in her essay, which is an examination of some common attitudes to animals. She argues that from the combination of "animal suffering is to be avoided" and "there is nothing wrong with killing animals" it follows that all animal life ought to be exterminated (since all sentient creatures will suffer to some degree at some point in their lives). Euthanasia is a contentious issue only because we place some value on living. If we did not, the least amount of suffering would justify it. Accordingly, if we deny that we have a duty to exterminate all animal life, we must concede that we are placing some value on animal life.

This argument seems to me valid, although one could still reply that the value of animal life is to be derived from the pleasures that life can have for them, so that, provided their lives have a balance of pleasure over pain, we are justified in rearing them. But his would imply that we ought to produce animals and let them live as pleasantly as possible, without suffering.

At this point, one can make the second of the two possible replies to the view that rearing and killing animals for food is all right so long as it is done humanely. This second reply is that so long as we think that a nonhuman may be killed simply so that a human can satisfy his taste for meat, we are still thinking of nonhumans as means rather than as ends in themselves. The factory farm is nothing more than the application of technology to this concept. Even traditional methods involve castration, the separation of mothers and their young, the breaking up of herds, branding or ear-punching, and of course transportation to the abattoirs and the final moments of terror when the animal smells blood and senses danger. If we were to try rearing animals so that they lived and died without suffering, we should find that to do so on anything like the scale of today's meat industry would be a sheer impossibility. Meat would become the prerogative of the rich.

I have been able to discuss only some of the contributions to this book, saying nothing about, for instance, the essays on killing for furs and for sport. Nor have I considered all the detailed questions that need to be asked once we start thinking about other species in the radically different way presented by this book. What, for instance, are we to do about genuine conflicts of interest like rats biting slum children? I am not sure of the answer, but the essential point is just that we *do* see this as a conflict of interests, that we recognize that rats have interests too. Then we may begin to think about other ways of resolving the conflict—perhaps by leaving out rat baits that sterilize the rats instead of killing them.

I have not discussed such problems because they are side issues compared with the exploitation of other species for food and for experimental purposes. On these central matters, I hope that I have said enough to show that this book, despite its flaws, is a challenge to every human to recognize his attitudes to nonhumans as a form of prejudice no less objectionable than racism or sexism. It is a challenge that demands not just a change of attitudes, but a change in our way of life, for it requires us to become vegetarians.

Can a purely moral demand of this kind succeed? The odds are certainly against it. The book holds out no inducements. It does not tell us that we will become healthier, or enjoy life more, if we cease exploiting animals. *Animal Liberation* will require greater altruism on the part of mankind than any other liberation movement, since animals are incapable of demanding it for themselves, or of protesting against their exploitation by votes, demonstrations, or bombs. Is man capable of such genuine altruism? Who knows? If this book does have a significant effect, however, it will be a vindication of all those who have believed that man has within himself the potential for more than cruelty and selfishness.

Postscript

Since this review is now appearing alongside philosophical discussions of rights and equality, it is worth noting that we can find indications of speciesism even amongst philosophers.

Richard Wasserstrom's "Rights, Human Rights, and Racial Discrimination" [reprinted in this volume, pp. 7–24], serves as an example. Wasserstrom defines "human rights" as those that humans have, and nonhumans do not have. He then argues that there are human rights, in this sense, to well-being and freedom. In defending the idea of a human right to well-being, Wasserstrom says that although we have no means of assessing the comparative worth of different people's enjoyment of, for instance, relief from acute physical pain, we know that denial of the opportunity to experience a good such as this makes it impossible to live a full or satisfying life. Wasserstrom then goes on to say: "In a real sense, the enjoyment of these goods differentiates human from nonhuman entities" [p. 119]. But this statement is incredible—for when we look back to find what the expression "these goods" is supposed to refer to, we find that the *only* example we have been given is relief from acute physical pain—and this, surely, is something that nonhumans may appreciate as well as humans.

Later, too, Wasserstrom points out that the grounds for discrimination between blacks and whites that racists sometimes offer are not relevant to the question of capacity for bearing acute pain, and therefore should be disregarded. So again Wasserstrom is taking capacity for perceiving acute pain as crucial. I would want to say that if Wasserstrom's argument is valid against discrimination on the basis of race—and I think it is—then an exactly parallel argument applies against the grounds usually offered for discrimination on the basis of species, since these grounds are also not relevant to the question of ability to bear acute pain. When Ray and Barrett, in the experiment I described in the review, gave electric shocks to over a thousand mice, they must have assumed that the mice *do* feel acute physical pain, since the aim of the experiment was to find out where the mice were most sensitive; and nothing else, surely, is relevant to the question of whether it is legitimate to use mice for this purpose.

I should make it quite clear, of course, that I do not believe Richard Wasserstrom is deliberately endorsing a speciesist position, or in any way condoning the infliction of acute physical pain on nonhumans. I draw attention to the point only in order to show how easy it is, even for a philosopher, to accept unthinkingly a prevailing ideology that places other animals outside the sphere of equal consideration. I would guess that most of Wasserstrom's readers, with similar predispositions, will not have noticed on a first reading that the only basis he offers for "human rights" applies to nonhumans too.

Suggestions for Further Reading (in paperback):

A. I. Melden, ed., *Human Rights* (Belmont, CA.: Wadsworth, 1970).

Jane English, ed., *Sex Equality* (Englewood Cliffs, NJ: Prentice-Hall, 1977).

Marshall Cohen, Thomas Nagel, and Thomas Scanlon, eds., *Equality and Preferential Treatment* (Princeton: Princeton University Press, 1976).

Peter Singer, *Animal Liberation* (New York: Avon Books, 1975).

Part II
Abortion and Fetal Research

Until 1973 nontherapeutic abortion was illegal in almost every part of the United States. A woman could obtain an abortion only if the pregnancy endangered her life, and in some states if the pregnancy was the result of rape or if the baby would probably be deformed. But abortion was not allowed simply because the baby was unwanted. These laws reflected a common moral assessment of abortion, which could be summarized in a syllogism: It is morally wrong to kill human beings; fetuses are human beings, although very tiny and helpless ones; therefore, it is wrong to kill fetuses. According to this way of thinking, abortion is simply murder, and ought to be illegal. And so it was.

Then in 1973 the Supreme Court of the United States upset this situation by declaring that the laws prohibiting abortion were unconstitutional. In the first place, the Court said, forbidding a woman to have an abortion violated her right to privacy, which was protected by the constitution. In the second place, the Court ruled that fetuses were not "persons" in the legal sense, and so they did not have a constitutionally protected right to life. The Court carefully distinguished the legal sense of "personhood" from the ordinary sense. Fetuses have never been legally persons because they could not own property, be a party to a lawsuit, and so forth. Therefore, the Court concluded that states may not prohibit abortion during the first 24 weeks of pregnancy. Only after the 24th week, when the fetus has become "viable"—that is, able to live outside the mother's body—may the states forbid elective abortions.

This decision caused a storm of controversy, and even today antiabortion forces are attempting to reverse it by means of a constitutional amendment. People who had fought for legalized abortion hailed the decision as a great step forward. From their point of view, women had now won the right to control their own bodies. It would no longer be necessary for women to alter their life plans because of unwanted children, or to suffer the emotional and economic hardship of having babies they could not afford. Desperate women would no longer have to seek unsafe, illegal abortions at the hands of backstreet "butchers." Of course, no one argued that abortion was the best solution to these problems; it would be preferable to prevent unwanted pregnancy by the use of contraception. Nevertheless, if an unwanted pregnancy did occur, the proabortion people argued that abortion should be available, and from this point of view the Supreme Court's decision was a victory.

From the other point of view, however, it was a moral horror. The decision meant that millions of innocent babies could now be slaughtered, simply upon their mothers' requests, and nothing could be done about it. The opponents of abortion were quick to point out that babies are people, not mere "things." By the eighth week of pregnancy, for example, the fetus is completely formed, with a face, fingers and toes, a skeleton, all its internal organs, a firm heartbeat, and even measurable brain activity. People unfamiliar with these facts were often shocked to see photographs of actual fetuses; while they may have vaguely expected to see globs of tissue, instead they saw little babies. Although the leaders of the antiabortion forces have often been Roman Catholics, their arguments have been addressed to all people, and not merely to members of one religious community.

In the aftermath of the Court's 1973 decision, public attention was drawn to a branch of medical research that had not previously received much attention—research involving fetuses. This research had been going on for more than two decades, and had been unusually productive. Viruses grown in cultures of fetal cells had led to the development of vaccines against polio and German measles, and research concerning the detection of diseases before birth had been spectacularly successful. When abortion was legalized, however, the number and kind of such experiments changed dramatically. Regardless of whether or not the fetus is considered a "person," there is no doubt that it is biologically a human being; so, if a fetus could be used for medical research after it had been aborted, the researcher would have the best possible subject—a human being. Fetal organs could be removed for experimental use, and whole aborted fetuses could be kept alive for several days in the laboratory for experimentation. *Legalized abortion, then, provided a bonanza of experimental material for medical laboratories.*

By and large, those who supported abortion found nothing objectionable in these developments. After all, they reasoned, if the fetus is going to die anyway, why not use it for experimental purposes first, if some good can be accomplished? However, those who had opposed legalized abortion were horrified. This, they said, was science gone mad; it confirmed their view that our society had simply lost its respect for human life. In Boston, one year after the Supreme Court decision legalizing abortion, four doctors who had been doing research using aborted fetuses were arrested and charged with the violation of a 19th century graverobbing statute. (Ultimately these charges were dropped.) Several states, including California, Ohio, and Massachusetts, passed laws forbidding fetal research. A Senate health subcommittee chaired by Senator Edward M. Kennedy held hearings. Finally a special commission—the National Commission for the Protection of Human Subjects of Biomedical and Behavioral Research—was appointed and given the responsibility of formulating guidelines for research in this area.

The readings which follow in this unit take up various aspects of the abortion controversy. The first selection is from Roe v. Wade, *the major Supreme Court case in which abortion was legalized. If you have never read an appeals court decision before, you may be surprised to find that it is not merely the announcement of a judicial verdict. It is more like a philosophical essay, in which issues are de-*

fined, distinctions made, arguments stated and assessed, and finally a conclusion reached. Thus, we can see not only what the Court decided but why that decision was thought best.

In the next selection Richard Wasserstrom, a Professor of Law and Philosophy at the University of California, Los Angeles, considers the crucial question of "The Status of the Fetus." He contends that the fetus should not be regarded as a person, but neither should it be regarded as a mere piece of tissue. Rather, in his view, the fetus should be placed in a special moral category, "in which its status is close to but not identical with that of a typical adult." If Wasserstrom is right, then abortion-on-demand is a very questionable practice. His paper was written as an advisory report to the National Commission, and includes his views about when and why fetal research should be permitted.

The papers by Judith Jarvis Thomson and R. M. Hare, both distinguished contemporary moral philosophers, are concerned specifically with the morality of abortion. Thomson's paper is perhaps the most famous and widely discussed defense of abortion by a philosopher. With great ingenuity she argues that abortion can be morally right even if the fetus is a human person with a right to life. This is a surprising view, since most people assume that if the fetus is a person with a right to life, then abortion must be wrong. However, Thomson argues that even if fetuses do have a right to life, women are not necessarily obligated to give over the use of their bodies to keep them alive.

"The Fetus as Guinea Pig," by Maggie Scarf, originally appeared in The New York Times Magazine. Scarf, a journalist who writes on the behavioral sciences, provides an overview of the issues connected with fetal research. Her article is followed by an excerpt from the guidelines for fetal research formulated by the National Commission. The chapter concludes with a critical review by

Peter Singer of the National Commission's work. Singer, a young Australian philosopher, believes that the Commission's conclusions are far too conservative, and that there is nothing wrong with research on fetuses provided they do not suffer and the parents do not object.

Roe v. Wade (1973)

United States Supreme Court

**Majority Opinion (Written by Justice
Harry A. Blackmun)**

. . . A recent review of the common law precedents argues
. . . that even post-quickening abortion was never established as a common law crime. This is of some importance
because while most American courts ruled, in holding or
dictum, that abortion of an unquickened fetus was not
criminal under their received common law, others followed Coke in stating that abortion of a quick fetus was a
"misprison," a term they translated to mean "mis-
demeanor." That their reliance on Coke on this aspect of
the law was uncritical and, apparently in all the reported
cases, dictum (due probably to the paucity of common law
prosecutions for post-quickening abortion), makes it now
appear doubtful that abortion was ever firmly established
as a common law crime even with respect to the destruction of a quick fetus. . . .

It is thus apparent that at common law, at the time of
the adoption of our Constitution, and throughout the
major portion of the 19th century, abortion was viewed
with less disfavor than under most American statutes currently in effect. Phrasing it another way, a woman enjoyed
a substantially broader right to terminate a pregnancy than
she does in most States today. At least with respect to the
early stage of pregnancy, and very possibly without such a
limitation, the opportunity to make this choice was present in this country well into the 19th century. Even later,
the law continued for some time to treat less punitively an
abortion procured in early pregnancy. . . .

Three reasons have been advanced to explain historically the enactment of criminal abortion laws in the 19th
century and to justify their continued existence.

It has been argued occasionally that these laws were the
product of a Victorian social concern to discourage illicit
sexual conduct. Texas, however, does not advance this justification in the present case, and it appears that no court
or commentator has taken the argument seriously. . . .

A second reason is concerned with abortion as a medical
procedure. When most criminal abortion laws were first
enacted, the procedure was a hazardous one for the
woman. This was particularly true prior to the development of antisepsis. Antiseptic techniques, of course, were
based on discoveries by Lister, Pasteur, and others first announced in 1867, but were not generally accepted and
employed until about the turn of the century. Abortion
mortality was high. Even after 1900, and perhaps until as
late as the development of antibiotics in the 1940's, standard modern techniques such as dilation and curettage
were not nearly so safe as they are today. Thus it has been
argued that a State's real concern in enacting a criminal
abortion law was to protect the pregnant woman, that is,
to restrain her from submitting to a procedure that placed
her life in serious jeopardy.

Modern medical techniques have altered this situation.
Appellants and various *amici* refer to medical data indicating that abortion in early pregnancy, that is, prior to the
end of first trimester, although not without its risk, is now
relatively safe. Mortality rates for women undergoing early
abortions, where the procedure is legal, appear to be as low
as or lower than the rates for normal childbirth. Consequently, any interest of the State in protecting the
woman from an inherently hazardous procedure, except
when it would be equally dangerous for her to forego it,
has largely disappeared. Of course, important state interests in the area of health and medical standards do remain.
The State has a legitimate interest in seeing to it that
abortion, like any other medical procedure, is performed
under circumstances that insure maximum safety for the
patient. This interest obviously extends at least to the performing physician and his staff, to the facilities involved,

to the availability of after-care, and to adequate provision for any complication or emergency that might arise. The prevalence of high mortality rates at illegal "abortion mills" strengthens, rather than weakens, the State's interest in regulating the conditions under which abortions are performed. Moreover, the risk to the woman increases as her pregnancy continues. Thus the State retains a definite interest in protecting the woman's own health and safety when an abortion is performed at a late stage of pregnancy.

The third reason is the State's interest—some phrase it in terms of duty—in protecting prenatal life. Some of the argument for this justification rests on the theory that a new human life is present from the moment of conception. . . .

Parties challenging state abortion laws have sharply disputed in some courts the contention that a purpose of these laws, when enacted, was to protect prenatal life. Pointing to the absence of legislative history to support the contention, they claim that most state laws were designed solely to protect the woman. Because medical advances have lessened this concern, at least with respect to abortion in early pregnancy, they argue that with respect to such abortions the laws can no longer be justified by any state interest. There is some scholarly support for this view of original purpose. The few state courts called upon to interpret their laws in the late 19th and early 20th centuries did focus on the State's interest in protecting the woman's health rather than in preserving the embryo and fetus. . . .

The Constitution does not explicitly mention any right of privacy. In a line of decisions, however, going back perhaps as far as *Union Pacific R. Co.* v *Botsford,* 141 U.S. 250, 251 (1891), the Court has recognized that a right of personal privacy, or a guarantee of certain areas or zones of privacy, does exist under the Constitution. In varying contexts the Court or individual Justices have indeed found at least the roots of that right in the First Amendment, . . . in the Fourth and Fifth Amendments . . . in the penumbras of the Bill of Rights . . . in the Ninth Amendment . . . or in the concept of liberty guaranteed by the first section of the Fourteenth Amendment, . . . These decisions make it clear that only personal rights that can be deemed "fundamental" or "implicit in the concept of ordered liberty," . . . are included in this guarantee of personal privacy. They also make it clear that the right has some extension to activities relating to marriage, . . . procreation, . . . contraception, . . . family relationships, . . . and child rearing and education, . . .

This right of privacy, whether it be founded in the Fourteenth Amendment's concept of personal liberty and restrictions upon state action, as we feel it is, or as the District Court determined, in the Ninth Amendment's reservation of rights to the people, is broad enough to encompass a woman's decision whether or not to terminate her pregnancy. . . .

. . . appellants and some *amici* argue that the woman's right is absolute and that she is entitled to terminate her pregnancy at whatever time, in whatever way, and for whatever reason she alone chooses. With this we do not agree. Appellants' arguments that Texas either has no valid interest at all in regulating the abortion decision, or no interest strong enough to support any limitation upon the woman's sole determination, is unpersuasive. The Court's decisions recognizing a right of privacy also acknowledge that some state regulation in areas protected by that right is appropriate. As noted above, a state may properly assert important interests in safe-guarding health, in maintaining medical standards, and in protecting potential life. At some point in pregnancy, these respective interests become sufficiently compelling to sustain regulation of the factors that govern the abortion decision. The privacy right involved, therefore, cannot be said to be absolute. . . .

We therefore conclude that the right of personal privacy includes the abortion decision, but that this right is not unqualified and must be considered against important state interests in regulation.

We note that those federal and state courts that have recently considered abortion law challenges have reached the same conclusion. . . .

Although the results are divided, most of these courts have agreed that the right of privacy, however based, is broad enough to cover the abortion decision; that the right, nonetheless, is not absolute and is subject to some limitations; and that at some point the state interests as to protection of health, medical standards, and prenatal life, become dominant. We agree with this approach.

The appellee and certain *amici* argue that the fetus is a "person" within the language and meaning of the Fourteenth Amendment. In support of this they outline at length and in detail the well-known facts of fetal development. If this suggestion of personhood is established, the appellant's case, of course, collapses, for the fetus' right to life is then guaranteed specifically by the Amendment. The appellant conceded as much on reargument. On the other hand, the appellee conceded on reargument that no case could be cited that holds that a fetus is a person within the meaning of the Fourteenth Amendment.

All this, together with our observation, *supra*, that throughout the major portion of the 19th century prevailing legal abortion practices were far freer than they are today, persuades us that the word "person," as used in the Fourteenth Amendment, does not include the unborn. . . . Indeed, our decision in *United States* v. *Vuitch*, 402 U.S. 62 (1971), inferentially is to the same effect, for we there would not have indulged in statutory interpretation favorable to abortion in specified circumstances if the necessary consequence was the termination of life entitled to Fourteenth Amendment protection.

. . . As we have intimated above, it is reasonable and appropriate for a State to decide that at some point in time another interest, that of health of the mother or that of potential human life, becomes significantly involved. The woman's privacy is no longer sole and any right of privacy she possesses must be measured accordingly.

. . . We need not resolve the difficult question of when life begins. When those trained in the respective disciplines of medicine, philosophy, and theology are unable to arrive at any consensus, the judiciary, at this point in the development of man's knowledge, is not in a position to speculate as to the answer.

It should be sufficient to note briefly the wide divergence of thinking on this most sensitive and difficult question. There has always been strong support for the

view that life does not begin until live birth. This was the
belief of the Stoics. It appears to be the predominant,
though not the unanimous, attitude of the Jewish faith. It
may be taken to represent also the position of a large seg-
ment of the Protestant community, insofar as that can be
ascertained; organized groups that have taken a formal
position on the abortion issue have generally regarded
abortion as a matter for the conscience of the individual
and her family. As we have noted, the common law found
greater significance in quickening. Physicians and their
scientific colleagues have regarded that event with less
interest and have tended to focus either upon conception
or upon live birth or upon the interim point at which the
fetus becomes "viable," that is, potentially able to live
outside the mother's womb, albeit with artificial aid. Viability is usually placed at about seven months (28 weeks)
but may occur earlier, even at 24 weeks. . . .

In areas other than criminal abortion the law has been
reluctant to endorse any theory that life, as we recognize
it, begins before live birth or to accord legal rights to the
unborn except in narrowly defined situations and except
when the rights are contingent upon live birth. . . . In
short, the unborn have never been recognized in the law as
persons in the whole sense.

In view of all this, we do not agree that, by adopting one
theory of life, Texas may override the rights of the pregnant woman that are at stake. We repeat, however, that
the State does have an important and legitimate interest in
preserving and protecting the health of the pregnant
woman, whether she be a resident of the State or a nonres-
ident who seeks medical consultation and treatment there,
and that it has still *another* important and legitimate
interest in protecting the potentiality of human life. These
interests are separate and distinct. Each grows in substan-
tiality as the woman approaches term and, at a point during pregnancy, each becomes "compelling."

With respect to the State's important and legitimate
interest in the health of the mother, the "compelling"
point, in the light of present medical knowledge, is at approximately the end of the first trimester. This is so because of the now established medical fact . . . that until
the end of the first trimester mortality in abortion is less

than mortality in normal childbirth. It follows that, from and after this point, a State may regulate the abortion procedure to the extent that the regulation reasonably relates to the preservation and protection of maternal health. Examples of permissible state regulation in this area are requirements as to the qualifications of the person who is to perform the abortion; as to the licensure of that person; as to the facility in which the procedure is to be performed, that is, whether it must be a hospital or may be a clinic or some other place of less-than-hospital status; as to the licensing of the facility; and the like.

This means, on the other hand, that, for the period of pregnancy prior to this "compelling" point, the attending physician, in consultation with his patient, is free to determine, without regulation by the State, that in his medical judgment the patient's pregnancy should be terminated. If that decision is reached, the judgment may be effectuated by an abortion free of interference by the State.

With respect to the State's important and legitimate interest in potential life, the "compelling" point is at viability. . . . State regulation protective of fetal life after viability thus has both logical and biological justifications. If the State is interested in protecting fetal life after viability, it may go so far as to proscribe abortion during that period except when it is necessary to preserve the life or health of the mother. . . .

To summarize and repeat:

1. A state criminal abortion statute of the current Texas type, that excepts from criminality only a *life saving* procedure on behalf of the mother, without regard to pregnancy stage and without recognition of the other interests involved, is violative of the Due Process Clause of the Fourteenth Amendment.

    (a) For the stage prior to approximately the end of the first trimester, the abortion decision and its effectuation must be left to the medical judgment of the pregnant woman's attending physician.

    (b) For the stage subsequent to approximately the end of the first trimester, the State, in promoting its interest in the health of the mother, may, if it chooses, regulate the abortion procedure in ways that are reasonably related to maternal health.

(c) For the stage subsequent to viability the State, in promoting its interest in the potentiality of human life, may, if it chooses, regulate, and even proscribe, abortion except where it is necessary, in appropriate medical judgment, for the preservation of the life or health of the mother.

2. The State may define the term "physician," as it has been employed in the preceding numbered paragraphs of this Part XI of this opinion, to mean only a physician currently licensed by the State, and may proscribe any abortion by a person who is not a physician as so defined.

. . . The decision leaves the State free to place increasing restrictions on abortion as the period of pregnancy lengthens, so long as those restrictions are tailored to the recognized state interests. The decision vindicates the right of the physician to administer medical treatment according to his professional judgment up to the points where important state interests provide compelling justifications for intervention. Up to those points the abortion decision in all its aspects is inherently, and primarily, a medical decision, and basic responsibility for it must rest with the physician. If an individual practitioner abuses the privilege of exercising proper medical judgment, the usual remedies, judicial and intraprofessional, are available. . . .

Dissent (Written by Justice Byron R. White)

At the heart of the controversy in these cases are those recurring pregnancies that pose no danger whatsoever to the life or health of the mother but are nevertheless unwanted for any one or more of a variety of reasons—convenience, family planning, economics, dislike of children, the embarrassment of illegitimacy, etc. The common claim before us is that for any one of such reasons, or for no reason at all, and without asserting or claiming any threat to life or health, any woman is entitled to an abortion at her request if she is able to find a medical advisor willing to undertake the procedure.

The Court for the most part sustains this position: During the period prior to the time the fetus becomes viable, the Constitution of the United States values the convenience, whim or caprice of the putative mother more than the life or potential life of the fetus; the Constitution, therefore, guarantees the right to an abortion as against any state law or policy seeking to protect the fetus from an abortion not prompted by more compelling reasons of the mother.

With all due respect, I dissent. I find nothing in the language or history of the Constitution to support the Court's judgment. . . . As an exercise of raw judicial power, the Court perhaps has authority to do what it does today; but in my view its judgment is an improvident and extravagant exercise of the power of judicial review which the Constitution extends to this Court.

The Court apparently values the convenience of the pregnant mother more than the continued existence and development of the life or potential life which she carries. . . .

It is my view, therefore, that the Texas statute is not constitutionally infirm because it denies abortions to those who seek to serve only their convenience rather than to protect their life or health. . . .

The Status of the Fetus

Richard Wasserstrom

What kind of an entity is a human fetus? I do not believe that the question of the morality of experimentation on living, non-viable fetuses can be sensibly considered without some attention being paid at the outset to that question. Although some of the relevant arguments do not depend, even implicitly, upon an answer to this question, the great majority of them do. That this is so can be seen, I think, from the fact that the question of experimentation is a very different one if the fetus is thought to be fundamentally like a piece of human tissue or organ, e.g., an appendix, than if the fetus is thought to be fundamentally like a fully developed, adult human being with normal capacities and abilities.

1. The Status of the Fetus

There are four different views that tend to be held concerning the status of the human fetus.

A. THAT THE FETUS IS IN MOST IF NOT ALL MORALLY RELEVANT RESPECTS LIKE A FULLY DEVELOPED, ADULT HUMAN BEING. At least two major arguments can be given in support of this position. The first is a theological argument which fixes conception as the time at which the entity acquires a soul. And since possesion of a soul is what matters morally and what distinguishes human beings from

---

This article first appeared in *Hastings Magazine*, June 1975.

other entities, the fetus is properly regarded as like all other persons. The second argument focuses upon the similarities between a developing fetus and a newly born infant. In briefest form, the argument goes as follows. It is clear that we regard a newly born infant as like an adult in all morally relevant respects. Infants as well as adults are regarded as persons who are entitled to the same sorts of protection, respect, etc. But there are no significant differences between newly born infants and fetuses which are quite fully developed and about to be born. What is more, there is no point in the developmental life of the fetus which can be singled out as the morally significant point at which to distinguish a fetus not yet at that point from one which has developed beyond it and hence is now to be regarded as a person. Therefore, fetuses are properly regarded from the moment of conception as having the same basic status as an infant. And since infants are properly regarded as having the same basic status as adults, fetuses should also be so regarded.

Now, of course, on this view abortion, whether before or after viability, raises enormous moral problems, since it is morally comparable to infanticide and homicide, generally. And the morality of abortion *per se* is beyond the scope of the present inquiry. This view is nonetheless directly relevant, even on the assumption that abortion prior to viability is morally permissible. For on this view, for instance, experimentation *ex utero* upon a non-viable living fetus is to be seen as analogous to experimentation upon, say, an adult human being who is in a coma and who will die within the next few hours. Thus, on this view, the moral problems of experimentation *ex utero* would be thought to be similar to those of experimentation upon adults whose deaths were imminent and who were themselves unconscious.

B. THAT THE FETUS IS IN MOST IF NOT ALL MORALLY RELEVANT RESPECTS LIKE A PIECE OF TISSUE OR A DISCRETE HUMAN ORGAN, FOR EXAMPLE, A BUNCH OF HAIR OR A KIDNEY. The argument in support of this view focuses upon all of the ways in which fetuses are different from typical adults with typical abilities. In particular, the absence of an ability to communicate, to act autonomously (morally, as well as physically), to be aware of one's own existence, and/or to experience sensations of pain and pleasure would singly and collectively be taken to be sufficient grounds for regarding the fetus as more like an organ growing within the woman's body than like any other kind of entity. It should be noted, too, that for our purposes this view includes all those positions which regard the status of the fetus as changing from something like a human organ to something else only at or after the moment of viability has been reached. For this inquiry is concerned only with experimentation upon non-viable fetuses.

On this view there are, I think, virtually no arguments against experimentation *ex utero* and only a few arguments against experimentation *in utero*. Whatever, for example, can properly be done to a severed human organ which still has certain life capacities—for example, it is capable of being transplanted into another human, or it still maintains some of its organ function—can properly be done to the non-viable fetus *ex utero* in those few hours before its life functions have ceased.

C. THAT THE FETUS IS IN MOST IF NOT ALL MORALLY RELEVANT RESPECTS LIKE AN ANIMAL, SUCH AS A DOG OR A MONKEY.   The fetus is, on this view, clearly not a person, nor is it just a collection of tissue or an organ. It is an entity which is at most entitled only to the same kind of respect that many (but not necessarily all) persons think is due to the "higher" animals. It is wrong to inflict needless cruelty on animals—perhaps because they do suffer or perhaps because of what this reveals about the character of the human imposing the cruelty. And fetuses are, basically, in the same class.

On this view, too, there are comparatively few worries about experimentation *ex utero* on non-viable fetuses. At most, the worries are of the same sort that apply to experimentation upon living animals. For the most part, it is proper to regard them as objects to be controlled, altered, killed, or otherwise used for the benefit of humans—subject only to concerns relating to the infliction of needless and perhaps intentional pain and suffering upon the entities being experimented upon, and (in the case of those higher animals we most identify with) to prohibitions upon their consumption as food.

D. THAT THE FETUS IS IN A DISTINCTIVE, RELATIVELY UNIQUE MORAL CATEGORY, IN WHICH ITS STATUS IS CLOSE TO BUT NOT IDENTICAL WITH THAT OF A TYPICAL ADULT.   On this view the status of the fetus is both different from and superior to that of the "higher" animals. It is, perhaps, closest to the status of the newly born infant in a culture in which infanticide is regarded as a very different activity from murder, or to the status of the insane, the mentally defective, or slaves—again in cultures which see them as less than persons but as clearly superior to animals. The case for regarding fetuses as belonging to a special, discrete class of entities rests, I think, largely on the fetus's potential to become in the usual case a fully developed adult human being. Conceding that the fetus is significantly different from an adult in respect to such things as its present capacity to act autonomously, to experience self-consciousness, and perhaps even to experience pain, this view emphasizes the distinctiveness of the human fetus as the entity capable in the ordinary course of events of becoming a fully developed person. This view sees the value of human life in the things of genuine value or worth that persons are capable of producing, creating, enjoying, and being, for example, works of art, interpersonal relations of love, trust and benevolence, and scientific and humanistic inquiries and reflections. Correspondingly, it sees the distinctive value of the fetus as being alone the kind of entity that can someday produce, create, enjoy and be these things of genuine value and worth.

It is, I think, especially important to notice the implications of this view for the morality of experimentation upon non-viable fetuses *ex utero.* For it is the non-viability of the fetus that goes, I believe, a long way toward making experimentation a substantially less troublesome act than it would otherwise be. That is to say, it is evident, I think, that on this view abortion is a morally worrisome act because it involves the destruction of an entity that possesses the potential to produce and be things of the highest value. However, if an abortion has been performed and if the fetus is still nonviable, then experimentation upon the fetus in no way affects the fetus's ability, or lack thereof, ever to realize any of its existing potential. On this view especially, abortion, not experimentation upon the non-viable fetus, is the fundamental, morally problematic activity.

II. Specific Issues Relating to Experimentation ex Utero

A. THE MAJOR ARGUMENTS AGAINST EXPERIMENTATION UPON NON-VIABLE, LIVING, HUMAN FETUSES EX UTERO. The arguments can be divided in a rough fashion into two groups: those that, on the one hand, oppose experimentation because of the possible deleterious consequences that are thought to follow from the legitimization of such a practice; and those that, on the other hand, oppose experimentation because of some feature of the situation that is seen to be itself wrong or improper. I begin with the former collection of arguments—those that concentrate upon the possible deleterious consequences.

One general argument concerning the possible deleterious consequences of permitting a practice of fetal experimentation is that if such a practice is permitted and well publicized then individuals and, in some related sense, the society will become less sensitive to values and claims which are entitled to the greatest respect. Thus, one specific version of this general line of attack is the argument that individuals will become less sensitive than they ought to be to the value of human life. Another specific claim is that individuals will become less sensitive than they ought to be to the rights and needs of persons who are, for one reason or other, incapable of looking after themselves, for example, infants, the aged, and the seriously ill or retarded. Still a third, related worry is that individuals will become less sensitive than they ought to be to the claims of those persons whose deaths are reasonably thought to be certain and imminent, such as persons in the last stages of terminal illnesses. And a fourth consequential concern is that individuals will become less sensitive than they ought to be to the rights of persons not to be the unwilling subjects of experimentation.

I think one thing that is of interest about all four of these arguments is that they can retain some if not all of their force irrespective of what is thought in fact to be the correct view about the kind of entity a fetus is. That is to say, consider the claim that permitting fetal research may lead individuals to become less sensitive than they ought to be to the rights and needs of persons who are, for one reason or another, incapable of looking after themselves. Even someone who is convinced that a fetus is basically like a human organ might nonetheless legitimately worry about the inferences that individuals would mistakenly draw from the permissibility of a practice of fetal research. As long as it is reasonable to believe that persons, in any significant number, might mistakenly suppose that the principle which justified fetal experimentation was a principle which justified experimentation upon any entity that was incapable of keeping itself alive without substantial human assistance, this is a deleterious consequence of a practice of fetal experimentation which would have to be taken into account. Of course, the more one thinks that a fetus is like other persons in most significant respects, the more one is also apt to think that individuals generally may confuse the case of the fetus with the case of those other entities whose claims to morally more sensitive treatment are nonetheless distinguishable.

A rather different consequential argument goes like this. Once it becomes permissible for experiments to be done on living, non-viable fetuses, such fetuses will come to be regarded as extremely useful in medical research. The increased demand for fetuses within the scientific community will lead to the creation of a variety of subtle as well as obvious incentives for persons both to have abortions and to have them in such a way that the fetus can be a useful object of experimentation. And this is undesirable for several reasons. To begin with, unless it is the case that abortion is a morally unproblematic action, it is wrong to develop a social practice which will encourage persons to have abortion. In addition, the fact that fetuses are useful objects of experimentation might lead members of the scientific and medical community unconsciously to distort or alter their views of when persons should have abortions. Doctors might in this way take into account non-medical reasons for advising patients to have abortions. And, finally, there is always the danger that the pressures and inducements would operate unequally throughout the society—persons from a low socioeconomic status would be the ones who were more likely to be attracted by the incentives and subjected to the pressures.

Still a third argument, which may or may not be consequentialist, points to the fact that many individuals will experience revulsion and will be in psychic turmoil when they learn of fetuses being treated in this way, that is, as objects of experimentation. The revulsion and turmoil are comparable to, though less universal than, that encountered at the thought of such things as cannibalism and the desecration of graves. If a large number of persons respond this way, then one argument against experimentation is that it will substantially impair social peace and harmony. Because they care so strongly, they will be led to act antagonistically toward the source of their discomfort. In addition, even if the numbers are not large, the severe quality of their reactions may justify prohibition simply on the ground that the gains of experimentation do not overbalance the pain and discomfort experienced by those who are so affected. . . .

B. THE MAJOR ARGUMENTS IN FAVOR OF THE PERMISSIBILITY OF EXPERIMENTATION UPON NON-VIABLE, LIVING FETUSES EX UTERO.   Some of the arguments depend quite directly upon what view is held concerning the status of the fetus, and others do not. More specifically, if the non-viable fetus is properly regarded as basically a human organ or piece of tissue, little if anything more than scientific curiosity is needed to justify experimentation. In the same way, if the non-viable fetus is basically regarded like a higher animal, such as a monkey, genuine scientific curiosity coupled with the avoidance of unnecessary suffering is all that is required.

The chief argument that applies, even if the nonviable fetus enjoys some other, more significant status, consists in a threefold claim. First, things of great usefulness vis-à-vis the preservation and improvement of human lives can be learned from these experiments, and, second, can *only* be learned from these experiments. Third, to describe the fetus as non-viable is to concede that no matter what is done, all signs of life will disappear from the fetus within a very short period of time, that is, not more than four or five hours. Thus, it is claimed, the conjunction of utility, need, and inevitability combine to establish the legitimacy of this kind of experimentation, irrespective of the status of the fetus.

One important objection that this argument must confront is this: if experimentation is justifiable under these conditions, then it is also justifiable in the case of a person who is unconscious, and who will die soon without regaining consciousness. . . .

At least two responses are possible. First, it might be argued that fetuses are just in a different class from adults. To be sure, there may not be anything intrinsically wrong with experimenting on an adult unconscious and in the last stages of a terminal illness. However, to permit experimentation would be an unwise exception to the doctrine of the sanctity of human life. Because fetuses are perceived to be different entities from fully developed persons, to permit experimentation on them is not to create the same kind of dangerous exception.

Second, it might be argued that the two cases are distinguishable in that there is no analogue to the concept of non-viability in the case of the adult. That is to say, medical science cannot identify with confidence those cases in which an individual will die soon without regaining consciousness, in the same way in which it can identify with confidence those fetuses that are not yet viable.

There is one argument in favor of experimentation that is worth noting. It is that if there is no good, moral reason to prohibit experimentation, then a decision to prohibit it encourages the practice of making social decisions on non-rational if not irrational grounds. And this is a generally unwise thing to do. That is to say, it might be maintained that experimentation should be prohibited just because it seems wrong or offensive even though no one can give a plausible account of why it ought to be so regarded. This argument is an answer to that way of proceeding. It is an argument for the importance of restricting sci-

entific inquiry only if there are good reasons and not, for
example, because of irrational or superstitious objections
to the investigations.

C. THE ISSUE OF CONSENT.   There is a general problem of
consent that arises: namely, that the fetus will not have
consented to anything. The question is whether that
should make a difference. . . . It will depend upon the view
that is taken of the status of the fetus, and the possible
answers will parallel those discussed above in the first part
of the paper. If the fetus is a person, then consent will be
required (but so, *a fortiori*, should consent have been required for the abortion), etc. I conclude, therefore, that no
new general problem is raised by the absence of the consent of the fetus to being the subject of experimentation.

   There is, however, a related issue that is worth mentioning. It is possible, I think, to hold a variety of views about
the status of the fetus and still believe that the mother, or
perhaps both parents, have a legitimate claim to have their
consent secured before any fetal experimentation occurs.
The justification cannot, of course, be that to require the
consent of the parents will protect the fetus from harm.
That is because having elected to terminate the pregnancy
the parents are already in a non-traditional, atypical relationship vis-á-vis the offspring. So it cannot be that the
consent of the parents should be required as a means of
protecting the fetus, or looking after its interests. Still, the
parents may have sensibilities and attitudes that are
deserving of respect—sensibilities that correspond to those
of living persons toward a deceased relative. It is not
exactly that they "own" the deceased, but that they do
have a legitimate claim to decide how the body of the deceased shall be dealt with. In the same way, I think, parents of an aborted fetus could see themselves as being in a
similar relationship to the fetus, such that they would feel
themselves injured in serious ways were the fetus to become the subject of experimentation without their agreement. For this reason, I believe that the consent of the
mother (in the case of an unmarried woman) or of both
parents to any experimentation should be required before
the abortion occurs, and that the nature of the proposed

experiments should be explained carefully and fully to them.

D. RECOMMENDATIONS CONCERNING EXPERIMENTATION EX UTERO.   My own view is that the fetus enjoys the kind of unique moral status described in Section I.D. above. Hence, abortion-on-demand seems to me to be a very troublesome moral issue. If the morality of the abortion is not in question, however, then I somewhat uncertainly conclude that experimentation *ex utero* may be permissible provided the following conditions are satisfied:

1. The consent of the mother (if unmarried) or of both parents should be procured before the abortion, and the experiments clearly described to those whose consent is required.
2. It should be determined by a body independent of those proposing the experiments that the experiments can reasonably be expected to yield important information or knowledge concerning the prevention of harm or the treatment of illness in other human beings. That same body should also determine that the desired information or knowledge is not reasonably obtainable in other ways.
3. Those medical persons who counsel a woman concerning abortion and secure the requisite consent should not be the same persons—or affiliated directly with those persons—who will be involved in the experimentation.
4. No experiments should be permitted on an aborted fetus which might in fact be viable, given the state of present medical ability.

III.   Specific Issues Relating to Experimentation in Utero

The cases that seem to me to be problematic are those in which there is a reasonable risk that the experiment will be harmful to the fetus and in which the experiments are not undertaken in order to benefit the particular fetus. Much of what has been said about experimentation *ex utero* applies to these cases as well. In addition, however, there are several new arguments that are relevant only in these cases.

The most significant one against experimentation *in utero* is that the fetus's non-viability has not yet been established in the same way in which it has been in the case of experimentation *ex utero*. That is to say, in the latter case, the abortion has already occurred and following upon that the fetus cannot survive no matter what is done. In the former case, however, the abortion has yet to take place, and until it does there is always the genuine possibility that the mother may change her mind and decide not to have the abortion at all.

Because this is so, the possibility of intervening injury resulting from the experimentation creates the following dilemma. On the one hand, if the mother changes her mind and decides not to have the abortion, the chances have thereby been increased that she will give birth to a child who is unnecessarily injured. It seems unfair to the child, the parents, and society to bring into the world a child with defects or disabilities that could have been prevented.

On the other hand, if the mother is required to proceed with the abortion because the experiments have been undertaken, the state is regarding the original consent to the abortion as irrevocable and it is, in essence, requiring her to submit to the abortion against her will.

There is, in addition, a related matter. The fact that potentially damaging experiments have been performed on the fetus will itself constitute an added inducement to the mother to go through with the abortion and not change her mind. That is to say, experimentation itself makes abortion more likely because the belief that the fetus has been injured will make the mother less likely to change her mind. If abortion is viewed as the kind of serious act that ought not be "artifically" encouraged, then the intervening experimentation may be objected to as just such an "artificial" inducement or encouragement to stay with the original decision to have the abortion.

For the above (and other) reasons I think it important that the decision to have an abortion be kept easily revocable, up until the time of the abortion. And for this reason I do not think that any experiments *in utero* should be permitted, where those experiments involve a substantial risk of injury to the fetus.

A Defense of Abortion[1]

Judith Jarvis Thomson

Most opposition to abortion relies on the premise that the fetus is a human being, a person, from the moment of conception. The premise is argued for, but, as I think, not well. Take, for example, the most common argument. We are asked to notice that the development of a human being from conception through birth into childhood is continuous; then it is said that to draw a line, to choose a point in this development and say "before this point the thing is not a person, after this point it is a person" is to make an arbitrary choice, a choice for which in the nature of things no good reason can be given. It is concluded that the fetus is, or anyway that we had better say it is, a person from the moment of conception. But this conclusion does not follow. Similar things might be said about the development of an acorn into an oak tree, and it does not follow that acorns are oak trees, or that we had better say they are. Arguments of this form are sometimes called "slippery slope arguments"—the phrase is perhaps self-explanatory—and it is dismaying that opponents of abortion rely on them so heavily and uncritically.

I am inclined to agree, however, that the prospects for "drawing a line" in the development of the fetus look dim. I am inclined to think also that we shall probably have to

From Judith Jarvis Thomson, "A Defense of Abortion," *Philosophy and Public Affairs*, vol. 1, no. 1 (copyright © 1971 by Princeton University Press). Reprinted by permission.

[1]I am very much indebted to James Thomson for discussion, criticism, and many helpful suggestions.

agree that the fetus has already become a human person well before birth. Indeed, it comes as a surprise when one first learns how early in its life it begins to acquire human characteristics. By the tenth week, for example, it already has a face, arms and legs, fingers and toes; it has internal organs, and brain activity is detectable.[2] On the other hand, I think that the premise is false, that the fetus is not a person from the moment of conception. A newly fertilized ovum, a newly implanted clump of cells, is no more a person than an acorn is an oak tree. But I shall not discuss any of this. For it seems to me to be of great interest to ask what happens if, for the sake of argument, we allow the premise. How, precisely, are we supposed to get from there to the conclusion that abortion is morally impermissible? Opponents of abortion commonly spend most of their time establishing that the fetus is a person, and hardly any time explaining the step from there to the impermissibility of abortion. Perhaps they think the step too simple and obvious to require much comment. Or perhaps instead they are simply being economical in argument. Many of those who defend abortion rely on the premise that the fetus is not a person, but only a bit of tissue that will become a person at birth; and why pay out more arguments than you have to? Whatever the explanation, I suggest that the step they take is neither easy nor obvious, that it calls for closer examination than it is commonly given, and that when we do give it this closer examination we shall feel inclined to reject it.

I propose, then, that we grant that the fetus is a person from the moment of conception. How does the argument go from here? Something like this, I take it. Every person has a right to life. So the fetus has a right to life. No doubt the mother has a right to decide what shall happen in and to her body; everyone would grant that. But surely a person's right to life is stronger and more stringent than the

---

[2]Daniel Callahan, *Abortion: Law, Choice and Morality* (New York, 1970), p. 373. This book gives a fascinating survey of the available information on abortion. The Jewish tradition is surveyed in David M. Feldman, *Birth Control in Jewish Law* (New York, 1968), part 5, the Catholic tradition in John T. Noonan, Jr., "An Almost Absolute Value in History," in *The Morality of Abortion*, ed. John T. Noonan, Jr. (Cambridge, Mass., 1970).

mother's right to decide what happens in and to her body, and so outweighs it. So the fetus may not be killed; an abortion may not be performed.

It sounds plausible. But now let me ask you to imagine this. You wake up in the morning and find yourself back to back in bed with an unconscious violinist. A famous unconscious violinist. He has been found to have a fatal kidney ailment, and the Society of Music Lovers has canvassed all the available medical records and found that you alone have the right blood type to help. They have therefore kidnapped you, and last night the violinist's circulatory system was plugged into yours, so that your kidneys can be used to extract poisons from his blood as well as your own. The director of the hospital now tells you, "Look, we're sorry the Society of Music Lovers did this to you—we would never have permitted it if we had known. But still, they did it, and the violinist now is plugged into you. To unplug you would be to kill him. But never mind, it's only for nine months. By then he will have recovered from his ailment, and can safely be unplugged from you." Is is morally incumbent on you to accede to this situation? No doubt it would be very nice of you if you did, a great kindness. But do you *have* to accede to it? What if it were not nine months, but nine years? Or longer still? What if the director of the hospital says, "Tough luck, I agree, but you've now got to stay in bed, with the violinist plugged into you, for the rest of your life. Because remember this. All persons have a right to life, and violinists are persons. Granted you have a right to decide what happens in and to your body, but a person's right to life outweighs your right to decide what happens in and to your body. So you cannot ever be unplugged from him." I imagine you would regard this as outrageous, which suggests that something really is wrong with that plausible-sounding argument I mentioned a moment ago.

In this case, of course, you were kidnapped; you didn't volunteer for the operation that plugged the violinist into your kidneys. Can those who oppose abortion on the ground I mentioned make an exception for a pregnancy due to rape? Certainly. They can say that persons have a right to life only if they didn't come into existence because of rape; or they can say that all persons have a right to life, but that some have less of a right to life than others, in particular, that those who came into existence because of rape have less. But these statements have a rather unpleasant sound. Surely the question of whether you have a right to life at all, or how much of it you have, shouldn't turn on the question of whether or not you are the product of a rape. And in fact the people who oppose abortion on the ground I mentioned do not make this distinction, and hence do not make an exception in case of rape.

Nor do they make an exception for a case in which the mother has to spend the nine months of her pregnancy in bed. They would agree that would be a great pity, and hard on the mother; but all the same, all persons have a right to life, the fetus is a person, and so on. I suspect, in fact, that they would not make an exception for a case in which, miraculously enough, the pregnancy went on for nine years, or even the rest of the mother's life.

Some won't even make an exception for a case in which continuation of the pregnancy is likely to shorten the mother's life; they regard abortion as impermissible even to save the mother's life. Such cases are nowadays very rare, and many opponents of abortion do not accept this extreme view. All the same, it is a good place to begin: a number of points of interest come out in respect to it.

1. Let us call the view that abortion is impermissible even to save the mother's life "the extreme view." I want to suggest first that it does not issue from the argument I mentioned earlier without the addition of some fairly powerful premises. Suppose a woman has become pregnant, and now learns that she has a cardiac condition such that she will die if she carries the baby to term. What may be done for her? The fetus, being a person, has a right to life, but as the mother is a person too, so has she a right to life. Presumably they have an equal right to life. How is it supposed to come out that an abortion may not be performed? If mother and child have an equal right to life, shouldn't we perhaps flip a coin? Or should we add to the mother's right to life her right to decide what happens in and to her body, which everybody seems to be ready to grant—the sum of her rights now outweighing the fetus' right to life?

The most familiar argument here is the following. We

are told that performing the abortion would be directly kill-ing[3] the child, whereas doing nothing would not be killing the mother, but only letting her die. Moreover, in killing the child, one would be killing an innocent person, for the child has committed no crime, and is not aiming at his mother's death. And then there are a variety of ways in which this might be continued. (1)But as directly killing an innocent person is always and absolutely impermissi-ble, an abortion may not be performed. Or, (2) as directly killing an innocent person is murder, and murder is always and absolutely impermissible, an abortion may not be per-formed.[4] Or, (3) as one's duty to refrain from directly kill-ing an innocent person is more stringent than one's duty to keep a person from dying, an abortion may not be per-formed. Or, (4) if one's only options are directly killing an innocent person or letting a person die, one must prefer letting the person die, and thus an abortion may not be performed.[5]

Some people seem to have thought that these are not further premises which must be added if the conclusion is to be reached, but that they follow from the very fact that an innocent person has a right to life.[6] But this seems to

---

[3]The term "direct" in the arguments I refer to is a technical one. Roughly, what is meant by "direct killing" is either killing as an end in itself, or killing as a means to some end, for example, the end of saving someone else's life. See note 6, below, for an example for its use.

[4]Cf. *Encyclical Letter of Pope Pius XI on Christian Marriage*, St. Paul Editions (Boston, n.d.), p. 32: "however much we may pity the mother whose health and even life is gravely imperiled in the performance of the duty allotted to her by nature, nevertheless what could ever be a sufficient reason for excusing in any way the direct murder of the innocent? This is precisely what we are dealing with here." Noonan *(The Morality of Abortion*, p. 43) reads this as follows: "What cause can ever avail to excuse in any way the direct killing of the inno-cent? For it is a question of that."

[5]The thesis in (4) is in an interesting way weaker than those in (1), (2), and (3): they rule out abortion even in cases in which both mother *and* child will die if the abortion is not performed. By contrast, one who held the view expressed in (4) could consistently say that one needn't prefer letting two persons die to kill-ing one.

[6]Cf. the following passage from Pius XII, *Address to the Italian Catholic Society of Midwives:* "The baby in the maternal breast has the right to life immediately from God.—Hence there is no man, no human authority, no science, no medical, eugenic, social, economic or moral 'indication' which can establish or grant a valid juridical ground for a direct deliberate disposition of an innocent human life, that is a disposition which looks to its destruction either as an end or as a means to another end perhaps in itself not illicit.—The baby, still not born, is a man in the same degree and for the same reason as the mother" (quoted in Noonan, *The Morality of Abortion*, p. 45)

me to be a mistake, and perhaps the simplest way to show this is to bring out that while we must certainly grant that innocent persons have a right to life, the theses in (1) through (4) are all false. Take (2), for example. If directly killing an innocent person is murder, and thus is impermissible, then the mother's directly killing the innocent person inside her is murder, and thus is impermissible. But it cannot seriously be thought to be murder if the mother performs an abortion on herself to save her life. It cannot seriously be said that she *must* refrain, that she *must* sit passively by and wait for her death. Let us look again at the case of you and the violinist. There you are, in bed with the violinist, and the director of the hospital says to you, "It's all most distressing, and I deeply sympathize, but you see this is putting an additional strain on your kidneys, and you'll be dead within the month. But you *have* to stay where you are all the same. Because unplugging you would be directly killing an innocent violinist, and that's murder, and that's impermissible." If anything in the world is true, it is that you do not commit murder, you do not do what is impermissible, if you reach around to your back and unplug yourself from that violinist to save your life.

The main focus of attention in writings on abortion has been on what a third party may or may not do in answer to a request from a woman for an abortion. This is in a way understandable. Things being as they are, there isn't much a woman can safely do to abort herself. So the question asked is what a third party may do, and what the mother may do, if it is mentioned at all, is deduced, almost as an afterthought, from what it is concluded that third parties may do. But it seems to me that to treat the matter in this way is to refuse to grant to the mother that very status of person which is so firmly insisted on for the fetus. For we cannot simply read off what a person may do from what a third party may do. Suppose you find yourself trapped in a tiny house with a growing child. I mean a very tiny house, and a rapidly growing child—you are already up against the wall of the house and in a few minutes you'll be crushed to death. The child on the other hand won't be crushed to death; if nothing is done to stop him from growing he'll be hurt, but in the end he'll simply burst open the house and walk out a free man. Now I could well understand it if a bystander were to say, "There's nothing we can do for you. We cannot choose between your life and his, we cannot be the ones to decide who is to live, we cannot intervene." But it cannot be concluded that you too can do nothing, that you cannot attack it to save your life. However innocent the child may be, you do not have to wait passively while it crushes you to death. Perhaps a pregnant woman is vaguely felt to have the status of house, to which we don't allow the right of self-defense. But if the woman houses the child, it should be remembered that she is a person who houses it.

I should perhaps stop to say explicitly that I am not claiming that people have a right to do anything whatever to save their lives. I think, rather, that there are drastic limits to the right of self-defense. If someone threatens you with death unless you torture someone else to death, I think you have not the right, even to save your life, to do so. But the case under consideration here is very different. In our case there are only two people involved, one whose life is threatened, and one who threatens it. Both are innocent: the one who is threatened is not threatened because of any fault, the one who threatens does not threaten because of any fault. For this reason we may feel that we bystanders cannot intervene. But the person threatened can.

In sum, a woman surely can defend her life against the threat to it posed by the unborn child, even if doing so involves its death. And this shows not merely that the theses in (1) through (4) are false; it shows also that the extreme view of abortion is false, and so we need not canvass any other possible ways of arriving at it from the argument I mentioned at the outset.

2. The extreme view could of course be weakened to say that while abortion is permissible to save the mother's life, it may not be performed by a third party, but only by the mother herself. But this cannot be right either. For what we have to keep in mind is that the mother and the unborn child are not like two tenants in a small house which has, by an unfortunate mistake, been rented to both: the mother owns the house. The fact that she does

adds to the offensiveness of deducing that the mother can do nothing from the supposition that third parties can do nothing. But it does more than this: it casts a bright light on the supposition that third parties can do nothing. Certainly it lets us see that a third party who says "I cannot choose between you" is fooling himself if he thinks this is impartiality. If Jones has found and fastened on a certain coat, which he needs to keep him from freezing, but which Smith also needs to keep him from freezing, then it is not impartiality that says "I cannot choose between you" when Smith owns the coat. Women have said again and again "This body is *my* body!" and they have reason to feel angry, reason to feel that it has been like shouting into the wind. Smith, after all, is hardly likely to bless us if we say to him, "Of course it's your coat, anybody would grant that it is. But no one may choose between you and Jones who is to have it."

We should really ask what it is that says "no one may choose" in the face of the fact that the body that houses the child is the mother's body. It may be simply a failure to appreciate this fact. But it may be something more interesting, namely the sense that one has a right to refuse to lay hands on people, even where it would be just and fair to do so, even where justice seems to require that somebody do so. Thus justice might call for somebody to get Smith's coat back from Jones, and yet you have a right to refuse to be the one to lay hands on Jones, a right to refuse to do physical violence to him. This, I think, must be granted. But then what should be said is not "no one may choose," but only "*I* cannot choose," and indeed not even this, but "*I* will not *act*," leaving it open that somebody else can or should, and in particular that anyone in a position of authority, with the job of securing people's rights, both can and should. So this is no difficulty. I have not been arguing that any given third party must accede to the mother's request that he perform an abortion to save her life, but only that he may.

I suppose that in some views of human life the mother's body is only on loan to her, the loan not being one which gives her any prior claim to it. One who held this view might well think it impartiality to say "I cannot choose."

But I shall simply ignore this possibility. My own view is that if a human being has any just, prior claim to anything at all, he has a just, prior claim to his own body. And perhaps this needn't be argued for here anyway, since, as I mentioned, the arguments against abortion we are looking at do grant that the woman has a right to decide what happens in and to her body.

But although they do grant it, I have tried to show that they do not take seriously what is done in granting it. I suggest the same thing will reappear even more clearly when we turn away from cases in which the mother's life is at stake, and attend, as I propose we now do, to the vastly more common cases in which a woman wants an abortion for some less weighty reason than preserving her own life.

3. Where the mother's life is not at stake, the argument I mentioned at the outset seems to have a much stronger pull. "Everyone has a right to life, so the unborn person has a right to life." And isn't the child's right to life weightier than anything other than the mother's own right to life, which she might put forward as ground for an abortion?

This argument treats the right to life as if it were unproblematic. It is not, and this seems to me to be precisely the source of the mistake.

For we should now, at long last, ask what it comes to, to have a right to life. In some views having a right to life includes having a right to be given at least the bare minimum one needs for continued life. But suppose that what in fact *is* the bare minimum a man needs for continued life is something he has no right at all to be given? If I am sick unto death, and the only thing that will save my life is the touch of Henry Fonda's cool hand on my fevered brow, then all the same, I have no right to be given the touch of Henry Fonda's cool hand on my fevered brow. It would be frightfully nice of him to fly in from the West Coast to provide it. It would be less nice, though no doubt well meant, if my friends flew out to the West Coast and carried Henry Fonda back with them. But I have no right at all against anybody that he should do this for me. Or again, to return to the story I told earlier, the fact that for

continued life that violinist needs the continued use of
your kidneys does not establish that he has a right to be
given the continued use of your kidneys. He certainly has
no right against you that *you* should give him continued
use of your kidneys. For nobody has any right to use your
kidneys unless you give him such a right; and nobody has
the right against you that you shall give him this right—if
you do allow him to go on using your kidneys, this is a
kindness on your part, and not something he can claim
from you as his due. Nor has he any right against anybody
else that *they* should give him continued use of your kidneys. Certainly he had no right against the Society of
Music Lovers that they should plug him into you in the
first place. And if you now start to unplug yourself, having
learned that you will otherwise have to spend nine years
in bed with him, there is nobody in the world who must
try to prevent you, in order to see to it that he is given
something he has a right to be given.

Some people are rather stricter about the right to life. In
their view, it does not include the right to be given anything, but amounts to, and only to, the right not to be
killed by anybody. But here a related difficulty arises. If
everybody is to refrain from killing that violinist, then
everybody must refrain from doing a great many different
sorts of things. Everybody must refrain from slitting his
throat, everybody must refrain from shooting him—and
everybody must refrain from unplugging you from him.
But does he have a right against everybody that they shall
refrain from unplugging you from him? To refrain from
doing this is to allow him to continue to use your kidneys.
It could be argued that he has a right against us that *we*
should allow him to continue to use your kidneys. That is,
while he had no right against us that we should give him
the use of your kidneys, it might be argued that he anyway
has a right against us that we shall not now intervene and
deprive him of the use of your kidneys. I shall come back
to third-party interventions later. But certainly the violinist has no right against you that *you* shall allow him to
continue to use your kidneys. As I said, if you do allow
him to use them, it is a kindness on your part, and not
something you owe him.

The difficulty I point to here is not peculiar to the right of life. It reappears in connection with all the other natural rights; and it is something which an adequate account of rights must deal with. For present purposes it is enough just to draw attention to it. But I would stress that I am not arguing that people do not have a right to life—quite to the contrary, it seems to me that the primary control we must place on the acceptability of an account of rights is that it should turn out in that account to be a truth that all persons have a right to life. I am arguing only that having a right to life does not guarantee having either a right to be given the use of or a right to be allowed continued use of another person's body—even if one needs it for life itself. So the right to life will not serve the opponents of abortion in the very simple and clear way in which they seem to have thought it would.

4. There is another way to bring out the difficulty. In the most ordinary sort of case, to deprive someone of what he has a right to is to treat him unjustly. Suppose a boy and his small brother are jointly given a box of chocolates for Christmas. If the older boy takes the box and refuses to give his brother any of the chocolates, he is unjust to him, for the brother has been given a right to half of them. But suppose that, having learned that otherwise it means nine years in bed with that violinist, you unplug yourself from him. You surely are not being unjust to him, for you gave him no right to use your kidneys, and no one else can have given him any such right. But we have to notice that in unplugging yourself, you are killing him; and violinists, like everybody else, have a right to life, and thus in the view we were considering just now, the right not to be killed. So here you do what he supposedly has a right you shall not do, but you do not act unjustly to him in doing it.

The emendation which may be made at this point is this: the right to life consists not in the right not to be killed, but rather in the right not to be killed unjustly. This runs a risk of circularity, but never mind: it would enable us to square the fact that the violinist has a right to life with the fact that you do not act unjustly toward him in unplugging yourself, thereby killing him. For if you do not kill him unjustly, you do not violate his right to life, and so it is no wonder you do him no injustice.

But if this emendation is accepted, the gap in the argument against abortion stares us plainly in the face: it is by no means enough to show that the fetus is a person, and to remind us that all persons have a right to life—we need to be shown also that killing the fetus violates its right to life, i.e., that abortion is unjust killing. And is it?

I suppose we may take it as a datum that in a case of pregnancy due to rape the mother has not given the unborn person a right to the use of her body for food and shelter. Indeed, in what pregnancy could it be supposed that the mother has given the unborn person such a right? It is not as if there were unborn persons drifting about the world, to whom a woman who wants a child says "I invite you in."

But it might be argued that there are other ways one can have acquired a right to the use of another person's body than by having been invited to use it by that person. Suppose a woman voluntarily indulges in intercourse, knowing of the chance it will issue in pregnancy, and then she does become pregnant; is she not in part responsible for the presence, in fact the very existence, of the unborn person inside? No doubt she did not invite it in. But doesn't her partial responsibility for its being there itself give it a right to the use of her body?[7] If so, then her aborting it would be more like the boy's taking away the chocolates, and less like your unplugging yourself from the violinist—doing so would be depriving if of what it does have a right to, and thus would be doing it an injustice.

And then, too, it might be asked whether or not she can kill it even to save her own life: If she voluntarily called it into existence, how can she now kill it, even in self-defense?

The first thing to be said about this is that it is something new. Opponents of abortion have been so concerned to make out the independence of the fetus, in order to establish that it has a right to life, just as its mother does, that they have tended to overlook the possible support they might gain from making out that the fetus is *depen-*

---

[7] The need for a discussion of this argument was brought home to me by members of the Society for Ethical and Legal Philosophy, to whom this paper was originally presented.

dent on the mother, in order to establish that she has a special kind of responsibility for it, a responsibility that gives it rights against her which are not possessed by any independent person—such as an ailing violinist who is a stranger to her.

On the other hand, this argument would give the unborn person a right to its mother's body only if her pregnancy resulted from a voluntary act, undertaken in full knowledge of the chance a pregnancy might result from it. It would leave out entirely the unborn person whose existence is due to rape. Pending the availability of some further argument, then, we would be left with the conclusion that unborn persons whose existence is due to rape have no right to the use of their mothers' bodies, and thus that aborting them is not depriving them of anything they have a right to and hence is not unjust killing.

And we should also notice that it is not at all plain that this argument really does go even as far as it purports to. For there are cases and cases, and the details make a difference. If the room is stuffy, and I therefore open a window to air it, and a burglar climbs in, it would be absurd to say, "Ah, now he can stay, she's given him a right to the use of her house—for she is partially responsible for his presnece there, having voluntarily done what enabled him to get in, in full knowledge that there are such things as burglars, and that burglars burgle." It would be still more absurd to say this if I had had bars installed outside my windows, precisely to prevent burglars from getting in, and a burglar got in only because of a defect in the bars. It remains equally absurd if we imagine it is not a burglar who climbs in, but an innocent person who blunders or falls in. Again, suppose it were like this: people-seeds drift about in the air like pollen, and if you open your windows, one may drift in and take root in your carpets or upholstery. You don't want children, so you fix up your windows with fine mesh screens, the very best you can buy. As can happen, however, and on very, very rare occasions does happen, one of the screens is defective; and a seed drifts in and takes root. Does the person-plant who now develops have a right to the use of your house? Surely not—despite the fact that you voluntarily opened your windows, you knowingly kept carpets and upholstered furniture, and you knew that screens were sometimes defective. Someone may argue that you are responsible for its rooting, that it does have a right to your house, because after all you *could* have lived out your life with bare floors and furniture, or with sealed windows and doors. But this won't do—for by the same token anyone can avoid a pregnancy due to rape by having a hysterectomy, or anyway by never leaving home without a (reliable!) army.

It seems to me that the argument we are looking at can establish at most that there are *some* cases in which the unborn person has a right to the use of its mother's body, and therefore *some* cases in which abortion is unjust killing. There is room for much discussion and argument as to precisely which, if any. But I think we should sidestep this issue and leave it open, for at any rate the argument certainly does not establish that all abortion is unjust killing.

5. There is room for yet another argument here, however. We surely must all grant that there may be cases in which it would be morally indecent to detach a person from your body at the cost of his life. Suppose you learn that what the violinist needs is not nine years of your life, but only one hour: all you need do to save his life is to spend one hour in that bed with him. Suppose also that letting him use your kidneys for that one hour would not affect your health in the slightest. Admittedly you were kidnapped. Admittedly you did not give anyone permission to plug him into you. Nevertheless it seems to me plain you *ought* to allow him to use your kidneys for that one hour—it would be indecent to refuse.

Again, suppose pregnancy lasted only an hour, and constituted no threat to life or health. And suppose that a woman becomes pregnant as a result of rape. Admittedly she did not voluntarily do anything to bring about the existence of a child. Admittedly she did nothing at all which would give the unborn person a right to the use of her body. All the same it might well be said, as in the newly emended violinist story, that she *ought* to allow it to remain for that hour—that it would be indecent in her to refuse.

Now some people are inclined to use the term "right" in such a way that it follows from the fact that you ought to

allow a person to use your body for the hour he needs, that
he has a right to use your body for the hour he needs, even
though he has not been given that right by any person or
act. They may say that it follows also that if you refuse,
you act unjustly toward him. This use of the term is
perhaps so common that it cannot be called wrong;
nevertheless it seems to me to be an unfortunate loosening
of what we would do better to keep a tight rein on. Suppose that box of chocolates I mentioned earlier had not
been given to both boys jointly, but was given only to the
older boy. There he sits, stolidly eating his way through
the box, his small brother watching enviously. Here we are
likely to say "You ought not to be so mean. You ought to
give your brother some of those chocolates." My own view
is that it just does not follow from the truth of this that
the brother has any right to any of the chocolates. If the
boy refuses to give his brother any, he is greedy, stingy,
callous—but not unjust. I suppose that the people I have
in mind will say it does follow that the brother has a right
to some of the chocolates, and thus that the boy does act
unjustly if he refuses to give his brother any. But the effect
of saying this is to obscure what we should keep distinct,
namely the difference between the boy's refusal in this
case and the boy's refusal in the earlier case, in which the
box was given to both boys jointly, and in which the small
brother thus had what was from any point of view clear
title to half.

A further objection to so using the term "right" that
from the fact that A ought to do a thing for B, it follows
that B has a right against A that A do it for him, is that it
is going to make the question of whether or not a man has
a right to a thing turn on how easy it is to provide him
with it; and it seems not merely unfortunate, but morally
unacceptable. Take the case of Henry Fonda again. I said
earlier that I had no right to the touch of his cool hand on
my fevered brow, even though I needed it to save my life. I
said it would be frightfully nice of him to fly in from the
West Coast to provide me with it, but that I had no right
against him that he should do so. But suppose he isn't on
the West Coast. Suppose he has only to walk across the
room, place a hand briefly on my brow—and lo, my life is

saved. Then surely he ought to do it, it would be indecent to refuse. Is it to be said "Ah, well, it follows that in this case she has a right to the touch of his hand on her brow, and so it would be an injustice in him to refuse"? So that I have a right to it when it is easy for him to provide it, though no right when it's hard? It's rather a shocking idea that anyone's rights should fade away and disappear as it gets harder and harder to accord them to him.

So my own view is that even though you ought to let the violinist use your kidneys for the one hour he needs, we should not conclude that he has a right to do so—we should say that if you refuse, you are, like the boy who owns all the chocolates and will give none away, self-centered and callous, indecent in fact, but not unjust. And similarly, that even supposing a case in which a woman pregnant due to rape ought to allow the unborn person to use her body for the hour he needs, we should not conclude that he has a right to do so; we should conclude that she is self-centered, callous, indecent, but not unjust, if she refuses. The complaints are no less grave; they are just different. However, there is no need to insist on this point. If anyone does wish to deduce "he has a right" from "you ought," then all the same he must surely grant that there are cases in which it is not morally required of you that you allow that violinist to use your kidneys, and in which he does not have a right to use them, and in which you do not do him an injustice if you refuse. And so also for mother and unborn child. Except in such cases as the unborn person has a right to demand it—and we were leaving open the possibility that there may be such cases—nobody is morally *required* to make large sacrifices, of health, of all other interests and concerns, of all other duties and commitments, for nine years, or even for nine months, in order to keep another person alive.

6. We have in fact to distinguish between two kinds of Samaritan: the Good Samaritan and what we might call the Minimally Decent Samaritan. The story of the Good Samaritan, you will remember, goes like this:

A certain man went down from Jerusalem to Jericho, and fell among thieves, which stripped him of his raiment, and wounded him, and departed, leaving him half dead.

And by chance there came down a certain priest that way; and when he saw him, he passed by on the other side.

And likewise a Levite, when he was at the place, came and looked on him, and passed by on the other side.

But a certain Samaritan, as he journeyed, came where he was; and when he saw him he had compassion on him.

And went to him, and bound up his wounds, pouring in oil and wine, and set him on his own beast, and brought him to an inn, and took care of him.

And on the morrow, when he departed, he took out two pence, and gave them to the host, and said unto him, "Take care of him; and whatsoever thou spendest more, when I come again, I will repay thee."   (Luke 10:30–35)

The Good Samaritan went out of his way, at some cost to himself, to help one in need of it. We are not told what the options were, that is, whether or not the priest and the Levite could have helped by doing less than the Good Samaritan did, but assuming they could have, then the fact they did nothing at all shows they were not even Minimally Decent Samaritans, not because they were not Samaritans, but because they were not even minimally decent.

These things are a matter of degree, of course, but there is a difference, and it comes out perhaps most clearly in the story of Kitty Genovese, who, as you will remember, was murdered while thirty-eight people watched or listened, and did nothing at all to help her. A Good Samaritan would have rushed out to give direct assistance against the murderer. Or perhaps we had better allow that it would have been a Splendid Samaritan who did this, on the ground that it would have involved a risk of death for himself. But the thirty-eight not only did not do this, they did not even trouble to pick up a phone to call the police. Minimally Decent Samaritanism would call for doing at least that, and their not having done it was monstrous.

After telling the story of the Good Samaritan, Jesus said "Go and do thou likewise." Perhaps he meant that we are morally required to act as the Good Samaritan did. Perhaps he was urging people to do more than is morally required of them. At all events it seems plain that it was not morally required of any of the thirty-eight that he rush out to give direct assistance at the risk of his own life, and that it is not morally required of anyone that he give long stretches of his life—nine years or nine months—to sustaining the life of a person who has no special right (we are leaving open the possibility of this) to demand it.

Indeed, with one rather striking class of exceptions, no one in any country in the world is *legally* required to do anywhere near as much as this for anyone else. The class of exceptions is obvious. My main concern here is not the state of the law in respect to abortion, but it is worth drawing attention to the fact that in no state in this country is any man compelled by law to be even a Minimally Decent Samaritan to any person; there is no law under which charges could be brought against the thirty-eight who stood by while Kitty Genovese died. By contrast, in most states in this country women are compelled by law to be not merely Minimally Decent Samaritans, but Good Samaritans to unborn persons inside them. This doesn't by itself settle anything one way or the other, because it may well be argued that there should be laws in this country—as there are in many European countries—compelling at least Minimally Decent Samaritanism.[8] But it does show that there is a gross injustice in the existing state of the law. And it shows also that the groups currently working against liberalization of abortion laws, in fact working toward having it declared unconstitutional for a state to permit abortion, had better start working for the adoption of Good Samaritan laws generally, or earn the charge that they are acting in bad faith.

I should think, myself, that Minimally Decent Samaritan laws would be one thing, Good Samaritan laws quite another, and in fact highly improper. But we are not here concerned with the law. What we should ask is not whether anybody should be compelled by law to be a Good

---

[8] For a discussion of the difficulties involved, and a survey of the European experience with such laws, see *The Good Samaritan and the Law,* ed. James M. Ratcliffe (New York, 1966).

Samaritan, but whether we must accede to a situation in which somebody is being compelled—by nature, perhaps—to be a Good Samaritan. We have, in other words, to look now at third-party interventions. I have been arguing that no person is morally required to make large sacrifices to sustain the life of another who has no right to demand them, and this even where the sacrifices do not include life itself; we are not morally required to be Good Samaritans or anyway Very Good Samaritans to one another. But what if a man cannot extricate himself from such a situation? What if he appeals to us to extricate him? It seems to me plain that there are cases in which we can, cases in which a Good Samaritan would extricate him. There you are, you were kidnapped, and nine years in bed with that violinist lie ahead of you. You have your own life to lead. You are sorry, but you simply cannot see giving up so much of your life to the sustaining of his. You cannot extricate yourself, and ask us to do so. I should have thought that—in light of his having no right to the use of your body—it was obvious that we do not have to accede to your being forced to give up so much. We can do what you ask. There is no injustice to the violinist in our doing so.

7. Following the lead of the opponents of abortion, I have throughout been speaking of the fetus merely as a person, and what I have been asking is whether or not the argument we began with, which proceeds only from the fetus' being a person, really does establish its conclusion. I have argued that it does not.

But of course there are arguments and arguments, and it may be said that I have simply fastened on the wrong one. It may be said that what is important is not merely the fact that the fetus is a person, but that it is a person for whom the woman has a special kind of responsibility issuing from the fact that she is its mother. And it might be argued that all my analogies are therefore irrelevant—for you do not have that special kind of responsibility for that violinist, Henry Fonda does not have that special kind of responsibility for me. And our attention might be drawn to the fact that men and women both *are* compelled by law to provide support for their children.

I have in effect dealt (briefly) with this argument in section 4 above; but a (still briefer) recapitulation now may be in order. Surely we do not have any such "special responsibility" for a person unless we have assumed it, explicitly or implicitly. If a set of parents do not try to prevent pregnancy, do not obtain an abortion, but rather take it home with them, then they have assumed responsibility for it, they have given it rights, and they cannot *now* withdraw support from it at the cost of its life because they now find it difficult to go on providing for it. But if they have taken all reasonable precautions against having a child, they do not simply by virtue of their biological relationship to the child who comes into existence have a special responsibility for it. They may wish to assume responsibility for it, or they may not wish to. And I am suggesting that if assuming responsibility for it would require large sacrifices, then they may refuse. A Good Samaritan would not refuse—or anyway, a Splendid Samaritan, if the sacrifices that had to be made were enormous. But then so would a Good Samaritan assume responsibility for that violinist; so would Henry Fonda, if he is a Good Samaritan, fly in from the West Coast and assume responsibility for me.

CONC

8. My argument will be found unsatisfactory on two counts by many of those who want to regard abortion as morally permissible. First, while I do argue that abortion is not impermissible, I do not argue that it is always permissible. There may well be cases in which carrying the child to term requires only Minimally Decent Samaritanism of the mother, and this is a standard we must not fall below. I am inclined to think it a merit of my account precisely that it does *not* give a general yes or a general no. It allows for and supports our sense that, for example, a sick and desperately frightened fourteen-year-old schoolgirl, pregnant due to rape, may of *course* choose abortion, and that any law which rules this out is an insane law. And it also allows for and supports our sense that in other cases resort to abortion is even positively indecent. It would be indecent in the woman to request an abortion, and indecent in a doctor to perform it, if she is in her seventh month, and wants the abortion just to avoid the nuisance of postponing a trip abroad. The very fact that the arguments I have

who decides?

been drawing attention to treat all cases of abortion, or
even all cases of abortion in which the mother's life is not
at stake, as morally on a par ought to have made them
suspect at the outset.

Secondly, while I am arguing for the permissibility of
abortion in some cases, I am not arguing for the right to
secure the death of the unborn child. It is easy to confuse
these two things in that up to a certain point in the life of
the fetus it is not able to survive outside the mother's
body; hence removing it from her body guarantees its
death. But they are importantly different. I have argued that
you are not morally required to spend nine months in bed,
sustaining the life of that violinist; but to say this is by no
means to say that if, when you unplug yourself, there is a
miracle and he survives, you then have a right to turn
round and slit his throat. You may detach yourself even if
this costs him his life; you have no right to be guaranteed
his death, by some other means, if unplugging yourself
does not kill him. There are some people who will feel
dissatisfied by this feature of my argument. A woman may
be utterly devastated by the thought of a child, a bit of
herself, put out for adoption and never seen or heard of
again. She may therefore want not merely that the child be
detached from her, but more, that it die. Some opponents
of abortion are inclined to regard this as beneath
contempt—thereby showing insensitivity to what is
surely a powerful source of despair. All the same, I agree
that the desire for the child's death is not one which anybody may gratify, should it turn out to be possible to detach the child alive.

At this place, however, it should be remembered that we
have only been pretending throughout that the fetus is a
human being from the moment of conception. A very early
abortion is surely not the killing of a person, and so is not
dealt with by anything I have said here.

Abortion
and the Golden Rule

R. M. Hare

I

If philosophers are going to apply ethical theory successfully to practical issues, they must first have a theory.
This may seem obvious; but they often proceed as if it
were not so. A philosopher's chief contribution to a practical issue should be to show us which are good and which
are bad arguments; and to do this he has to have some way
of telling one from the other. Moral philosophy therefore
needs a basis in philosophical logic—the logic of the moral
concepts. But we find, for example, Professor Judith Jarvis
Thomson, in an article on abortion which has been justly
praised for the ingenuity and liveliness of her examples,
proceeding as if this were not necessary at all.[1] She simply
parades the examples before us and asks what we would
say about them. But how do we know whether what we
feel inclined to say has any secure ground? May we not
feel inclined to say it just because of the way we were
brought up to think? And was this necessarily the right
way? It is highly diverting to watch the encounter in the
same volume between her and Mr. John Finnis, who, being

From R. M. Hare, "Abortion and the Golden Rule," *Philosophy & Public Affairs*
4, no. 3 (Spring 1975). Copyright © 1975 by R. M. Hare. Reprinted by the permission of the author and Princeton University Press.
[1]Judith Jarvis Thomson, "A Defense of Abortion," *Philosophy & Public Affairs* I,
no. 1 (Fall 1971). Reprinted in *The Rights and Wrongs of Abortion*, ed. Marshall
Cohen, Thomas Nagel, and Thomas Scanlon (Princeton, N.J., 1974), hereafter
cited as *RWA*.

a devout Roman Catholic, has intuitions which differ from
hers (and mine) in the wildest fashion.[2] I just do not know
how to tell whether Mr. Finnis is on safe ground when he
claims that suicide is "a paradigm case of an action that is
always wrong"; nor Professor Thomson when she makes
the no doubt more popular claim that we have a right to
decide what happens in and to our own bodies.[3] How
would we choose between these potentially conflicting intuitions? Is it simply a contest in rhetoric?

In contrast, a philosopher who wishes to contribute to
the solution of this and similar practical problems should
be trying to develop, on the basis of a study of the moral
concepts and their logical properties, a theory of moral
reasoning that will determine which arguments we ought
to accept. Professor Thomson might be surprised to see me
saying this, because she thinks that I am an emotivist,[4] in
spite of the fact that I devoted two of the very first papers I
ever published to a refutation of emotivism.[5] Her examples are entertaining, and help to show up our prejudices;
but they will do no more than that until we have a way of
telling which prejudices ought to be abandoned.

II

I shall abjure two approaches to the question of abortion
which have proved quite unhelpful. The first puts the
question in terms of the "rights" of the fetus or the
mother; the second demands, as a necessary condition for
solving the problem, an answer to the question, Is the
fetus a person? The first is unhelpful at the moment be-

---

[2]John Finnis, "The Rights and Wrongs of Abortion: A Reply to Judith Thomson,"
Philosophy & Public Affairs 2, no. 2 (Winter 1973); reprinted in *RWA.*
[3]Finnis, "Rights and Wrongs," p. 129; *RWA,* p. 97. Thomson, "Defense," pp. 53f.;
RWA, pp. 9f.
[4]Judith Jarvis Thomson and Gerald Dworkin, *Ethics* (New York, 1968), p. 2. Cf.
David A. J. Richards, "Equal Opportunity and School Financing: Towards a
Moral Theory of Constitutional Adjudication," *Chicago Law Review* 41 (1973):
71, for a similar misunderstanding. I am most grateful to Professor Richards
for clearing up this misunderstanding in his article, "Free Speech and Obscenity
Law," University of Pennsylvania Law Review 123 (1974), fn. 255.
[5]"Imperative Sentences," *Mind* 58 (1949), reprinted in my *Practical Inferneces*
(London, 1971); "Freedom of the Will," *Aristotelian Society Supp.* 25 (1951), reprinted in my *Essays on the Moral Concepts* (London, 1972).

cause nobody has yet proposed an even plausible account of how we might argue conclusively about rights. Rights are the stamping-ground of intuitionists, and it would be difficult to find any claim confidently asserted to a right which could not be as confidently countered by a claim to another right, such that both rights cannot simultaneously be complied with. This is plainly true in the present controversy, as it is in the case of rights to property—one man has a right not to starve, another a right to hold on to the money that would buy him food. Professor Thomson evidently believes in property rights, because she curiously bases the right of a woman to decide what happens in and to her own body on her ownership of it. We might ask whether, if this is correct, the property is disposable; could it be held that by the marriage contract a wife and a husband yield up to each other some of their property rights in their own bodies? If so, might we find male chauvinists who were prepared to claim that, if the husband wants to have an heir, the wife cannot claim an absolute liberty to have an abortion? As a question of law, this could be determined by the courts and the legislature; but as a question of morals . . . ?

In the law, cash value can be given to statements about rights by translating them into statements about what it is or is not lawful to do. An analogous translation will have to be effected in morals, with "right" (adjective), "wrong," and "ought" taking the place of "lawful" and "unlawful," before the word "rights" can be a dependable prop for moral arguments. It may be that one day somebody will produce a theory of rights which links the concept firmly to those of "right," "wrong," and "ought"—concepts whose logic is even now a *little* better understood. The simplest such theory would be one which said that A has a right, in one sense of the word, to do X if and only if it is not wrong for A to do X; and that A has a right, in another sense, to do X if and only if it is wrong to prevent A from doing X; and that A has a right to do X in a third sense if and only if it is wrong not to assist A to do X (the extent of the assistance, and the persons from whom it is due, being unspecified and, on many occasions of the use of this ambiguous word "rights," unspecifiable). It is often unclear, when people claim that women have a right to do what they like with their own bodies, which of these senses is being used. (Does it, for example, mean that it is not wrong for them to terminate their own pregnancies, or that it is wrong to stop them doing this, or that it is wrong not to assist them in doing this?) For our present purposes it is best to leave these difficulties on one side and say that *if* at some future time a reliable analysis of the various senses of "rights" in terms of "wrong" or "ought" is forthcoming, then arguments about rights will be restatable in terms of what it is wrong to do, or what we ought or ought not to do. Till that happy day comes, we shall get the issues in better focus if we discuss them directly in terms of what we ought or ought not to do, or what it would be right or wrong to do, to the fetus or the mother in specified circumstances.

III

The other unhelpful approach, that of asking whether the fetus is a person, has been so universally popular that in many of the writings it is assumed that this question is the key to the whole problem. The reason for this is easy to see; if there is a well-established moral principle that the intentional killing of other innocent persons is always murder, and therefore wrong, it looks as if an easy way to determine whether it is wrong to kill fetuses is to determine whether they are persons, and thus settle once for all whether they are subsumable under the principle. But this approach has run into well-known difficulties, the basic reason for which is the following. If a normative or evaluative principle is framed in terms of a predicate which has fuzzy edges (as nearly all predicates in practice have), then we are not going to be able to use the principle to decide cases on the borderline without doing some more normation or evaluation. If we make a law forbidding the use of wheeled vehicles in the park, and somebody thinks he can go in the park on roller skates, no amount of cerebration, and no amount of inspection of roller skates, are going to settle for us the question of whether roller skates are wheeled vehicles "within the meaning of the Act" if the

Act has not specified whether they are; the judge has to decide whether they are *to be* counted as such. And this is a further determination of the law.[6] The judge may have very good reasons of public interest or morals for his decision; but he cannot make it by any physical or metaphysical investigation of roller skates to see whether they are *really* wheeled vehicles. If he had not led too sheltered a life, he knew all he needed to know about roller skates before the case ever came into court.

In the same way the decision to say that the fetus becomes a person at conception, or at quickening, or at birth, or whenever takes your fancy, and that thereafter, because it is a person, destruction of it is murder, is inescapably a moral decision, for which we have to have moral reasons. It is not necessary, in order to make this point, to insist that the word "person" is a moral word; though in many contexts there is much to be said for taking this line. It is necessary only to notice that "person," even if descriptive, is not a fully determinate concept; it is loose at the edges, as the abortion controversy only too clearly shows. Therefore, if we decide that, "within the meaning of" the principle about murder, a fetus becomes a person as soon as it is conceived, we are deciding a moral question, and ought to have a moral reason for our decision. It is no use looking more closely at the fetus to satisfy ourselves that it is *really* a person (as the people do who make so much of the fact that it has arms and legs); we already have all the information that we need about the fetus. What is needed is thought about the moral question, How ought a creature, about whose properties, circumstances, and probable future we are quite adequately informed, to be treated? If, in our desire to get out of addressing ourselves to this moral question—to get it settled for us without any moral thought on our part—we go first to the physicians for information about whether the fetus is really a person, and then, when they have told us all they can, to the metaphysicians, we are only indulging in the well-known vice

---

[6]Cf. Aristotle, *Nicomachean Ethics* 5, 1137^{b}20. I owe the roller-skate example to H.L.A. Hart.

of philosophers (which my fellow linguistic philosophers, at any rate, ought to be on their guard against, because that is the mainstay of our training)—the vice of trying to settle substantial questions by verbal maneuvers.

I am not saying that physiological research on the fetus has no bearing on moral questions about abortion. If it brought to light, for example, that fetuses really do suffer on the same scale as adults do, then that would be a good moral reason for not causing them to suffer. It will not do to show that they wriggle when pricked, for so do earthworms; and I do not think that the upholders of the rights of unborn children wish to extend these rights to earthworms. Encephalograms are better; but there are enormous theoretical and practical difficulties in the argument from encephalograms to conscious experiences. In default of these latter, which would have to be of such a sort as to distinguish fetuses radically from other creatures which the antiabortionist would not lift a finger to protect, the main weight of the antiabortionist argument is likely to rest, not on the sufferings of the fetus, but on harms done to the interests of the person into whom the fetus would normally develop. These will be the subject of most of the rest of this paper.

Approaching our moral question in the most general way, let us ask whether there is *anything* about the fetus *or* about the person it may turn into that should make us say that we ought not to kill it. If, instead of asking this question, somebody wants to go on asking, indirectly, whether the fetus is a person, and whether, *therefore*, killing it is wrong, he is at liberty to do so; but I must point out that the reasons he will have to give for saying that it is a person, and that, therefore, killing it is wrong (or that it is not a person and, therefore, killing it is not wrong) will be the very same moral reasons as I shall be giving for the answer to my more direct question. Whichever way one takes it, one cannot avoid giving a reasoned answer to this moral question; so why not take it the simplest way? To say that the fetus is (or is not) a person gives *by itself* no moral reason for or against killing it; it merely incapsulates any reasons we may have for including the fetus within a certain category of creatures that it is, or is not, wrong to kill (i.e., persons or nonpersons). The word "person" is doing no work here (other than that of bemusing us).

IV

Is there then anything about the fetus which raises moral problems about the legitimacy of killing it? At this point I must declare that I have no axe to grind—I am not a fervent abortionist nor a fervent antiabortionist—I just want fervently to get to the root of the matter. It will be seen, as the argument goes on, that the first move I shall make is one which will give cheer to the antiabortionists; but, before they have had time to celebrate, it will appear that this move brings with it, inescapably, another move which should encourage the other side. We shall end up somewhere in between, but perhaps with a clearer idea of how, in principle, to set about answering questions about particular abortions.

The single, or at least the main, thing about the fetus that raises the moral question is that, if not terminated, the pregnancy is highly likely to result in the birth and growth to maturity of a person just like the rest of us. The world "person" here reenters the argument, but in a context and with a meaning that does not give rise to the old troubles; for it is clear at least that we ordinary adults are persons. If we knew beyond a peradventure that a fetus was going to miscarry anyway, then little would remain of the moral problem beyond the probably minimal sufferings caused to the mother and just possibly the fetus by terminating the pregnancy now. If, on the other hand, we knew (to use Professor Tooley's science-fiction example)[7] that an embryo kitten would, if not aborted but given a wonder drug, turn into a being with a human mind like ours, then that too would raise a moral problem. Perhaps Tooley thinks not; but we shall see. It is, to use his useful expression, the "potentiality" that the fetus has of becom-

---

[7]"Abortion and Infanticide," *Philosophy & Public Affairs* 2, no. 1 (Fall 1972): 60; *RWA*, p. 75. It will be clear what a great debt I owe to this article.

ing a person in the full ordinary sense that creates the
problem. It is because Tooley thinks that, once the "potentiality principle" (see below) is admitted, the conserva-
tives or extreme antiabortionists will win the case hands
down, that he seeks reasons for rejecting it; but, again, we
shall see.

We can explain why the potentiality of the fetus for becoming a person raises a moral problem if we appeal to a
type of argument which, in one guise or another, has been
the formal basis of almost all theories of moral reasoning
that have contributed much that is worth while to our
understanding of it. I am alluding to the Christian (and indeed pre-Christian) "Golden Rule," the Kantian Categorical Imperative, the ideal observer theory, the rational con-
tractor theory, various kinds of utilitarianism, and my
own universal prescriptivism.[8] I would claim that the last
of these gives the greatest promise of putting what is
common to all these theories in a perspicuous way, and so
revealing their justification in logic; but it is not the purpose of this paper to give this justification. Instead, since
the problem of abortion is discussed as often as not from a
Christian standpoint, and since I hope thereby to find a
provisional starting point for the argument on which many
would agree, I shall use that form of the argument which
rests on the Golden Rule that we should do to others as we
wish them to do to us.[9] It is a logical extension of this
form of argument to say that we should do to others what
we are glad was done to us. Two (surely readily admissible) changes are involved here. The first is a mere difference in the two tenses which cannot be morally relevant.
Instead of saying that we should do to others as we wish
them (in the future) to do to us, we say that we should do

---

[8]See my "Rules of War and Moral Reasoning," *Philosophy & Public Affairs* 1,
no. 2 (Winter 1972), fn. 3; reprinted in *War and Moral Responsibility,* ed. Marshall Cohen, Thomas Nagel, and Thomas Scanlon (Princeton, N.J., 1974). See
also my review of John Rawls, *A Theory of Justice,* in *Philosophical Quarterly* 23
(1973): 154f.; and my "Ethical Theory and Utilitarianism" in *Contemporary
British Philosophy,* series 4, ed. H. D. Lewis (London, forthcoming).
[9]St. Matthew 7:12. There have been many misunderstandings of the Golden
Rule, some of which I discuss in my "Euthanasia: A Christian View," *Proceedings of the Center for Philosophic Exchange,* vol. 6 (SUNY at Brockport,
1975).

to others as we wish that they had done to us (in the past). The second is a change from the hypothetical to the actual: instead of saying that we should do to others as we wish that they had done to us, we say that we should do to others as we are glad that they did do to us. I cannot see that this could make any difference to the spirit of the injunction, and logical grounds could in any case be given, based on the universal prescriptivist thesis, for extending the Golden Rule in this way.

The application of this injunction to the problem of abortion is obvious. If we are glad that nobody terminated the pregnancy that resulted in *our* birth, then we are enjoined not, *ceteris paribus*, to terminate any pregnancy which will result in the birth of a person having a life like ours. Close attention obviously needs to be paid to the *"ceteris paribus"* clause, and also to the expression " like ours." The "universalizability" of moral judgments, which is one of the logical bases of the Golden Rule, requires us to make the same moral judgment about qualitatively identical cases, and about cases which are *relevantly* similar. Since no cases in this area are going to be qualitatively *identical*, we shall have to rely on relevant similarity. Without raising a very large topic in moral philosophy, we can perhaps avoid the difficulty by pointing out that the relevant respects here are going to be those things about our life which make us glad that we were born. These can be stated in a general enough way to cover all those persons who are, or who are going to be or would be, glad that they were born. Those who are not glad they were born will still have a reason for not aborting those who would be glad; for even the former wish that, if they had been going to be glad; for even the former wish that, if they had been going to be glad that they were born, nobody should have aborted them. So, although I have, for the sake of simplicity, put the injunction in a way that makes it apply only to the abortion of people who will have a life just like that of the aborter, it is generalizable to cover the abortion of any fetus which will, if not aborted, turn into someone who will be glad to be alive.

I now come back to Professor Tooley's wonder kitten. He says that if it became possible by administering a wonder drug to an embryo kitten to cause it to turn into a being with a human mind like ours, we should still not feel under any obligation either to administer the drug to kittens or to refrain from aborting kittens to whom the drug had been administered by others. He uses this as an argument against the "potentiality principle," which says that if there are any properties which are possessed by adult human beings and which endow any organisms possessing them with a serious right to life, then "at least one of those properties will be such that any organism *potentially* possessing that property has a serious right to life even now, simply by virtue of that potentiality, where an organism possesses a property potentially if it will come to have that property in the normal course of its development."[10] Putting this more briefly and in terms of "wrong" instead of "rights," the potentiality principle says that if it would be wrong to kill an adult human being because he has a certain property, it is wrong to kill an organism (e.g., a fetus) which will come to have that property if it develops normally.

There is one minor objection to what Tooley says which we can pass over quickly. The administration of wonder drugs is not normal development, so Tooley ought not to have used the words "in the normal course of its development"; they spoil his "kitten" example. But let us amend our summary of his principle by omitting the words "if it develops normally" and substituting "if we do not kill it," I do not think that this substitution makes Tooley's argument any weaker than it is already.

Now suppose that I discovered that I myself was the result of the administration of the wonder drug to a kitten embryo. To make this extension of the example work, we have to suppose that the drug is even more wonderful and can make kitten embryos grow into beings with human bodies as well as minds; but it is hard to see how this could make any moral difference, especially for Tooley, who rests none of his argument on bodily shape. If this happened, it would not make my reasons for being glad that I was not aborted cease to apply. I certainly prescribe that they should not have aborted an embryo kitten which the wonder drug was going to turn into *me*. And so, by the

Golden Rule, I must say that I should not abort an embryo kitten to whom the wonder drug had been administered and which therefore was going to turn into a creature just like me. And, for what it is worth, this is what I would say. The fact that I confidently assert this, whereas Tooley confidently asserts the opposite—so confidently, in fact, that he thinks that this single example is enough to establish his entire case against the potentiality principle, and produces no other—just shows how inadequate intuitions are as a guide to moral conclusions. The fantastic nature of his example (like that of some of Professor Thomson's) makes it even more difficult to be certain that we are saying what we *should* say about it. Our intuitions are the result of our upbringings, and we were not brought up on cases where kittens can be turned into beings with human minds, or where people get kidnapped and have distinguished violinists with kidney failure plugged into their bloodstreams, as in Professor Thomson's example.

The problem becomes more difficult if we ask whether the same argument could be used to establish that it would be wrong, if this wonder drug were invented, not to administer it to all the embryo kittens one could get hold of. I shall postpone discussion of this problem until we have discussed the similar problem of whether the potentiality principle, once established, will not force upon us an extreme conservative position not only about abortion but also about contraception, and even forbid chastity. If we allow the potentiality of procreating human beings to place upon us obligations to procreate them, shall we not have a duty to procreate all the human beings that we can, and will not even monks and nuns have to obey King Lear's injunction to "let copulation thrive"?[11] To the general problem which this raises I shall return. We shall see that it is simply the familiar problem about the right population policy, which has to be faced whatever view we take of the present question.

---

[10]Tooley, "Abortion and Infanticide," pp. 55–56; *RWA*, pp. 70–71 (my italics).
[11]Act 4, sc. 6.

V

I propose to take it as established, that the potentiality principle is *not* refuted by Tooley's one example, and that it therefore holds the field until somebody produces a better argument against it—which I do not expect to happen, because the potentiality principle itself can be based on the Golden Rule, as the examples already considered show, and the Golden Rule has a secure logical foundation which I have already mentioned, though I have not had room to expound it.

Why does Tooley think that, if the potentiality principle is once granted, the extreme conservative position on abortion becomes impregnable? Obviously because he has neglected to consider some other potential beings. Take, to start with, the next child that this mother will have if this pregnancy is terminated but will not have if this pregnancy is allowed to continue. Why will she not have it? For a number of alternative reasons. The most knockdown reason would be that the mother would die or be rendered sterile if this pregnancy were allowed to continue. Another would be that the parents had simply decided, perhaps for morally adequate reasons, that their family would be large enough if and when this present fetus was born. I shall be discussing later the morality of family limitation; for the moment I shall assume for the sake of argument that it is morally all right for parents to decide, after they have had, say, fifteen children, not to have any more, and to achieve this modest limitation of their family by remaining completely chaste.

In all these cases there is, in effect, a choice between having this child now and having another child later. Most people who oppose abortion make a great deal of the wrongness of stopping the birth of this child but say nothing about the morality of stopping the birth of the later child. My own intuition (on which I am by no means going to rely) is that they are wrong to make so big a distinction. The basis of the distinction is supposed to be that the fetus already exists as a single living entity all in one place, whereas the possible future child is at the moment represented only by an unfertilized ovum and a sperm which may or may not yet exist in the father's testes. But will this basis support so weighty a distinction?

First, why is it supposed to make a difference that the genetic material which causes the production of the future child and adult is in two different places? If I have a duty to open a certain door, and two keys are required to unlock it, it does not seem to me to make any difference to my duty that one key is already in the lock and the other in my trousers. This, so far, is an intuition, and I place no reliance on it; I introduce the parallel only to remove some prejudices. The real argument is this: when I am glad that I was born (the basis, it will be remembered, of the argument that the Golden Rule therefore places upon me an obligation not to stop others being born), I do not confine this gladness to gladness that they did not abort me. I am glad, also, that my parents copulated in the first place, without contraception. So from my gladness, in conjunction with the extended Golden Rule, I derive not only a duty not to abort, but also a duty not to abstain from procreation. In the choice-situation that I have imagined, in which it is either this child or the next one but not both, I cannot perform both these duties. So, in the words of a wayside pulpit report to me by Mr. Anthony Kenny, "if you have conflicting duties, one of them isn't your duty." But which?

I do not think that any general answer can be given to this question. If the present fetus is going to be miserably handicapped if it grows into an adult, perhaps because the mother had rubella, but there is every reason to suppose that the next child will be completely normal and as happy as most people, there would be reason to abort this fetus and proceed to bring to birth the next child, in that the next child will be much gladder to be alive than will this one. The Golden Rule does not directly guide us in cases where we cannot help failing to do to *some* others what we wish were done to us, because if we did it to some, we should thereby prevent ourselves from doing it to others. But it can guide us indirectly, if further extended by a simple maneuver, to cover what I have elsewhere called "multilateral" situations. We are to do to the others affected, taken together, what we wish were done to us if we had to be all of them by turns in random order.[12] In this case, by terminating this pregnancy, I get, on this scenario, no life at all in one of my incarnations and a happy life in the other; but by not terminating it, I get a miserable life in one and no life at all in the other. So I should choose to terminate. In order to reach this conclusion it is not necessary to assume, as we did, that the present fetus will turn into a person who will be positively miserable; only that the person's expectation of happiness is so much less than the expectation of the later possible person that the other factors (to be mentioned in a moment) are outweighed.

In most cases, the probability that there will be another child to replace this one is far lower than the probability that this fetus will turn into a living child. The latter probability is said in normal cases to be about 80 percent; the probability of the next child being born may be much lower (the parents may separate; one of them may die or become sterile; or they may just change their minds about having children). If I do not terminate in such a normal case, I get, on the same scenario, an 80 percent chance of a normal happy life in one incarnation and no chance at all of any life in the other; but if I do terminate, I get a much lower chance of a normal happy life in the second incarnation and no chance at all in the first. So in this case I should not terminate. By applying this kind of scenario to different cases we get a way of dramatizing the application of the Golden Rule to them. The cases will all be different, but the relevance of the differences to the moral decision becomes clearer. It is these differences in probabilities of having a life, and of having a happy one, that justify, first of all the presumptive policy, which most people would follow, that abortions in general ought to be avoided, and secondly the exceptions to this policy that many people would now allow—though of course they will differ in their estimation of the probabilities.

I conclude, therefore, that the establishment of the potentiality principle by no means renders impregnable the

---

[12]See C. I. Lewis, *An Analysis of Knowledge and Valuation* (La Salle, 1946), p. 547; D. Haslett, *Moral Rightness* (The Hague, 1974), chap. 3. Cf. my *Freedom and Reason* (Oxford, 1963), p. 123.

extreme conservative position, as Tooley thinks it does. It merely creates a rebuttable or defeasible presumption against abortion, which is fairly easily rebutted if there are good indications. The interests of the mother may well, in many cases, provide such good indications, although, because hers is not the only interest, we have also to consider the others. Liberals can, however, get from the present form of argument all that they could reasonably demand, since in the kinds of cases in which they would approve of termination, the interests of the mother will usually be predominant enough to tip the balance between those of the others affected, including potential persons.

The effect of this argument is to bring the morality of contraception and that of abortion somewhat closer together. Important differences will remain, however. There is the fact that the fetus has a very good chance of turning into a normal adult if allowed to develop, whereas the chance that a single coitus will have the result is much lower. Further, if a general duty to produce children be recognized (as the view I have suggested requires), to kill a fetus means the nonfulfilment of this duty for a much longer period (the period from its begetting to the begetting of the next child, if any); whereas, if you do not beget a child now, you may five minutes later. Thirdly, parents become attached to the child in the womb (hence the argument, "We should all think differently if wombs were transparent"), and therefore an abortion may (whatever the compensating good) do some harm to them in addition to that (if any) done to the prospective child that is aborted; this is not so if they merely refrain from procreation. These differences are enough to account for the moral gap between contraception and abortion which will be found in the intuitions of most people; one has to be very extreme in one's views either to consider contraception as sinful as abortion or to think of abortion as *just* another alternative to contraception.

VI

We must now consider some possible objections to this view. Some of these rest on supposed conflicts with received opinion. I shall not deal at great length with these, for a number of reasons. The first is that it would be hard at the moment to point to any at all generally received opinion about abortion. But even if we could, it is a difficult question in moral philosophy, which I have discussed at length elsewhere,[13] how much attention should be paid to received opinion on moral issues. I shall sum up my view, without defending it. There are two levels of moral thinking. The first (level 1) consists in the application of learnt principles, which, in order to be learnt, have to be *fairly* general and simple; the second (level 2) consists in the criticism, and possibly the modification, of these general principles in the light of their effect in particular cases, actual and imagined. The purpose of this second, reflective kind of thinking is to select those general principles for use in the first kind of thinking which will lead to the nearest approximation, if generally accepted and inculcated, to the results that would be achieved if we had the time and the information and the freedom from self-deception to make possible the practice of level-2 thinking in every single case. The intuitions which many moral philosophers regard as the final court of appeal are the result of their upbringing—i.e. of the fact that just these level-1 principles were accepted by those who most influenced them. In discussing abortion, we ought to be doing some level-2 thinking; it is therefore quite futile to appeal to those level-1 intuitions that we happen to have acquired. It is a question, not of what our intuitions *are,* but of what they *ought* to be—a question which can usefully be dramatized by asking, What opinions about abortion ought we to be teaching to our children?

This may help to answer two objections which often crop up. The first claims that common opinion makes a larger moral distinction between failure to procreate and killing a fetus than the present view would warrant. Sometimes this distinction is said to be founded on the more general one between omissions and acts. There are strong

---

[13]See "The Argument from Received Opinion," in my *Essays on Philosophical Method* (London, 1971); "Principles," *Aristotelian Society* 72 (1972–73); and my "Ethical Theory and Utilitarianism."

arguments against the moral relevance of this last distinction;[14] and if we are always careful to compare like with like in our examples, and apply the Golden Rule to them, we shall not obtain any morally relevant difference between acts and omissions, provided that we are engaged in level-2 thinking. However, it may well be that the level-1 principles, which we selected as a result of this thinking, *would* use the distinction between acts and omissions. The reason for this is that, although this distinction is philosophically very puzzling and even suspect, it is operable by the ordinary man at the common-sense level; moreover, it serves to separate from each other classes of cases which a more refined thinking would also separate, but would do so only as a result of a very protracted investigation which did not itself make use of the act-omission distinction. So the act-omission distinction serves as a useful surrogate for distinctions which really are morally relevant, although it itself is not. Thus there may be no morally relevant distinction, so far as the Golden Rule goes, between killing and failing to keep alive *in otherwise identical cases;* but if people have ingrained in them the principle that it is wrong to kill innocent adults, but not always so wrong to fail to keep them alive, they are more likely in practice to do the right thing than if their ingrained principles made no such distinction. This is because most cases of killing differ from most cases of failing to keep alive in *other* crucial ways, such that the former are very much more likely to be wrong than the latter. And in the case of abortion and failure to procreate, it is *possible* (I do not say that it is so) that the best level-1 principles for practical use would make bigger distinctions at birth and at conception than a refined level-2 thinking could possibly support. The reason is that conception and birth are dividing lines easily discerned by the ordinary man, and that therefore a level-1 principle which uses these dividing lines in order to draw the moral line (what moral line?) *may* lead in practice to the morally best results. But if we are arguing (as we are) whether or not this

---

[14]Tooley, "Abortion and Infanticide," p. 59; *RWA*, p. 74. See also J.C.B. Glover's forthcoming book on the morality of killing.

is so, appeals to the intuitions of the ordinary man are entirely beside the point.

Secondly, we have the "thin end of the wedge" or "slippery-slope" objection. If we sanction contraception, why not abortion; and if abortion, why not infanticide; and if infanticide, why not the murder of adults? As an argument against the too ready abandonment of accepted general level-1 principles this argument has some force; for, psychologically speaking, if the ordinary man or the ordinary doctor has got hold of some general principles about killing, which serve well enough in the ordinary run, and then somebody tells him that these principles ought not to be followed universally, it may well be that he will come to disregard them in cases where he ought not. The argument can be overplayed—I do not think that many doctors who have come to accept abortion are thereby made any more prone to murder their wives; but at this level the argument has *some* force, especially if, in the upbringing of the ordinary man and the ordinary doctor, enormous stress has been laid on general principles of great rigidity—such principles are naturally susceptible to thin ends of wedges. But when we are disputing at level 2 about our level-1 principles ought to be, the argument has little force. For it may be that we could devise other, equally simple principles which would be wedge-resistant and would draw lines in different places; it may be that we *ought* to do this, if the new places were more likely, if generally recognized, to lead most often to the right results in practice. Tooley recommends such a moral line very shortly *after* birth, and his arguments have a great attraction.[15] For the present, it is enough to say that if the line proved wedge-resistant and if it separated off, in a workable manner, nearly all the cases that would be pronounced wrong by level-2 thinking from nearly all those which would be pronounced permissible, then it would be no argument against this proposal that it conflicted with

[15]Tooley, p. 64; *RWA*, p. 79. If the potentiality principle be granted, the number of permissible infanticides is greatly reduced, but not to nothing. See my "Survival of the Weakest" in *Documentation in Medical Ethics 2* (1973); reprinted in *Moral Problems in Medicine*, ed. S. Gorovitz et al. (New York, forthcoming).

people's intuitions. These intuitions, like earlier ones which made a big distinction at quickening, are the results of attempts to simplify the issues for a laudable practical purpose; they cannot without circularity be used in an appraisal of themselves. As Tooley implies, we have to find real moral reasons for distinguishing cases. If, as is sure to happen, the distinctions that result are very complicated, we have to simplify them for ordinary use as best we can; and there is no reason to assume that the simplifications which will be best are those which have been current hitherto—certainly not in a context in which circumstances have changed as radically as they have with regard to abortion.

VII

It might be objected, as we have seen, that the view I have advocated would require unlimited procreation, on the ground that not to produce any single child whom one might have produced lays one open to the charge that one is not doing to that child as one is glad has been done to oneself (viz. causing him to be born). But there are, even on the present view, reasons for limiting the population. Let us suppose that fully-grown adults were producible ad lib., not by gestation in human mothers or in the wombs of cats or in test tubes, but instantaneously by waving a wand. We should still have to formulate a population policy for the world as a whole, and for particular societies and families. There would be a point at which the additional member of each of these units imposed burdens on the other members great enough in sum to outweigh the advantage gained by the additional member. In utilitarian terms, the classical or total utility principle sets a limit to population which, although higher than the average utility principle, is nevertheless a limit.[16] In terms of the Golden Rule, which is the basis of my present argument, even if the "others" to whom we are to do what we wish, or what we are glad, to have done to us are to include potential

---

[16]See my review of Rawls, pp. 244f.

people, good done to them may be outweighed by harm done to other actual or potential people. If we had to submit to all their lives or nonlives in turn, we should have a basis for choosing a population policy which would not differ from that yielded by the classical utility principle. How restrictive this policy would be would depend on assumptions about the threshold effects of certain increases in population size and density. I think myself that even if potential people are allowed to be the objects of duties, the policy will be fairly restrictive; but this is obviously not the place to argue for this view.

One big gap in the argument of this paper is my failure to deal with the question of whether, when we are balancing the interests of the potential person into whom this fetus will turn against the interests of other people who might be born, we ought to limit the second class to other members of the same family, or include in it *any* potential person who might in some sense "replace" the first-mentioned potential person. This major question would seem to depend for its answer on a further question: To what extent will the birth or non-birth of *this* person make more or less likely the birth or non-birth of the others? This is a demographic question which at the moment baffles me; but it would obviously have to be gone into in any exhaustive account of the morality of abortion. I have, however, written (possibly too hastily) as if only other potential members of the same family need be considered. That was enough to illustrate the important principle that I was trying to explain.

VIII

Lastly, a logician might object that these potential people do not exist, and cannot be identified or individuated, and therefore cannot be the objects of duties. If I had put my own view in terms of rights or interests, the same objection could be expressed by saying that only actual people have these. Two points can be made against this objection at once. The first is a perhaps superficial one: it would be strange if there were an act whose very performance made it impossible for it to be wrong. But if the objection were correct, the act of aborting a possible person would be such an act; by preventing the existence of the object of the wrongdoing, it would remove its wrongness. This seems too easy a way of avoiding crime.

Secondly, there seems to be no objection in principle to condemning hypothetical acts: it would have been wrong for Nixon to stay on any longer in the presidency. And it seems a fairly safe principle that if it makes sense to make value-judgments about an act that was done, it makes equal sense to make opposite judgments about the hypothetical omission to do that act. "Nixon did right to resign" makes sense; and so therefore, does "Nixon would have done wrong not to resign." But we do commend actions which resulted in our own existence—every Sunday in thousands of churches we give thanks for our creation as well as for our preservation and all the blessings of this life; and Aristotle says that we ought to show the same gratitude to our earthly fathers as "causes of our being."[17] So it is at least meaningful to say of God or of our fathers that if they had not caused us to exist, they would not have been doing as well for us as they could. And this is all that my argument requires.

Coming now to the purely logical points, we notice that the nonactuality of the potential person (the supposed object of the duty to procreate or not abort) is a separate issue from his nonidentifiability. Unfortunately "identifiable" is an ambiguous word; in one sense I can identify the next man to occupy my carrel at the library by describing him thus, but in another sense I cannot identify him because I have no idea who he is. The person who will be born if these two people start their coitus in precisely five minutes is identified by that description; and so, therefore, is the person who would have been born if they had started it five minutes ago. Moreover (this is an additional point) if we had enough mechanical and other information, we could specify the hair color and all the other traits of that person, if we wished, with as much precision as we could the result of a lottery done on a computer whose ran-

---

[17] *Nicomachean Ethics* 8, 1161ª17, 1163ª6, 1165ª23.

domizing mechanism we could minutely inspect. In this sense, therefore, the potential person is identifiable. We do not know who he will be, in the sense that we do not know what actually now existing person he will be, because he will not be identical with any actually now existing person. But it is hard to see how his inability to meet this logically unmeetable demand for identifiability with some already existing person affects the argument; he is identifiable in the sense that identifying reference can be made to him. So it cannot be nonidentifiability that is the trouble.

Is it then nonactuality? Certainly not *present* nonactuality. We can do harm to and wrong succeeding generations by using up all the world's resources or by releasing too much radioactive material. But suppose that this not merely made them miserable, but actually stopped them being born (e.g. that the radioactive material made everybody sterile all at once). As before it seems that we can be thankful that our fathers did not do this, thereby stopping us coming into existence; why cannot we say, therefore, that if we behave as well as our fathers, we shall be doing well by our children or grandchildren, or that if we were to behave in this respect worse than our fathers, we would be doing worse by our children or grandchildren. It seems strange to say that if we behaved only a little worse, so that the next generation was half the size it would have been, we had done badly for that generation, but that if we behaved much worse, so that the succeeding generation was reduced to nil, we had not done badly for it at all.

This is obviously a very perplexing matter, and needs much more discussion. All I can hope to do here is to cast doubt on the assumption that some people accept without question, viz. that one cannot harm a person by preventing him coming into existence. True, he does not exist to be harmed; and he is not *deprived* of existence, in the sense of having it taken away from him, though he is *denied* it. But if it would have been a good for him to exist (because this made possible the goods that, once he existed, he was able to enjoy), surely it was a harm to him not to exist, and so not to be able to enjoy these goods. He did not suffer; but there were enjoyments he could have had and did not.

IX

I conclude, then, that a systematic application of the Christian Golden Rule yields the following precepts about abortion. It is prima facie and in general wrong in default of sufficient countervailing reasons. But since the wrongness of it consists, in the main, of stopping a person coming into existence and not in any wrong done to the fetus as such, such countervailing reasons are not too hard to find in many cases. And if the termination of this pregnancy facilitates or renders possible or probable the beginning of another more propitious one, it really does not take much to justify it.

I have not discussed what the law on abortion ought to be; that question would have to be the subject of another paper. I have been speaking only about the morality of terminating individual pregnancies. I will end as I began by saying that my argument has been based on a developed ethical theory, though I have not had room to expound this theory (I have done it in my books). This theory provides the logical basis of the Golden Rule. Though not *founded on* a utilitarian principle, it also provides the basis for a certain sort of utilitarianism that escapes the vices which have been decried in some other sorts.[18] But I shall not now try to defend these last assertions. If they are challenged, and if the view that I have advanced in this paper is challenged, the issue can only be fought out on the terrain of ethical theory itself. That is why it is such a pity that so many people—even philosophers—think that they can discuss abortion without making up their minds about the fundamental problems of moral philosophy.

---

[18]See my "Ethical Theory and Utilitarianism."

The Fetus as Guinea Pig

Maggie Scarf

I can remember a situation in which a woman entered the hospital with a miscarriage. It was a case of spontaneous abortion, and she came in because she'd been told it was about to happen. The baby, however, was born alive. It weighed less than 500 grams, or just under a pound—which was below the legal definition of a live birth (this was in Baltimore). No birth certificate was made out, therefore, and it wasn't legally born. Since it *was* alive, however, it was taken over to the premature unit where it survived for two days. Eventually, being at that very borderline weight, it did die. . . . As it happened, the woman had given birth on December 31; and so the two days of infant care had been during the first two days of the New Year. The parents, when they received the hospital bill, were unable to claim any tax deduction. The father was incensed and he took the position that since there never had been any legally born "person"—no birth certificate and no death certificate—they couldn't hold him responsible for the costs of treatment. Why should he be made to pay for the care of a child who had never even existed? The hospital, on its own part, was put in the odd position of having spent forty-eight hours treating an individual who wasn't even, technically speaking, born. They finally did cancel the charges, I believe, and they agreed to forget the whole thing. . . .

From *The New York Times Magazine*, October 19, 1975. © 1975 by the New York Times Company. Reprinted by permission.

Dr. Richard E. Behrman, Medical Director, Babies Hospital (Columbia University), in an interview.

When does a fetus become "a person"? At what point in the slow continuum of fetal growth—from fertilization, to implantation in the uterine wall, to the time of the first heartbeat, to "quickening" (when the mother first perceives movement within her womb), to "viability" (the stage of fetal maturation at which the organism becomes capable of surviving outside the mother's support system, outside the uterus), to birth itself—does it become possible to say that, yes, from here onward, the fetus is to be regarded as a fully human individual, endowed with status as a person and a set of protectable human rights?

Legally, the position of the fetus was stated clearly in *Roe v. Wade,* one of the Supreme Court decisions on the abortion issue, which was handed down in 1973. The Court said that the fetus is not to be regarded as a "person in the whole sense" prior to the age of viability. Viability, as defined in the *Roe–Wade* decision, is the point in fetal development at which the growing organism is "potentially able to live outside the mother's womb, albeit with artificial aid"; the Court placed the stage of fetal viability at "seven months, twenty-eight weeks," but noted that it could occur earlier, as early as twenty-four weeks. The Court took the view, in short, that a fetus that is born alive is not to be construed as a "person"; the fetus that can maintain a biologically independent existence—that can live, grow and develop outside the womb—is to be so regarded.

As one may readily see, the *Roe–Wade* decision has a curious impact upon our perception of the fetus prior to the age of viability. It places that fetus not only in an odd legal limbo, but in a metaphysical and moral one as well. For, by defining the fetus in the first two trimesters of pregnancy as "not a person in the whole sense," the Court leaves open the entire question of what it actually is—and, more importantly, what may be done with it.

Since the time of the Supreme Court abortion decisions, live and dead fetuses, fetal tissues, fetal organs and similar materials have become widely available for use in a dizzying array of scientific investigations. At the same time,

antiabortion forces, who believe that fetal work "legiti-
mizes" abortion practices, as well as people who are
simply opposed to this experimentation on moral and
ethical grounds, have been pressing for legislation that will
impede or halt fetal research entirely. Opponents of this
work have decried it as a form of "mad science" and an
assault on human values and human dignity. Scientists,
for their part, have been protesting what they view as per-
secutory tactics, spearheaded by "anti-science" fanatics.

In 1974, in response to a surge of public concern over
fetal and other kinds of research that utilized "human subjects," Congress enacted legislation to establish a National
Commission for the Protection of Human Subjects of
Biomedical and Behavioral Research. The commission,
whose members were selected by the Secretary of Health,
Education and Welfare, was entrusted with the task of
studying the various types of human research and suggesting possible regulations for experimentation that might go
on in the future. While the National Commission was to
have no legal power to enforce its decisions, the Congres-
sional legislation did require the Secretary of H.E.W. to respond to whatever report it made (either negatively or
positively) when he drew up his guidelines for the protection of human subjects.

The same act of Congress that established the National
Commission also provided for a ban on all experimentation involving life, whole fetuses, before or after an induced abortion—and it instructed the commission to investigate fetal research in advance of all other kinds of
human research, as its very first order of business. As if
these moves were not sobering enough for scientists working in this area, the Department of Health, Education and
Welfare then suggested that a voluntary "moratorium" on
any even mildly questionable fetal studies be entered into
by investigators whose research they were supporting.

It was thus in an atmosphere of some apprehension and
a good deal of bitter misunderstanding that the National
Commission for the Protection of Human Subjects was
appointed; it consisted of three lawyers, three physician-
investigators, two medical ethicists, two psychologists and
one "public representative." Perhaps the thorniest issue
they had to consider was that of the fetus's humanity:

Does fetal work involve research on "human beings," or are fetuses, prior to viability, "nonpeople," and therefore perfectly legitimate subjects for use in potentially valuable scientific studies?

The question of what the fetus is, as one philosopher working as a consultant to the National Commission remarked to me, is not so much a moral and ethical as it is a pre-ethical issue. "You have to define what it is you're talking about," he explained, "before you can define whatever you're doing as right or wrong. . . ." The word "person" is variously defined, but generally signifies a being characterized by the ability to experience consciousness of self, to communicate, to experience sensations of pain and pleasure, to reason, to behave autonomously both in the moral and physical sense, and so forth. If the fetus cannot do that, then to what else may it best be equated? Is the fetus, for instance, more nearly similar to an animal than it is to a fully human "person"? The ancient philosophers, in point of fact, did so characterize it—they took the view that the developing organism moved from the merely vegetative stage to the animal and finally to the rational level. If it is true, as recent researchers at Albert Einstein Medical School have suggested, that "brain life"—the capacity for human intelligence, including consciousness, self-awareness and other generally recognized cerebral functions—does not come into being until after the twenty-eighth week of the fetal life, then can experimentation on the fetus up until the end of the seventh month of pregnancy be seen as nothing too different from experimentation on a monkey or a rabbit? We, as a society, certainly do permit and find morally justifiable a wide range of biomedical investigations that make use of living animal subjects. And such experimentation has yielded impressive medical and scientific benefits—the human community has clearly profited from them.

Perhaps the fetus might, in the early months of pregnancy, more profitably be viewed as something that is simply a part of the mother's body—something similar to her gall bladder or her appendix. If she should choose, due to some pressing set of reasons, to have her gall bladder, appendix or her fetus removed, then she might give consent to have the excised part of her body studied. Isn't her permission—since the fetus was once a part of her—all the moral justification the investigator needs in order to proceed with an experiment?

Many scientists think so. But in a paper on fetal experimentation prepared for the National Commission, Dr. Leon Kass of the Kennedy Institute of Bioethics at Georgetown University said flatly: "The assertion that the fetus is a part of the mother is simply false. The fetus, in its varying stages, is a self-developing, self-hanging whole, which assimilates and transforms food supplied by the mother, and grows and differentiates itself according to the plan encoded in its own DNA. . . ." Other experts consulting with the commission have attacked the validity of maternal consent on different grounds. If the mother has determined to abort her fetus, they argue, isn't the meaning of her consent highly equivocal? Generally speaking, in cases involving experimentation on a living, human child, the parent's proxy consent is required—*i.e.*, the parent of a four-year-old child suffering from leukemia would have to give consent if the physician wished to treat the child with a new and unproven drug. The parent is assumed, in such an instance, to "speak for the child," to be the one who has the child's best interests at heart. In a situation in which the mother has already decided upon abortion, however, her own interests (wanting to terminate her pregnancy) would appear to be in some conflict with the interests of the fetus. Is she, then, the person who may most properly "speak on behalf of the fetus," the person who can be assumed to hold the best interests of that fetus closest to heart?

Paul Ramsey, the Princeton theologian and ethical philosopher, has suggested that a good deal of biomedical research involving the human fetus can be seen as similar to experimentation upon unconscious or dying patients. For the fetus, like the unconscious or dying person, is a nonconsenting, vulnerable and helpless human subject. In his recent book *The Ethics of Fetal Research* (Yale University Press, 1975), he carried this analogy further: "In cases of induced abortion," he wrote, "the fetal human being resembles not only the dying; it also closely resembles the condemned (even if necessarily and justly, but tragically, still the condemned)."

Dr. Ramsey, sixty-three, has been serving as one of the battery of consultants to the National Commission for the Protection of Human Subjects over the course of the past year. "One might argue," he pointed out, during the course of a talk we had in his Princeton office, "that capital punishment presented us with a similar 'golden opportunity' to do high-risk medical experimentation. After all, the condemned prisoner, like the living previable fetus, was going to die anyhow. . . . So why is it that we didn't research someone in that position to death? Such experimentation could, you know, have been seen as 'ennobling' the death of the human subject by using him to make great contributions to mankind. . . ."

Ramsey smiled briefly: "I think we all know that would be a morally degrading use of the condemned for us, as a society, to make."

I suggested to Ramsey that the classes of persons to whom he was comparing the fetus—that is, the unconscious, the dying, the condemned—were all among the more "helpless" kinds of human beings. This seemed to beg the whole question of the "personhood" of the fetus; and hence its eligibility for the customary human rights and protections. "I myself," he responded at once, "am of the opinion that the unborn fetus is a protectable human being."

Professor Ramsey leaned forward: "What we're *really* discussing here is not an object called the live but nonviable fetus. We're *really* discussing a tragical case of a dying baby—and the concern I am expressing is about the dying; that is, about imposing research upon this dying creature, who cannot consent. All of a sudden here are these 'things' that can be used for scientific experimentation—and the human fetus may soon become the most unprotected primate in medical research."

Fetal research is not something new under the sun—embryonic human tissues taken from live but nonviable, spontaneously expelled fetuses were, for example, vitally necessary for culturing the viruses that led to the creation of polio vaccine back in the 1940s. What is *is* new is the extraordinary growth and vitality of this area of study: Fetal experimentation is a "hot" field in medicine, not only because of some striking recent advances, but because the ready availability of fetuses and fetal organs—as a result of the 1973 abortion decisions—has itself stimulated a good deal of work.

Some medical ethicists have, as a matter of fact, contended that if we as a society do condone abortion, then there can be no earthly reason for refusal to condone experimentation on the fetus. If, as in the *Roe–Wade* decision, we are making the claim that a mother has the right to abort her previable fetus because the fetus is not yet a "person in the whole sense," with its own set of rights and protections, then why defend and protect the fetus from experimental procedures? Drs. Willard Gaylin and Marc Lappé, of the Institute of Society, Ethics and the Life Sciences, have asserted that such a position—*i.e.*, permitting abortion but drawing the line at much or all fetal experimentation—has "an element of the irrational about it." Writing in the *Atlantic Monthly* in May of 1975, the two authors observed that the fact that some people do hold the mutually contradictory positions "perplex[es] many of us. Such absolute and complete defense of the dignity and autonomous rights of the fetus seems bizarre, when . . . in abortion, we condone procedures which subject the fetus to dismemberment, salt-induced osmotic shock, or surgical extirpation. No experimentation so far imagined would do the same. If society can condone abortion procedures which subject the live fetus to these unimaginable acts of violence, how can it balk at giving a mother an aspirin prior to those procedures in order to determine if the drug crosses the placenta—with the hope that the knowledge thereby gained will prevent damage to future, wanted babies? . . ."

Why not indeed? Critics of the Gaylin–Lappé position have pointed out that their moral justification for experimentation on the live fetus seems to be predicated on the fact that we're going to be committing "unimaginable acts of violence" upon it anyhow. In other words, because the worst will be visited upon the fetus ultimately, lesser acts along the way ought (rationally speaking) to be tolerated. This is a worrisome kind of argument to use in defense of any type of research.

It is true, furthermore, that experimentation can sometimes involve a good deal more than simply having mothers swallow aspirins just prior to abortion procedures. In that instance, the moral costs of the research would appear—in my own view—to be low, and the possible benefits to be high; there are, however, other instances in which the weighing-up of costs and benefits might tilt the argument strongly in the other direction. An experiment called "An Artificial Placenta," for example, involved an attempt to simulate the role of the placenta in supplying oxygen to the immature fetus. For that experiment, eight fetuses were obtained by hysterotomy—an abortion procedure often used after the fifth month of pregnancy—which is much like a Caesarian operation. The living fetuses, ranging in weight from 300 to 980 grams, were then placed in tanks filled with warmed, saline solution (to mimic amniotic fluid). Small cannulas, or tubes, were inserted in the umbilical arteries and veins—for pumping in and removing oxygenated blood. The researchers had constructed an elaborate circulation system, which, they hoped, would prove able to play the mother's role in supplying oxygen to the fetus. In the case of the wanted fetus, this could be the means of assisting the premature infant to survive until its lungs had matured enough to allow for breathing; the experiment described here was simply intended to test out the oxygenation circuitry. The following is taken from the investigators' report, and details the death of the largest (980 grams) fetus used in the study:

> For the whole 5 hours of life, the fetus did not respire. Irregular gasping movements, twice a minute, occurred in the middle of the experiment but there was no proper respiration. Once the perfusion [*i.e.*, the pumping-in of oxygenated blood] was stopped, however, the gasping respiratory efforts increased to 8 to 10 per minute. . . . After stopping the circuit, the heart slowed, became irregular and eventually stopped. . . . The fetus was quiet, making occasional stretching limb movements very like the ones reported in other human work . . . The fetus died 21 minutes after leaving the circuit.

"An Artificial Placenta" is a study that has provoked a storm of ethical criticism: Not only does it smack uncomfortably of research on the dying, but it brings to mind old tales of mad science, the "living beings preserved in tanks." This makes it all the more interesting to note that, shortly after this research was completed, it won the Foundation Prize Award from the American Association of Obstetricians and Gynecologists.

A more recent fetal investigation, which has not yet attracted much attention and criticism—but which undoubtedly will—was reported upon in a 1975 paper innocuously entitled: "Oxidation of Glucose and D-*beta*-OH Butyrate by the Early Human Fetal Brain." This research was directed toward ascertaining whether or not the fetal brain is capable of utilizing the breakdown products of fat bodies when the usual source of "brain energy" (which is glucose, a sugar) happens to be in short supply. It was already known that when an adult was starving, D-*beta*-OH butyrate, a breakdown product of fat stored in the liver, could be taken up and used by the cerebral tissues; thus, when the adult brain was not being nourished by its usual energy source, glucose, it could survive on derivatives of the body's stored fats. But, given a state of fetal emergency—say, if a diabetic mother were failing to provide adequate glucose to the growing organism—was it possible for the fetus's brain to function in the same way?

In order to answer this question, twelve human fetuses between twelve and twenty-one weeks of gestation were studied. The fetuses were, at these ages, nonviable; all died soon after delivery. Once the fetal heartbeat had ceased, a catheter was inserted into the major artery leading to the brain (the carotid). The head of the fetus was then, as the investigators phrased it "isolated surgically from the other organs"; in other words, the fetuses' heads were cut off. The fetal brains were then perfused, first with the glucose, and then with D-*beta*-OH butyrate, and the rate at which the cerebral tissues took up each of these substances was carefully measured. In this way, it was possible to demonstrate that the fetal brain can support metabolism of D-*beta*-OH butyrate as an alternative "brain fuel" in the event that normal glucose supplies are unavailable. (It should be explained that while the fetuses were officially dead at the outset of this experiment—heartbeat having ceased—their brain tissues were living, for death at the cellular level had not yet occurred.)

Shades of *Donovan's Brain*! It is undeniably somewhat strange to read, in the researchers' account of this experimentation, that the fetal heads were placed in something they referred to as an "organ chamber." And one cannot help but wonder if, on balance, it is worth doing this kind of experiment in order to obtain this bit of knowledge of fetal physiology. Some types of scientific research, particularly those that may serve to harden or brutalize the investigator (and the society he or she serves as well) may simply not be worth the moral price they exact.

But this is my own opinion; others would view this work as totally unobjectionable biomedical research. As the author and bioethicist Dr. Joseph Fletcher complained (in *The Ethics of Genetic Control*, Anchor Press, 1974): "Many people's belief propositions are entirely visceral, not rational—witness, for example, the repugnance some people feel at perfusion of a separated fetus head while feeling none at the perfusion of its kidney. Where we start is essentially important in understanding our own moral judgments and others. . . ." In Fletcher's opinion, as stated repeatedly both in his book and in a paper prepared for the National Commission, the great advances in health and welfare that may accrue to the human race as a direct result of this experimentation are justification enough for such research on the human fetus.

According to Dr. Maurice J. Mahoney, Associate Professor of Human Genetics and Pediatrics at Yale University, experimentation involving the use of the whole, living fetus after an abortion—or, as may also occur, during the abortion procedure itself—represents well under 1 percent of published fetal research. Dr. Mahoney, another of the consultants working with the National Commission, has compiled an overview of all fetal work carried out between the years 1969 and 1975. "Most fetal research has actually addressed itself to diagnosing the fetus that is sick inside the uterus," he told me, "and to finding ways to help and treat that fetus." He himself, Dr. Mahoney said, takes a negative view of the small amount of fetal experimentation that falls into the "artificial placenta" and "several heads" category. "I think there's something about invading the human body in these ways that makes most of us feel uncomfortable." Nevertheless, he noted, even such morally dubious studies as these have been motivated by sincere attempts to solve real and urgent medical problems.

Is it possible that the living fetus suffers during experimental procedures? Could the eight fetal subjects used in the "artificial placenta" research, for example, have been experiencing pain during their hours in the fluid-filled tank? It seems to be impossible to answer this question with total certainty.

However, in the opinion of every medical expert that I spoke to, it seems extraordinarily improbable that the fetus—at least before the age of twenty-eight weeks— could have the capacity to suffer. The central nervous system is apparently still too underdeveloped. The nerve endings in the skin have not yet extended outward with any of the degree of the affluence to be seen later on; the surface of the brain is relatively smooth, showing little in the way of the convolutions seen in the mature human brain cortex. The nerve endings have not yet developed their fatty myelin sheaths—and without these sheaths, which play some crucial role in the transmission of nervous "messages" from one nerve cell to the next, it is hard to imagine sensations of pain "getting through."

The fetus's "incapacity for experiencing pain" is one of the four major reasons set forth by Sissela Bok in support of continuing—though carefully regulated—research involving living fetal subjects. Dr. Bok, who is a lecturer on Medical Ethics at Harvard Medical School, is another of the consultants working with the National Commission for the Protection of Human Subjects. In a position paper prepared for the commission last March, she cited four major reasons for *not* permitting experimentation on nonconsenting human subjects. These were: (1) because we would not want to cause harm or suffering to the victim, (2) because we would not want to cause grief to those who were bound to the victim by ties of affection, love or economic dependence, (3) because we would not want to permit brutalization of the researcher and (4) because we would not want to permit the brutalization of society— since we all have a stake in the protection of human life.

In the case of the nonviable fetus, Bok pointed out, the organism is not capable of experiencing pain, and is dying as well—the researcher can, therefore, do it no serious harm. If consent for experimentation is given by the mother or both parents, no suffering will be caused on the part of those who might otherwise experience sadness, loss and anguish. The researcher will not be brutalized by the work he is doing, because he is experimenting on a "not-yet-viable" subject—an organism related to the human community in potential, but not yet in fact. Lastly, the society that permits such research will not be brutalized —as we would be, were we to permit experimentation on other kinds of vulnerable, nonconsenting subjects, such as the unconscious or dying person, the infant, the condemned prisoner—because we will not have violated our own strong sense of the worth, protectability and value of the individual human life.

In a conversation with Dr. Bok at her home in Cambridge, I asked when, in her estimation, the developing fetus becomes a "person." Bok, who has the wide blue eyes and blond haircut of a Dutch schoolgirl—so that the force and determination of her personality take one slightly by surprise—shook her head quickly. "I think that's a wrong question to ask," she said. "People have become simply mesmerized by that question, and it's really a question that has no answer. Because we are, after all, talking about something that is biologically "human" not only after fertilization, but before—the ovum cell and the sperm cells are certainly both living and human even before they meet.

"But if we are talking about 'personhood,' then I believe it's impossible to speak of the fertilized egg, early in gestation, as 'a man,' " she continued, "although I realize that some theologicans and others do. . . . It's as if one were to have to contemplate having funerals for two- or three-month fetuses that had miscarried or investigations for murder each time a fetus died *in utero* for reasons that weren't completely clear."

What is essential to do, suggested Dr. Bok, is to draw a line—"an artificial line, admittedly, because as I said, nature hasn't provided us with a biological one"—at some point early in pregnancy, and to say that beyond that stage of development no experimentation will be allowable. The line must, she stated, be drawn at a time in pregnancy when there can be no question whatsoever about the possible viability of the fetus to be used as subject in biomedical research. "I think," she added, "that we'll always have to be very careful anyhow, and that it will be essential for us to continue having experimentation committees that can oversee and regulate all proposals for this kind of research."

Last May, the National Commission for the Protection of Human Subjects headed by Dr. Kenneth J. Ryan, submitted a full report on their deliberations and conclusions concerning research on the fetus to the Secretary of Health, Education and Welfare (and most of their recommendations were subsequently adopted and incorporated into new guidelines set by the Secretary in August). They suggested that the total ban on experimentation involving the living human fetus be lifted; they also called for the end of the moratorium on H.E.W.-supported fetal research. At the same time, they set the "age of viability" at twenty weeks (four and a half months) and 500 grams; this was much more conservative than the Supreme Court's definition had been. What this means, in essence, is that any fetus above the age of twenty weeks is "possibly viable," and therefore not a candidate for use in biomedical studies.

The commission also proposed a set of guidelines that would serve to restrict and carefully regulate (in some instances, prohibit outright) certain types of fetal experimentation. One kind of research procedure, for example, involves injecting the pregnant mother—who has already decided upon abortion—with drugs whose effects upon the fetus are not fully known. Then, following upon abortion procedures and the fetus's death, an autopsy is performed in order to ascertain the extent to which the drug was able (if it was able) to cross the placental membrane and affect the fetus. This kind of information is often invaluable to the physician treating the pregnant woman who plans to bring her baby to term.

In research such as this, the commission has now ruled against the "testing out" of potentially harmful drugs on fetuses whose mothers have decided upon abortion. The fetus whose mother plans to abort it, the commission has asserted, is no different in itself and in its own essence from a fetus whose mother plans to bring it to term; the only distinction between them is our knowledge of the impending abortion. This ought not, in the commission's opinion, serve to render the fetus-to-be-aborted into a testing animal. Mothers do sometimes change their minds about going ahead with a planned abortion—and for this reason, the commission has proscribed all experimentation involving the fetus *in utero* that entails anything more than "minimal risk."

It is interesting to note at this point that fetal work carried out by the defendants in the "Boston Grave-Robbing Case" would be permissible under the commission's new ruling, even though it is now about to be prosecuted by law. The case involved an attempt to find out what kinds of antibiotics might best be prescribed for pregnant women who had syphilis and who were allergic to penicillin. The syphilis, left alone, would invade the fetus and cause congenital defects; the penicillin, while capable of treating the fetus *in utero*, could not be tolerated by the pregnant mother. The question was what other antibiotic might most effectively be used in its place. In order to find out, researchers performed routine experimentation with fourteen pregnant women, all planning abortions, who agreed to accept injections of two different antibiotics while their fetuses were still *in utero*. Later on, after the nonviable fetuses were aborted and had died, the investigators did autopsies to find out which of the two substitute antibiotics had penetrated the placental barrier most effectively. The doctors who performed this research apparently neglected to get the mothers' signed permission to do the autopsies, which left them vulnerable to prosecution under grave-robbing statutes. Three of the doctors were indicted more than a year and a half ago, but their trial date has not yet been set.

One of the most sensitive issues to be discussed by the National Commission was the whole problem of research involving the intact, living fetus—in practical terms, an aborted fetus that is alive after delivery, but not viable and predictably going to die. Such a fetus must, the report of the commissioners stated, be viewed as a "dying subject." Stating that "issues of violation of integrity are . . . central," the commission recommended that "out of consideration for the dying subject," no experimental procedures be permitted that would alter the duration of the fetus's existence, either shortening its life by methods that might literally research it to death, or prolonging its life. (Enforcement of this regulation would, obviously, serve to prohibit research of the type reported upon in "An Artificial Placenta.")

In a section of their report entitled "Deliberations and Conclusions," the commissioners reviewed some of the complex problems that were debated during their effort to set some reasonable medical-social policy in this truly formidable area. But it is fascinating to note that nowhere in their summing-up document does the commission try to define the nature of the fetus (nonhuman? prehuman? animal-like? "somewhat-human"? "person"?); aside from the fact that the fetus is discussed under the rubric of "human subject," they remain silent on this question. But consultant Paul Ramsey, his sharp blue eyes glittering humorously, observed: ". . . the fact that the National Commission has drawn up *any* protective legislation concerning the human fetus has demonstrated that they do consider it to be a vulnerable, nonconsenting subject of research which is entitled to rights and protections of *some kinds*. It seems to me," he added, with a sly pursing of his lips, "that once you've conceded that much—I mean that you are talking about something which is, in some sense, 'human' and protectable—why you've obviously conceded quite a lot."

Why do fetal experimentation at all? Why not, given that this research has ruffled so many moral feathers and aroused such antipathy among certain portions of the population, simply drop the enterprise altogether? The issue need not be linked to the question of abortion—we could, for example, think of continuing to permit abortions to women who want them during the early weeks of pregnancy, but prohibit the use of the abortuses (or the products of spontaneous miscarriages) as material for study in biomedical experimentation. Is there, in fact, some technological imperative urging us implacably onward? Is this research really necessary?

The fact is that fetal experimentation has become important in medicine because it seems to be exploding in a number of different directions, and many real advances have already been made. One of the most important among these, according to Professor Richard E. Behrman, M.D., chairman of the Department of Pediatrics at Columbia and director of its Babies Hospital, has been the development of *amniocentesis.*

The word means, literally, "piercing of the amnion," sac enclosing the fetus; and the procedure involves sending a fine needle through the mother's belly and into her womb. By withdrawing a sample of the amniotic fluid and subjecting it to careful analysis, physicians are able to diagnose the presence of any of several dozen known genetic (and other) fetal diseases. For instance, Down's syndrome—called *mongolism*—one of the common causes of mental retardation, can readily be detected *in utero* by this means, and the prospective parents can then be forewarned of the danger and make their own choice about whether or not to terminate that pregnancy. "Now the whole development in this area did involve fetal research," observed Dr. Behrman. "I mean, someone did have to take the risk of putting that needle into the mother's uterus. And it had to be done not only in instances where the fetus was thought to be suffering from a disease, but in cases where it was known to be perfectly healthy—so that we could make the necessary comparisons between the 'sick' and the 'normal' fetal cell."

The development of amniocentesis, Behrman continued, was crucial to the discovery of effective treatments for Rh-diseased fetuses and infants. Rh-disease, known also as Rh-incompatibility, used to result in the births of scores of severely damaged—retarded and deaf—children, and in the delivery of many dead infants as well. The problem arises when a mother and her fetus are of differing blood types, and cells in the mother's blood have become sensitized to the red blood cells of her developing offspring.

What occurs is essentially an immune reaction on the mother's part. She forms antibodies that literally attack and destroy the red blood cells of the fetus much as they would attack and annihilate an invading virus. By means of amniocentesis doctors are now, however, able to detect the distressed fetus before too much harm has taken place, and take steps to treat it while it remains lodged in the womb.

Fetal research whose effects will be felt in the future is directed mainly toward precise measurement of several dimensions of behavior *in utero:* For instance, the fetus's ability to perceive sound (and the subsequent effects upon heart-rate and brain activity), its swallowing and breathing and gasping patterns, its pattern of urination and its periods of apparent sleep are all currently under study. More exact knowledge of these fetal functions can make a life-and-death difference in circumstances where an early delivery may be indicated and the doctor is uncertain about the maturity of the fetus and therefore its capacity to survive outside the womb. Such information may also be vital to the earlier detection of fetuses that have become ill inside the uterus.

A number of fetal scientists, sensitive to recent criticisms, assert that a failure to pursue such research at this point would be an abandonment of the fetal patient; they add, too, that there has been far too little public awareness of the real gains that have been made in fetal medicine. For instance, researchers have learned to peer directly into the womb and identify structural defects in the developing fetus (such as *hydrocephalus*, or "water on the brain," and *anencephaly*, the failure of the brain to develop). These increasingly sophisticated diagnostic techniques do suggest that more sophisticated methods of treatment will be in the offing.

And many questions about fetal life and development, some of them of a pressing nature, remain unanswered. In numerous instances, for example, it is not known how the drugs a pregnant woman is taking are going to affect her fetus. If the mother is taking antidepressants (which cause changes in her mood by effecting alterations in her brain chemistry), are those drugs entering the brain of the growing fetus as well? And if so, do they affect brain development and functioning—and in what ways? Much more needs to be learned about the effects of maternal psychotropic drug-taking, maternal smoking and environmental pollutants that the mother may be ingesting. A recent study has, for instance, linked the taking of common aspirin with the incidence of stillbirths.

Thus far, it appears to me, the real advances in fetal knowledge have not come from the more brutal, invasive "cutting and chopping" experimentation, or research protocols that call for maintaining live fetuses in amnionlike brine; but rather from the standard kinds of medical research that are more or less directed toward caring for and helping the particular fetuses involved. The major gains (thus far) have really been in areas in which the fetus was the "subject to be treated," not the "object to be studied." Undoubtedly, however, we are now moving into a time in which critical choices are going to have to be faced and made. We do, on the one hand, share a strong presumption that experimentation on dying people is wrong, and that human life is not to be treated casually. On the other hand, many of us also do have doubts regarding the "personhood" of the fetus and realize that we may be balancing its welfare against that of untold numbers of babies who will live to enter the human community, and who can be benefited vastly from this research. On the one side are our concerns about permitting medical researchers to make use of something human; on the other, the promise of great scientific good to be obtained. There is an element of ultimate conflict in this whole, peculiar situation.

Guidelines for Fetal Research

National Commission for the Protection of Human Subjects

1. *Therapeutic research directed toward the fetus* may be conducted or supported, and should be encouraged, by the Secretary, DHEW, provided such research (a) conforms to appropriate medical standards, (b) has received the informed consent of the mother, the father not dissenting, and (c) has been approved by existing review procedures with adequate provision for the monitoring of the consent process. (Adopted unanimously.)
2. *Therapeutic research directed toward the pregnant woman* may be conducted or supported, and should be encouraged by the Secretary, DHEW, provided such research (a) has been evaluated for possible impact on the fetus, (b) will place the fetus at risk to the minimum extent consistent with meeting the health needs of the pregnant woman, (c) has been approved by existing review procedures with adequate provision for the monitoring of the consent process, and (d) the pregnant woman has given her informed consent. (Adopted unanimously.)
3. *Nontherapeutic research directed toward the pregnant woman* may be conducted or supported by the Secretary, DHEW, provided such research (a) has been evaluated for possible impact on. the fetus, (b) will impose minimal or no risk to the well-being of the fetus, (c) has been approved by existing review

procedures with adequate provision for the monitoring of the consent process, (d) special care has been taken to assure that the woman has been fully informed regarding possible impact on the fetus, and (e) the woman has given informed consent. (Adopted unanimously.)

It is further provided that nontherapeutic research directed at the pregnant woman may be conducted or supported (f) only if the father has not objected, both where abortion is not at issue (adopted by a vote of 8 to 1) and where an abortion is anticipated (adopted by a vote of 5 to 4).

4. *Nontherapeutic research directed toward the fetus in utero* (other than research in anticipation of, or during, abortion) may be conducted or supported by the Secretary, DHEW, provided (a) the purpose of such research is the development of important biomedical knowledge that cannot be obtained by alternative means, (b) investigation on pertinent animal models and nonpregnant humans has preceded such research, (c) minimal or no risk to the well-being of the fetus will be imposed by the research, (d) the research has been approved by existing review procedures with adequate provision for the monitoring of the consent process, (e) the informed consent of the mother has been obtained, and (f) the father has not objected to the research. (Adopted unanimously.)

5. *Nontherapeutic research directed toward the fetus in anticipation of abortion* may be conducted or supported by the Secretary, DHEW, provided such research is carried out within the guidelines for all other nontherapeutic research directed toward the fetus *in utero.* Such research presenting special problems related to the interpretation or application of these guidelines may be conducted or supported by the Secretary, DHEW, provided such research has been approved by a national ethical review body. (Adopted by a vote of 8 to 1.)

6. *Nontherapeutic research directed toward the fetus during the abortion procedure and nonthereapeutic*

research directed toward the nonviable fetus ex utero may be conducted or supported by the Secretary, DHEW, provided (a) the purpose of such research is the development of important biomedical knowledge that cannot be obtained by alternative means, (b) investigation on pertinent animal models and nonpregnant humans (when appropriate) has preceded such research, (c) the research has been approved by existing review procedures with adequate provision for the monitoring of the consent process, (d) the informed consent of the mother has been obtained, and (e) the father has not objected to the research; and provided further that (f) the fetus is less than 20 weeks gestational age, (g) no significant procedural changes are introduced into the abortion procedure in the interest of research alone, and (h) no intrusion into the fetus is made which alters the duration of life. Such research presenting special problems related to the interpretation or application of these guidelines may be conducted or supported by the Secretary, DHEW, provided such research has been approved by a national ethical review body. (Adopted by a vote of 8 to 1).

7. *Nontherapeutic research directed toward the possibly viable infant* may be conducted or supported by the Secretary, DHEW, provided (a) the purpose of such research is the development of important biomedical knowledge that cannot be obtained by alternative means, (b) investigation on pertinent animal models and nonpregnant humans (when appropriate) has preceded such research, (c) no additional risk to the well-being of the infant will be imposed by the research, (d) the research has been approved by existing review procedures with adequate provision for the monitoring of the consent process, and (e) informed consent of either parent has been given and neither parent has objected. (Adopted unanimously.)

8. *Review Procedures.* Until the Commission makes its recommendations regarding review and consent

procedures, the review procedures mentioned above are to be those presently required by the Department of Health, Education, and Welfare. In addition, provision for monitoring the consent process shall be required in order to ensure adequacy of the consent process and to prevent unfair discrimination in the selection of research subjects, for all categories of research mentioned above. A national ethical review, as required in Recommendations (5) and (6), shall be carried out by an appropriate body designated by the Secretary, DHEW, until the establishment of the National Advisory Council for the Protection of Subjects of Biomedical and Behavioral Research. In order to facilitate public understanding and the presentation of public attitudes toward special problems reviewed by the national review body, appropriate provision should be made for public attendance and public participation in the national review process. (Adopted unanimously, one abstention.)

9. *Research on the Dead Fetus and Fetal Tissue.* The Commission recommends that use of the dead fetus, fetal tissue and fetal material for research purposes be permitted, consistent with local law, the Uniform Anatomical Gift Act and commonly held convictions about respect for the dead. (Adopted unanimously, one abstention.)

10. The design and conduct of a nontherapeutic research protocol should not determine recommendations by a physician regarding the advisability, timing or method of abortion. (Adopted by a vote of 6 to 2.)

11. Decisions made by a personal physician concerning the health care of a pregnant woman or fetus should not be compromised for research purposes, and when a physician of record is involved in a prospective research protocol, independent medical judgment on these issues is required. In such cases, review panels should assure that procedures for such independent medical judgment are adequate, and all

conflict of interest or appearance thereof between appropriate health care and research objectives should be avoided. (Adopted unanimously.)

12. The Commission recommends that research on abortion techniques continue as permitted by law and government regulation. (Adopted by a vote of 6 to 2.)

13. The Commission recommends that attention be drawn to Section 214(d) of the National Research Act (Pub. L. 93–348) which provides that:

> No individual shall be required to perform or assist in the performance of any part of a health service program or research activity funded in whole or in part by the Secretary of Health, Education, and Welfare, if his performance or assistance in the performance of such part of such program or activity would be contrary to his religious beliefs or moral convictions.

(Adopted unanimously.)

14. No inducements, monetary or otherwise, should be offered to procure an abortion for research purposes. (Adopted unanimously.)

15. Research which is supported by the Secretary, DHEW, to be conducted outside the United States should at the minimum comply in full with the standards and procedures recommended herein. (Adopted unanimously.)

Fetal Research

Peter Singer

Although some research on human fetuses had been done prior to the legalization of abortion, the 1973 Supreme Court decision striking down anti-abortion laws brought the issue to the surface. Since 1973 there has been a steady stream of women coming to hospitals for abortions, and it did not take researchers long to realize the possibilities inherent in this situation.

Assume that you have developed a new drug, known to be safe for adults but untested for its effects on the fetus if taken by a pregnant woman. To test the drug on pregnant animals would not give reliable information about humans, since there are variations in drug susceptibility between different species, as the thalidomide case tragically showed. To test the drug on normal pregnant women and then check for deformities when they give birth is out of the question. But if there are women about to undergo abortion, one could give them a drug just prior to the operation and then test the fetus, after abortion, to see if the drug has crossed the placenta. If it has not, it will not harm a developing fetus.

Further research possibilities arise from the fact that some methods of abortion result in the fetus being removed from the uterus intact and still alive. It is possible to keep such a fetus alive for several hours or even a day or two. Studies of the *living fetus* outside the uterus can yield knowledge not otherwise obtainable about the develop-

From *The New York Review of Books*, August 5, 1976. Reprinted by permission of the author.

ment of the fetus, and it has been claimed that this could lead to major advances in, for example, detecting and preventing abnormal births, and in saving premature infants. It is this class of research—on the nonviable but still living fetus outside the uterus—that has aroused the greatest feeling among some sections of the public, and has caused the most intense debate among bioethicists; and this is quite proper, because such a fetus lacks even the minimal protection of the presence of its mother.

As a result of public disquiet, Congress in July 1974 declared a moratorium on all research on fetuses until the National Commission for the Protection of Human Subjects could consider the issue and make recommendations. The outcome is the *Report and Recommendations*, together with a huge *Appendix* separately published and containing the texts of papers and reports prepared for or reviewed by the commission.

The *Appendix* shows that the commission received a great deal of advice and information, some straightforwardly factual, some addressing the ethical issues. On factual questions there are reports on the nature and extent of research on fetuses, on the boundary between viable and nonviable fetuses, on the legal issues, on the role of fetal research in medical advances, and on the extent to which women change their minds about having an abortion. There are nine separate papers, by theologians, specialists in bioethics, and philosophers, on ethical issues.

Despite the wide sweep of the factual studies undertaken for the commission there is a notable absence of testimony on one point which is surely significant, though the commission apparently did not think so: whether the previable fetus is conscious or capable of feeling pain. The commission did not ask any expert to deal directly with this question, and consequently the factual studies contain only a few incidental remarks which bear on it. According to one study prepared for the commission, the fetus responds to touch as early as seven weeks; this may, however, be a reflex action. A British government-appointed committee on the use of fetuses in research has stated that the parts of the brain on which consciousness depends are very poorly developed and show no sign of electrical activity in a fetus of less than 300 grams, which is reached around eighteen weeks (this was the weight it used as the boundary for permissible research, since it gave a safe margin against the possibility that the fetus could be viable). Paul Ramsey, in *The Ethics of Fetal Research*, challenges this assertion, though without supporting his contrary view by any medical references. In the present state of medical knowledge the question remains an open one.

As for its ethical deliberations, the commission appears to have gone about its task in the following manner. Starting with the assumption that the fetus is a human being, which is therefore broadly entitled to the same protection as other human beings, the commission then affirmed the general principle that "manifest risks imposed upon non-consenting subjects cannot be tolerated," and only research involving minimal or no risk is permissible in such cases. To underline its view, the commission explicitly stated that the fact that a fetus is about to be aborted does not change its status: "the same principles apply whether or not abortion is contemplated."

Anyone who was engaged in fetal research and had read this far might have begun winding up his project at once; in the following paragraph, however, the commission took back much of what it had just said by telling us that some members were of the opinion that the decision to abort does make a difference, not to the status of the fetus, but to what constitutes "minimal risk." For instance, it is one thing to administer a drug with unknown long-term effects to a fetus undergoing abortion, and quite a different thing to administer it to a fetus likely to grow into a child. Unable to reach agreement on how to define "minimal risk," the commission dealt with this problem by recommending that a "national ethical review body" be set up, to which questions of interpretation could be referred.

Finally the commission took a step back toward its earlier position by adding that even if considerations of long-term harm are less important for a nonviable fetus outside the uterus than for a normal fetus, still "considerations of respect for the dignity of the fetus continue to be of paramount importance" and "issues of violation of integrity" are central. Therefore the commission recommended the prohibition of non-therapeutic experiments which would either shorten or lengthen the life of the fetus.

Is the ethical issue really as difficult as the commission has made it appear? I cannot see that it is. If the fetus is going to die anyway, without ever possessing self-awareness or the capacity to make decisions of any kind, the only thing that we can do for it is to ensure that it does not suffer in the time that it remains alive. If there is any possibility that the fetus is suffering, then suffering should be ended by total anesthesia for the remainder of the life of the fetus. So long as this provision is scrupulously observed, I cannot see that the commission's prohibition on shortening or lengthening the life of the fetus can make any difference to the fetus at all.

For those inclined to reject this solution, I suggest the following thought-experiment: suppose that for some reason we can do nothing to save a dog which is dying. There is an experiment we can perform on it before it dies which has reasonable prospects of leading to a significant medical advance. The experiment can be performed under total anesthesia and the dog will die before recovering from the anesthetic. Is there any rational basis for objecting to such an experiment? So long as we are sure the dog will feel nothing, I cannot see any. Nor do I think it makes any difference whether the experiment shortens or prolongs the unconscious animal's life.

Is there any morally relevant difference between doing this experiment on a dying dog and doing it on a dying human fetus? One difference is that the human parents are more likely to be aware of what is happening than the canine parents. This difference is extrinsic to the comparison of fetus and dog as research subjects in themselves, and I shall consider it shortly. Extrinsic factors apart, though, I cannot find any morally relevant difference that can be defended apart from differences based on specifically religious arguments. It is the dog that is the more intelligent, sensitive, and autonomous being. How could any comparison not unthinkingly prejudiced in favor of our own species attribute greater dignity or integrity to the dying fetus than to the dying dog?

Some might say that we must respect the potential of the fetus to become a fully fledged person. But the biological potential of the fetus becomes irrelevant the moment the decision to abort is irrevocable, for at that moment it is determined that the fetus will never realize its distinctively human potential. Or some might say that just the fact that the fetus is human gives it a special claim to protection. This seems to be the view of both the commission and of Paul Ramsey. Both state that the fetus is human and that this gives it a special claim to protection. Neither questions the basis of this special protection.

Ramsey and the commission, as well as those who testified to the commission, accept without question that research on the fetus is to be undertaken only if there is no "animal work" that could be done to yield the same information. In accepting this they are accepting that thousands of perfectly healthy animals will be subjected to experimentation involving suffering as well as death. They appear to regard this as so obviously preferable to experimenting upon an unconscious fetus that they see no need to give reasons for their choice.

Yet to say that merely being a member of our species entitles a being to special protection, even when the being will never have any of the capacities that are commonly thought to elevate our species above others, is to discriminate on the basis of species alone, a form of discrimination no more defensible than discrimination on the basis of race alone.[1]

The only possible legitimate basis for giving a dying human fetus greater protection than we give to a dying nonhuman animal is that which arises from the interests of the human parents. While our duties to a dying fetus or animal are satisfied by ensuring that it not suffer, in the case of the dying human fetus we may also have duties to the parents that we are not likely to have in the case of a dying animal. This leads us to the issue of parental consent.

---

[1] For further discussion of this point, see my *Animal Liberation* (A New York Review Book, 1975), chapters 1 and 6.

Normally if research is contemplated on a child too young to consent to the experiment, the consent of the parents is needed. This is regarded as protection for the child, since it is assumed that the parents will act in the child's interest. This assumption becomes dubious, however, in the case of a fetus that the parents have decided to abort. Hence the necessity of obtaining parental consent in these circumstances has been challenged.

The commission takes the view that, notwithstanding the decision to abort, a woman will have some interest in and concern for the fetus, and so her consent should be obtained. By a majority the commission would give the father the right to veto research, though his explicit assent is not required.

Ramsey first condemns as "morally outrageous" the idea of giving a woman who elects to have an abortion for social or economic reasons the role of deciding whether the fetus should be experimented upon. But he ends up recommending that the woman's consent be sought after all, on the pragmatic ground that if the woman is to give genuine consent she and her physician will have to discuss the condemned fetus itself and not merely the relief of the woman's condition. Ramsey believes this may lead to a change of mind about the abortion, or if not that, at least to a drastic reduction in the amount of research performed on aborted fetuses. Either outcome would meet with Ramsey's approval, though this cynical view of the consent requirement scarcely befits the "ethic of principles and not consequences" for which Ramsey claims to stand.

Once we accept that the only interest the aborted fetus has is in not suffering, the question of parental consent becomes soluble too. As long as the prohibition of experiments that could involve suffering is strictly enforced we do not need a parent to act as protector of the fetus, for the fetus has all the protection it needs. This means, of course, that causing a fetus to suffer must not only be prohibited but that all fetal research must be carefully monitored by independent observers. Under such conditions, there would be no need to ask the parents who have decided on abortion to consent on behalf of the fetus.

It is understandable that parents will in many cases be

concerned about the fate of the fetus they are delivering into the hands of the medical profession. They may have serious doubts about the researcher's assurance that the fetus will feel nothing. In view of the demonstrable callousness of some medical researchers toward nonhuman experimental subjects, such doubts may be well founded. Or parents may have deep-seated emotions that go beyond the desire to ensure that the fetus does not suffer—an abhorrence, perhaps, of the whole idea of strangers using their still-living offspring for any purpose at all. Such attitudes may be difficult to justify rationally, but this does not mean that they may be disregarded.

The decision to have an abortion is often difficult, even when it seems the right decision in the circumstances. If either parent is anxious about the prospect of an experiment being performed on the fetus, they should not have this anxiety added to the difficulty of the decision to abort. For the parents' own peace of mind, their consent should be required in all cases, even though it could be shown that the fetus would not suffer in any way. At the same time, as I have said, no fetal research should be undertaken unless such a showing is made.

We have seen that despite the complication of the consent issue, it is possible to reach plausible conclusions about the limits of ethical research on the fetus without taking the zig-zagging path of the commission or the species-biased and over-restrictive view of Ramsey. The failure of both the vis-à-vis "animal models" is, as I said earlier, an instance of a general weakness in bioethics.

Suggestions for Further Reading (in paperback):

Joel Feinberg, ed., *The Problem of Abortion* (Belmont, CA: Wadsworth, 1973).

Robert Perkins, ed., *Abortion: Pro and Con* (Cambridge, MA: Schenkman, 1974).

Marshall Cohen, Thomas Nagel, and Thomas Scanlon, eds., *The Rights and Wrongs of Abortion* (Princeton, NJ: Princeton University Press, 1975).

Paul Ramsey, *The Ethics of Fetal Research* (New Haven, CT: Yale University Press, 1975).

Part III
Poverty and Hunger

The two economic facts raise moral questions of the most fundamental sort. The first is the fact that some people are very rich, while others are very poor. In the United States, for example, the top 5 percent of the people own 20 percent of the wealth, while the bottom 20 percent of the people own only 5 percent of the wealth. Is this fair? Do the rich really deserve to have more than the poor, or is the unequal distribution of wealth merely the result of unjust social arrangements that should be changed? The second related fact is that some people in the world are so poor that they are starving; many even starve to death. It is not clear just how wide-spread world hunger is, but the Food and Agriculture Organization of the United Nations estimates that approximately 15,000 people die of malnutrition or related causes every day. What responsibility do those of us in the more affluent countries have toward starving people? Can it be morally right, for example, for us to spend money on luxuries that could be used to save other people from starvation?

In the opening selection of this unit, Joel Feinberg considers the question of the distribution of wealth. Feinberg, who teaches at the University of Arizona, is one of the most respected social philosophers in the United States. In "Justice and Economic Income," he examines five principles that have been proposed as basic to the just distribution of wealth: the principle of perfect equality, that all people should have equal wealth; the principle of need, that everyone should have enough to satisfy their basic needs; the principle that wealth should be distributed according to people's merits or achievements; the principle that people should receive a share of society's wealth according to their contribution to society; and finally, the principle of labor, that people should be rewarded according to their effort. Feinberg's conclusion is that the principle of need is fundamental to a just distribution of goods, and that the principles of contribution and effort may enter to determine the distribution of left-

over goods *after* *everyone's basic needs have been satisfied.*

*What principles actually determine the distribution of
wealth in the United States? The answer is quite complicated. Our economy is in some ways like a free-market
economy (or capitalist economy), where people are allowed to increase or decrease their holdings by making
business deals with others. The words "business deal"
should not be construed too narrowly here. There are all
kinds of business deals: when a performer agrees to sing
for pay, that is a business deal, and when a teacher agrees
to tutor someone in mathematics for pay, that is also a
business deal. By such trades, people increase or decrease
their holdings, or they exchange one kind of holding for
another (e.g., a person may exchange money for entertainment or a knowledge of math).*

*The kinds of business deals a person is able to make
depends, however, on various factors. One person may be
born with musical talent or a glorious voice, and may be
able to perform for pay, and so amass considerable
wealth, while another person who has no musical ability
cannot earn money in this way. It has been argued that
this introduces an important element of unfairness into
the system because the fact that some people are talented
or very intelligent, is largely a matter of luck. People do
not deserve the talent or intelligence which enables them
to accumulate wealth in a free-market system. Moreover,
some people are lucky enough to be born into wealthy
families, and this also creates differences between people
that are matters of luck. These facts create serious problems for the moral justification of capitalism.*

*Our economy is not, however, a purely free-market af-
fair. The government places various sorts of restrictions
on what businesses may do, and people are not allowed
to keep all the money they obtain through the operation
of the system. Some of their holdings (indeed, quite a
large portion) are taken from them as taxes and redistrib-*

uted to others in the form of welfare programs. This is, at least on face value, a government effort to provide the basic needs for all citizens along the lines of Feinberg's principle of need.

If Feinberg is right, then our economic system should probably be changed to make it even less of a free-market system. In the second selection in this unit the Nobel Prizewinning economist Milton Friedman argues in defense of free-market capitalism. He contends that the distribution of wealth produced by this system is just, and that under such a system there will be less poverty than under alternative arrangements. Capitalism, he says, is a system that allows people to make free choices about what they do with their money, time, and effort. Some people will risk what they have in the hope of gaining more; others will choose to play it safe. But, Friedman argues, why shouldn't those who choose to take risks be allowed to keep what they gain from doing so, if they are willing to forfeit what they might lose? Suppose a million people choose to put one dollar each into a lottery in the hope of winning, and as a result some lucky person ends up a millionaire. This creates an unequal distribution of wealth—one person is now a millionaire—but is there anything wrong with it? Is any injustice done to the more cautious people who chose not to enter the lottery? If we insist on taking away the new millionaire's money through taxation, and then redistributing it to others in the form of social services, aren't we simply denying people the right to have such lotteries? These questions are relevant because risky business ventures can be compared to lotteries in which people gamble some of their holdings on the chance of gaining more. The example of the lottery also shows how great inequalities of wealth might be created without violating anyone's rights. The moral is that respecting people's freedom may require us to respect their right to make deals among themselves which allow some to become richer than others. This is the basic ethical argument in defense of the free-market system.

In contrast with Friedman, the philosopher Bernard Gendron is a radical critic of capitalism. In his article "Capitalism and Poverty," Gendron argues that capitalism makes it harder, not easier, to eliminate poverty. He begins by discussing what poverty is—what standard should be used to determine who is poor and who is not—and this becomes a more complicated question than expected. The usual approach is to set a fixed level of income, and think that anyone falling below that level is "poor." Using this approach, as the society gets richer and the average income rises, fewer and fewer people are considered poor. However, Gendron points out that there are problems with this: what counts as poverty seems to change as time passes. Today we would say that any American citizen who cannot get medical treatment is poor; yet Cleopatra did not have access to such good treatment, and we certainly would not call her poor. It would seem that as more and more goods and services are available in the society, more and more is required to keep individuals above the poverty line, and so the poverty line rises, too. This is a complicated issue, and Gendron's article is one of the few treatments of it.

The last three articles in the unit deal with the moral questions arising out of the fact that many people in the world are starving. What is our responsibility toward them? In "Famine, Affluence, and Morality," Peter Singer argues that each of us has a moral obligation to give large parts of our income to relieve hunger. He starts with the basic principle that if we can prevent a great moral evil from happening without sacrificing anything comparably important, we should do so. This principle is hard to deny, but accepting it and acting on it would require a drastic change in our lifestyles. We commonly spend money on such things as fancy clothes and phonograph records when that money could go to save people from starving to death. The implication is that we must think the clothes, records, and so on, are more important than food for the starving. Of course most of us do not think that; so why don't we give the money for famine relief rather than spending it on trivia?

If Singer is right, we cannot say that famine relief is simply a matter for government action, and excuse ourselves. We ought to give what we have to supply food. Garrett Hardin takes a radically different view. In "Lifeboat Ethics: The Case Against Helping the Poor," he argues that sending food does more harm than good. The earth, he says, is like a lifeboat which will support only a certain number of people, and we have already exceeded that number. We could feed the starving now, but this only helps in the short run; the people that we save would only reproduce more people which would have to be fed, and then more. Sooner or later there would be even more massive starvation. The problem is that the poor countries have exceeded their "carrying capacity;" that is, the countries simply cannot support their populations. Attempts to help them will not work in the long run, and only weaken the kindhearted but misguided people who give up what they have in quest of an impossible cause. Hardin presents a grim picture of a tragic situation in which nothing can be done.

The final selection in this unit, written by Nick Eberstadt of the Harvard Center for Population Studies, questions whether in fact the picture is as grim as Hardin maintains. Eberstadt views the situation as difficult, but not impossible; intelligently administered relief programs can reduce, if not eliminate, the tragedy of starvation. Like most important practical issues, the question of our responsibility to the starving populations depends on factual matters—is Hardin or Eberstadt right about the possibility of effective relief programs?—as well as philosophical perspectives.

Justice and Economic Income

Joel Feinberg

The term "distributive justice" traditionally applied to burdens and benefits directly distributed by political authorities, such as appointed offices, welfare doles, taxes, and military conscription, but it has now come to apply also to goods and evils of a nonpolitical kind that can be distributed by private citizens to other private citizens. In fact, in most recent literature, the term is reserved for *economic* distributions, particularly the justice of differences in economic income between classes, and of various schemes of taxation which discriminate in different ways between classes. Further, the phrase can refer not only to acts of distributing but also to de facto states of affairs, such as *the fact that* at present "the five percent at the top get 20 percent [of our national wealth] while the 20 percent at the bottom get about five percent."[1] There is, of course, an ambiguity in the meaning of "distribution." The word may refer to the *process* of distributing, or the *product* of some process of distributing, and either or both of these can be appraised as just or unjust. In addition, a "distribution" can be understood to be a "product" which is *not* the result of any deliberate distributing process, but

Joel Feinberg, *Social Philosophy*, © 1973, pp. 107–117. Reprinted by permission of Prentice-Hall, Inc., Englewood Cliffs, NJ.
[1]"T.R.B. from Washington" in *The New Republic*, Vol. CLX, No. 12 (March 22, 1969), p. 4.

simply a state of affairs whose production has been too complicated to summarize or to ascribe to any definite group of persons as their deliberate doing. The present "distribution" of American wealth is just such a state of affairs.

Are the 5 percent of Americans "at the top" really different from the 20 percent "at the bottom" in any respect that would justicize the difference between their incomes? It is doubtful that there is any characteristic—relevant or irrelevant—common and peculiar to all members of either group. *Some* injustices, therefore, must surely exist. Perhaps there are some traits, however, that are more or less characteristic of the members of the privileged group, that make the current arrangements at least approximately just. What could (or should) those traits be? The answer will state a standard of relevance and a principle of material justice for questions of economic distributions, at least in relatively affluent societies like that of the United States.

At this point there appears to be no appeal possible except to *basic attitudes*, but even at this level we should avoid premature pessimism about the possibility of rational agreement. Some answers to our question have been generally discredited, and if we can see why those answers are inadequate, we might discover some important clues to the properties any adequate answer must possess. Even philosophical adversaries with strongly opposed initial attitudes may hope to come to eventual agreement if they share *some* relevant beliefs and standards and a common commitment to consistency. Let us consider why we all agree (that is the author's assumption) in rejecting the view that differences in race, sex, IQ, or social "rank" are the grounds of just differences in wealth or income. Part of the answer seems obvious. People cannot by their own voluntary choices determine what skin color, sex, or IQ they shall have, or which hereditary caste they shall enter. To make such properties the basis of discrimination between individuals in the distribution of social benefits would be "to treat people differently in ways that profoundly affect their lives because of differences for which they have no responsibility."[2] Differences in a given respect are *relevant* for the aims of distributive justice, then, only if they are differences for which their possessors can be held responsible; properties can be the grounds of just discrimination between persons only if those persons had a *fair opportunity* to acquire or avoid them. Having rejected a number of material principles that clearly fail to satisfy the "fair opportunity" requirement, we are still left with as many as five candidates for our acceptance. (It is in theory open to us to accept two or more of these five as valid principles, there being no a priori necessity that the list be reduced to one.) These are: (1) the principle of perfect equality; (2) the principle[s] of need; (3) the principles of merit and achievement; (4) the principle of contribution (or due return); (5) the principle of effort (or labor). I shall discuss each of these briefly.

I. Equality

The principle of perfect equality obviously has a place in any adequate social ethic. Every human being is equally a human being, and that minimal qualification entitles all human beings equally to certain absolute human rights: positive rights to noneconomic "goods" that by their very natures cannot be in short supply, negative rights not to be treated in cruel or inhuman ways, and negative rights not to be exploited or degraded even in "humane" ways. It is quite another thing, however, to make the minimal qualification of humanity the ground for an absolutely equal distribution of a country's *material wealth* among its citizens. A strict equalitarian could argue that he is merely applying Aristotle's formula of proportionate equality (presumably accepted by all parties to the dispute) with a criterion of relevance borrowed from the human rights theorists. Thus, distributive justice is accomplished between *A* and *B* when the following ratio is satisfied:

---

[2]W. K. Frankena, "Some Beliefs About Justice," *The Lindley Lecture,* Department of Philosophy Pamphlet (Lawrence: University of Kansas, 1966), p. 10.

$$\frac{A\text{'s share of } P}{B\text{'s share of } P} = \frac{A\text{'s possession of } Q}{B\text{'s possession of } Q}$$

Where P stands for economic goods, Q must stand simply for "humanity" or "a human nature," and since every human being possesses *that* Q equally, it follows that all should also share a society's economic wealth (the P in question) equally.

The trouble with this argument is that its major premise is no less disputable than its conclusion. The standard of relevance it borrows from other contexts where it seems very little short of self-evident, seems controversial, at best, when applied to purely economic contexts. It seems evident to most of us that merely being human entitles *everyone*—bad men as well as good, lazy as well as industrious, inept as well as skilled—to a fair trial if charged with a crime, to equal protection of the law, to equal consideration of his interests by makers of national policy, to be spared torture or other cruel and inhuman treatment, and to be permanently ineligible for the status of chattel slave. Adding a right to an equal share of the economic pie, however, is to add a benefit of a wholly different order, one whose presence on the list of goods for which mere humanity is the sole qualifying condition is not likely to win wide assent without further argument.

It is far more plausible to posit a human right to the satisfaction of (better: to an opportunity to satisfy) one's *basic* economic needs, that is, to enough food and medicine to remain healthy, to minimal clothing, housing, and so on. As Hume pointed out,[3] even these rights cannot exist under conditions of extreme scarcity. Where there is not enough to go around, it cannot be true that everyone has a right to an equal share.[4] But wherever there is moderate abundance or better—wherever a society produces more than enough to satisfy the *basic needs of everyone*—there it seems more plausible to say that mere possession of basic human needs qualifies a person for the

---

[3]David Hume, *Enquiry Concerning the Principles of Morals* Part III (LaSalle, Ill.: The Open Court Publishing Company, 1947). Originally published in 1777.
[4]Except in the "manifesto sense" of "right" discussed on p. 67.

opportunity to satisfy them. It would be a rare and calloused sense of justice that would not be offended by an affluent society, with a large annual agricultural surplus and a great abundance of manufactured goods, which permitted some of its citizens to die of starvation, exposure, or easily curable disease. It would certainly be *unfair* for a nation to produce more than it needs and not permit some of its citizens enough to satisfy their basic biological requirements. Strict equalitarianism, then, is a perfectly plausible material principle of distributive justice when confined to affluent societies and basic biological needs, but it loses plausibility when applied to division of the "surplus" left over after basic needs are met. To be sure, the greater the degree of affluence, the higher the level at which we might draw the line between "basic needs" and merely "wanted benefits, and insofar as social institutions create "artificial needs," it is only fair that society provide all with the opportunity to satisfy them.[5] But once the line has been drawn between what is needed to live a minimally decent life by the realistic standards of a given time and place and what is only added "gravy," it is far from evident that justice still insists upon absolutely equal shares of the total. And it is evident that justice does *not* require strict equality wherever there is reason to think that unequal distribution causally determines greater production and is therefore in the interests of everyone, even those who receive the relatively smaller shares.

Still, there is no way to *refute* the strict equalitarian who requires exactly equal shares for everyone whenever that can be arranged without discouraging total productivity to the point where everyone loses. No one would insist upon equal distributions that would diminish the size of the total pie and thus leave smaller slices for *everyone*; that would be opposed to reason. John Rawls makes this condition part of his "rational principle" of justice: "Inequalities are arbitrary unless it is reasonable to expect that they will work out to everyone's advan-

---

[5]This point is well made by Katzner, "An Analysis of the Concept of Justice," pp. 173–203.

tage. . . ."[6] We are left then with a version of strict
equalitarianism that is by no means evidently true and yet
is impossible to refute. That is the theory that purports to
apply not only to basic needs but to the total wealth of a
society, and allows departures from strict equality when,
but only when, they will work out to everyone's advantage. Although I am not persuaded by this theory, I think
that any adequate material principle will have to attach
great importance to keeping differences in wealth within
reasonable limits, even after all basic needs have been met.
One way of doing this would be to raise the standards for a
"basic need" as total wealth goes up, so that differences
between the richest and poorest citizens (even when there
is no real "poverty") are kept within moderate limits.

II. Need

The principle of need is subject to various interpretations,
but in most of its forms it is not an independent principle
at all, but only a way of mediating the application of the
principle of equality. It can, therefore, be grouped with the
principle of perfect equality as a member of the equalitarian family and contrasted with the principles of merit,
achievement, contribution, and effort, which are all members of the nonequalitarian family. Consider some differences in "needs" as they bear on distributions. Doe is a
bachelor with no dependents; Roe has a wife and six children. Roe must satisfy the needs of eight persons out of his
paycheck, whereas Doe need satisfy the needs of only one.
To give Roe and Doe equal pay would be to treat Doe's
interests substantially *more* generously than those of anyone in the Roe family. Similarly, if a small private group is
distributing food to its members (say a shipwrecked crew
waiting rescue on a desert island), it would not be fair to
give precisely the same quantity to a one hundred pounder
as to a two hundred pounder, for that might be giving one
person all he needs and the other only a fraction of what
he needs—a difference in treatment not supported by any

---

[6]John Rawls, "Justice as Fairness," *The Philosophical Review*, LXVII (1958), 165.

relevant difference between them. In short, to distribute goods in proportion to basic needs is not really to depart from a standard of equality, but rather to bring those with some greater initial burden or deficit up to the same level as their fellows.

The concept of a "need" is extremely elastic. In a general sense, to say that S needs X is to say simply that if he doesn't have X he will be harmed. A "basic need" would then be for an X in whose absence a person would be harmed in some crucial and fundamental way, such as suffering injury, malnutrition, illness, madness, or premature death. Thus we all have a basic need for foodstuffs of a certain quantity and variety, fuel to heat our dwellings, a roof over our heads, clothing to keep us warm, and so on. In a different but related sense of need, to say that S needs X is to say that without X he cannot achieve some specific purpose or perform some specific function. If they are to do their work, carpenters need tools, merchants need capital and customers, authors need paper and publishers. Some helpful goods are not strictly needed in this sense: an author with pencil and paper does not really need a typewriter to write a book, but he may need it to write a book speedily, efficiently, and conveniently. We sometimes come to rely upon "merely helpful but unneeded goods" to such a degree that we develop a strong habitual dependence on them, in which case (as it is often said) we have a "psychological" as opposed to a material need for them. If we don't possess that for which we have a strong psychological need, we may be unable to be happy, in which case a merely psychological need for a functional instrument may become a genuine need in the first sense distinguished above, namely, something whose absence is harmful to us. (Cutting across the distinction between material and psychological needs is that between "natural" and "artificial" needs, the former being those that can be expected to develop in any normal person, the latter being those that are manufactured or contrived, and somehow implanted in, or imposed upon, a person.) The more abundant a society's material goods, the higher the level at which we are required (by the force of psychological needs) to fix the distinction between "necessities" and "luxuries"; what *everyone* in a given society regards as "necessary" tends to become an actual, basic need.

III. Merit and Achievement

The remaining three candidates for material principles of distributive justice belong to the nonequalitarian family. These three principles would each distribute goods in accordance, not with need, but with *desert;* since persons obviously differ in their deserts, economic goods would be distributed unequally. The three principles differ from one another in their conceptions of the relevant *bases of desert* for economic distributions. The first is the principle of *merit.* Unlike the other principles in the nonequalitarian family, this one focuses not on what a person has *done* to deserve his allotment, but rather on what kind of person he is—what characteristics he has.

Two different types of characteristic might be considered meritorious in the appropriate sense: skills and virtues. Native skills and inherited aptitudes will not be appropriate desert bases, since they are forms of merit ruled out by the fair opportunity requirement. No one deserves credit or blame for his genetic inheritance, since no one has the opportunity to select his own genes. Acquired skills may seem more plausible candidates at first, but upon scrutiny they are little better. First, all acquired skills depend to a large degree on native skills. Nobody is born knowing how to read, so reading is an acquired skill, but actual differences in reading skill are to a large degree accounted for by genetic differences that are beyond anyone's control. Some of the differences are no doubt caused by differences in motivation afforded different children, but again the early conditions contributing to a child's motivation are also largely beyond his control. We may still have some differences in acquired skills that are to be accounted for solely or primarily by differences in the degree of practice, drill, and perseverance expended by persons with roughly equal opportunities. In respect to these, we can propitiate the requirement of fair opportunity, but only by nullifying the significance of acquired skill as such, for now skill is a relevant basis of desert only to the extent that it is a product of one's own effort. Hence, *effort* becomes the true basis of desert (as claimed by our fifth principle, discussed below), and not simply skill as such.

Those who would propose rewarding personal *virtues* with a larger than average share of the economic pie, and punishing defects of character with a smaller than average share, advocate assigning to the economic system a task normally done (if it is done at all) by noneconomic institutions. What they propose, in effect, is that we use retributive criteria of distributive justice. Our criminal law, for a variety of good reasons, does not purport to punish people for what they are, but only for what they do. A man can be as arrogant, rude, selfish, cruel, insensitive, irresponsible, cowardly, lazy, or disloyal as he wishes; unless he *does* something prohibited by the criminal law, he will not be made to suffer legal punishment. At least one of the legal system's reasons for refusing to penalize character flaws as such would also explain why such defects should not be listed as relevant differences in a material principle of distributive justice. The apparatus for detecting such flaws (a "moral police"?) would be enormously cumbersome and impractical, and its methods so uncertain and fallible that none of us could feel safe in entrusting the determination of our material allotments to it. We could, of course, give roughly equal shares to all except those few who have *outstanding* virtues—gentleness, kindness, courage, diligence, reliability, warmth, charm, considerateness, generosity. Perhaps these are traits that deserve to be rewarded, but it is doubtful that larger economic allotments are the appropriate vehicles of rewarding. As Benn and Peters remind us, "there are some sorts of 'worth' for which rewards in terms of income seem inappropriate. Great courage in battle is recognized by medals, not by increased pay."[7] Indeed, there is something repugnant, as Socrates and the Stoics insisted, in paying a man to be virtuous. Moreover, the rewards would offer a pecuniary motive for certain forms

_____

[7]Benn and Peters, *Social Principles and the Democratic State*, p. 139.

of excellence that require motives of a different kind, and would thus tend to be self-defeating.

The most plausible nonequalitarian theories are those that locate relevance not in meritorious traits and excellences of any kind, but rather in prior doings: not in what one is, but in what one has done. Actions, too, are sometimes called "meritorious," so there is no impropriety in denominating the remaining families of principles in our survey as "meritarian." One type of action-oriented meritarian might cite *achievement* as a relevant desert basis for pecuniary rewards, so that departures from equality income are to be justicized only by distinguished achievements in science, art, philosophy, music, athletics, and other basic areas of human activity. The attractions and disadvantages of this theory are similar to those of theories which I rejected above that base rewards on skills and virtues. Not all persons have a fair opportunity to achieve great things, and economic rewards seem inappropriate as vehicles for exposing expressing recognition and admiration of noneconomic achievements.

IV. Contribution or "Due Return"

When the achievements under consideration are themselves contributions to our general economic well-being, the meritarian principle of distributive justice is much more plausible. Often it is conjoined with an economic theory that purports to determine exactly what percentage of our total economic product a given worker or class has produced. Justice, according to this principle, requires that each worker get back exactly that proportion of the national wealth that he has himself created. This sounds very much like a principle of "commutative justice" directing us to *give back* to every worker what is really his own property, that is, the product of his own labor.

The French socialist writer and precursor of Karl Marx, Pierre Joseph Proudhon (1809–1865), is perhaps the classic example of this kind of theorist. In his book, *What Is Property?* (1840), Proudhon rejects the standard socialist slogan, "From each according to his ability, to each according to his needs,"[8] in favor of a principle of distributive justice based on contribution, as interpreted by an economic theory that employed a pre-Marxist "theory of surplus value." The famous socialist slogan was not intended, in any case, to express a principle of distributive justice. It was understood to be a rejection of all considerations of "mere" justice for an ethic of human brotherhood. The early socialists thought it unfair, in a way, to give the great contributors to our wealth a disproportionately small share of the product. But in the new socialist society, love of neighbor, community spirit, and absence of avarice would overwhelm such bourgeois notions and put them in their proper (subordinate) place.

Proudhon, on the other hand, based his whole social philosophy not on brotherhood (an ideal he found suitable only for small groups such as families) but on the kind of distributive justice to which even some capitalists gave lip service:

> The key concept was "mutuality" or "reciprocity." "Mutuality, reciprocity exists," he wrote, "when all the workers in an industry, instead of working for an entrepreneur who pays them and keeps their products, work for one another and thus collaborate in the making of a common product whose profits they share among themselves."[9]

Proudhon's celebrated dictum that "property is theft" did not imply that all *possession* of goods is illicit, but rather that the system of rules that permitted the owner of a factory to hire workers and draw profits ("surplus value") from *their* labor robs the workers of what is rightly theirs. "This profit, consisting of a portion of the proceeds of labor that rightfully belonged to the laborer himself, was 'theft.' "[10] The injustice of capitalism, according to

---

[8]Traced to Louis Blanc. For a clear brief exposition of Proudhon's view which contrasts it with that of other early socialists and also that of Karl Marx, see Robert Tucker's "Marx and Distributive Justice," in *Nomos VI: Justice*, ed. C. J. Friedrich and J. W. Chapman (New York: Aldine-Atherton Press, 1963), pp. 306–25.
[9]Tucker, "Marx and Distributive Justice," p. 310.
[10]Tucker, "Marx and Distributive Justice," p. 311.

Proudhon, consists in the fact that those who create the wealth (through their labor) get only a small part of what they create, whereas those who "exploit" their labor, like voracious parasites, gather in a greatly disproportionate share. The "return of contribution" principle of distributive justice, then, cannot work in a capitalist system, but requires a *fédération mutualiste* of autonomous producer-cooperatives in which those who create wealth by their work share it in proportion to their real contributions.

Other theorists, employing different notions of what produces or "creates" economic wealth, have used the "return of contribution" principle to support quite opposite conclusions. The contribution principle has even been used to justicize quite unequalitarian capitalistic status quos, for it is said that capital as well as labor creates wealth, as do ingenious ideas, inventions, and adventurous risk-taking. The capitalist who provided the money, the inventor who designed a product to be manufactured, the innovator who thought of a new mode of production and marketing, the advertiser who persuaded millions of customers to buy the finished product, the inventor who risked his savings on the success of the enterprise—these are the ones, it is said, who did the most to produce the wealth created by a business, not the workers who contributed only their labor, and of course, these are the ones who tend, on the whole, to receive the largest personal incomes.

Without begging any narrow and technical questions of economics, I should express my general skepticism concerning such facile generalizations about the comparative degrees to which various individuals have contributed to our social wealth. Not only are there impossibly difficult problems of measurement involved, there are also conceptual problems that appear beyond all nonarbitrary solution. I refer to the elements of luck and chance, the social factors not attributable to any assignable individuals, and the contributions of population trends, uncreated natural resources, and the efforts of people now dead, which are often central to the explanation of any given increment of social wealth.

The difficulties of separating out causal factors in the production of social wealth might influence the partisan of the "return of contribution" principle in either or both of two ways. He might become very cautious in his application of the principle, requiring that deviations from average shares be restricted to very clear and demonstrable instances of unusually great or small contributions. But the moral that L. T. Hobhouse[11] drew from these difficulties is that *any* individual contribution will be very small relative to the immeasurably great contribution made by political, social, fortuitous, natural, and "inherited" factors. In particular, strict application of the "return of contribution" principle would tend to support a larger claim for the *community* to its own "due return," through taxation and other devices.

In a way, the principle of contribution is not a principle of mere *desert* at all, no matter how applied. As mentioned above, it resembles a principle of commutative justice requiring repayment of debts, return of borrowed items, or compensation for wrongly inflicted damages. If I lend you my car on the understanding that you will take good care of it and soon return it, or if you steal it, or damage it, it will be too *weak* to say that I "deserve" to have my own car, intact, back from you. After all, the car is *mine* or my due, and questions of ownership are not settled by examination of deserts; neither are considerations of ownership and obligation commonly out-balanced by considerations of desert. It is not merely "unfitting" or "inappropriate" that I should not have my own or my due; it is downright *theft* to withhold it from me. So the return of contribution is not merely a matter of merit deserving reward. It is a matter of a maker demanding that which he has created and is thus properly his. The ratio—*A's* share of *X* is to *B's* share of *X* as *A's* contribution to *X* is to *B's* contribution to *X*—appears, therefore, to be a very strong and plausible principle of distributive justice, whose main deficiencies,

---

[11]L. T. Hobhouse, *The Elements of Social Justice* (London: George Allen and Unwin Ltd., 1922). See especially pp.161–63.

when applied to economic distributions, are of a practical (though severe) kind. If Hobhouse is right in claiming that there are social factors in even the most pronounced individual contributions to social wealth, then the principle of due return serves as a moral basis in support of taxation, and other public claims to private goods. In any case, if $A's$ contribution, though apparently much greater than $B's$, is nevertheless only the tiniest percentage of the total contribution to X (whatever that may mean and however it is to be determined), it may seem like the meanest quibbling to distinguish very seriously between A and B at all.

V. Effort

The principle of due return, as a material principle of distributive justice, does have some vulnerability to the fair opportunity requirement. Given unavoidable variations in genetic endowments and material circumstances, different persons cannot have precisely the same opportunities to make contributions to the public weal. Our final candidate for the status of a material principle of distributive justice, the *principle of effort,* does much better in this respect, for it would distribute economic products not in proportion to successful achievement but according to the degree of effort exerted. According to the principle of effort, justice decrees that hard-working executives and hard-working laborers receive precisely the same remuneration (although there may be reasons having nothing to do with justice for paying more to the executives), and that freeloaders be penalized by allotments of proportionately lesser shares of the joint products of everyone's labor. The most persuasive argument for this principle is that it is the closest approximation to the intuitively valid principle of due return that can pass the fair opportunity requirement. It is doubtful, however, that even the principle of effort fully satisfies the requirement of fair opportunity, since those who inherit or acquire certain kinds of handicap may have little oppportunity to *acquire the motivation* even to do their best. In any event, the principle of effort does seem to have intuitive cogency giving it at least some weight as a factor determining the justice of distributions.

In very tentative conclusion, it seems that the principle of equality (in the version that rests on needs rather than that which requires "perfect equality") and the principles of contribution and effort (where nonarbitrarily applicable, and only *after* everyone's basic needs have been satisfied) have the most weight as determinants of economic justice, whereas all forms of the principle of merit are implausible in that role. The reason for the priority of basic needs is that, where there is economic abundance, the claim to life itself and to minimally decent conditions are, like other human rights, claims that all men make with perfect equality. As economic production increases, these claims are given ever greater consideration in the form of rising standards for distinguishing basic needs from other wanted goods. But no matter where that line is drawn, when we go beyond it into the realm of economic surplus or "luxuries," nonequalitarian considerations (especially contribution and effort) come increasingly into play.

Capitalism and Freedom

Milton Friedman

A central element in the development of a collectivist sentiment in this century, at least in Western countries, has been a belief in equality of income as a social goal and a willingness to use the arm of the state to promote it. Two very different questions must be asked in evaluating this egalitarian sentiment and the egalitarian measures it has produced. The first is normative and ethical: what is the justification for state intervention to promote equality? The second is positive and scientific: what has been the effect of the measures actually taken?

The Ethics of Distribution

The ethical principle that would directly justify the distribution of income in a free market society is, "To each according to what he and the instruments he owns produces." The operation of even this principle implicitly depends on state action. Property rights are matters of law and social convention. As we have seen, their definition and enforcement is one of the primary functions of the state. The final distribution of income and wealth under the full operation of this principle may well depend markedly on the rules of property adopted.

From Milton Friedman, *Capitalism and Freedom*, pp. 161–176. © 1962 by the University of Chicago Press. Reprinted by permission.

What is the relation between this principle and another that seems ethically appealing, namely, equality of treatment? In part, the two principles are not contradictory. Payment in accordance with product may be necessary to achieve true equality of treatment. Given individuals whom we are prepared to regard as alike in ability and initial resources, if some have a greater taste for leisure and others for marketable goods, inequality of return through the market is necessary to achieve equality of total return or equality of treatment. One man may prefer a routine job with much time off for basking in the sun to a more exacting job paying a higher salary; another man may prefer the opposite. If both were paid equally in money, their incomes in a more fundamental sense would be unequal. Similarly, equal treatment requires that an individual be paid more for a dirty, unattractive job than for a pleasant rewarding one. Much observed inequality is of this kind. Differences of money income offset differences in other characteristics of the occupation or trade. In the jargon of economists, they are "equalizing differences" required to make the whole of the "net advantages," pecuniary and non-pecuniary, the same.

Another kind of inequality arising through the operation of the market is also required, in a somewhat more subtle sense, to produce equality of treatment, or to put it differently to satisfy men's tastes. It can be illustrated most simply by a lottery. Consider a group of individuals who initially have equal endowments and who all agree voluntarily to enter a lottery with very unequal prizes. The resultant inequality of income is surely required to permit the individuals in question to make the most of their initial equality. Redistribution of the income after the event is equivalent to denying them the opportunity to enter the lottery. This case is far more important in practice than would appear by taking the notion of a "lottery" literally. Individuals choose occupations, investments, and the like partly in accordance with their taste for uncertainty. The girl who tries to become a movie actress rather than a civil servant is deliberately choosing to enter a lottery, so is the individual who invests in penny uranium stocks rather than government bonds. Insurance is a way of expressing a taste for certainty. Even these examples do not indicate fully the extent to which actual inequality may be the result of arrangements designed to satisfy men's tastes. The very arrangements for paying and hiring people are affected by such preferences. If all potential movie actresses had a great dislike of uncertainty, there would tend to develop "co-coperatives" of movie actresses, the members of which agreed in advance to share income receipts more or less evenly, thereby in effect providing themselves insurance through the pooling of risks. If such a preference were widespread, large diversified corporations combining risky and non-risky ventures would become the rule. The wildcat oil prospector, the private proprietorship, the small partnership, would all become rare.

Indeed, this is one way to interpret governmental measures to redistribute income through progressive taxes and the like. It can be argued that for one reason or another, costs of administration perhaps, the market cannot produce the range of lotteries or the kind of lottery desired by the members of the community, and that progressive taxation is, as it were, a government enterprise to do so. I have no doubt that this view contains an element of truth. At the same time, it can hardly justify present taxation, if only because the taxes are imposed *after* it is already largely known who have drawn the prizes and who the blanks in the lottery of life, and the taxes are voted mostly by those who think they have drawn the blanks. One might, along these lines, justify one generation's voting the tax schedules to be applied to an as yet unborn generation. Any such procedure would, I conjecture, yield income tax schedules much less highly graduated than present schedules are, at least on paper.

Though much of the inequality of income produced by payment in accordance with product reflects "equalizing" differences or the satisfaction of men's tastes for uncertainty, a large part reflects initial differences in endowment, both of human capacities and of property. This is the part that raises the really difficult ethical issue.

It is widely argued that it is essential to distinguish between inequality in personal endowments and in property, and between inequalities arising from inherited wealth and from acquired wealth. Inequality resulting from differences in personal capacities, or from differences in wealth accumulated by the individual in question, are considered appropriate, or at least not so clearly inappropriate as differences resulting from inherited wealth.

This distinction is untenable. Is there any greater ethical justification for the high returns to the individual who inherits from his parents a peculiar voice for which there is a great demand than for the high returns to the individual who inherits property? The sons of Russian commissars surely have a higher expectation of income—perhaps also of liquidation—than the sons of peasants. Is this any more or less justifiable than the higher income expectation of the son of an American millionaire? We can look at this same question in another way. A parent who has wealth that he wishes to pass on to his child can do so in different ways. He can use a given sum of money to finance his child's training as, say, a certified public accountant, or to set him up in business, or to set up a trust fund yielding him a property income. In any of these cases, the child will have a higher income than he otherwise would. But in the first case, his income will be regarded as coming from human capacities; in the second, from profits; in the third, from inherited wealth. Is there any basis for distinguishing among these categories of receipts on ethical grounds? Finally, it seems illogical to say that a man is entitled to what he has produced by personal capacities or to the produce of the wealth he has accumulated, but that he is not entitled to pass any wealth on to his children; to say that a man may use his income for riotous living but may not give it to his heirs. Surely, the latter is one way to use what he has produced.

The fact that these arguments against the so-called capitalist ethic are invalid does not of course demonstrate that the capitalist ethic is an acceptable one. I find it difficult to justify either accepting or rejecting it, or to justify any alternative principle. I am led to the view that it cannot in and of itself be regarded as an ethical principle; that it must be regarded as instrumental or a corollary of some other principle such as freedom.

Some hypothetical examples may illustrate the fundamental difficulty. Suppose there are four Robinson Crusoes, independently marooned on four islands in the same neighborhood. One happened to land on a large and fruitful island which enables him to live easily and well. The others happened to land on tiny and rather barren islands from which they can barely scratch a living. One day, they discover the existence of one another. Of course, it would be generous of the Crusoe on the large island if he invited the others to join him and share its wealth. But suppose he does not. Would the other three be justified in joining forces and compelling him to share his wealth with them? Many a reader will be tempted to say yes. But before yielding to this temptation, consider precisely the same situation in different guise. Suppose you and three friends are walking along the street and you happen to spy and retrieve a $20 bill on the pavement. It would be generous of you, of course, if you were to divide it equally with them, or at least blow them to a drink. But suppose you do not. Would the other three be justified in joining forces and compelling you to share the $20 equally with them? I suspect most readers will be tempted to say no. And on further reflection, they may even conclude that the generous course of action is not itself clearly the "right" one. Are we prepared to urge on ourselves or our fellows that any person whose wealth exceeds the average of all persons in the world should immediately dispose of the excess by distributing it equally to all the rest of the world's inhabitants? We may admire and praise such action when undertaken by a few. But a universal "potlatch" would make a civilized world impossible.

If any event, two wrongs do not make a right. The unwillingness of the rich Robinson Crusoe or the lucky finder of the $20 bill to share his wealth does not justify the use of coercion by the others. Can we justify being judges in our own case, deciding on our own when we are entitled to use force to extract what we regard as our due from others? Or what we regard as not their due? Most differences of status or position or wealth can be regarded as the product of chance at a far enough remove. The man who is hard working and thrifty is to be regarded as "deserving"; yet these qualities owe much to the genes he was fortunate (or unfortunate?) enough to inherit.

Despite the lip service that we all pay to "merit" as compared to "chance," we are generally much readier to accept inequalities arising from chance then those clearly attributable to merit. The college professor whose colleague wins a sweepstake will envy him but is unlikely to bear him any malice or to feel unjustly treated. Let the colleague receive a trivial raise that makes his salary higher than the professor's own, and the professor is far more likely to feel aggrieved. After all, the goddess of chance, as of justice, is blind. The salary raise was a deliberate judgment of relative merit.

The Instrumental Role of Distribution According to Product

The operative function of payment in accordance with product in a market society is not primarily distributive, but allocative. The central principle of a market economy is co-operation through voluntary exchange. Individuals co-operate with others because they can in this way satisfy their own wants more effectively. But unless an individual receives the whole of what he adds to the product, he will enter into exchanges on the basis of what he can receive rather than what he can produce. Exchanges will not take place that would have been mutually beneficial if each party received what he contributed to the aggregate product. Payment in accordance with product is therefore necessary in order that resources be used most effectively, at least under a system depending on voluntary cooperation. Given sufficient knowledge, it might be that compulsion could be substituted for the incentive of reward, though I doubt that it could. One can shuffle inanimate objects around; one can compel individuals to be at certain places at certain times; but one can hardly compel individuals to put forward their best efforts. Put another way, the substitution of compulsion for co-operation changes the amount of resources available.

Though the essential function of payment in accordance with product in a market society is to enable resources to be allocated efficiently without compulsion, it is unlikely to be tolerated unless it is also regarded as yielding distributive justice. No society can be stable unless there is a basic core of value judgments that are unthinkingly accepted by the great bulk of its members. Some key institutions must be accepted as "absolutes," not simply as instrumental. I believe that payment in accordance with product has been, and, in large measure, still is, one of these accepted value judgments or institutions.

One can demonstrate this by examining the grounds on which the internal opponents of the capitalist system have attacked the distribution of income resulting from it. It is a distinguishing feature of the core of central values of a society that it is accepted alike by its members, whether they regard themselves as proponents or as opponents of the system of organization of the society. Even the severest internal critics of capitalism have implicitly accepted payment in accordance with product as ethically fair.

The most far-reaching criticism has come from the Marxists. Marx argued that labor was exploited. Why? Because labor produced the whole of the product but got only part of it; the rest is Marx's "surplus value." Even if the statements of fact implicit in this assertion were accepted, the value judgment follows only if one accepts the capitalist ethic. Labor is "exploited" only if labor is entitled to what it produces. If one accepts instead the socialist premise, "to each according to his need, from each according to his ability"—whatever that may mean—it is necessary to compare what labor produces, not with what it gets but with its "ability," and to compare what labor gets, not with what it produces but with its "need."

Of course, the Marxist argument is invalid on other grounds as well. There is, first, the confusion between the total product of all co-operating resources and the amount added to product—in the economist's jargon, marginal product. Even more striking, there is an unstated change in the meaning of "labor" in passing from the premise to the conclusion. Marx recognized the role of capital in producing the product but regarded capital as embodied labor. Hence, written out in full, the premises of the Marxist syllogism would run: "Present and past labor produce the whole of the product. Present labor gets only part of the product." The logical conclusion is presumably "Past labor is exploited," and the inference for action is that past labor should get more of the product, though it is by no means clear how, unless it be in elegant tombstones.

The achievement of allocation of resources without compulsion is the major instrumental role in the market place of distribution in accordance with product. But it is not the only instrumental role of the resulting inequality. The role that inequality plays in providing independent foci of power to offset the centralization of political power, as well as the role that it plays in promoting civil freedom by providing "patrons" to finance the dissemination of unpopular or simply novel ideas. In addition, in the economic sphere, it provides "patrons" to finance experimentation and the development of new products—to buy the first experimental automobiles and television sets, let alone impressionist paintings. Finally, it enables distribution to occur impersonally without the need for "authority"—a special facet of the general role of the market in effecting co-operation and co-ordination without coercion.

Facts of Income Distribution

A capitalist system involving payment in accordance with product can be, and in practice is, characterized by considerable inequality of income and wealth. This fact is frequently misinterpreted to mean that capitalism and free enterprise produce wider inequality than alternative systems and, as a corollary, that the extension and development of capitalism has meant increased inequality. This misinterpretation is fostered by the misleading character of most published figures on the distribution of income, in particular their failure to distinguish short-run from long-run inequality. Let us look at some of the broader facts about the distribution of income.

One of the most striking facts which runs counter to many people's expectation has to do with the sources of income. The more capitalistic a country is, the smaller the fraction of income paid for the use of what is generally regarded as capital, and the larger the fraction paid for human services. In underdeveloped countries like India,

Egypt, and so on, something like half of total income is property income. In the United States, roughly one-fifth is property income. And in other advanced capitalist countries, the proportion is not very different. Of course, these countries have much more capital than the primitive countries but they are even richer in the productive capacity of their residents; hence, the larger income from property is a smaller fraction of the total. The great achievement of capitalism has not been the accumulation of property, it has been the opportunities it has offered to men and women to extend and develop and improve their capacities. Yet the enemies of capitalism are fond of castigating it as materialist, and its friends all too often apologize for capitalism's materialism as a necessary cost of progress.

Another striking fact, contrary to popular conception, is that capitalism leads to less inequality than alternative systems of organization and that the development of capitalism has greatly lessened the extent of inequality. Comparisons over space and time alike confirm this view. There is surely drastically less inequality in Western capitalist societies like the Scandinavian countries, France, Britain, and the United States, than in a status society like India or a backward country like Egypt. Comparison with communist countries like Russia is more difficult because of paucity and unreliability of evidence. But if inequality is measured by differences in levels of living between the privileged and other classes, such inequality may well be decidedly less in capitalist than in communist countries. Among the Western countries alone, inequality appears to be less, in any meaningful sense, the more highly capitalist the country is: less in Britain than in France, less in the United States than in Britain— though these comparisons are rendered difficult by the problem of allowing for the intrinsic heterogeneity of populations; for a fair comparison, for example, one should perhaps compare the United States, not with the United Kingdom alone but with the United Kingdom plus the West Indies plus its African possessions.

With respect to changes over time, the economic progress achieved in the capitalist societies has been accompanied by a drastic diminution in inequality. As late as 1848, John Stuart Mill could write, "Hitherto [1848] it is questionable if all the mechanical inventions yet made have lightened the day's toil of any human being. They have enabled a greater population to live the same life of drudgery—and imprisonment, and an increased number of manufacturers and others to make fortunes. They have increased the comforts of the middle classes. But they have not yet begun to effect those great changes in human destiny, which it is in their nature and in their futurity to accomplish."[1] This statement was probably not correct even for Mill's day, but certainly no one could write this today about the advanced capitalist countries. It is still true about the rest of the world.

The chief characteristic of progress and development over the past century is that it has freed the masses from backbreaking toil and has made available to them products and services that were formerly the monopoly of the upper classes, without in any corresponding way expanding the products and services available to the wealthy. Medicine aside, the advances in technology have for the most part simply made available to the masses of the people luxuries that were always available in one form or another to the truly wealthy. Modern plumbing, central heating, automobiles, television, radio, to cite just a few examples, provide conveniences to the masses equivalent to those that the wealthy could always get by the use of servants, entertainers, and so on.

Detailed statistical evidence on these phenomena, in the form of meaningful and comparable distributions of income, is hard to come by, though such studies as have been made confirm the broad conclusions just outlined. Such statistical data, however, can be extremely misleading. They cannot segregate differences in income that are equalizing from those that are not. For example, the short working life of a baseball player means that the annual income during his active years must be much higher than

---

[1]*Principles of Political Economy* (Ashley edition; London: Longmans, Green & Co., 1909), p. 751.

in alternative pursuits open to him to make it equally attractive financially. But such a difference affects the figures in exactly the same way as any other difference in income. The income unit for which the figures are given is also of great importance. A distribution for individual income recipients always shows very much greater apparent inequality than a distribution for family units: many of the individuals are housewives working part-time or receiving a small amount of property income, or other family members in a similar position. Is the distribution that is relevant for families one in which the families are classified by total family income? Or by income per person? Or per equivalent unit? This is no mere quibble. I believe that the changing distribution of families by number of children is the most important single factor that has reduced inequality of levels of living in this country during the past half century. It has been far more important than graduated inheritance and income taxes. The really low levels of living were the joint product of relatively low family incomes and relatively large numbers of children. The average number of children has declined and, even more important, this decline has been accompanied and largely produced by a virtual elimination of the very large family. As a result, families now tend to differ much less with respect to number of children. Yet this change would not be reflected in a distribution of families by the size of total family income.

A major problem in interpreting evidence on the distribution of income is the need to distinguish two basically different kinds of inequality; temporary, short-run differences in income, and differences in long-run income status. Consider two societies that have the same distribution of annual income. In one there is great mobility and change so that the position of particular families in the income hierarchy varies widely from year to year. In the other, there is great rigidity so that each family stays in the same position year after year. Clearly, in any meaningful sense, the second would be the more unequal society. The one kind of inequality is a sign of dynamic change, social mobility, equality of opportunity; the other, of a status society. The confusion of these two kinds of inequality is particularly important, precisely because competitive free-enterprise capitalism tends to substitute the one for the other. Non-capitalist societies tend to have wider inequality than capitalist, even as measured by annual income; in addition, inequality in them tends to be permanent, whereas capitalism undermines status and introduces social mobility.

Government Measures Used to Alter the Distribution of Income

The methods that governments have used most widely to alter the distribution of income have been graduated income and inheritance taxation. Before considering their desirability, it is worth asking whether they have succeeded in their aim.

No conclusive answer can be given to this question with our present knowledge. The judgment that follows is a personal, though I hope not utterly uninformed, opinion, stated, for sake of brevity, more dogmatically than the nature of the evidence justifies. My impression is that these tax measures have had a relatively minor, though not negligible, effect in the direction of narrowing the differences between the average position of groups of families classified by some statistical measures of income. However, they have also introduced essentially arbitrary inequalities of comparable magnitude between persons within such income classes. As a result, it is by no means clear whether the net effect in terms of the basic objective of equality of treatment or equality of outcome has been to increase or decrease equality.

The tax rates are on paper both high and highly graduated. But their effect has been dissipated in two different ways. First, part of their effect has been simply to make the pretax distribution more unequal. This is the usual incidence effect of taxation. By discouraging entry into activities highly taxed—in this case activities with large risk and non-pecuniary disadvantages—they raise returns in those activities. Second, they have stimulated both legislative and other provisions to evade the tax—so-called "loopholes" in the law such as percentage depletion, exemption of interest on state and municipal bonds, specially favorable treatment of capital gains, expense accounts, other indirect ways of payment, conversion of ordinary income to capital gains, and so on in bewildering number and kind. The effect has been to make the actual rates imposed far lower than the nominal rates, and perhaps more important, to make the incidence of taxes capricious and unequal. People at the same economic level pay very different taxes depending on the accident of the source of their income and the opportunities they have to evade the tax. If present rates were made fully effective, the effect on incentives and the like might well be so serious as to cause a radical loss in the productivity of the society. Tax avoidance may therefore have been essential for economic well-being. If so, the gain has been bought at the cost of a great waste of resources, and of the introduction of widespread inequity. A much lower set of nominal rates, plus a more comprehensive base through more equal taxation of all sources of income could be both more progressive in average incidence, more equitable in detail, and less wasteful of resources.

This judgment that the personal income tax has been arbitrary in its impact and of limited effectiveness in reducing inequality is widely shared by students of the subject, including many who strongly favor the use of gradauted taxation to reduce inequality. They too urge that the top bracket rates be drastically reduced and the base broadened.

A further factor that has reduced the impact of the graduated tax structure on inequality of income and wealth is that these taxes are much less taxes on being wealthy than on becoming wealthy. While they limit the use of the income from existing wealth, they impede even more strikingly—so far as they are effective—the accumulation of wealth. The taxation of the income from the wealth does nothing to reduce the wealth itself, it simply reduces the level of consumption and additions to wealth that the owners can support. The tax measures give an incentive to avoid risk and to embody existing wealth in relatively stable forms, which reduces the likelihood that existing accumulations of wealth will be dissipated. On the other side, the major route to new accumulations is through large current incomes of which a large fraction is saved and invested in risky activities, some of which will yield high returns. If the income tax were effective, it would close this route. In consequence, its effect would be to protect existing holders of wealth from the competition of newcomers. In practice, this effect is largely dissipated by the avoidance devices already referred to. It is notable how large a fraction of the new accumuations have been in oil, where the percentage depletion allowances provide a particularly easy route to the receipt of tax-free income.

In judging the desirability of graduated income taxation it seems to me important to distinguish two problems even through the distinction cannot be precise in application: first, the raising of funds to finance the expenses of those governmental activities it is decided to undertake (including perhaps measures to eliminate poverty); second, the imposition of taxes for redistributive purposes alone. The former might well call for some measure of graduation, both on grounds of assessing costs in accordance with benefits and on grounds of social standards of equity. But the present high nominal rates on top brackets of income and inheritance can hardly be justified on this ground—if only because their yield is so low.

I find it hard, as a liberal, to see any justification for graduated taxation solely to redistribute income. This seems a clear case of using coercion to take from some in order to give to others and thus to conflict head-on with individual freedom.

All things considered, the personal income tax structure that seems to me best is a flat-rate tax on income above an exemption, with income defined very broadly and deductions allowed only for strictly defined expenses of earning income. I would combine this program with the abolition of the corporate income tax, and with the requirement that corporations be required to attribute their income to stockholders, and that stockholders be required to include such sums on their tax returns. The most important other desirable changes are the elimination of percentage depletion on oil and other raw materials, the elimination of tax exemption of interest on state and local securities, the elimination of special treatment of capital gains, the co-ordination of income, estate, and gift taxes, and the elimination of numerous deductions now allowed.

An exemption, it seems to me, can be a justified degree of graduation. It is very different for 90 percent of the population to vote taxes on themselves and an exemption for 10 percent than for 90 percent to vote punitive taxes on the other 10 percent—which is in effect what has been done in the United States. A proportional flat-rate-tax would involve higher absolute payments by persons with higher incomes for governmental services, which is not clearly inappropriate on grounds of benefits conferred. Yet it would avoid a situation where any large numbers could vote to impose on others taxes that did not also affect their own tax burden.

The proposal to substitute a flat-rate income tax for the present graduated rate structure will strike many a reader as a radical proposal. And so it is in terms of concept. For this very reason, it cannot be too strongly emphasized that it is not radical in terms of revenue yield, redistribution of income, or any other relevant criterion. Our present income tax rates range from 20 percent to 91 percent, with the rate reaching 50 percent on the excess of taxable incomes over $18,000 for single taxpayers or $36,000 for married taxpayers filing joint returns. Yet a flat rate of 23½ percent on taxable income as presently reported and presently defined, that is, above present exemptions and after all presently allowable deductions, would yield as much revenue as the present highly graduated rate.[2] In fact, such a flat rate, even with no change whatsoever in other features of the law, would yield a higher revenue be-

---

[2]This point is so important that it may be worth giving the figures and calculations. The latest year for which figures are available as this is written is the taxable year 1959 in U.S. Internal Revenue Service, *Statistics of Income for 1959.* For that year: Aggregate taxable income reported on

Individual tax returns	$166,540 million
Income Tax before tax credit	39,092 million
Income tax after tax credit	38,645 million

A flat rate tax of 23½ percent on the aggregate taxable income would have yielded (.235) × $166,540 million = $39,137 million.

If we assume the same tax credit, the final yield would have been about the same as that actually attained.

cause a larger amount of taxable income would be reported for three reasons: there would be less incentive than now to adopt legal but costly schemes that reduce the amount of taxable income reported (so-called tax avoidance); there would be less incentive to fail to report income that legally should be reported (tax evasion); the removal of the disincentive effects of the present structure of rates would produce a more efficient use of present resources and a higher income.

If the yield of the present highly graduated rates is so low, so also must be their redistributive effects. This does not mean that they do no harm. On the contrary. The yield is so low partly because some of the most competent men in the country devote their energies to devising ways to keep it so low; and because many other men shape their activities with one eye on tax effects. All this is sheer waste. And what do we get for it? At most, a feeling of satisfaction on the part of some that the state is redistributing income. And even this feeling is founded on ignorance of the actual effects of the graduated tax structure, and would surely evaporate if the facts were known.

To return to the distribution of income, there is a clear justification for social action of a very different kind than taxation to affect the distribution of income. Much of the actual inequality derives from imperfections of the market. Many of these have themselves been created by government action or could be removed by government action. There is every reason to adjust the rules of the game so as to eliminate these sources of inequality. For example, special monopoly privileges granted by government, tariffs, and other legal enactments benefiting particular groups, are a source of inequality. The removal of these, the liberal will welcome. The extension and widening of educational opportunities has been a major factor tending to reduce inequalities. Measures such as these have the operational virtue that they strike at the sources of inequality rather than simply alleviating the symptoms.

The distribution of income is still another area in which government has been doing more harm by one set of measures than it has been able to undo by others. It is another example of the justification of government intervention in

Capitalism and Poverty

Bernard Gendron

In recent controversies on the extent of poverty in America, the defenders of American capitalism have repeatedly made the following claim: the incidence of poverty in America, during the past few decades, has been decreasing consistently at a remarkable rate, and the day is rapidly approaching when poverty will virtually have been eliminated within its borders. Let's refer to this as the *meliorist thesis.* How are we radicals to respond to it? It is to this question that I address myself.

Surprisingly, few radical texts contest the meliorist thesis directly. Indeed, few radical books, though otherwise lengthy, devote more than a few pages, or even a few paragraphs, to poverty.[1] One radical reader, for example, organizes the ills of America under six categories: inequality, alienation, racism, sexism, irrationality, and imperialism.[2] Poverty only gets passing mention in the section on inequality. Are we to take this as an indication

---

From *Radical Philosopher's News Journal*, January 4, 1975. Reprinted by permission of the author.

[1]Cf. Baran and Sweezy, *Monopoly Capital,* (New York, Monthly Review Press, 1966); Howard Sherman, *Radical Political Economy* (New York, Basic Books, 1972); David Mermelstein (ed.)., *Economics: Mainstream Readings and Radical Critiques,* (New York, Random House, 1970); Tom Christoffel, David Finkelher, and Dan Gilbarg (ed.), *Up Against the American Myth* (New York: Holt, Rinehart and Winston, 1970); Ernest Mandel, *Marxist Economic Theory,* (London, Merlin Press, 1968).

[2]Richard Edwards, Michael Reich, and Thomas Weisskopf (ed.), *The Capitalist System* (Englewood Cliffs, Prentice-Hall, 1972).

that radicals concede the meliorist thesis? If so, what are they going to do with Marx's prediction of "increasing misery" for the working clases? Will radicals, as Ronald Meek suggests, regretfully admit that on this issue Marx was seriously mistaken?[3] But can the thesis of increasing misery be eliminated without serious damage to the Marxist system? Or is "increasing misery" to be interpreted in noneconomic terms, that is, in terms of increasing alienation, racism, sexism? But, if radicals concede that economic misery can be substantially reduced in capitalism, why shouldn't they also concede that alienation and other forms of noneconomic misery also can be substantially reduced in capitalism? Perhaps radicals, while agreeing with the meliorist thesis, can salvage the increasing misery doctrine by applying it to the global impact of American capitalism, rather than exclusively to its domestic impact. So understood, the doctrine says that globally American capitalism is generating more poverty than it is eliminating. It says that the price of decreasing poverty at home is increasing poverty in countries under the sway of American imperialism. But this move has its difficulties. First, the standards which warrant the claim that poverty is declining in the U.S. will also warrant the claim that it is declining in countries dominated by U.S. firms. Secondly, insofar as the international expansion of U.S. firms is motivated by the search for cheap labor, it should, *mutatis mutandis*, contribute to the lowering rather than the raising of the wages of domestic workers.

All this, it appears, shows that the radical critique of American capitalism will suffer intolerably if it concedes the meliorist thesis. The meliorist thesis must be attacked. But first let us see what underlies it.

I

The standard justification of the meliorist thesis goes somewhat as follows:

---

[3]Ronald L. Meek, "Marx's 'Doctrine of Increasing Misery'", in *Economics and Ideology* (London, Chapman and Hall Ltd., 1967).

(1) American *per capita* income has been increasing significantly and sustainedly over the past few decades.
(2) The real incomes of the lower economic groups, during the past few decades, have increased at the same rate as the national average.
(3) As the real incomes of lower economic groups increase, the incidence of poverty among them proportionately decreases.
(4) Therefore, the incidence of poverty in America has been decreasing significantly and sustainedly over the past few decades.

There are readily available arguments to justify each of these premises. In defenses of premise (1), one may point to the fact that average individual and family income in America (in 1968 dollars) has increased from $4700 in 1929, to $5800 in 1947, to $7400 in 1962 and to $8900 in 1968.[4] Premise (2) is based on statistics showing that the relative income shares of the various income groups, divided into quintiles, have only changed marginally in the past few decades.[5] Premise (3) is supported by the Social Security Administration measure of poverty—hereon referred to as the 'SSA meassure,"—which is the official and most widely used measure. Applying the SSA measure tells us this: any family of four is, or was, or will be in poverty, if it is, or was, or will be, receiving a yearly income of less than $3100 in constant 1963 dollars, or equivalently, a yearly income of less than $4000 in constant 1970 dollars. This poverty income line is arrived at by multiplying by three the value of the minimally nutritionally adequate food budget, on the assuption that twice as much income is required to satisfy non-nutritional basic needs than is required to satisfy nutritional needs.[6]

Obviously, as real incomes go up across the board, the

[4]Herman P. Miller, *Rich Man, Poor Man*, (New York, Thomas Y. Crowell, 1971), p. 41.
[5]*Ibid.*, pp. 49–50.
[6]Bradley Schiller, *The Economics of Poverty and Discrimination*, (Englewood Cliffs, Prentice-Hall, 1973), pp. 14–15; Miller, *op cit.*, pp. 117–118.

incidence of families earning less than $3100 1963 dollars,
and hence less than the SSA poverty cut-off income, goes
down proportionately; thus the warrant for premise (3). So
if we accept premises (1) and (2), and we accept the SSA
measure of poverty, we cannot resist the conclusion that
poverty has been significantly and substainedly reduced in
America during the past few decades. Indeed, according to
the SSA, the record is quite impressive. The percentage of
persons falling below the SSA poverty line has decreased
from 59 percent in 1929, to 32 percent in 1947, to 20 percent in 1963, and to 12.6 percent in 1970.[7]

II

The argument for the meliorist thesis is challenging
enough. How can it be met by radicals? There is little reason to object to premises (1) and (2); indeed radicals concede quite willingly that the American economy is a
growth economy with a constant rate of inequality. So,
this leaves us only with premise (3).

In order to refute (3), radicals must attack the SSA measure of poverty, on which (3) depends. Now, there have
been countless criticisms of the SSA measure, but not all
are relevant to the issue at hand. For example, it has been
argued *ad nauseam* that the SSA poverty line is too low,
and hence that there are many more persons living in poverty than the SSA will admit. For its minimal food
budget, the SSA uses the "economy" food plan of the Department of Agriculture, which allowed (in 1970) 91 cents
per day per person. But this is admittedly an "emergency"
food plan, and not suitable for permanent diet. And, even
on an emergency basis, it can be assumed to be nutritionally adequate only on the conditions that prices are average, that much time will be spent for comparison shop-
ping, that only the most nutritious foods will be bought,
that all the meals will be taken at home, and that they

[7]Schiller, *op cit.*, pp. 19–20; S. M. Miller and Pamela Roby, *The Future of Inequality*, (New York, Basic Books, 1970), pp. 47–48.

will be cooked with care. But, for lower income groups, none of these conditions are borne out. The SSA further assumes, what appears to be manifestly false, that manual workers require no more nutrients than do sedentary workers. In addition, there is convincing evidence that the ratio of total consumption to food consumption among lower income groups is closer to 4:1 rather than 3:1 as is supposed by the SSA.[8]

We can all agree: the SSA poverty income line is too low. We may, as many radicals have done, opt for the Bureau of Labor Statistics (BLS) low income budget, as a preferable base for demarcating the poor from the non-poor; if we so move, we will conclude that there are at least 60-percent more persons in poverty than is allowed by the SSA measure.[9] These moves against the SSA measure are all fine; but they are misdirected if aimed at those features of the SSA measure which supports the meliorist thesis. For, showing that some higher poverty line (e.g., that of the BLS) is superior to the SSA poverty line does not, by itself, inflict any damage on the meliorist thesis supported by the SSA measure. That there are many more poor than is officially believed does not entail that poverty has not been declining consistently and significantly in the past fifty years. What needs to be attacked are not the SSA's particular indices of poverty, but the general conception of poverty, or the general approach to the measurement of poverty, which underlies the choice of these indices. For there are many alternatives to the SSA measure which share its approach to, or conception of, poverty. If the BLS measure of poverty presupposes the same general conception and approach as does the SSA measure, then, from the anti-meliorist point of view, the BLS measure is just as objectionable as the SSA measure.

---

[8]Miller and Roby, *op. cit.*, p. 28; Miller, *op. cit.*, pp. 119–120; Schiller, *op cit.*, p. 16; Martin Rein, "Problems in the Definition and Measurement of Poverty", in Peter Townsend (ed.) *The Concept of Poverty*, (New York, American Elsevier, 1970), pp. 53–58. David Caplevits, *The Poor Pay More*, (New York, Free Press, 1967).

[9]Cf. Baran and Sweezy, *op. cit.*, pp. 285–289; Edwards, Reich, and Weisskopf, *op. cit.*, p. 212; Christoffel, Finkelher, and Gilbarg, *op. cit.*, pp. 10–11.

III

But what conception of, or approach to, poverty underlies the SSA measure? Let us begin by stipulating that anyone is poor who lacks the economic wherewithal necessary for the satisfaction of his/her subsistence needs. The expressions "economic wherewithal" and "subsistence needs" are of course open to a variety of interpretations or applications. These interpretations and applications in turn generate different approaches to, or conceptions of, poverty.

The SSA measure embodies what I shall call the *fixed absolute income approach* to poverty. According to it, something is a subsistence need if and only if it is a biological need. A biological need is any need, which does not come into being as a consequence of conditioning, learning, or socialization, and which is required for the satisfaction of some inherited want or drive, for the actualization of some inherited capacity, or for the fulfillment of some inherited organ function. The proponents of the SSA measure seem to assume that there is a large core of biological needs shared by all, or nearly all, humans; they further seem to assume that non-universal biological needs will be distributed similarly from society to society, place to place, and time to time. Hence, insofar as subsistence needs are equated with biological needs, the identity and distribution of subsistence needs will remain the same from society to society, place to place, and time to time. Consequently, the standards for demarcating between poverty and nonpoverty, insofar as they are formulated by reference to the set of subsistence needs, will be constant over time and place; the standards are absolute rather than *culturally* or *temporally relative.*

Now, the satisfaction of these culturally and temporally invariant needs requires a certain amount of consumable goods and services, such as food, shelter, clothing, education, transportation, medicine, security, recreation, etc. According to the SSA, the poor are those who lack the purchasing power for acquiring these minimum goods and services. Since purchasing power is assumed to be a function of real income, then the poor are those whose real income is substantially inadequate for purchasing the market basket containing all and only those goods and services necessary for the satisfaction of their biological needs. Further, it is assumed that the size or value (or equivalently the real cost) of this market basket remains more or less constant over time and place, and hence that the real income just sufficient for purchasing it remains more or less constant over time and place. From this it follows that the line demarcating the poor from the non-poor is a *fixed income line,* determined by *culturally* and *temporally invariant* (or *"absolute"*) standards. Such is the fixed absolute income approach to poverty which appears to buttress the SSA measure of poverty.

IV

It is obvious that a *fixed absolute income* approach to poverty will support the meliorist thesis when the former is applied to a growing economy in which all income groups share in the gains. Hence, this approach must be rejected by radicals. What alternative approach would they propose?

Obviously, it is the SSA's insistence on the *fixety* of the poverty income line which leads it to the meliorist thesis. Radicals, on the other hand, insist that the poverty income line must be upgraded proportionately as the capitalist economy grows. They are thus in support of a *variable income* approach. But what can justify this? Why should the standards for being non-poor go up? Why should we get continuously fussier about who are to count as the non-poor? Aren't we weakening the evaluative force of the expression "is poor" if we keep diluting the measures for determining who is poor? What alternative conception of poverty will justify the upgrading of the poverty income line with the growth of the capitalist economy?

Now, the most obvious way to support a variable income approach is by appeal to some relative income approach; that is, one can most straightforwardly defend the practice of continually upgrading the poverty income line in a growing capitalist economy, by claiming that subsistence needs are culturally and temporally variant, and that they grow as the capitalist economy grows. This appears to be Marx's view:

> The worker's natural wants, such as food, clothing, fuel, and housing, vary according to climatic and other physical conditions of his country... On the other hand, the number and extent of his socially necessary wants... are themselves the product of historical development and depend, therefore, to a great extent on the degree of civilization of a country...[10]

Presumably, according to Marx, the class of subsistence needs includes not only biological needs, but also historically created needs, i.e., needs resulting from the varying conditioning and socialization practices of societies at different historical stages. And, presumably, at least in capitalist societies, the class of historically created subsistence needs grows as per capita incomes increase across the board. This appears generally to be the view of radicals (e.g., Baran and Sweezy, Mermelstein and Mandel), as well as of anti-meliorist liberals.

This view however is not without its difficulties. For, once we include among subsistence needs, needs which are nonbiological and historically created, we run into the difficulties of demarcating between subsistence and non-subsistence needs. Which historical needs, at a given time and place, are to count as subsistence needs and which are not? Is any strongly felt need a subsistence need? If someone feels very deprived for not having a sportscar like his friends do, is he thereby poor? Suppose that he feels just as poor and deprived as does a ghetto family head? Is he thereby just as poor? This seems wrong. There is simply more to being poor than feeling poor.

This difficulty, however, can be met straightforward as follows. In any society, there is a standard view of what is to count as a minimally decent life. A decent life is a life

---

[10]Karl Marx, Volume I, *Capital*, (New York, International Publishers, 1967), 170–171.

which persons with average income can afford, with some leeway for savings and luxury goods. Now, in this view, the subsistence needs of a given society are precisely those needs which must be satisfied if one is to live the standard decent life of that society. Hence, anyone is poor whose income is substantially inadequate to purchase those goods and services necessary for the living of a minimally decent lifes thus, anyone is poor whose income is substantially below the appropriately designated average income.

Now, any appropriately designated average income will inevitably go up as per capita income goes up across the board; hence, the standard for a minimally decent life will inevitably increase with across-the-board increases in per capita income. So, in a growing economy, the incidence of poverty will not decrease, if there is no decrease in the percentage of persons receiving substantially less than the growing, appropriately designated average income. That is, in a growing economy, the incidence of poverty will not decrease, if there is no decrease in the percentage of persons receiving substantially less than the income necessary for meeting the continuous rising standards for decent living. On this, consider the words of H. P. Miller:

> The essential fallacy of the fixed poverty line is that it fails to recognize the relative nature of "needs." The poor will not be satisfied with a given level of living year after year when the levels of those around them are going up at the rate of about 3 percent per year. Old-timers may harken back to the "good old days" when people were happy without electricity, flush toilets, automobiles, and television sets; but they must also realize that once it becomes possible for all to have these "luxuries," they will be demanded and will quickly assume the status of "needs."[11]

Or, in the words of an Economic Report to the President:

> As average incomes rise, society amends its assessment of basic needs. Individuals who cannot afford more than a

---

[11]Miller, *op cit.*, p. 120.

small fraction of the items enjoyed by the majority are likely to feel deprived. Consequently, an absolute standard that seems appropriate today will inevitably be rejected tommorrow, just as we now reject poverty definitions appropriate a century ago.[12]

The approach to poverty just presented, as an alternative to the *fixed absolute income approach*, may be labeled the *variable relative income approach*. That is, according to it, the subsistence needs, which provide the standards for demarcating the poor from the non-poor, are relative to time and place; consequently, the poverty income line will vary in accordance with time and place. Unlike the fixed absolute income approach the variable relative income approach, when applied to a growing capitalist economy does not support the meliorist view, that the incidence of poverty is sustainedly going down as per capita income is sustainedly going up. On the contrary, insofar as it has been well established, by critics of American capitalism, that there has been in the long run no decrease in the extent of economic inequality in America (or other capitalist countries), then the variable relative income approach warrants the anti-meliorist conclusion that there has been, in the long run, no significant decreases in the incidence of poverty in America or other capitalist countries. Obviously, this is because, for the most plausible version of the variable income approach, there is a direct correlation between the extent of poverty in a given society and the extent of inequality in that society; that is, a direct correlation between the incidence of poverty and the proportion of persons making less than some appropriate average income. This is why radical critics of the way in which America has coped with the problem of poverty tend to speak interchangeably of poverty and inequality. Mermelstein exhibits this most explicitly:

Ultimately, poverty is a condition of life, the real meaning of which is socially defined—*when there are no rich, there*

---

[12]Miller and Roby, *op cit.*, p. 42.

can be no poor. By setting limits which allow poor persons to purchase television sets, officialdom believes that it has made due allowances for this social content of poverty. This is not so. It merely creates an upward adjustment to the boundary line of poverty. In a relatively rich society as the United States, poverty is as much psychological as it is physical, in the sense that an individual evaluates his life by contrasting it with others in that society. *Therefore, poverty will persist indefinitely as long as income and wealth remain sharply unequal.* Changes must take place in these distributions of income and wealth if poverty is to be eradicated. [13]

Suppose for example that it is agreed that any family is poor which receives less than half the median family income (as has been proposed by Victor Fuchs). So determined, the poverty line for families in America went up from $2100 in 1947 to $3400 in 1965. Nonetheless, the incidence of poverty among families went up from 18.9 percent in 1947 to 20 percent in 1965; hence, the warrant for anti-meliorism. [14]

V

For the moment, the confrontation between orthodox meliorist views and radical anti-meliorist view reduces to the confrontation between the fixed absolute income and the variable relative income approaches to poverty. Which of these is most defensible? First, we may ask, which of these coheres best with our intuitions? The surprising answer is neither coheres well with our intuitions, and each must be rejected on these grounds.

Consider first the fixed absolute income approach. It generates conclusions and predictions which are grossly in disagreement with our perceptions of the variations in the incidence of poverty from time to time, and from culture to culture. For example within the framework of an indus-

---

[13]Mermelstein, *op cit.,* p. 270.
[14]Miller and Roby, *op cit.,* p. 36.

trial growth economy, any fixed income measure, developed in the year Y to apply to the year Y, will tend to overestimate the numbers of the poor when it is applied to years following Y. The half-century work of the British sociologist, B. S. Rowntree, nicely illustrates this point. Rowntree made studies of the incidence of poverty in the city of York in the years 1899, 1936, and 1950. By appeal to a well-defined measure, he concluded in 1899 that 28 percent of the York population was poor. He came back in 1936, upgraded his measure, and found that 17 percent of the York population was poor. When he returned in 1950, he further upgraded his measure and again found that a sizable portion of the York population was poor. Had he used the 1899 measure in 1936, he would have found only 4 percent of the population to be poor. By applying the 1899 measure in 1950, he would have found virtually no poverty in York; with the 1936 measure he would have concluded that in 1950 only 2.7 percent of the York population was poor.[15] But, the claim that York had virtually no poverty in 1950, or that it had only a 4 percent poverty population in 1936, surely would have conflicted with the perceptions of anyone who had carefully observed the York scene in those years. On the other hand, had the 1950 poverty income measure been applied in 1899, it surely would have led to some unintuitive finding, for example that over 70 percent of the York population was poor. Another illustration: Franklin Roosevelt, in 1936, said that one third of the country was "ill-housed, ill-clad, ill-nourished." If he was right, then in 1936, the poverty income line was at $2,000 (in 1970 dollars). If the same measure had been used in 1970, then only 4.6 percent of the American population would have been construed poor.[16] The Roosevelt measure was liberal when used in his time; but it had to be upgraded in 1970 in order to be in harmony with the contemporary perceptions of poverty.

Similar difficulties confront a fixed income measure when applied to different regions or cultures. A fixed in-

---

[15]Oscar Oranti, *Poverty Amidst Affluence*, (New York, The Twentieth Century Fund, 1966), pp. 31–38.
[16]Schiller, *op cit.*, p. 7.

come measure of poverty formulated in some region R to apply to region R, will tend to overestimate the numbers of the poor when transposed to some region less developed economically than R, and will tend to underestimate the numbers of the poor when transposed to some region more developed than R.

So, it appears, no fixed income approach can cohere without perceptions of the variations of poverty over space and time. Unfortunately, no relative income approach will succeed in this respect either, although for opposite reasons. Consider, for example, the view that the poverty income line should be half the median income. This leads to patently absurd conclusions for societies that are both egalitarian and economically backward, as well as for societies which are both inegalitarian and highly affluent. To illustrate: Take a pre-industrial society whose median family income is $80 per year, and 1 percent of whose families earn less than the median income. As we note widespread malnutrition, disease, winter discomfort, and insecurity, we might rationally estimate that over half the population is poor. Still, the relative income criterion introduced above would sanction the odd conclusion that only 1 percent of the population is poor, and hence that poverty has been virtually eliminated in that society. Or, take a futuristic postindustrial society, whose median family income is $40,000 1970 dollars, and 20 percent of whose families receive an income between $16,000 and $20,000. These 20 percent may desperately want things which they cannot afford (e.g. yachts, palatial homes); they may be compulsively consumptive; but surely they are not poor. And yet the relative income criterion introduced above would sanction the conclusion that these 20 percent of the families are all poor. Here again the relative income approach clashes with our intuitions. Generally, to the extent that a society is egalitarian and indigent, to that extent do relative income approaches tend to underestimate the numbers of the poor; and to the extent that a society is affluent and inegalitarian, to that extent do they tend to overestimate the numbers of the poor. This is true particularly for any approach which looks to inequality for the criterion, or the major cause, or poverty.

VI

It follows that no fixed income approach and no relative income approach will work. This means that we must reject the fixed absolute income approach, presupposed by the SSA in its support of the meliorist thesis, as well as the variable relative income approach, presupposed generally by radicals in their critique of the meliorist thesis; it goes without saying that we should reject any fixed relative income approach, which no one in his or her right mind would subscribe to anyway. This leaves us with one alternative; the *variable absolute income* approach. According to it, the set of subsistence needs, which provides the standards for demarcating poverty from nonpoverty, is identical to the set of culturally invariant biological needs; yet, it allows that the real costs for satisfying these invariant biological needs will fluctuate considerably from society to society, and from economic stage to economic stage. Can such an approach be defended? And if so, can it help resolve the controversy between orthodox supporters of the meliorist thesis and their radical opponents? On both counts, I think it can. Indeed, not only does it cohere with our perceptions of the variations of poverty over space and time, but it explains why these perceptions are in fact correct. And, though in the abstract it is neutral on the controversy between meliorists and anti-meliorists, it does tend to support the radical critique of the meliorist thesis, once it is conjoined with fairly obvious claims concerning recent trends in advanced capitalism.

We can agree that subsistence needs, as biological needs, are culturally and temporally invariant. Nonetheless, we can still allow that the content of the market basket just sufficient for satisfying these invariant needs, and hence the real income just sufficient for avoiding poverty, will fluctuate quite dramatically from society to society, and time to time; we can even allow for the possibility that in some societies the minimal income necessary for satisfying these invariant needs will increase sustainedly as the economy grows. The reason for this is fairly obvious. Though invariantly present from culture to culture, subsistence needs can be satisfied in a number of varying

ways from culture to culture. Indeed, socio-economic systems can be differentiated in terms of the sorts of opportunities and means which they provide for the satisfaction
of biological needs, and in terms of the obstacles which
they put up. The means or instruments provided by one
socio-economic system for satisfying biological needs, may
be more costly to appropriate than those provided by
another, either because they are more complicated or inferior, or because they require more resources or are
otherwise more costly to produce, or because they satisfy a
whole variety of nonsubsistence needs at the same time
that they satisfy subsistence needs. Or, the obstacles to
the satisfaction of biological needs generated by one
socio-economic system may be more expensive to overcome than those generated by another. For these reasons,
the costs of staying out of poverty in one system may be
higher than in another; and so the poverty income line in
one system may be higher than that in another. Furthermore, it is possible that there are socio-economic systems which, as they grow economically, create increasingly more expensive instruments or means for satisfying
biological needs, and create increasingly more plentiful
and more expensive obstacles to the satisfaction of these
needs. In these systems, the costs of staying out of poverty, and hence the real poverty income line, will go up
sustainedly.

Now, within the framework of a variable absolute income approach, can it be argued persuasively, in defense of
an anti-meliorist position, that advanced capitalist
societies, and particularly America, tend continuously to
raise the costs of avoiding poverty as they grow economically; that is, can it be argued that modern capitalist
societies, and particularly America, tend as they grow
economically to create more costly instruments to appropriate and more costly obstacles to overcome, for the satisfaction of biological needs? I think it can. For it can be
maintained with some plausibility that modern capitalism
supports the following trends which add continuously to
the costs of staying out of poverty: (a) increasing urbanization, (b) growing city ghettoes, (c) the continued expansion
of the monopoly and oligopoly sectors, (d) the continued

expansion of the welfare state, (e) sustained technological growth, and (f) the maintenance of a constant level of economic inequality. Consider how each of these trends contributes to increasing costs for satisfying invariant biological needs.

INCREASING URBANIZATION.   Urban living adds to the obstacles to the satisfaction of biological needs. There are health hazards, such as garbage, human waste, pollution, and overcrowdirg; safety hazards, such as crime, fire, and heavy traffic; these require the provision of a variety of services and goods not required, or less required, in rural environments. Housing in the city can no longer be built just to keep out the elements; it must satisfy complex safety standards, sanitation standards, and security standards. Cities have no natural recreational environments and must institute them. And city living greatly increases the need for transportation.

GROWING CITY GHETTOES.   The ghetto presents added obstacles to the satisfaction of biological needs. Pollution and crime are worse; the population is more dense; stress is higher; the health hazards greater. The services provided to cope with these problems are uniformly worse. Transportation systems are out of line and jobs far away. Recreational facilities are more scarce. Foods and durables, provided mainly by small shops, are more expensive.

THE CONTINUED EXPANSION OF THE MONOPOLY AND OLIGOPOLY SECTORS.   Monopolization and oligopolization increase the real costs of commodities in three ways: through planned obsolescence, through increased advertising, and through intense attempts at product differentiation.

THE CONTINUED EXPANSION OF THE WELFARE STATE.   The emergence of the welfare state is supposed to have been a boon to the lower economic strata; actually it has added to the real costs of staying out of poverty. The new expenditures of the welfare state have been funded either by raising regressive taxes (such as sales and property taxes) or by adding "regressive" elements to the "progressive" income tax. Between 1962 and 1968, social security taxes went up 60 percent for the lowest income groups, sales taxes went up 30 percent and property taxes went up 48 percent. And the federal income tax since the New Deal has continued to enroach on lower real incomes. And a very large part of the tax-funded expenditures, e.g., for defense, for roads, for higher education, for research and development, are much more conducive to the interests of upper income strata than they are to the interests of lower income strata.[17]

UNCHANGING INEQUALITY IN A GROWING ECONOMY. The standards for production in inegalitarian capitalist market societies are set by the consumption habits of the more affluent. Capitalist systems, in determining which sorts of goods or services to produce for the satisfaction of biological needs, will tend to produce the sorts of goods or services preferred by the more affluent. They will stress the production of beef, to satisfy protein needs, of cars and airplanes, for the satisfaction of transportational needs, and of TV sets, for the satisfaction of recreational needs. But the goods or services preferred by the more affluent, for the satisfaction of biological needs, will tend to be more costly to produce and to appropriate than the alternatives, the car being more costly than mass transportation, beef more costly than nonmeat proteins, and TV more costly than informal neighborhood entertainment. In part, this is because the goods and services preferred by the more affluent, for satisfying biological needs, tend at the same time to provide many nonnecessary amenities; the automobile, for example, is not only for some an indispensable means of job transportation, but is also an instrument of escape, a source of thrills, a status symbol, and a hideway for teenage lovers. Thus, the more unequal a capitalist market society is, the more costly is the purchase of the means for satisfying biological needs. And, as the society grows econnomically, and its rich get

---

[17]Philip Stern, *The Rape of the Tax Payer*, (New York, Random House, 1973), pp. 24–25.

richer, in the absence of any reduction in income inequality, then the commodities meant for the satisfaction of biological needs, suited as they are for the tastes of the more affluent, will tend to become increasingly more costly to produce and to appropriate.

CONTINUED TECHNOLOGICAL GROWTH.   Technological growth, at least within capitalism, continually changes, and sometimes upgrades, the requirements for job training; it tends to transform lower-skilled jobs into meaningless, repetitive tasks; and it contributes to the spread of external diseconomies, such as pollution, urban blight, noise, and stress.

So, within the framework of a variable absolute income approach, one can argue quite plausibly for a radical anti-meliorist position in the following way:

> In advanced capitalist societies, there are sustained trend toward increasing urbanization, ghettoization, monopolization and oligopolization, welfarism, and technological growth, and no trend toward the reduction of income inequalities.

> But the costs of staying out of poverty (i.e., the costs of satisfying invariant subsistence needs) will grow as the economy grows, wherever there exists increasing urbanization, ghettoization, monopolization, welfarism, growing technology, and no improvement in the distribution of income.

> Therefore, in advanced capitalist societies, the costs of staying out of poverty (i.e., of satisfying invariant subsistence needs) grows as the economy grows. Consequently, there is no long term tendency in advanced capitalist societies for the incidence of poverty to decrease significantly as the economy grows.

VII

Now, to summarize. The purpose of this paper has been to analyze the meliorist thesis and the radical responses to it, and to provide the groundwork for a successful radical critique of it. The meliorist position was shown to presuppose a fixed absolute income approach to poverty, and the radical anti-meliorist position to be usually defended by appeal, explicitly or implicitly, to a variable relative income approach. On balance, however, neither of these two approaches is compatible with our perceptions concerning changes in the incidence of poverty over space and time; hence, neither can count as an adequate approach to poverty. The fixed absolute income approach fails because of its assumption that the costs of satisfying subsistence needs, and thus of avoiding poverty, remain fixed over time and place; consequently, it underestimates the incidence of poverty for relatively advanced socio-economic systems, and it overestimates it for relatively backward socio-economic systems. The variable relative income approach fails because of its assumption that subsistence needs fluctuate significantly over time and place; consequently, it overestimates the incidence of poverty for relatively advanced and inegalitarian socio-economic systems, and it underestimates it for relatively backward and egalitarian socio-economic systems.

The only approach compatible with our perceptions is the variable absolute income approach. It allows for the continued upgrading of the poverty line, in societies where the real costs for appropriating the instruments necessary for the satisfaction of subsistence needs, and for overcoming the obstacles to the satisfaction of these needs, are continuously on the increase. And it allows for the possibility of a high incidence of poverty in conjunction with much equality, and for a low incidence of poverty in conjunction with much inequality.

Unlike the other two approaches, the variable absolute income approach is, in the abstract, neutral on the controversy between meliorist defenders of modern capitalism and their radical critics. However, in conjunction with a number of very plausible factual claims concerning trends of various sorts in advanced capitalist societies, it does support the radical anti-meliorist position that the incidence of poverty is decreasing only marginally in advanced capitalist societies.

The disagreement between meliorists and their radical opponents have to date been primarily conceptual; the disagreement has been primarily over what is to count as a subsistence need. Supporters of the meliorist thesis allow the expression "subsistence needs" to stand only for biological needs, whereas radical critics allow it to stand for any historical need whose satisfaction is necessary to meet customary standards for a decent life. Unfortunately, as long as radicals continue to confront the meliorist thesis on conceptual grounds, they will continue to lose the argument; for as long as they refuse to conceive of subsistence needs exclusively as biological needs, they will run counter to our everyday intuitions concerning the variations in poverty over space and time. On the other hand, radicals will win the arguments if they confront the meliorist thesis on factual grounds. Meliorists go wrong, not because they misconstrue the nature of subsistence needs, but because they make the wrong (factual) assumptions concerning the variations in the costs for satisfying these needs over time and space.

This essay has shown then that we radicals can quite successfully criticize American capitalism for its failure to alleviate minimally the problems of poverty. However, insofar as we subscribe to the variable absolute income approach (rather than some relative approach), we will have to tone down our predilections toward historicism, and deemphasize the role we give to income inequality, in our investigations of poverty in capitalism. We will have to admit that there are sets of transhistorical needs against which the successes and failures of different social systems can be measured. And we will have to concede that income inequality is neither the criterion for measuring the extent of poverty nor the primary cause of poverty; it is just one of many factors having some influence on the extent of poverty.

Famine, Affluence, and Morality

Peter Singer

As I write this, in November 1971, people are dying in East
Bengal from lack of food, shelter, and medical care. The
suffering and death that are occurring there now are not
inevitable, not unavoidable in any fatalistic sense of the
term. Constant poverty, a cyclone, and a civil war have
turned at least nine million people into destitute refugees;
nevertheless, it is not beyond the capacity of the richer
nations to give enough assistance to reduce any further
suffering to very small proportions. The decisions and actions of human beings can prevent this kind of suffering.
Unfortunately, human beings have not made the necessary
decisions. At the individual level, people have, with very
few exceptions, not responded to the situation in any significant way. Generally speaking, people have not given
large sums to relief funds; they have not written to their
parliamentary representatives demanding increased government assistance; they have not demonstrated in the
streets, held symbolic fasts, or done anything else directed
toward providing the refugees with the means to satisfy
their essential needs. At the government level, no government has given the sort of massive aid that would enable
the refugees to survive for more than a few days. Britain, for instance, has given rather more than most coun-

tries. It has, to date, given £14,750,000. For comparative
purposes, Britain's share of the nonrecoverable development costs of the Anglo-French Concorde project is already in excess of £275,000,000, and on present estimates
will reach £440,000,000. The implication is that the
British government values a supersonic transport more
than thirty times as highly as it values the lives of the
nine million refugees. Australia is another country which,
on a per capita basis, is well up in the "aid to Bengal"
table. Australia's aid, however, amounts to less than one-
twelfth of the cost of Sydney's new opera house. The total
amount given, from all sources, now stands at about
£65,000,000. The estimated cost of keeping the refugees
alive for one year is £464,000,000. Most of the refugees
have now been in the camps for more than six months.
The World Bank has said that India needs a minimum of
£300,000,000 in assistance from other countries before the
end of the year. It seems obvious that assistance on this
scale will not be forthcoming. India will be forced to
choose between letting the refugees starve or diverting
funds from her own development program, which will
mean that more of her own people will starve in the future.[1]

These are the essential facts about the present situation
in Bengal. So far as it concerns us here, there is nothing
unique about this situation except its magnitude. The Bengal emergency is just the latest and most acute of a series
of major emergencies in various parts of the world, arising
both from natural and from man-made causes. There are
also many parts of the world in which people die from
malnutrition and lack of food independent of any special
emergency. I take Bengal as my example only because it is
the present concern, and because the size of the problem
has ensured that it has been given adequate publicity.
Neither individuals nor governments can claim to be unaware of what is happening there.

---

[1]There was also a third possibility: that India would go to war to enable the
refugees to return to their lands. Since I wrote this paper, India has taken this
way out. The situation is no longer that described above, but this does not affect
my argument, as the next paragraph indicates.

What are the moral implications of a situation like this? In what follows, I shall argue that the way people in relatively affluent countries react to a situation like that in Bengal cannot be justified; indeed, the whole way we look at moral issues—our moral conceptual scheme—needs to be altered, and with it, the way of life that has come to be taken for granted in our society.

In arguing for this conclusion I will not, of course, claim to be morally neutral. I shall, however, try to argue for the moral position that I take, so that anyone who accepts certain assumptions, to be made explicit, will, I hope, accept my conclusion.

I begin with the assumption that suffering and death from lack of food, shelter, and medical care are bad. I think most people will agree about this, although one may reach the same view by different routes. I shall not argue for this view. People can hold all sorts of eccentric positions, and perhaps from some of them it would not follow that death by starvation is in itself bad. It is difficult, perhaps impossible, to refute such positions, and so for brevity I will henceforth take this assumption as accepted. Those who disagree need read no further.

My next point is this: if it is in our power to prevent something bad from happening, without thereby sacrificing anything of comparable moral importance, we ought, morally, to do it. By "without sacrificing anything of comparable moral importance" I mean without causing anything else comparably bad to happen, or doing something that is wrong in itself, or failing to promote some moral good, comparable in significance to the bad thing that we can prevent. This principle seems almost as uncontroversial as the last one. It requires us only to prevent what is bad, and not to promote what is good, and it requires this of us only when we can do it without sacrificing anything that is, from the moral point of view, comparably important. I could even, as far as the application of my argument to the Bengal emergency is concerned, qualify the point so as to make it: if it is in our power to prevent something very bad from happening, without thereby sacrificing anything morally significant, we ought, morally, to do it. An application of this principle would be as follows: if I am walking past a shallow pond and see a child drowning in it, I ought to wade in and pull the child out. This will mean getting my clothes muddy, but this is insignificant, while the death of the child would presumably be a very bad thing.

The uncontroversial appearance of the principle just stated is deceptive. If it were acted upon, even in its qualified form, our lives, our society, and our world would be fundamentally changed. For the principle takes, firstly, no account of proximity or distance. It makes no moral difference whether the person I can help is a neighbor's child ten yards from me or a Bengali whose name I shall never know, ten thousand miles away. Secondly, the principle makes no distinction between cases in which I am the only person who could possibly do anything and cases in which I am just one among millions in the same position.

I do not think I need to say much in defense of the refusal to take proximity and distance into account. The fact that a person is physically near to us, so that we have personal contact with him, may make it more likely that we *shall* assist him, but this does not show that we *ought* to help him rather than another who happens to be further away. If we accept any principle of impartiality, universalizability, equality, or whatever, we cannot discriminate against someone merely because he is far away from us (or we are far away from him). Admittedly, it is possible that we are in a better position to judge what needs to be done to help a person near to us than one far away, and perhaps also to provide the assistance we judge to be necessary. If this were the case, it would be a reason for helping those near to us first. This may once have been a justification for being more concerned with the poor in one's own town than with famine victims in India. Unfortunately for those who like to keep their moral responsibilities limited, instant communication and swift transportation have changed the situation. From the moral point of view, the development of the world into a "global village" has made an important, though still unrecognized, difference to our moral situation. Expert observers and supervisors, sent out by famine relief organizations or permanently stationed in famine-prone areas, can direct our aid to a refugee in Bengal almost as effectively as we could get it to someone in our own block. There would seem, therefore, to be no possible justification for discriminating on geographical grounds.

There may be a greater need to defend the second implication of my principle—that the fact that there are millions of other people in the same position, in respect to the Bengali refugees, as I am, does not make the situation significantly different from a situation in which I am the only person who can prevent something very bad from occurring. Again, of course, I admit that there is a psychological difference between the cases; one feels less guilty about doing nothing if one can point to others, similarly placed, who have also done nothing. Yet this can make no real difference to our moral obligations.[2] Should I consider that I am less obliged to pull the drowning child out of the pond if on looking around I see other people, no further away than I am, who have also noticed the child but are doing nothing? One has only to ask this question to see the absurdity of the view that numbers lessen obligation. It is a view that is an ideal excuse for inactivity; unfortunately most of the major evils—poverty, overpopulation, pollution—are problems in which everyone is almost equally involved.

The view that numbers do make a difference can be made plausible if stated in this way: if everyone in circumstances like mine gave £5 to the Bengal Relief Fund, there would be enough to provide food, shelter, and medical care for the refugees; there is no reason why I should give more than anyone else in the same circumstances as I am; therefore I have no obligation to give more than £5. Each premise in this argument is true, and the argument

---

[2] In view of the special sense philosophers often give to the term, I should say that I use "obligation" simply as the abstract noun derived from "ought," so that "I have an obligation to" means no more, and no less, than "I ought to." This usage is in accordance with the definition of "ought" given by the *Shorter Oxford English Dictionary*: "the general verb to express duty or obligation." I do not think any issue of substance hangs on the way the term is used; sentences in which I use "obligation" could all be rewritten, although somewhat clumsily, as sentences in which a clause containing "ought" replaces the term "obligation."

looks sound. It may convince us, unless we notice that it
is based on a hypothetical premise, although the conclusion is not stated hypothetically. The argument would be
sound if the conclusion were: if everyone in circumstances
like mine were to give £5, I would have no obligation to
give more than £5. If the conclusion were so stated, however, it would be obvious that the argument has no bearing
on a situation in which it is not the case that everyone
else gives £5. This, of course, is the actual situation. It is
more or less certain that not everyone in circumstances
like mine will give £5. So there will not be enough to provide the needed food, shelter, and medical care. Therefore
by giving more than £5 I will prevent more suffering than I
would if I gave just £5.

It might be thought that this argument has an absurd
consequence. Since the situation appears to be that very
few people are likely to give substantial amounts, it follows that I and everyone else in similar circumstances
ought to give as much as possible, that is, at least up to the
point at which by giving more one would begin to cause
serious suffering for oneself and one's dependents—perhaps even beyond this point to the point of marginal utility, at which by giving more one would cause oneself
and one's dependents as much suffering as one would prevent in Bengal. If everyone does this, however, there will
be more than can be used for the benefit of the refugees,
and some of the sacrifice will have been unnecessary.
Thus, if everyone does what he ought to do, the result will
not be as good as it would be if everyone did a little less
than he ought to do, or if only some do all that they ought
to do.

The paradox here arises only if we assume that the actions in question—sending money to the relief funds—are
performed more or less simultaneously, and are also unexpected. For if it is to be expected that everyone is going to
contribute something, then clearly each is not obliged to
give as much as he would have been obliged to had others
not been giving too. And if everyone is not acting more or
less simultaneously, then those giving later will know
how much more is needed, and will have no obligation to
give more than is necessary to reach this amount. To say

this is not to deny the principle that people in the same circumstances have the same obligations, but to point out that the fact that others have given, or may be expected to give, is a relevant circumstance: those giving after it has become known that many others are giving and those giving before are not in the same circumstances. So the seemingly absurd consequence of the principle I have put forward can occur only if people are in error about the actual circumstances—that is, if they think they are giving when others are not, but in fact they are giving when others are. The result of everyone doing what he really ought to do cannot be worse than the result of everyone doing less than he ought to do, although the result of everyone doing what he reasonably believes he ought to do could be.

If my argument so far has been sound, neither our distance from a preventable evil nor the number of other people who, in respect to that evil, are in the same situation as we are, lessens our obligation to mitigate or prevent that evil. I shall therefore take as established the principle I asserted earlier. As I have already said, I need to assert it only in its qualified form: if it is in our power to prevent something very bad from happening, without thereby sacrificing anything else morally significant, we ought, morally, to do it.

The outcome of this argument is that our traditional moral categories are upset. The traditional distinction between duty and charity cannot be drawn, or at least, not in the place we normally draw it. Giving money to the Bengal Relief Fund is regarded as an act of charity in our society. The bodies which collect money are known as "charities." These organizations see themselves in this way—if you send them a check, you will be thanked for your "generosity." Because giving money is regarded as an act of charity, it is not thought that there is anything wrong with not giving. The charitable man may be praised, but the man who is not charitable is not condemned. People do not feel in any way ashamed or guilty about spending money on new clothes or a new car instead of giving it to famine relief. (Indeed, the alternative does not occur to them.) This way of looking at the matter cannot be justified. When we buy new clothes not to keep ourselves warm but to look "well-dressed" we are not providing for any important need. We would not be sacrificing anything significant if we were to continue to wear our old clothes, and give the money to famine relief. By doing so, we would be preventing another person from starving. It follows from what I have said earlier that we ought to give money away, rather than spend it on clothes which we do not need to keep us warm. To do so is not charitable, or generous. Nor is it the kind of act which philosophers and theologians have called "supererogatory"—an act which it would be good to do, but not wrong not to do. On the contrary, we ought to give the money away, and it is wrong not to do so.

I am not maintaining that there are no acts which are charitable, or that there are no acts which it would be good to do but not wrong not to do. It may be possible to redraw the distinction between duty and charity in some other place. All I am arguing here is that the present way of drawing the distinction, which makes it an act of charity for a man living at the level of affluence which most people in the "developed nations" enjoy to give money to save someone else from starvation, cannot be supported. It is beyond the scope of my argument to consider whether the distinction should be redrawn or abolished altogether. There would be many other possible ways of drawing the distinction—for instance, one might decide that it is good to make other people as happy as possible but not wrong not to do so.

Despite the limited nature of the revision in our moral conceptual scheme which I am proposing, the revision would, given the extent of both affluence and famine in the world today, have radical implications. These implications may lead to further objections, distinct from those I have already considered. I shall discuss two of these.

One objection to the position I have taken might be simply that it is too drastic a revision of our moral scheme. People do not ordinarily judge in the way I have suggested they should. Most people reserve their moral condemnation for those who violate some moral norm, such as the norm against taking another person's property.

They do not condemn those who indulge in luxury instead of giving to famine relief. But given that I did not set out to present a morally neutral description of the way people make moral judgments, the way people do in fact judge has nothing to do with the validity of my conclusion. My conclusion follows from the principle which I advanced earlier, and unless that principle is rejected, or the arguments shown to be unsound, I think the conclusion must stand, however strange it appears.

It might, nevertheless, be interesting to consider why our society, and most other societies, do judge differently from the way I have suggested they should. In a well-known article, J. O. Urmson suggests that the imperatives of duty, which tell us what we must do, as distinct from what it would be good to do but not wrong not to do, function so as to prohibit behavior that is intolerable if men are to live together in society.[3] This may explain the origin and continued existence of the present division between acts of duty and acts of charity. Moral attitudes are shaped by the needs of society, and no doubt society needs people who will observe the rules that make social existence tolerable. From the point of view of a particular society, it is essential to prevent violations of norms against killing, stealing, and so on. It is quite inessential, however, to help people outside one's own society.

If this is an explanation of our common distinction between duty and supererogation, however, it is not a justification of it. The moral point of view requires us to look beyond the interests of our own society. Previously, as I have already mentioned, this may hardly have been feasible, but it is quite feasible now. From the moral point of view, the prevention of the starvation of millions of people outside our society must be considered at least as pressing as the upholding of property norms within our society.

It has been argued by some writers, among them Sidgwick and Urmson, that we need to have a basic moral

---

[3]J. O. Urmson, "Saints and Heroes," in *Essays in Moral Philosophy*, ed. Abraham I. Melden (Seattle and London, 1958), p. 214. For a related but significantly different view see also Henry Sidgwick, *The Methods of Ethics*, 7th edn. (London, 1907), pp. 220–221, 492–493.

code which is not too far beyond the capacities of the ordinary man, for otherwise there will be a general breakdown of compliance with the moral code. Crudely stated,
this argument suggests that if we tell people that they
ought to refrain from murder and give everything they do
not really need to famine relief, they will do neither,
whereas if we tell them that they ought to refrain from
murder and that it is good to give to famine relief but not
wrong not to do so, they will at least refrain from murder.
The issue here is: Where should we drawn the line between conduct that is required and conduct that is good
although not required, so as to get the best possible result?
This would seem to be an empirical question, although a
very difficult one. One objection to the Sidgwick-Urmson
line of argument is that it takes insufficient account of the
effect that moral standards can have on the decisions we
make. Given a society in which a wealthy man who gives
five percent of his income to famine-relief is regarded as
most generous, it is not surprising that a proposal that we
all ought to give away half our incomes will be thought to
be absurdly unrealistic. In a society which held that no
man should have more than enough while others have less
than they need, such a proposal might seem narrow-
minded. What it is possible for a man to do and what he is
likely to do are both, I think, very greatly influenced by
what people around him are doing and expecting him to
do. In any case, the possibility that by spreading the idea
that we ought to be doing very much more than we are to
relieve famine we shall bring about a general breakdown of
moral behavior seems remote. If the stakes are an end to
widespread starvation, it is worth the risk. Finally, it
should be emphasized that these considerations are relevant only to the issue of what we should require from
others, and not to what we ourselves ought to do.

The second objection to my attack on the present distinction between duty and charity is one which has from
time to time been made against utilitarianism. It follows
from some forms of utilitarian theory that we all ought,
morally, to be working full time to increase the balance of
happiness over misery. The position I have taken here
would not lead to this conclusion in all circumstances, for

if there were no bad occurrences that we could prevent without sacrificing something of comparable moral importance, my argument would have no application. Given the present conditions in many parts of the world, however, it does follow from my argument that we ought, morally, to be working full time to relieve great suffering of the sort that occurs as a result of famine or other disasters. Of course, mitigating circumstances can be adduced—for instance, that if we wear ourselves out through overwork, we shall be less effective than we would otherwise have been. Nevertheless, when all considerations of this sort have been taken into account, the conclusion remains: we ought to be preventing as much suffering as we can without sacrificing something else of comparable moral importance. This conclusion is one which we may be reluctant to face. I cannot see, though, why it should be regarded as a criticism of the position for which I have argued, rather than a criticism of our ordinary standards of behavior. Since most people are self-interested to some degree, very few of us are likely to do everything that we ought to do. It would, however, hardly be honest to take this as evidence that it is not the case that we ought to do it.

It may still be thought that my conclusions are so wildly out of line with what everyone else thinks and has always thought that there must be something wrong with the argument somewhere. In order to show that my conclusions, while certainly contrary to contemporary Western moral standards, would not have seemed so extraordinary at other times and in other places, I would like to quote a passage from a writer not normally thought of as a way-out radical, Thomas Aquinas.

Now, according to the natural order instituted by divine providence, material goods are provided for the satisfaction of human needs. Therefore the division and appropriation of property, which proceeds from human law, must not hinder the satisfaction of man's necessity from such goods. Equally, whatever a man has in superabundance is owed, of natural right, to the poor for their sustenance. So Ambrosius says, and it is also to be found in the *Decretum Gratiani*: "The bread which you withhold belongs to the hungry; the clothing you shut away, to the naked; and the money you bury in the earth is the redemption and freedom of the penniless."[4]

I now want to consider a number of points, more practical than philosophical, which are relevant to the application of the moral conclusion we have reached. These points challenge not the idea that we ought to be doing all we can to prevent starvation, but the idea that giving away a great deal of money is the best means to this end.

It is sometimes said that overseas aid should be a government responsibility, and that therefore one ought not to give to privately run charities. Giving privately, it is said, allows the government and the noncontributing members of society to escape their responsibilities.

This argument seems to assume that the more people there are who give to privately organized famine relief funds, the less likely it is that the government will take over full responsibility for such aid. This assumption is unsupported, and does not strike me as at all plausible. The opposite view—that if no one gives voluntarily, a government will assume that its citizens are uninterested in famine relief and would not wish to be forced into giving aid—seems more plausible. In any case, unless there were a definite probability that by refusing to give one would be helping to bring about massive government assistance, people who do refuse to make voluntary contributions are refusing to prevent a certain amount of suffering without being able to point to any tangible beneficial consequence of their refusal. So the onus of showing how their refusal will bring about government action is on those who refuse to give.

I do not, of course, want to dispute the contention that governments of affluent nations should be giving many times the amount of genuine, no-strings-attached aid that they are giving now. I agree, too, that giving privately is not enough, and that we ought to be campaigning actively

[4]*Summa Theologica*, II–II, Question 66, Article 7, in *Aquinas, Selected Political Writings*, ed. A. P. d'Entreves, trans. J. G. Dawson (Oxford, 1948), p. 171.

for entirely new standards for both public and private contributions to famine relief. Indeed, I would sympathize with someone who thought that campaigning was more important than giving oneself, although I doubt whether preaching what one does not practice would be very effective. Unfortunately, for many people the idea that "it's the government's responsibility" is a reason for not giving which does not appear to entail any political action either.

Another, more serious reason for not giving to famine relief funds is that until there is effective population control, relieving famine merely postpones starvation. If we save the Bengal refugees now, others, perhaps the children of these refugees, will face starvation in a few years' time. In support of this, one may cite the now well-known facts about the population explosion and the relatively limited scope for expanded production.

This point, like the previous one, is an argument against relieving suffering that is happening now, because of a belief about what might happen in the future; it is unlike the previous point in that very good evidence can be adduced in support of this belief about the future. I will not go into the evidence here. I accept that the earth cannot support indefinitely a population rising at the present rate. This certainly poses a problem for anyone who thinks it important to prevent famine. Again, however, one could accept the argument without drawing the conclusion that it absolves one from any obligation to do anything to prevent famine. The conclusion that should be drawn is that the best means of preventing famine, in the long run, is population control. It would then follow from the position reached earlier that one ought to be doing all one can to promote population control (unless one held that all forms of population control were wrong in themselves, or would have significantly bad consequences). Since there are organizations working specifically for population control, one would then support them rather than more orthodox methods of preventing famine.

A third point raised by the conclusion reached earlier relates to the question of just how much we all ought to be giving away. One possibility, which has already been mentioned, is that we ought to give until we reach the level of marginal utility—that is, the level at which, by giving more, I would cause as much suffering to myself or my dependents as I would relieve by my gift. This would mean, of course, that one would reduce oneself to very near the material circumstances of a Bengali refugee. It will be recalled that earlier I put forward both a strong and a moderate version of the principle of preventing bad occurrences. The strong version, which required us to prevent bad things from happening unless in doing so we would be sacrificing something of comparable moral significance, does seem to require reducing ourselves to the level of marginal utility. I should also say that the strong version seems to me to be the correct one. I proposed the more moderate version—that we should prevent bad occurrences unless, to do so, we had to sacrifice something morally significant—only in order to show that even on this surely undeniable principle a great change in our way of life is required. On the more moderate principle, it may not follow that we ought to reduce ourselves to the level of marginal utility, for one might hold that to reduce oneself and one's family to this level is to cause something significantly bad to happen. Whether this is so I shall not discuss, since, as I have said, I can see no good reason for holding the moderate version of the principle rather than the strong version. Even if we accepted the principle only in its moderate form, however, it should be clear that we would have to give away enough to ensure that the consumer society, dependent as it is on people spending on trivia rather than giving to famine relief, would slow down and perhaps disappear entirely. There are several reasons why this would be desirable in itself. The value and necessity of economic growth are now being questioned not only by conservationists, but by economists as well.[5] There is no doubt, too, that the consumer society has had a distorting effect on the goals and purposes of its members. Yet looking at the matter purely from the point of view of overseas aid, there must be a limit to the extent to

---

[5]See, for instance, John Kenneth Galbraith, *The New Industrial State* (Boston, 1967); and E.J. Mishan, *The Costs of Economic Growth* (London, 1967).

which we should deliberately slow down our economy; for it might be the case that if we gave away, say, forty percent of our Gross National Product, we would slow down the economy so much that in absolute terms we would be giving less than if we gave twenty-five percent of the much larger GNP that we would have if we limited our contribution to this smaller percentage.

I mention this only as an indication of the sort of factor that one would have to take into account in working out an ideal. Since Western societies generally consider one percent of the GNP an acceptable level for overseas aid, the matter is entirely academic. Nor does it affect the question of how much an individual should give in a society in which very few are giving substantial amounts.

It is sometimes said, though less often now than it used to be, that philosophers have no special role to play in public affairs, since most public issues depend primarily on an assessment of facts. On questions of fact, it is said, philosophers as such have no special expertise, and so it has been possible to engage in philosophy without committing oneself to any position on major public issues. No doubt there are some issues of social policy and foreign policy about which it can truly be said that a really expert assessment of the facts is required before taking sides or acting, but the issue of famine is surely not one of these. The facts about the existence of suffering are beyond dispute. Nor, I think, is it disputed that we can do something about it, either through orthodox methods of famine relief or through population control or both. This is therefore an issue on which philosophers are competent to take a position. The issue is one which faces everyone who has more money than he needs to support himself and his dependents, or who is in a position to take some sort of political action. These categories must include practically every teacher and student of philosophy in the universities of the Western world. If philosophy is to deal with matters that are relevant to both teachers and students, this is an issue that philosophers should discuss.

Discussion, though, is not enough. What is the point of relating philosophy to public (and personal) affairs if we do not take our conclusions seriously? In this instance, taking our conclusion seriously means acting upon it. The philosopher will not find it any easier than anyone else to alter his attitudes and way of life to the extent that, if I am right, is involved in doing everything that we ought to be doing. At the very least, though, one can make a start. The philosopher who does so will have to sacrifice some of the benefits of the consumer society, but he can find compensation in the satisfaction of a way of life in which theory and practice, if not yet in harmony, are at least coming together.

Lifeboat Ethics: The Case Against Helping the Poor

Garrett Hardin

Environmentalists use the metaphor of the earth as a "spaceship" in trying to persuade countries, industries and people to stop wasting and polluting our natural resources. Since we all share life on this planet, they argue, no single person or institution has the right to destroy, waste, or use more than a fair share of its resources.

But does everyone on earth have an equal right to an equal share of its resources? The spaceship metaphor can be dangerous when used by misguided idealists to justify suicidal policies for sharing our resources through uncontrolled immigration and foreign aid. In their enthusiastic but unrealistic generosity, they confuse the ethics of a spaceship with those of a lifeboat.

A true spaceship would have to be under the control of a captain, since no ship could possibly survive if its course were determined by committee. Spaceship Earth certainly has no captain; the United Nations is merely a toothless tiger, with little power to enforce any policy upon its bickering members.

If we divide the world crudely into rich nations and poor nations, two thirds of them are desperately poor, and only one third comparatively rich, with the United States the

---

wealthiest of all. Metaphorically each rich nation can be seen as a lifeboat full of comparatively rich people. In the ocean outside each lifeboat swim the poor of the world, who would like to get in, or at least to share some of the wealth. What should the lifeboat passengers do?

First, we must recognize the limited capacity of any lifeboat. For example, a nation's land has a limited capacity to support a population and as the current energy crisis has shown us, in some ways we have already exceeded the carrying capacity of our land.

Adrift in a Moral Sea

So here we sit, say fifty people in our lifeboat. To be generous, let us assume it has room for ten more, making a total capacity of sixty. Suppose the fifty of us in the lifeboat see 100 others swimming in the water outside, begging for admission to our boat or for handouts. We have several options: we may be tempted to live by the Christian ideal of being "our brother's keeper," or by the Marxist ideal of "to each according to his needs." Since the needs of all in the water are the same, and since they can all be seen as "our brothers," we could take them all into our boat, making a total of 150 in a boat designed for sixty. The boat swamps, everyone drowns. Complete justice, complete catastrophe.

Since the boat has an unused excess capacity of ten more passengers, we could admit just ten more to it. But which ten do we let in? How do we choose? Do we pick the best ten, the neediest ten, "first come, first served"? And what do we say to the ninety we exclude? If we do let an extra ten into our lifeboat, we will have lost our "safety factor," an engineering principle of critical importance. For example, if we don't leave room for excess capacity as a safety factor in our country's agriculture, a new plant disease or a bad change in the weather could have disastrous consequences.

Suppose we decide to preserve our small safety factor and admit no more to the lifeboat. Our survival is then possible, although we shall have to be constantly on guard against boarding parties.

While this last solution clearly offers the only means of our survival, it is morally abhorrent to many people. Some say they feel guilty about their good luck. My reply is simple: "Get out and yield your place to others." This may solve the problem of the guilt-ridden person's conscience, but it does not change the ethics of the life-boat. The needy person to whom the guilt-ridden person yields his place will not himself feel guilty about his good luck. If he did, he would not climb aboard. The net result of conscience-stricken people giving up their unjustly held seats is the elimination of that sort of conscience from the lifeboat.

This is the basic metaphor within which we must work out our solutions. Let us now enrich the image, step by step, with substantive additions from the real world, a world that must solve real and pressing problems of over-population and hunger.

The harsh ethics of the lifeboat become even harsher when we consider the reproductive differences between the rich nations and the poor nations. The people inside the lifeboats are doubling in numbers every eighty-seven years; those swimming around outside are doubling, on the average, every thirty-five years, more than twice as fast as the rich. And since the world's resources are dwindling, the difference in prosperity between the rich and the poor can only increase.

As of 1973, the U.S. had a population of 210 million people, who were increasing by 0.8 percent per year. Outside our lifeboat, let us imagine another 210 million people, (say the combined populations of Colombia, Ecuador, Venezuela, Morocco, Pakistan, Thailand and the Philippines) who are increasing at a rate of 3.3 percent per year. Put differently, the doubling time for this aggregate population is twenty-one years, compared to eighty-seven years for the U.S.

Multiplying the Rich and the Poor

Now suppose the U.S. agreed to pool its resources with those seven countries, with everyone receiving an equal share. Initially the ratio of Americans to non-Americans in this model would be one-to-one. But consider what the ratio would be after eighty-seven years, by which time the Americans would have doubled to a population of 420 million. By then, doubling every twenty-one years, the other group would have swollen to 354 billion. Each American would have to share the available resources with more than eight people.

But, one could argue, this discussion assumes that current population trends will continue, and they may not. Quite so. Most likely the rate of population increase will decline much faster in the U.S. than it will in the other countries, and there does not seem to be much we can do about it. In sharing with "each according to his needs," we must recognize that needs are determined by population size, which is determined by the rate of reproduction, which at present is regarded as a sovereign right of every nation, poor or not. This being so, the philanthropic load created by the sharing ethic of the spaceship can only increase.

The Tragedy of the Commons

The fundamental error of spaceship ethics, and the sharing it requires, is that it leads to what I call "the tragedy of the commons." Under a system of private property, the men who own property recognize their responsibility to care for it, for if they don't they will eventually suffer. A farmer, for instance, will allow no more cattle in a pasture than its carrying capacity justifies. If he overloads it, erosion sets in, weeds take over, and he loses the use of the pasture.

If a pasture becomes a commons open to all, the right of each to use it may not be matched by a corresponding responsibility to protect it. Asking everyone to use it with discretion will hardly do, for the considerate herdsman who refrains from overloading the commons suffers more than a selfish one who says his needs are greater. If everyone would restrain himself, all would be well; but it takes only one less than everyone to ruin a system of voluntary restraint. In a crowded world of less than perfect human beings, mutual ruin is inevitable if there are no controls. This is the tragedy of the commons.

One of the major tasks of education today should be the

creation of such an acute awareness of the dangers of the commons that people will recognize its many varieties. For example, the air and water have become polluted because they are treated as commons. Further growth in the population or per capita conversion of natural resources into pollutants will only make the problem worse. The same holds true for the fish of the oceans. Fishing fleets have nearly disappeared in many parts of the world, technological improvements in the art of fishing are hastening the day of complete ruin. Only the replacement of the system of the commons with a responsible system of control will save the land, air, water and oceanic fisheries.

The World Food Bank

In recent years there has been a push to create a new commons called a World Food Bank, an international depository of food reserves to which nations would contribute according to their abilities and from which they would draw according to their needs. This humanitarian proposal has received support from many liberal international groups, and from such prominent citizens as Margaret Mead, U.N. Secretary General Kurt Waldheim, and Senators Edward Kennedy and George McGovern.

A world food bank appeals powerfully to our humanitarian impulses. But before we rush ahead with such a plan, let us recognize where the greatest political push comes from, lest we be disillusioned later. Our experience with the "Food for Peace program," or Public Law 480, gives us the answer. This program moved billions of dollars worth of U.S. surplus grain to food-short, population-long countries during the past two decades. But when P.L. 480 first became law, a headline in the business magazine *Forbes* revealed the real power behind it: "Feeding the World's Hungry Millions: How It Will Mean Billions for U.S. Business."

And indeed it did. In the years 1960 to 1970, U.S. taxpayers spent a total of $7.9 billion on the Food for Peace program. Between 1948 and 1970, they also paid an additional $50 billion for other economic-aid programs, some of which went for food and food-producing machinery and technology. Though all U.S. taxpayers were forced to contribute to the cost of P.L. 480, certain special interest groups gained handsomely under the program. Farmers did not have to contribute the grain; the Government, or rather the taxpayers, bought it from them at full market prices. The increased demand raised prices of farm products generally. The manufacturers of farm machinery, fertilizers and pesticides benefited by the farmers' extra efforts to grow more food. Grain elevators profited from storing the surplus until it could be shipped. Railroads made money hauling it to ports, and shipping lines profited from carrying it overseas. The implementation of P.L. 480 required the creation of a vast Government bureaucracy, which then acquired its own vested interest in continuing the program regardless of its merits.

Extracting Dollars

Those who proposed and defended the Food for Peace program in public rarely mentioned its importance to any of these special interests. The public emphasis was always on its humanitarian effects. The combination of silent selfish interests and highly humanitarian apologists made a powerful and successful lobby for extracting money from taxpayers. We can expect the same lobby to push now for the creation of a World Food Bank.

However great the potential benefit to selfish interests, it should not be a decisive argument against a truly humanitarian program. We must ask if such a program would actually do more good than harm, not only momentarily but also in the long run. Those who propose the food bank usually refer to a current "emergency" or "crisis" in terms of world food supply. But what is an emergency? Although they may be infrequent and sudden, everyone knows that emergencies will occur from time to time. A well-run family, company, organization or country prepares for the likelihood of accidents and emergencies. It expects them, it budgets for them, it saves for them.

Learning the Hard Way

What happens if some organizations or countries budget for accidents and others do not? If each country is solely responsible for its own well-being, poorly managed ones will suffer. But they can learn from experience. They may mend their ways, and learn to budget for infrequent but certain emergencies. For example, the weather varies from year to year, and periodic crop failures are certain. A wise and competent government saves out of the production of the good years in anticipation of bad years to come. Joseph taught this policy to Pharaoh in Egypt more than 2,000 years ago. Yet the great majority of the governments in the world today do not follow such a policy. They lack either the wisdom or the competence, or both. Should those nations that do manage to put something aside be forced to come to the rescue each time an emergency occurs among the poor nations?

"But it isn't their fault!" Some kindhearted liberals argue. "How can we blame the poor people who are caught in an emergency? Why must they suffer for the sins of their governments?" The concept of blame is simply not relevant here. The real question is, what are the operational consequences of establishing a world food bank? If it is open to every country every time a need develops, slovenly rulers will not be motivated to take Joseph's advice. Someone will always come to their aid. Some countries will deposit food in the world food bank, and others will withdraw it. There will be almost no overlap. As a result of such solutions to food shortage emergencies, the poor countries will not learn to mend their ways, and will suffer progressively greater emergencies as their populations grow.

Population Control the Crude Way

On the average, poor countries undergo a 2.5 percent increase in population each year; rich countries, about 0.8 percent. Only rich countries have anything in the way of food reserves set aside, and even they do not have as much as they should. Poor countries have none. If poor countries received no food from the outside, the rate of their population growth would be periodically checked by crop failures and famines. But if they can always draw on a world food bank in time of need, their population can continue to grow unchecked, and so will their "need" for aid. In the short run, a world food bank may diminish that need, but in the long run it actually increases the need without limit.

Without some system of worldwide food sharing, the proportion of people in the rich and poor nations might eventually stabilize. The over-populated poor countries would decrease in numbers, while the rich countries that had room for more people would increase. But with a well-meaning system of sharing, such as a world food bank, the growth differential between the rich and the poor countries will not only persist, it will increase. Because of the higher rate of population growth in the poor countries of the world, 88 percent of today's children are born poor, and only 12 percent rich. Year by year the ratio becomes worse, as the fast reproducing poor outnumber the slow-reproducing rich.

A world food bank is thus a commons in disguise. People will have more motivation to draw from it than to add to any common store. The less provident and less able will multiply at the expense of the abler and more provident, bringing eventual ruin upon all who share in the commons. Besides, any system of "sharing" that amounts to foreign aid from the rich nations to the poor nations will carry the taint of charity, which will contribute little to the world peace so devoutly desired by those who support the idea of a world food bank.

As past U.S. foreign-aid programs have amply and depressingly demonstrated, international charity frequently inspires mistrust and antagonism rather than gratitude on the part of the recipient nation.

Chinese Fish and Miracle Rice

The modern approach to foreign aid stresses the export of technology and advice, rather than money and food. As an ancient Chinese proverb goes: "Give a man a fish and he will eat for a day; teach him how to fish and he will eat for the rest of his days." Acting on this advice, the Rockefeller and Ford Foundations have financed a number of programs for improving agriculture in the hungry nations. Known as the "Green Revolution," these programs have led to the development of "miracle rice" and "miracle wheat," new strains that offer bigger harvests and greater resistance to crop damage. Norman Borlaug, the Nobel Prize winning agronomist who, supported by the Rockefeller Foundation, developed "miracle wheat," is one of the most prominent advocates of a world food bank.

Whether or not the Green Revolution can increase food production as much as its champions claim is a debatable but possibly irrelevant point. Those who support this well-intended humanitarian effort should first consider some of the fundamentals of human ecology. Ironically, one man who did was the late Alan Gregg, a vice president of the Rockefeller Foundation. Two decades ago he expressed strong doubts about the wisdom of such attempts to increase food production. He likened the growth and spread of humanity over the surface of the earth to the spread of cancer in the human body, remarking that "cancerous growths demand food; but, as far as I know, they have never been cured by getting it."

Overloading the Environment

Every human born constitutes a draft on all aspects of the environment: food, air, water, forests, beaches, wildlife, scenery and solitude. Food can, perhaps, be significantly increased to meet a growing demand. But what about clean beaches, unspoiled forests, and solitude? If we satisfy a growing population's need for food, we necessarily decrease its per capita supply of the other resources needed by men.

India, for example, now has a population of 600 million, which increases by 15 million each year. This population already puts a huge load on a relatively impoverished environment. The country's forests are now only a small fraction of what they were three centuries ago, and floods and erosion continually destroy the insufficient farmland that remains. Every one of the 15 million new lives added to India's population puts an additional burden on the environment, and increases the economic and social costs of crowding. However humanitarian our intent, every Indian life saved through medical or nutritional assistance from abroad diminishes the quality of life for those who remain, and for subsequent generations. If rich countries make it possible, through foreign aid, for 600 million Indians to swell to 1.2 billion in a mere twenty-eight years, as their current growth rate threatens, will future generations of Indians thank us for hastening the destruction of their environment? Will our good intentions be sufficient excuse for the consequences of our actions?

My final example of a commons in action is one for which the public has the least desire for rational discussion—immigration. Anyone who publicly questions the wisdom of current U.S. immigration policy is promptly charged with bigotry, prejudice, ethnocentrism, chauvinism, isolationism or selfishness. Rather than encounter such accusations, one would rather talk about other matters, leaving immigration policy to wallow in the crosscurrents of special interests that take no account of the good of the whole, or the interests of posterity.

Perhaps we still feel guilty about things we said in the past. Two generations ago the popular press frequently referred to Dagos, Wops, Polacks, Chinks and Krauts, in articles about how America was being "overrun" by foreigners of supposedly inferior genetic stock. But because the implied inferiority of foreigners was used then as justification for keeping them out, people now assume that restrictive policies could only be based on such misguided notions. There are other grounds.

A Nation of Immigrants

Just consider the numbers involved. Our Government acknowledges a net inflow of 400,000 immigrants a year. While we have no hard data on the extent of illegal entries, educated guesses put the figure at about 600,000 a year. Since the natural increase (excess of births over deaths) of the resident population now runs about 1.7 million per year, the yearly gain from immigration amounts to at least 19 percent of the total annual increase, and may be as much as 37 percent if we include the estimate for illegal immigrants. Considering the growing use of birth control devices, the potential effect of educational campaigns by such organizations as Planned Parenthood Federation of America and Zero Population Growth, and the influence of inflation and the housing shortage, the fertility rate of Anerican women may decline so much that immigration could account for all the yearly increase in population. Should we not at least ask if that is what we want?

For the sake of those who worry about whether the "quality" of the average immigrant compares favorably with the quality of the average resident, let us assume that immigrants and nativeborn citizens are of exactly equal quality, however one defines that term. We will focus here only on quantity; and since our conclusions will depend on nothing else, all charges of bigotry and chauvinism become irrelevant.

Immigration Vs. Food Supply

World food banks *move food to the people,* hastening the exhaustion of the environment of the poor countries. Unrestricted immigration, on the other hand, *moves people to the food,* thus speeding up the destruction of the environment of the rich countries. We can easily understand why poor people should want to make this latter transfer, but why should rich hosts encourage it?

As in the case of foreign-aid programs, immigration receives support from selfish interests and humantarian impulses. The primary selfish interest in unimpeded immigration is the desire of employers for cheap labor, particularly in industries and trades that offer degrading work. In the past, one wave of foreigners after another was brought into the U.S. to work at wretched jobs for wretched wages. In recent years the Cubans, Puerto Ricans and Mexicans have had this dubious honor. The interests of the employers of cheap labor mesh well with the guilty silence of the country's liberal intelligentsia. White Anglo-Saxon Protestants are particularly reluctant to call for a closing of the doors to immigration for fear of being called bigots.

But not all countries have such reluctant leadership.

Most educated Hawaiians, for example, are keenly aware
of the limits of their environment, particularly in terms of
population growth. There is only so much room on the
islands, and the islanders know it. To Hawaiians, immigrants from the other forty-nine states present as great a
threat as those from other nations. At a recent meeting of
Hawaiian government officials in Honolulu, I had the
ironic delight of hearing a speaker, who like most of his
audience was of Japanese ancestry, ask how the country
might practically and constitutionally close its doors to
further immigration. One member of the audience countered: "How can we shut the doors now? We have many
friends and relatives in Japan we'd like to bring here some
day so that they can enjoy Hawaii too." The Japanese-
American speaker smiled sympathetically and answered:
"Yes, but we have children now, and someday we'll have
grandchildren too. We can bring people here from Japan
only by giving away some of the land that we hope to pass
on to our grandchildren some day. What right do we have
to do that?"

At this point, I can hear U.S. liberals asking: "How can
you justify slamming the door once you're inside? You say
that immigrants should be kept out. But aren't we all
immigrants, or the descendents of immigrants? If we insist
on staying, must we not admit all others?" Our craving for
intellectual order leads us to seek and prefer symmetrical
rules and morals: a single rule for me and everybody else;
the same rule yesterday, today, and tomorrow. Justice, we
feel, should not change with time and place.

We Americans of non-Indian ancestry can look upon
ourselves as the descendants of thieves who are guilty
morally, if not legally, of stealing this land from its Indian
owners. Should we then give back the land to the now living American descendants of those Indians? However
morally or logically sound this proposal may be, I, for one,
am unwilling to live by it and I know no one else who is.
Besides, the logical consequence would be absurd. Suppose
that, intoxicated with a sense of pure justice, we should
decide to turn our land over to the Indians. Since all our
wealth has also been derived from the land, wouldn't we
be morally obliged to give that back to the Indians too?

Pure Justice Vs. Reality

Clearly, the concept of pure justice produces an infinite regression to absurdity. Centuries ago, wise men invented statutes of limitations to justify the rejection of such pure justice, in the interest of preventing continual disorder. The law zealously defends property rights, but only relatively recent property rights. Drawing a line after an arbitrary time has elapsed may be unjust, but the alternatives are worse.

We are all the descendants of thieves, and the world's resources are inequitably distributed. But we must begin the journey to tomorrow from the point where we are today. We cannot remake the past. We cannot safely divide the wealth equitably among all peoples so long as people reproduce at different rates. To do so would guarantee that our grandchildren, and everyone else's grandchildren, would have only a ruined world to inhabit.

To be generous with one's own possessions is quite different from being generous with those of posterity. We should call this point to the attention of those who, from a commendable love of justice and equality, would institute a system of the commons, either in the form of a world food bank, or of unrestricted immigration. We must convince them if we wish to save at least some parts of the world from environmental ruin.

Without a true world government to control reproduction and the use of available resources, the sharing ethic of the spaceship is impossible. For the foreseeable future, our survival demands that we govern our actions by the ethics of a lifeboat, harsh though they may be. Posterity will be satisfied with nothing less.

Myths of the Food Crisis

Nick Eberstadt

How little we know about the world food problem is frightening. There are really no accurate figures on food production for any poor country; the margin of error in the estimate for India alone could feed or starve twelve million people. Nutritionists' estimates of the "average" daily adult protein requirement have ranged from 20 grams a day to over 120. Perhaps most astonishing, we do not know the world's population within 400 million people. In short, we do not know how much food there is, how much food people need, or even how many people there are.

If we wish to help the world's poor, a question which naturally arises is: whom should we listen to for our information and advice? The sad answer seems to be that almost all our sources are inaccurate and unreliable. Because of the dearth of information and the high stakes involved (literally, control over millions of lives), this field has produced a litter of instant experts, who demonstrate an aggressive arrogance in situations requiring humility and caution. Their "facts" are often half true, sometimes entirely false; their judgments tend to be sweeping, majestic, and impossible to stand by for more than a year.

Thus Lester Brown, a popular food guru who is frequently quoted in *Give Us This Day* ..., writes in 1971 that the Green Revolution of high-yielding seeds and in-

From *The New York Review of Books*, February 19, 1976. Reprinted by permission of the author.

creased agricultural inputs (pesticides, fertilizer, irrigation)
is "likely to be a greater force for change than any
technology or ideology ever introduced into the poor countries."[1] By 1973 Brown finds that the Green Revolution is
an "opportunity lost,"[2] too heavily dependent on high-
priced items, enriching rich farmers while impoverishing
poor ones. Similarly, other experts pronounce either that
we have vanquished hunger or are doomed to live in an age
of scarcity, depending on how the next six months of crops
look.

Almost invariably, the flashiest, most arrogant, and most
inaccurate of our various food informants teach and advise
the public. There is a reason for this, and it has to do with
the realities of big business and the nature of journalism.
Like steel or computers, news is an industry, and it must
subordinate the quality of its product to its promotion. A
million people starving is better business for the press
than a thousand people starving, but a billion people starving is best of all! Here the interests of the instant experts
and the press dovetail: the expert gives an outrageous
quote (last year one man predicted fifty million Indians
might starve in 1975) and gets his name promoted, the
press publishes a horror story and sells news. This is the
Catch-22 of food reporting: if you read prognostications,
they are probably not worth taking seriously for the very
reasons that got them into the papers.
     The misinformation network promoting the food crisis
is more than intellectually unpleasant. Because the net-
work "informs" the rich world, and the rich world so often
makes crucial decisions over lives in the poor world, news
about food can be an outright threat to many of the
world's poorest people. Bangladesh is a case in point. The
cameramen who photograph those living corpses for your
evening consumption work hard to evoke a nation of un-
recognizable monsters starving by the roadside. Unless

---

[1] Lester R. Brown, "The Social Impact of the Green Revolution," *International Conciliation*, 1971, quoted in Keith Griffin, *The Political Economy of Agrarian Change* (Harvard University Press, 1974.)
[2] Lester R. Brown, *In the Human Interest* (Norton, 1974).

you have been there, you would find it hard to imagine
that the people of Bangladesh are friendly and energetic,
and perhaps 95 percent of them eat enough to get by. Or
that Bangladesh has the richest cropland in the world, and
that a well-guided aid program could help turn it from a
famine center into one of the world's great breadbaskets.
To most people in America the situation must look hopeless and our involvement, therefore, pointless. If the situation is so bad, why shouldn't we cut off our food and
foreign aid to Bangladesh, and use it to save people who
aren't going to die anyhow? So *The New York Times* literally holds lives in its hands.

And how does it treat them? If *Give Us This Day . . .* is
any indication, clumsily. This series of *Times* articles on
famine, food production, and the 1974 Rome Food Conference, which have been slapped together into a book, is not
even one of the more objectionable books on the food
problem; nevertheless its analysis is shallow and its
statements frequently inaccurate. By comparing it with
one of the most sensitive and accurate publications on
food in recent years, an issue of *Science* magazine which
has just been turned into a book, we can perhaps see how
serious are the fallacies behind some of the food myths we
accept daily as fact.

Myths from 1972

Give Us This Day . . . has two spectacular conclusions
about the food crisis of June 1972–June 1973. First, a cooling trend in weather is causing crop failures. Besides making much of our northern cropland unusable, this meteoro-
logical aberration might destroy future crops in more tem-
perate zones by playing havoc with the winds and rains.
Second, the explosive price increases for food are proof
that we have entered an age of permanent food shortage,
in which demand will be inexorably driven ahead of supply by affluence in the rich world and population in the
poor. Luckily for all of us, who must eat, this analysis is
superficial and inaccurate.

It is true that we have been blessed by unusually mild
weather in the last twenty years, and that a well-known

meteorologist, Reid Bryson, has guessed the odds against its continuing another twenty to be about 10,000 to one. But as Louis Thompson points out in the *Science* collection, "weather variability is a much more important consideration in grain production than a cooling trend." Crop yields could actually be higher with slightly cooler weather; "it is when weather variability [is highest] that yields are lowest. Even if the weather does trend toward the coolness of a century ago, yields will not be significantly reduced unless weather becomes more variable."

There are, moreover, few signs that we are entering an age of permanent food scarcity. Quite the opposite: as food prices rose, so did investment and production, and prices then fell. All things considered, the world market exhibited surprisingly flexible and rapid response to a sudden stimulus.

There was a time, not so long ago, when the poor perished en masse if grain prices went wild. The world is different today: social conditions in the poor world and grain prices in the international marketplace seldom correlate; for the grain market is dominated by the rich world, which has the money to buy. During 1972 and 1973, corn, wheat, rice, and soybeans all more than doubled their 1971 prices; four new famines struck in 1972 (Philippines, Burundi, Nicaragua, Sudan), while fifteen had occurred in 1971.

Americans may have assumed famine was striking down the rest of the world during the "food shortage" because for the first time in twenty years *their* food prices were rising faster than their cost of living. But the immediate cause of the rise was a huge grain purchase not by the starving but by Russia, which had committed itself to raising meat consumption, and had fallen short of feedstocks. India never could have made this kind of purchase: it would have cost 3 percent of its gross national product, almost 25 percent of its annual government revenue. As Jean Mayer notes sadly in "Management of Famine Relief" in the *Science* collection, "There has been a serious famine somewhere practically every year since the end of World War II," and these tragedies are likely to recur in the future. But they are are also likely to have little bearing on the price we pay for bread and steak.

What did the "food shortage" of 1972–1973 prove? It showed how heartless administrators can become when humanitarianism is no longer to their advantage. Three years ago 50 percent of the American food shipped to the poor world was aid; last year the proportion was 15 percent.[3] During the 1960s we had been tryi quite literally, to *give* our surpluses away; for years Americahad been producing more food than it could get rid of. It saw its stockpiles as a liability which cost half a billion dollars a year to maintain.

What to America was a liability, however, was for the grain-buying nations (practically the rest of the world) protection against widespread hunger in the event of a disaster. In 1961 world grain reserves could feed the entire earth for ninety-five days. As America happily depleted its stockpiles, the figure fell steadily; in 1974 it was twenty-seven days. The grain market is volatile, poorly supervised, and thin (only about 20 percent of the world's wheat and 3 percent of its rice is sold internationally), and the thinner it gets, the more pronounced the dislocations when they hit. Unless concern for humanity, the profit motive, or some combination of the two moves America to build up its stockpiles, dislocations are likely to recur. It must be stressed, however, that these dislocations are caused by bureaucratic shortcomings and market imperfections, not by inexorable trends.

Malnutrition Myths

Every bureaucracy exaggerates to its advantage the size of the problems it must tackle, and the hunger relief organizations are no exception. In a field where not only basic information, such as caloric intake requirements, but also basic definitions, such as "undernutrition" or "chronic malnutrition," are highly conjectural, these organizations can bully their facts. Conceptually, malnutrition is a deviation from an ideal, and few things in this world are per-

---

[3]Emma Rothschild, "Food Politics," *Foreign Affairs*, January 1976.

fect. Remember that ad about 50 percent of all American housewives suffering from iron poor blood; if you wish to assume that anyone who does not receive daily a sufficient and proper balance of proteins, carbohydrates, fats, minerals, and vitamins is malnourished, you can say that almost everyone in the poor world and most in the rich world suffer from malnutrition.

This is roughly what the United Nation's Food and Agricultural Organization (FAO) did with its first World Food Survey in 1945, in which it "proved" that 60 percent of the planet, then estimated to be about 1.5 billion people, were inadequately nourished. To prove this, as Thomas Poleman points out in the *Science* collection, all they had to do was leave the typical 10 percent understatement of food supplies in the poor world uncorrected, and posit that the average human being needed 2,500 kilocalories of energy a day.[4] This is only 100 less than required for the U.S. Food and Nutrition Board's "reference man," a moderately active adult male weighing 70 kilograms (154 pounds).

More recently FAO has altered caloric intake requirement and food supply estimates to "prove" that a more conservative 10 percent of the world's population, about 400 million people (94 percent of them living in poor countries), are malnourished, although they add that "a less conservative definition of malnutrition might double this figure." Thus 400 million people has become the mag-

---

[4]Poleman demonstrates how difficult it is to interpret what scanty evidence does exist on malnutrition by using food figures from Sri Lanka. Between the lowest class (representing 43 percent of the survey population) and the next lowest (37 percent) a 10 gram protein and 200 kilocalorie energy gap existed, but diet compositions were identical.

"What does this mean? Because the FAO now (quite reasonably) reckons energy needs in South Asia average 1,900 kilocalories daily and protein adequacy to be a function of energy adequacy, it could mean either of two things. If the standard factor of 15 percent is applied to account for wastage between purchase and ingestion, the 200 kilocalorie gap could be interpreted as implying enforced reduced activity among the poor or actual physical deterioration (or both).

Alternatively, one might postulate caloric adequacy among the element of society which is too poor to waste anything, and which because of the high rate of unemployment in Sri Lanka leads a less active life and thus has lower energy needs. Thus you can have it either way: depending on your assumptions you can prove beyond a statistical doubt that 43 percent of the Ceylonese population suffer protein calorie malnutrition or none do."

ical answer to any question about how many hungry people live in the world. Again and again in this latter-day numerology that figure is faithfully recorded in the pages of *Give Us This Day* .... Occasionally, it is even improved upon: the Overseas Development Council, for example, places the number of people who "go hungry" for some part of the year at over one billion.

When these numbers are used to describe the extent of serious hunger, they overstate the problem by a whole order of magnitude. Malnutrition is a misleading term; it is like sickness. Its shades of severity range from vitamin deficiencies to chronic protein calorie malnutrition to the Gomez-3 variety, just as respiratory ailments range from sore throats to terminal tuberculosis. Few of us can say our health or diet is biologically optimal; many, on the other hand, can say it is biologically acceptable. Malnutrition is usefully defined in functional rather than aesthetic terms—as a state, say, in which a 1 percent increase in food consumption leads to more than a 1 percent increase in activity and energy. A body which is truly hungry devotes its energy to maintaining itself; it can "afford" practically no other activity. If it is given extra calories, it will resume normal physical activities at a rate higher than that of the increase in nutrition. But such a definition eliminates a great deal of what is defined as malnutrition in the world.

Whom does this leave? Most importantly, it leaves the chronically malnourished—those who are physically threatened by malnutrition. A World Health Organization estimate puts the number of severely malnourished children under five in the world at ten million. While all figures in the food field may be regarded with skepticism, WHO is a health organization, and need not inflate its hunger figures for its own good. If ten million infants are chronically malnourished, this would imply, in view of the ratio of children to adults in the poor world, a total population of about seventy million chronically malnourished people. This figure, however, would tend to be on the high side, for children under five need more protein and calories for their body weight than adults do—pound for pound, often up to 60 percent more. For seventy million people to be threatened with death through starvation in a world as rich as ours is so shocking and outrageous that it may tend to obscure the fact that this is less than 2 percent of the world's population—a lower proportion, in all likelihood, than ever before.

It is, moreover, a proportion which is small enough to be eliminated altogether. Here, however, is where the hunger relief lobby's rhetoric and inflated figures hurt its clients. Food relief and development projects for seventy million people, spread across perhaps ninety countries, are a manageable undertaking, and with some international cooperation could be attempted fairly easily. If on the other hand the number of starving were believed to be a billion the task might seem unmanageable or hopeless, and for the governments involved, politically dangerous to boot. Fear of social change among the ruling elites is no small consideration in attempts to eliminate hunger. During much of the Sahelian drought Chad's president actually *refused* food aid. A large proportion of his people were hungry, and hungry people, he knew, were inactive people, in no condition to rebel against a well-fed army.

Where do the desperately hungry live? The answer may seem surprising. Although millions do live in India, Pakistan, and Bangladesh, since a quarter of the poor world's population inhabit the subcontinent, many more proportionately live in some of the poor nations of the Caribbean, Latin America, Southeast Asia, and especially Africa. India may be the workhorse for famine metaphors, but the fact is that at least twenty-six nations—including Haiti, Colombia, North Vietnam, and Algeria—are estimated to have lower per capita protein consumption, and it is Zaire, not Bangladesh, whose inhabitants receive less protein than any other nation.

India, we often forget, is one of the world's great civilizations and great powers; for a state of 600 million simply to function at all it must have reached an impressive stage of political and economic development. Poor as it is, India has a highly sophisticated system of social services. As one Indian official quoted in *Give Us This Day . . .* explains it,

"For a person to starve in Calcutta, he would have to be in social isolation—either a crazy person, or an old and sick person who literally couldn't cry out for help." There are many nations, especially in Africa, which virtually lack social services altogether—where to live is to live in social isolation. It is here, far from newsmen's hotels and photographer's cameras, that people literally *do* die of hunger.

This is reflected in the death rates. Although India's states of health and nutrition horrify Westerners, and rightly, life expectancy there is about fifty-three years, higher than that of nineteenth-century European nobility. Life expectancy in Sahelian Africa, on the other hand, is under forty, and in some areas under thirty. Death rates for the Sahelian region as a whole are 50 percent higher than India's. In the last three years up to half a million people may have died quietly in remote corners of Ethiopia from such diseases as cholera that were exacerbated by famine. Yet we never heard from those places. They had no public health officers, reporters, or diplomats to represent them. India has the world's third largest population of scientists and college graduates, as well as the ninth largest industrial sector, fourth largest army, and sixth largest atomic force; the corruption, waste, and red tape of relief efforts notwithstanding, the Indian poor are immeasurably better off because the rest of the world hears about it when India is hit by famine, and sends food, at least part of which is not funnelled away from those who most need it.

With all the talk about starvation, it is seldom if ever mentioned how extremely difficult it is to die from it. People are not docile about dying; they fight to live, and man is an exceptionally rugged animal. He has always been able to survive conditions which quickly killed off other mammals. Conditions must be fantastically adverse for people to succumb to death from hunger. During the recent Sahelian famines tribes lived on practically nothing for seasons, and sometimes even years, before the death rates started going up. And when they went up, as Michael Latham explains in the *Science* collection, very few of the deaths were ostensibly caused by "starvation or malnutrition, but deaths from measles, respiratory infections, and other infectious diseases were ... very much above pre-famine levels."[5]

To say that one dies from starvation is to say that the body wards off tuberculosis, diptheria, small pox, dysentery, and whatever else while its defenses progressively break down; it is a very unlikely situation. This is why so few poor governments see death by starvation as a serious problem, and concentrate on medical relief rather than food. It may seem carping or even inhumane to point out that death by starvation is more of an emotional codeword than an actual condition, but one must realize that the casual mass exploitation of the concept by the *Times* and others has made us take starvation for granted. When someone is in danger of starving to death, he or she is facing conditions none of us in the rich world can understand or even imagine.

The Causes of Hunger

Do people starve because they must starve?

The plausible and widely accepted answer is, yes. A popular Malthusian syllogism explains why: people starve when there is too little food to go around; because of constant population expansion there is already too little food to go around, and there will be even less in the future; therefore, people must starve, and starve in ever greater numbers. What is most puzzling about this syllogism is that it stands undisputed when so many facts could upset it.

There is no logistical justification for hunger of any kind anywhere; enough food is produced each year to feed everyone on earth comfortably. The Japanese get by with less than 600 pounds of grain per person annually[6] (they

---

[5]It should be noted that hunger usually picks off children, not adults. Children need both more food and more special kinds of food, pound for pound, than adults, and when things get tough they are likely, pound for pound, to get less. They are often not strong enough or old enough to go out and feed themselves, and so instead they die: almost half the deaths in Central Africa are among children under five, and in Indonesia a one-year-old has worse odds of surviving another year than a sixty-one-year-old. With food, as with so many other things in life, those most desperately in need of your help cannot assault you for it; at best they can wheedle and beg.

[6]FAO, *Food Balance Sheets.*

are, in fact, among the best nourished people on earth), yet there is less food available per person in Japan than in the world as a whole. For 1974 somewhere between 590 and 720 pounds of foodgrain, depending on whose figures one believes (a reasonable middle estimate might be 650 pounds), were available for each person in the world, not including reserves. Put another way if 1.3 billion tons of grain are produced and one person could get by on 500 pounds, the world could feed—and feed well—5.2 billion people, 800 million more than the highest estimates for today's population.

The availability of food per person, moreover, is increasing, not declining. In 1972–1973, the year that supposedly signaled the beginning of a chronic world food shortage, the most reasonable estimate for grain production per person on earth was 632 pounds; yet in 1960, a year of supposed plenty, the comparable figure was under 600. At 500 pounds of grain per person the world in 1960 could have supported 300 million more people than the highest population estimates claimed existed; by 1973, despite the fact that world population had grown by almost a billion in the meantime, the new "margin of safety" was 600 million.

Why, then, *do* people starve?

Re-examine the Malthusian syllogism: it blames today's hunger not on the wealth of the rich, but on the sexual habits of the poor. It neatly avoids the issue of inequality, when it is inequality and inequality alone that can be blamed for hunger today.

People in the rich world (Europe and Russia, countries settled by descendants of the English, Israel, Japan) consume 40 percent more calories and 70 percent more protein than the rest of the world, and use almost three times as much grain.[7] Inequality in consumption, moreover, is rising: food production per capita for the world as a whole has risen about 9 percent since 1960. But during those same fifteen years inequality in calorie consumption has

---

[7]The rich consume their grain primarily indirectly (feedstocks converted into animal protein). The poor's consumption is mainly direct (gruels, breads, noodles, rice dishes).

risen 4 percent, in protein consumption 18 percent, and in grain use about 20 percent.[8]

Although grain use in the poor world averages about 430 pounds per capita, inequality here is marked: Argentina, one of the rich of the poor world nations, uses about 900 pounds per person (more than West Germany) while Bangladesh must make do with about 300. Even the poorest nations in the world, however, probably produce enough food to provide adequately for all their people. The data on age, sex, weight, and activity levels in the poor world suggest that any poor nation with thirty-nine grams of protein a day and 285 pounds of grain a year per capita has enough so that its inhabitants need not suffer from malnutrition of any sort. Only two nations in the world (Liberia and Zaire) might fall below these minimums, although the margins of error in their food-production estimates are sufficiently large that they may not.

As James Gavan and John Dixon point out in their essay "India: A Perspective on the Food Situation" in the *Science* collection, it is unequal food distribution—not lack of production—that causes hunger in India. Even in the famine years of 1965 and 1966 the nation had 13 percent more food than it needed to feed everyone adequately. Similarly, Bangladesh today probably produces enough food to prevent malnutrition altogether, but the rich consume 30 percent more calories than the poor (as well as twice as much protein and several times as much grain). A flourishing black market—approved by the government— ships perhaps as much as a third of all marketed grain into India, for in Bangladesh the rupee is a prized currency.

The FAO, in its *State of Food and Agriculture 1974*, repeats its claim that "malnutrition ... is strongly correlated with poverty." It is perhaps more significant that marked social inequality, which is also "strongly corre-

---

[8]Like death, food consumption is a biological process and hence an equalizer of men: one can spend 100 times as much money as someone else, or use 500 times as much energy, but one cannot, over any length of time, eat three times as much food. In a world of inequality, however, levelers cut both ways: I can survive on one-hundredth of your income and one-five-hundredth of your energy use, but I shall die if my calorie consumption is only 30 percent of yours consistently.

lated" with extreme poverty, in fact probably causes malnutrition. Brazil has vast numbers of the underfed (its
northeast region is said to be one of the grimmest in the
world) while China has very few; yet China's per capita
GNP is only a third as high as Brazil's.

Production Myths

With holocaust through atomic warfare at least temporarily less likely and the threat of environmental self-
destruction apparently overrated, the *Times* collection is
not the only publication that has now picked up the baton
of Malthusianism. Malthusians believe they have two un-
answerable propositions: first, that the poor world is procreating away all its advances in crop production; second,
that the world's population is doubling every thirty-five
years, and it is impossible for food production to keep pace
with this. Fortunately for the poor of the world, neither
proposition stands up.

   It is true that per capita increases in food production
since World War II have been about five times as rapid in
the rich countries as in the poor (1.5 versus 0.3 percent per
year), that total food production has risen just slightly
faster in the poor world than in the rich, and that the
poor world's population has been growing twice as rapidly.
But does this mean the poor are converting grain into
babies and saving none to improve their lives?

   Not necessarily. The economies of rich nations and poor
nations work very differently: in the former, economic
growth is practically divorced from population growth. In
the latter, labor rather than technology is the primary factor stimulating growth, so that growth of the economic
hinges on growth of the labor force. One could argue that a
poor nation with 3.3 and 3.0 percent rates of growth per
annum for food production and population could quad-
ruple its annual per capita faod increase by lowering population growth to 2 percent. But poor nations are characterized by low productivity per worker. Under existing
conditions it is more likely that lowering the growth of
the labor force by a third wd cut the growth of output by a

third, and hence slash the already pitifully low rate of increase in food consumption by a third.[9]

It is the poorest of the poor who depend most on population growth for their economic welfare, and for them it is not irrational to produce more children. People will be better fed in poor countries not simply by making them lower their birth rates (if accomplished through coercion, as now seems likely will be tried in India's Punjab, this could lead to economic as well as political tragedy). What is needed instead are the institutional changes which would make it in the interest of the poor to lower their own birth rates. To be 95 percent sure that one will see a son reach adulthood, one must have at least six children in India today; with better health care, more of the children born would grow up, and parents would be less inclined to produce "spare" children. Education raises one's aspirations and decreases the desire for children. Jobs for women open up opportunities for self-fulfillment outside the nursery. In every nation where equality of income has increased, fertility has decreased, perhaps because parents no longer need to depend on their children as a source of income and old-age security. Similarly, improving workers' productivity eliminates their main reason for having large families: it is no longer necessary to have an array of sons in the fields for a family to scratch out a living.

In agriculture, raising worker productivity means increasing crop yields per acre. Few people realize the potential which lies here. We think Bangladesh a basket case because it uses every inch of its land, sends 85 percent of its work force to the fields, and still seems to grow too little food to get by. But how many of us know that rice yields per hectare in Bangladesh are only 53 percent as great as the world average, 24 percent as great as America's, and only 15 percent as great as can be obtained on experimen-

---

[9]Simon Kuznets is one of the few American economists who have worked on this problem. See his *Modern Economic Growth* (Yale University Press, 1966), *Economic Growth of Nations* (Harvard University Press, 1971), and *Population, Capital, and Growth* (Norton, 1974).

tal stations in *Bangladesh*? Were Bangladesh merely to
raise its rice yields to the world average, its per capita production would be over 530 pounds, higher than Japan's at
the beginning of the 1960s. There is no technical reason
why this could not be done.

Moreover, the world yields for most crops are only a
fraction of the maximums that have actually been obtained: for wheat the fraction is one-third; for maize and
sorghum, one-fourth; for rice, one-fifth. In agricultural col-
leges, research stations, and crop improvement centers
today there is already enough know-how literally to flood
the world with food. Roger Revelle has estimated that the
earth could feed between thirty-eight and forty-eight billion people on a European diet, were we to plow all unused
but cultivable land around the world and farm it with the
methods and technology practiced in Iowa today.[10]

If this estimate's range seems too precise, its order of
magnitude is certainly correct. And this order of magnitude understates the world's feeding potential. As various articles in the *Science* collection's sections on research
and basic biology show,[11] tropical soils may hold more agricultural promise than we thought, pest control may save
a larger portion of the crop, and genetic improvements not
yet undertaken may lead to substantial increments in
yields. The best wheat field on earth, for example, yields
only half its genetic potential; the best banana grove, only
a tenth. Demographers now say we should expect about
seven billion people by the year 2000; it would be highly
unrealistic to say that we could feed *seventy* billion by
then, but it would not be inaccurate to say we could have
the technology to do so.

I have argued that the present food situation is not as desperate as reported, and the future not as hopeless as predicted; that our misunderstanding of food realities demon-

[10]*Scientific American,* September 1974.
[11]S. H. Wittwer, "Food Production: Technology and the Resource Base"; W. B.
Ennis, Jr., W.. Dowler, W. Klassen, "Crop Protection to Increase Food Supplies";
P. A. Sanchez and S. W. Buol, "Soils of the Tropics and the World Food Crisis"; I.
Zeitlich, "Improving the Efficiency of Photosynthesis."

strates how little we actually know about the problem. If, as I assumed at the beginning of this article, we wish to help the poor, where do we go from here? We could start by examining why we know least about the world's poor themselves. Why do we know so little about their lives and their problems? It is certainly not because of a shortage of research funds and fact-finding commissions. Why, moreover, do the myriad fact-findings groups always seem to require high budgets, limousines, interpreters, and the best hotel suites in town? The answer is symptomatic of the problem: it is below our dignity to learn about the poor by working with them or living with them. We are ignorant about the poor of the earth because we are separated from them by a social and economic gap that they are unable to cross, and that we are unwilling to.

In the recent past we have seen the birth of a world economy and the development of an international division of labor. Although m complex factors have produced this division, and there are variations within it, it is still true that on one side have been those whose economic surplus was being expropriated, on the other those who were expropriating it. This international division of labor allowed the countries which are now rich to develop and multiply their productive resources; while growth was stifled and perverted in many of the countries which are now poor. As perhaps a quarter of the world's population was propelled up to a level of material comfort enjoyed a few generations before only by the aristocracy, fully half the world saw its standard of living stagnate and in some cases (Indonesia, perhaps Bangladesh) even decline.[12] It is impossible to separate the issue of unequal food distribution (which is the question behind the food crisis, not some absolute lack of food) from the acceleration of inequality which the development of the world economy has encouraged. Historically, the food crisis is merely the most recent in a long

---

[12]See Immanuel Wallerstein, *The Modern World System* (Academic Press, 1975); Samir Amin, *Accumulation on a World Scale* (Monthly Review Press, 1972); A. Emmanuel, *Unequal Exchange* (Monthly Review Press, 1973). For the effect of the world economy on particular areas, see the work of Clifford Geertz (Indonesia), André Gunder Frank (Latin America), and Giovanni Arrighi (Africa).

series of manifestations of inequality between the rich and
the poor worlds.

This inequality, however, cannot be separated from productivity, for it is differing rates of growth in productivity
that have caused it. An American may use five times as
much grain as an Indian, but this is so because he can buy
five times as much, and he can buy five times as much
because, farmer to farmer, he produces *seventy-five* times
as much. The plaintive calls for Americans to keep their
standard of living high but to go without hamburger, or for
nations to redistribute their food supplies without altering
the balance of productive resources, have gone unheeded
because inequality cannot be eliminated by welfare-style
transfers of income. Inequality is inextricably linked with
production: the only way the nations of the world can become more equal is through making their productivities
more equal.

How, then, can the poor world's productivity be raised?
As Pierre Crosson explains in the *Science* collection, three
conditions must be satisfied to expand food production: 1)
technology must exist; 2) farmers must know how to use
it efficiently; 3) they must have incentives to use it. The
first condition is already satisfied. You don't need tractors,
spray planes, and other trappings of the Green Revolution
to raise yields. With know-how and little else (a few simple hand tools, some good seeds, a little pesticide, manure
or ferti;izer) a diligent but poor farmer can produce at least
one crop a year with yields higher than those now har-
vested in rich countries.

This is not easy, but it can be done, and men such as
Reverend Carl Reither, a missionary in the town of Feni,
Bangladesh, and Dr. Dale Haws, an agronomist in the
Philippines, have shown farmers how to do it. (To my
knowledge, nothing has yet been written about the extraordinary Rev. Reither. On Haws's low-investment harvest, see *Research Highlights* for 1974.[13]) Poor countries,

---

[13]International Rice Research Institute, Los Baños, Philippines; see also my
forthcoming "Los Baños Diary," *R. F. Illustrated,* published by the Rockefeller Foundation, New York.

moreover, are tropical countries. With an investment in irrigation and drainage which in most cases pays for itself in less than two years, the poor farmer can be harvesting three crops a year to our one.

Fulfilling the second condition depends on reaching the smallest, poorest farmer. There are no general rules for doing this. Voluntary farmer association, which flourished in Japan, have failed in the Philippines. The brutal *kolkhoz* system of rounding up peasants, dropping them on a farm, and making them work for the state, which is still holding back Russian agriculture, is said to have had some limited success in Tanzania. Information does not seek out its audience; word of mouth, open-air meetings, even color TV will not bring a message across to peasant farmers unless a number of other factors encourage them to be receptive, including their culture, their degree of political development, the position of farmers in the social system, and the inclinations of their leaders. South Korea and Taiwan are currently touted as models for poor world agricultural development, their experience supposedly proving that income redistribution is a precondition for progress and that political development is an important form of economic development. An educated, disciplined mass party or voting public, so the argument runs, is only a step away from an educated, disciplined labor force.

There is truth in these claims, but a crucial—and almost totally ignored—reason that agriculture has been so successful in those countries since World War II is that they were Japanese colonies before the war. Where the other imperial powers wanted export earnings from their colonies, Japan needed food, and built the roads, market system, and the rest of the "infrastructure" to deliver it. Small farmers in South Korea and Taiwan were reached not through social justice but foreign fiat; yields began to rise sharply long before land reform programs even existed.

The farmer's life is not only strenuous, boring, and poorly paid, but brutal. Through most of the world (India's Punjab experience perhaps being a significant exception) successful efforts to reach him and raise his productivity

have been accompanied by some sort of coercion. The
lower his level of political culture (his ability, if you will,
to be moved to act by the existing political channels), the
greater has been the use of force in changing his situation,
for better or worse.

The third condition implies that if national needs are to be
fulfilled it must be in the interest of the small farmer to
fulfill them, since he produces the lion's share of crops in
every poor nation. This means regulating the power and
the privileges of the classes that exploit him. Class
privilege in the Philippines, for example, causes yields to
stagnate and population to explode. Most of the labor is
tenant or landless, and the tenure systems puts the burden
risk on the *campesino;* if the crop fails, he pays, and if it
thrives it is the landlord who prospers. Thus, the only
really safe investment a peasant can make is children:
they don't eat much, or need clothes or schooling, and
they start earning their living at about age five. Because
unemployment rates are high, it is good to have many
children so that one or two are always employed; because
infant mortality is high, it is good to have many children
so that few might grow up to support you when you are too
weak to work. On the other hand, in Japan, a former poor
nation, the conflict between national needs and individual
aspirations was largely eliminated regarding agricultural
production. Land is more equally distributed, irrigation,
pesticides, fertilizers, good seeds, credit, guaranteed mar-
kets, high support prices are easily available. It is in the
farmer's interest to raise a good crop.

On millions of small farms throughout the world, op-
timum production and social justice are closely linked:
you probably can't have one for any length of time without
the other.[14] This is because, in the world economy, it is

---

[14]There are of course exceptions: Costa Rica exports more meat every year while
growing numbers at home go hungry; South Vietnam in the last six months
may have seen its crop production and its numbers of malnourished fall simultaneously. We may suspect, however, that the exceptions are temporary exceptions: in the first case, the contradiction between justice and production may
eventually damage production, in the second, where the contradiction between
justice and production reportedly is being solved, we might expect production
to be enhanced.

the structure rather than the fact of poverty that per-
petuates poverty. As Mao Tse-tung, the great economic-
development genius of our age, has proven, within at least
one poor nation vast reserves of unused productive power
can be liberated by altering the social system. A little bit
of justice goes a long way in production. Land reform, for
example, has been credited with raising production in
many countries where it is enacted; although the claim is
no doubt exaggerated, we can see why it should be conducive to higher yields. With effective land redistribution,
many more farmers get a homestead. Thus, rural unemployment (commonly 30 percent) tends to disappear.
With land (and thus money) of their own, the former poor
buy more food and become stronger; hence the quantity
and the quality of the labor force simultaneously increase.

Moreover, the labor force now has reason to work hard
and seek out new ways to improve yields. Output im-
proves, and because it is more evenly distributed, so do
health and education, which in turn further improve output. Farm demand leads now to appropriate industriali-
zation—shoes, hammocks, roofs (not El Dorados)—
which in turn leads to greater demand for farm goods, and
so on. It has been estimated that Brazil could raise its
crop output immediately by 20 percent simply by rearranging factors of production (i.e., land reform).[15] Such an
estimate, however, takes into account neither the current
political and social obstacles to rearranging those factors
nor the present and future social dividends which would
be reaped. Clearly both are very great.

When we put the proportion of poor and hungry around
the world in historical perpective we can prove that things
have never been better. But if we choose to compare the
number of people who could be well fed with the number
who are well fed, we can also prove that things have never
been worse. Little as we know about the food crisis, we
know that it is a social, not a technical, problem; the

---

[15]W. R. Cline, *Economic Consequences of Land Reform in Brazil*, quoted in
Keith Griffin, *The Political Economy of Agrarian Change* (Harvard University
Press, 1974).

Part IV
Punishment

Often when people break the law they are punished. The punishment may involve the loss of property or the loss of certain privileges—for example, the penalty for violating the traffic code may be a fine or the loss of a driver's license. In the case of more serious offenses, the penalty can be imprisonment, and for some crimes the punishment can even be death. These practices are so familiar that we may accept them without question. Yet, upon reflection, they do require justification. In taking away the money, the freedom, and the lives of convicted persons, the state is doing them great harm; and whenever harm is done, some justification is required. So why is the state justified in inflicting such treatment on lawbreakers? What, if any, is the justification of punishment?

There are two traditional answers to this question, the retributivist *answer and the* utilitarian *answer. As the name suggests, retributivists view punishment as retribution: it is a way of "paying back" offenders for their wrongful deeds. Suppose, for example, a man has assaulted a helpless old woman and stolen her money. The retributivist would say that he* deserves *to be punished for this. It is simple justice that, having behaved in such a way, he should have to suffer for it. For the retributivist, the mere fact that the lawbreaker has violated society's rules is sufficient justification for punishing him.*

The utilitarian looks at the matter very differently. Since punishment involves treating people in ways that are harmful to them, the utilitarian argues that it cannot be justified unless it can be shown that some good comes of it. In order to be justified, punishment must have good consequences. In fact, the utilitarian might add, the practice of punishing lawbreakers does have good consequences: as a result of it, most citizens respect and obey the law. Because theft is punished, fewer people steal; because murder is punished, fewer people commit murder. Thus, punishment is justified because it serves a useful purpose: it deters people from committing crimes.

Objections have been raised to both theories. Retributivism, it is argued, is nothing more than the endorsement of naked revenge dressed up in nice language. The retributivist may say it is "simple justice" that those who "deserve" punishment should suffer; but the reality behind such words is the old bloodthirsty mentality that demands "getting even," the demand to inflict harm on your "enemies" even if no good will come of it. When viewed in this light, retributivism seems a much less attractive theory of punishment than utilitarianism.

But the utilitarian justification of punishment also has its difficulties. Suppose, for example, that an innocent person was widely believed to have committed a crime. Then the "punishment" of that innocent person would have just as much deterrent effect as would the punishment of a guilty person. Now if punishment is justified by its deterrent effects, there is as much justification for punishing the innocent person as there would be for punishing the real culprit. Therefore the utilitarian theory seems to lead to the thoroughly unacceptable conclusion that we could be justified in punishing innocent people, if only they are widely believed to be guilty. The general problem is that in concentrating all its attention on the effects of punishment, the utilitarian theory overlooks the crucial matter of guilt and innocence—after all, guilt and innocence are matters of what has happened in the past, not of what will happen (as a result of punishment) in the future.

But the most common view today does not emphasize either retribution or simple deterrence. The emphasis in this third theory is on rehabilitation of the individual criminal. According to this view, we should not think of the social response to crime in terms of "punishment." The word "punishment" has all sorts of misleading associations; it suggests that we are mainly interested in hurting (punishing) the lawbreaker. According to the advocates of rehabilitation, we should be less concerned with punishment and more concerned with the underlying causes of crime. People commit crimes because they are unable to function satisfactorily according to societal standards. Perhaps they have emotional or psychological problems that make them aggressive or violent; perhaps, being unable to read or write, they are not able to hold jobs; perhaps they were brought up in impoverished environments. There are many other possible causes of criminal behavior. In each case, we do not need to "punish" the individuals, but to attend to their needs and correct the problems that led to their becoming lawbreakers in the first place. Prisons should therefore be places where lawbreakers are rehabilitated. Inmates with emotional or psychological problems should receive professional care; those who are illiterate should be taught to read; those without job skills should acquire them.

The rehabilitation theory has come to dominate the thinking of educated people in the United States within the past 100 years. It actually could be considered a variant of the utilitarian theory since it emphasizes the results of incarceration. The most common complaint about our prisons is that, unfortunately, not very many prisoners are actually rehabilitated—but this complaint makes sense only if we suppose that prisons should be places of rehabilitation. The rehabilitation ideology makes a great deal of difference, too, in how the penal system operates. For example, instead of being sentenced to definite periods of time in prison ("five years, period"), convicted persons are given indefinite sentences ("from two to eight years"). The reason for the use of indefinite sentencing is closely connected to the rehabilitation theory. The purpose of incarceration is to rehabilitate criminals, but we can't know just how long that will take; therefore, they are given indeterminate sentences and judgments are made later (usually by a parole board) concerning whether they are "ready" to be released.

The first selection in this chapter is "The Justification of Punishment," by the British philosopher R. S. Downie, who discusses the merits of the traditional theories of punishment. The second selection is from a book, **Struggle for Justice,** *prepared by the American Friends Service Committee—the Quakers. The Quakers undertook a study of the American prison system and reached the surprising conclusion that the whole concern with rehabilitation should be abandoned. Rehabilitationism was found to be defective in both theory and practice. One problem is that we do not know enough about the causes of crime to formulate really workable rehabilitation programs. Consider, for example, the whitecollar crime of accountants who embezzle funds: what exactly should be done to "rehabilitate" them in prison? They are perfectly literate; they have impressive job skills; and the assumption that they have emotional or psychological problems may be simply false—they may be just plain greedy, in the ordinary sense. Moreover, the desire to rehabilitate people is often nothing more than the desire to impose white, middleclass values associated with the work ethic on them, and it becomes questionable whether or not it is right to try to remake the personalities and values of people in another image.*

The ineffectiveness of rehabilitation programs is often traceable to factors that are part and parcel of the rehabilitation ideology, such as indeterminate sentencing. Most prisoners feel that it is unfair to sentence them to indefinite terms like "two to eight years," and their resentment may very well be justified; after all, if their crimes were only serious enough to merit two years in prison, why should we hold over their heads the threat of keeping them there for four times that long? Resentment over indeterminate sentencing is an important factor contributing to the ineffectiveness of rehabilitation programs; yet such sentencing practices are a direct result of the re-

habilitationist ideology. The Quakers concluded that we ought to go back to viewing the prisons as places of punishment, where prisoners are sent for definite terms. The prisons should, of course, be operated humanely, and help of various kinds should be available to prisoners on a voluntary basis—but that is all.

The last three selections in the unit deal with a specific and controversial form of punishment—the death penalty. Victor H. Evjen lists the various arguments against capital punishment, and Jacques Barzun presents an argument in favor of it. The final selection is an extract from the Supreme Court's decision in Gregg v. Georgia.

Until recent times, death has been a very common punishment all over the world. In England at the beginning of the nineteenth century there were still over 225 separate offenses, including many that we would consider trivial, punishable by death. It was only during the nineteenth century that imprisonment began to replace death as the punishment for most crimes; pickpockets, for example, began to be imprisoned rather than hanged. During the twentieth century most executions have been for such serious crimes as murder and rape; at least this has been true in the western countries. The recent history of capital punishment, then, has been to use it less and less, to punish fewer and fewer crimes.

Meanwhile, critics of the death penalty have been arguing that it should be abolished altogether. They contend that it is not an effective deterrent to crime, and that it is an inherently brutal punishment unworthy of a civilized people. Moreover, they point out that when a mistake is made—and there inevitably are mistakes—and an innocent person is executed, it is impossible ever to undo that terrible injustice. Proponents counter that the threat of death must be a great deterrent to such crimes as murder; and besides, some crimes are so heinous that no penalty short of death could suffice.

318

A parallel argument was developing over whether or not capital punishment is compatible with the United States Constitution. For one thing, the fourteenth amendment guarantees all citizens the "equal protection" of the law, but the death penalty was being used mainly against poor or black defendants. If a person was white, and had enough money to hire good lawyers, the gas chamber or the electric chair or the hangman's rope could usually be avoided. Moreover, the eighth amendment forbids "cruel and unusual" punishment, and it was argued that the death penalty is such a punishment.

By 1967 the constitutionality of capital punishment had become so questionable that all executions had ceased, pending a resolution of the argument by the Supreme Court. There were no executions in the United States for the next ten years. Then in 1972 the Court declared that all existing statutes imposing the death penalty were unconstitutional, because they permitted the penalty to be applied in an arbitrary and discriminatory manner. In other words, the Court agreed with the complaint that a disproportionate number of executed criminals were members of minority groups or were poor. But the Court did not rule on the crucial question of whether capital punishment is inherently "cruel and unusual." Following the 1972 decision, many states rushed to write new statutes, under which the death penalty would be applied in a more evenhanded manner, and the new laws were then tested in court. Finally, in 1976 the Supreme Court approved of these new statutes, and declared that capital punishment is not contrary to the "cruel and unusual" clause of the eighth amendment. This declaration was made in a series of decisions handed down at the same time; Gregg v. Georgia was one of the most important of them.

The 1976 decision meant that the individual states were now free to start executing people, but the same

The Justification of Punishment

R. S. Downie

Traditionally two very general sorts of justification have been offered for the practice of punishment: retributivist and utilitarian. According to the theory of retribution, punishment is justified insofar as it is a morally fitting response to the violation of a law. Sometimes the theory is expressed in the ambiguous form: punishment is justified by guilt. This form of words is ambiguous because it may mean that guilt is a necessary condition of punishment, or it may mean that guilt is a necessary and a sufficient condition of punishment. The first of these claims is entirely innocuous—it is indeed part of the definition of punishment that it is for an offence (real or supposed)—and can be conceded by all without further ado. But insofar as the first claim simply states part of the definition of punishment it cannot constitute any part of its justification. Hence, insofar as the retributive theory sets out to be justificatory it logically must involve the more radical of the two claims—that guilt is a necessary and a sufficient condition of the infliction of punishment on an offender. Is the theory plausible?

It might be said against it that it does not reflect actual practice either in the law or in more informal normative orders such as schools or the family. In these institutions we find such practices as the relaxation of punishment for first offenders, warnings, pardons, and so on. Hence, it may seem that actual penal practice is at variance with the retributive theory if it is saying that guilt is a necessary and a sufficient condition of punishment. Only in games, it may be said, do we find a sphere where the infringement of rules is a necessary and a sufficient condition of the infliction of a penalty, and even in games there may be a 'playing the advantage' rule.

It is not clear, however, that the retributivist need be disturbed by this objection. He might take a high-handed line with the objection and say that if it is the case that actual penal practice does not reflect his theory then so much the (morally) worse for actual practice. Whatever people in fact do, he might argue, it is morally fitting that guilt be a necessary and a sufficient condition of the infliction of punishment.

A less high-handed line, and one more likely to conciliate the opponents of the retributivist theory, is to say that the statement of the theory so far provided is to be taken as a very general one. When it is said that guilt is a necessary and a sufficient condition of punishment it is not intended that punishment should in every case follow inexorably. There are cases where extenuating circumstances may be discovered and in such cases it would be legitimate to recommend mercy or even to issue a pardon. It is unfair to the retributivist to depict his theory as the inflexible application of rules. There is nothing in the theory which forbids it the use of all the devices in the law and in less formal institutions whereby punishment may in certain circumstances be mitigated. Even the sternest of retributivists can allow for the concept of mercy. Perhaps the objection may be avoided completely if the theory is stated more carefully as: guilt and nothing other than guilt may justify the infliction of punishment. To state the theory in this way is to enable it to accommodate the complex operation of extenuating factors which modify the execution of actual systems of law. But to say this is not yet to explain why guilt and nothing other than guilt may justify the infliction of punishment. Indeed, we might ask the retributivist to tell us why we should punish anyone at all.

Retributivists give a variety of answers to this question. One is that punishment annuls the evil which the offender has created. It is not easy to make sense of this claim. No amount of punishment can undo an offence that has been committed: what has been has been. Sometimes metaphors of punishment washing away sin are used to explain how punishment can annul evil. But such ideas can mislead. Certainly, the infliction of punishment may, as a matter of psychological fact, remove some people's *feelings* of guilt. But we may query whether this is necessarily a good thing. Whether or not it is, however, it is not the same as annulling the evil committed.

A second retributivist idea is that the offender has had some sort of illicit pleasure and that the infliction of pain will redress the moral balance. People speak of the criminal as 'paying for what he has done' or as 'reaping a harvest of bitterness'; the infliction of suffering is regarded as a fitting response to crime. But this view may be based on a confusion of the idea that 'the punishment must fit the crime', which is acceptable if it means only that punishment ought to be proportionate, with the idea that punishment is a fitting response to crime, which is not so obviously acceptable. It may be that the traditional *lex talionis* is based on a confusion of the two ideas. At any rate, it is the idea of punishment as the 'fitting response' which is essential to the retributivist position.

A third claim sometimes made by the retributivists is that an offender has a right to punishment. This claim is often mocked by the critics of retributivism on the grounds that it is an odd right that would gladly be waived by the holder! It might be thought that the view can be defended on the grounds that the criminal's right to punishment is merely the right correlative to the authority's duty to punish him. Such a defence is not plausible, however, for, even supposing there is a right correlative to a legal authority's duty to punish criminals, it is much more plausible to attribute this right to the society which is protected by the deterrent effect of punishment.

There are two arguments, more convincing than the first, which can be put forward in defence of the view that the offender has a right to punishment. One of these requires us to take the view in conjunction with the premise that punishment annuls evil. If punishment can somehow wash away the guilt of the offender then it is plausible to say that the offender has a right to be punished. The difficulty with this argument, however, is that it simply transfers the problems. It is now intelligible to say that the offender has a right to punishment, but, as we have already seen, it is not at all clear what it means to say that punishment annuls evil.

The other argument invites us to consider what the alternative is to punishing the criminal. The alternative, as we shall shortly see, may be to 'treat' him and attempt a 'cure' by means of various psychological techniques. Now this would be rejected as morally repugnant by many retributivists, on the grounds that an offender has freely decided to break the law and should be regarded as a self-determining rational being who knew what he was doing. An offender, so described, may be said to have a right to *punishment* (as distinct from psychological treatment, moral indoctrination, or brain-washing in the interests of the State). Such an argument produces a favourable response from many criminals who, when they have served their time in prison, feel that the matter is then over and that they ought to be protected from the attentions of moral doctors and the like. So stated, there may be some truth in the 'right to punishment' doctrine, however easy it is for the sophisticated to mock it.

So far we have been concerned to suggest detailed criticism of the retributivist theory. But there are two general criticisms which are commonly made of it at the moment (for it is a most unfashionable theory in philosophical and other circles). The first is that insofar as its claims are intelligible and prima facie acceptable, they are disguised utilitarian claims.

This criticism is valid against certain ways in which retributivists sometimes state their claims. For example, they have sometimes regarded the infliction of punishment as the 'emphatic denunciation by the community of a crime'. But we might well ask why society should bother to denounce crime unless it hopes by that means to do some good and diminish it. A second example of a retributivist claim which easily lends itself to utilitarian interpretation is that the infliction of punishment reforms the criminal by shocking him into a full awareness of his moral turpitude. The question here is not whether this claim is in fact plausible (criminologists do not find it so) but whether the justification of punishment it offers is essentially retributivist. It seems rather to be utilitarian, and in this respect like the more familiar version of the reform theory we shall shortly examine.

It seems, then, that this criticism does have some force against certain retributivist claims, or against certain ways of stating retributivist claims. But the criticism does not do radical damage to retributivism. Provided the theory is stated in such a way that it is clear that the justification of punishment is necessarily only that it is a fitting response to an offender, then the fact that punishment may sometimes also do good need not count against retributivism. It is, however, an implication of retributivism that it must sometimes be obligatory to punish when punishment is not expected to do any good beyond itself.

It is precisely this implication which is used as the basis for the second criticism of retributivism. This criticism is a straightforward moral judgement, that the theory is morally objectionable in that it requires us to inflict punishment, which is by definition unpleasant and therefore as such evil, for no compensating greater good. The critics therefore invite us to reject the theory as a barbarous residue of old moral ideas.

In the context of philosophical analysis it is important to avoid taking sides in moral argument, as far as this can be done. But it may be worth pointing out that perhaps the great majority of ordinary people have sympathy with some form of retributivism. Contemporary philosophers often appeal to what the 'ordinary moral agent' would do or say in certain circumstances, or what the morality of 'common sense' would hold on certain topics, but if they make this appeal in settling questions of the justification of punishment they may find that the ordinary person adheres to some form of retributivism. Since there is generally something to be said for an appeal in moral matters to what people ordinarily think, let us consider whether the implication of retributivism is really so morally repugnant.

The implication is that on some occasions it will be

obligatory to punish an offender even though this will do no good beyond itself, and that even when some further good is in fact accomplished by the punishment this is irrelevant to its justification. Now it may be that this implication is thought to be morally objectionable because the clause 'no good beyond itself' is equated with 'no good at all'. But a retributivist will claim that the mere fact of inflicting punishment on an offender is good in itself. It is not that a *further* good will result (although it may do so) but that the very fact of the punishment is fitting and to that extent good.

This argument may be made more convincing by an example. Let us suppose that a Nazi war criminal responsible for the cruel torture and deaths of many innocent people has taken refuge in South America where he is living *incognito*. Let us suppose that he has become a useful and prosperous member of the community in which he is living. Let us suppose that the whereabouts of this criminal are discovered and it becomes possible to bring him to justice and punish him. It is very doubtful whether such punishment will have any utilitarian value at all; the criminal will not in any way be 'reformed' by treatment, and the deterrence of other war criminals seems an unrealistic aim. We can at least imagine that the punishment of such a criminal will have minimal utilitarian value and may even have disvalue in utilitarian terms. Nevertheless, many people might still feel that the criminal ought to be brought to justice and punished, that irrespective of any further good which may or may not result from the punishment, it is in itself good that such a man should be punished for his crimes. To see some force in this special pleading is to see that retributivism is not completely without moral justification although it can never on its own constitute a complete theory of the justification of punishment.

I have tried to find merits in the retributivist theory because it is frequently dismissed with contempt by philosophers and others at the present time, but we shall now consider theories of the justification of punishment with more obvious appeal. These are all different forms of utilitarianism and they therefore have in common the claim that the justification of punishment necessarily rests in the value of its consequences. There are two common forms of utilitarian justification: in terms of deterrence and in terms of reform.

According to the deterrence form of the utilitarian theory the justification of punishment lies in the fact that the threats of the criminal law will deter potential wrong-doers. But since threats are not efficacious unless they are carried out, proved wrong-doers must in fact have unpleasant consequences visited on them. The increase in the pain of the criminal, however, is balanced by the increase in the happiness of society, where crime has been checked. The theory is modified to account for two classes of people for whom the threats of the law cannot operate; the cases of infants and madmen on the one hand, and on the other hand cases in which accident, coercion and other 'excusing conditions' affected the action. In such cases the threats of the law would clearly have little effect and punishment would therefore do no social good.

A deterrent theory of this general sort has often been accepted by utilitarian philosophers from the time of Bentham, but it is frequently criticized. The most common criticism is that it does not rule out the infliction of 'punishment' or suffering on the innocent. Utilitarians, that is, argue that where excusing conditions exist punishment would be wasted or would be socially useless. But their argument shows only that the threat of punishment would not be effective in particular cases where there are excusing conditions; the infliction of 'punishment' in such cases would still have deterrent values on *others* who might be tempted to break the law. Moreover, people who have committed a crime may hope to escape by pleading excusing conditions and hence there would be social efficacy in punishing those with excuses. Presumably this is the point of 'strict liability' in the civil law. But if the deterrent theory commits us to such implications it is at variance with our ordinary views, for we do not accept that the punishment of the lunatic (say) is permissible whatever its social utility.

Utilitarians have sometimes tried to meet this objection by arguing that a system of laws which did not provide for excusing conditions might cause great misery to society. There would be widespread alarm in any society in which no excusing conditions were allowed to affect judicial decisions in criminal cases, and indeed (a utilitarian might argue) such a system might not receive the co-operation of society at large, without which no judicial system can long operate. The utilitarian reply, then, is that while punishment is justified by its deterrent value we must allow excusing conditions since they also have social utility.

It is doubtful, however, whether this reply is adequate. For if excusing conditions are allowed only insofar as they have social utility there remains the possibility that some unusual cases may crop up in which the infliction of suffering or 'punishment' on an innocent person would have social utility which would far outweigh the social utility of excusing him. This is not only a logical possibility on the deterrent theory but a very real possibility in communities in which the 'framing' of an innocent person might prevent rioting of a racial or religious kind. But this implication of the deterrent theory is at odds with widely accepted moral views. Rather it would be held that the rights of the individual must come before the good of society. This does not mean that the rights of the individual must never be sacrificed to the general good but only that there are certain basic rights, the rights of man, or rights which belong to persons as such, which must never be violated no matter what social good will accrue. It is the weakness of the deterrent version of the utilitarian justification of punishment that it cannot accommodate this truth. Here the deterrent theory contrasts adversely with the retributive theory which does stress the rights of the individual against those of society.

Despite this criticism, however, the deterrent theory cannot be entirely dismissed for it does have relevance at the level of legislation. Whereas it is a failure if it is regarded as an attempt to provide a complete justification of punishment it does succeed in bringing out one of the functions of punishment—that of acting as a deterrent to the potential criminal.

The second conception in terms of which utilitarians try to justify the infliction of punishment is that of 'reform'.

They argue that when a criminal is in prison or in some other detention centre a unique opportunity is created for equipping him with a socially desirable set of skills and attitudes. The claim is that such a procedure will have a social utility which outweighs that of conventional punishment.[1] The theory is often based on a psychological or sociological study of the effects of certain kinds of deprivation, cultural starvation, and general lack of education on the individual's outlook, and the hope is that these may be put right by re-education or psychological treatment in the period when there would otherwise be conventional punishment.

There are certain oddities about the reform theory if it is intended to be a justification for punishment. The first is that the processes of reform need not involve anything which is painful or unpleasant in the conventional sense. Some critics of the theory would rule it out on that ground alone. In reply, the advocates of the theory might say that insofar as the criminal is *compelled* to undergo reform the process can count as 'punishment' in the conventional sense; at least the criminal is deprived of his liberty and that is in itself unpleasant whatever else may happen to him during his period of enforced confinement. A different line of defence might be to concede that reform is not punishment in the conventional sense and to go on to point out that the reform theory is an attempt to replace punishment with a practice which has greater utilitarian justification. According to this line, punishment cannot be justified on utilitarian grounds and the utilitarian must therefore replace punishment with a practice which is justifiable.

There is a second respect in which the reform theory has consequences which are at variance with traditional ideas on punishment. The processes of reform may involve what might be called 'treatment'. It happens to be true that

---

[1] This theory must be distinguished from that mentioned in the discussion of retributivism—that conventional punishment reforms by 'shocking' the criminal into an awareness of what he has done. Apart from the question of its consistency with the tenets of retributivism this claim does not seem to be supported by the facts; conventional punishment is said by criminologists in fact to increase the criminal's resentment against society.

many advocates of the theory are influenced by psychological doctrines to the effect that the criminal is suffering from a disease of social maladjustment from which he should be cured. Hence, the processes of reform may include more than re-education in the conventional sense; they may involve what is nearer to brainwashing (and from a strictly utilitarian point of view there is everything to be said in favour of this if it is in fact effective). A merit of the retributive theory is to insist that persons as ends in themselves should be protected against undue exposure to the influence of moral 'doctors' no matter how socially effective their treatment may be.

The third respect in which the theory departs from traditional ideas is that it gives countenance to the suggestion that the criminal may legitimately be detained until he is reformed. But in some advanced cases of social disease the cure may take some time. And what of the incurables? Here again the retributive theory reminds us of the inhumanity of treating people simply as social units to be moulded into desirable patterns.

So far we have considered three oddities of the reform theory, but none of these, of course, invalidates it. The first point simply brings out the nature of the reform theory, and the second and third are hardly implications in the strict sense but merely probable consequences if the practice which the theory reflects is developed in a certain direction. The fatal defect of the theory is rather that it is inadequate as an account of the very many complex ways in which the sanctions of the criminal law are intended to affect society. The reform theory concentrates on only one kind of case, that of the person who has committed an offence or a number of offences and who might do so again. Moreover, it is plausible only for a certain range of cases in this class; those requiring treatment rather than conventional punishment. But it must be remembered that the criminal law is also intended for those, such as murderers, traitors, and embezzlers, for whom the possibility of a second offence is limited. Moreover, the criminal law serves also to deter ordinary citizens who might occasionally be tempted to commit offences. The inadequacy of the reform theory lies in its irrelevance to such important types of cases.

It is clear, then, that no one of the accounts of punishment provides on its own an adequate justification of punishment. The retributive theory, which is often taken to be an expression of barbarism, in fact provides a safeguard against the inhumane sacrifice of the individual for the social good, which is the moral danger in the utilitarian theory. Bearing in mind this moral doctrine about the rights of the individual we can then incorporate elements from both the deterrent and the reform versions of utilitarian justification. Only by drawing from all three doctrines can we hope to reflect the wide range of cases to which the criminal law applies.

Critique of Rehabilitation

American Friends Service Committee

Prior to the latter part of the eighteenth century, imprisonment in the Western world was usually used only for pretrial detention or short jail terms. Instead, the usual sanctions imposed after conviction were capital punishment (even for trivial offenses), dismemberment, banishment, flogging, and monetary fines. One of the gentlest punishments was public humiliation in the stocks.

The transformation from imprisonment as an exceptional measure to its use as the typical sanction for crime was the product of the complex economic, political, intellectual, social, and humanitarian changes that pervaded nineteenth-century life. The revolution against indiscriminate use of the death penalty demanded the development of alternative measures. Abandoned ships were pressed into service and at least one prison (California's San Quentin) was built where it was because that was the point at which a prison hulk was swept ashore during a storm. Transportation of criminals, as from England to Australia, proved to be a short-term expedient both because of the predictable opposition of the receiving colonies and because colonization at government expense ul-

Reprinted with the permission of Hill and Wang (now a division of Farrar, Straus & Giroux, Inc.) From *Struggle For Justice: A Report on Crime and Punishment in America*, Prepared for the American Friends Service Committee, Copyright © 1971 by Hill and Wang.

timately proved more of an inducement than a deterrent to crime.

The prison as we now know it is perhaps most of all the product of the Industrial Revolution, which created a need for cheap labor and for a time made the criminal as much an asset as a liability. Before business and union pressures curbed such "unfair competition," the exploitation of convict labor often enabled penal institutions to break even or perhaps show a profit.

Concomitant with these economic determinants of a productive penology were the burgeoning concepts of democracy and the inalienable rights of man. Democratic theory required the assimilation of deviance into the dominant culture and provided a new view of the criminal as someone to be reformed as well as punished. The new concept of the prison was rationalized both by the English utilitarian theorists and, on this side of the Atlantic, by the humanitarian reformers exemplified by the Pennsylvania Quakers. The utilitarians perceived crime as a natural phenomenon flowing directly from humanity's self-seeking nature. Since human beings are motivated to maximize pleasure and minimize pain, they can be expected to transgress when they see it is to their advantage to do so. To insure public safety, punishment for a criminal act needed only to offer sufficiently more pain than the transgression was worth, thereby deterring the offender from further crime and warning other potential offenders.

The Quakers in Pennsylvania differed largely by placing increased emphasis on reformation. They developed a solitary confinement system that, by holding the convict in total isolation and thus quarantining him from other prisoners, was supposed to encourage his meditation, reflection, and penitence. Though the expensiveness of this system never allowed it to be given a thorough trial, an attempt was made to perpetuate the isolation of convicts through such devices as the Auburn (silent) system.

The concept of a prison centered on forced convict labor was an apparently happy marriage of reformism and practicality. To view labor as therapy and idleness as the root of crime was an appealing notion for an economically expanding America with its Puritan moral heritage. The fact that the prisoner insofar as feasible paid the costs of his own imprisonment with his labor made long-term imprisonment economically and politically practicable. From the outset, however, there was an inherent dilemma in this approach. If prison was to reform, it had to provide incentives for conformity and hard work. But if it was to deter criminality, it must threaten a regime more unpleasant than that of the worst-off segments in the free society outside. This practical dilemma confined penal administration within narrow limits, for the rewards it could offer, whether monetary or psychological, were necessarily petty.

In the latter part of the nineteenth century and increasingly in the twentieth century, the decline of the prison as a productive economic institution has vitiated most of the purported therapy of "hard labor." Idleness or meaningless made-work is today the characteristic regime of many, perhaps most, inmates. More important, the concept of reformation as something achieved through penitence or the acquisition of working skills and habits has been de-emphasized because of developments in social and behavioral science. Varying scientific or pseudoscientific approaches to crime, although in conflict with one another and unconfirmed by hard scientific data, view criminals as distinct biological, psychological, or social-cultural types.

Such theories all share a more or less deterministic premise, holding that man's behavior is caused by social or psychological forces located outside his consciousness and therefore beyond his control. Rehabilitation, therefore, is deemed to require expert help so as to provide the inmate with the understanding and guidance that it is assumed he cannot achieve on his own.

The individualized treatment model, the outcome of this historical process, has for nearly a century been the ideological spring from which almost all actual and proposed reform in criminal justice has been derived. It would be hard to exaggerate the power of this idea or the extent of its influence. In recent years it has been the conceptual foundation of such widely divergent approaches to criminal justice as the President's Crime Commission Report, the British *Why Prison?—A Quaker View of Imprison-*

ment and Some Alternatives, and the American Law Institute's Model Penal Code. Like other conceptions that become so entrenched that they slip imperceptibly into dogma, the treatment model has been assumed rather than analyzed, preached rather than evaluated.

The underlying rationale of this treatment model is deceptively simple. It rejects inherited concepts of criminal punishment as the payment of a debt owed to society, a debt proportioned to the magnitude of the offender's wrong. Instead it would save the offender through constructive measures of reformation, protect society by keeping the offender locked up until that reformation is accomplished, and reduce the crime rate not only by using cure-or-detention to eliminate recidivism, but hopefully also by the identification of potential criminals in advance so that they can be rendered harmless by preventive treatment. Thus the dispassionate behavioral expert displaces judge and theologian. The particular criminal act becomes irrelevant except insofar as it has diagnostic significance in classifying and treating the actor's particular criminal typology. Carried to an extreme, the sentence for all crimes would be the same: an indeterminate commitment to imprisonment, probation, or parole, whichever was dictated at any particular time by the treatment program. Any sentence would be the time required by the treatment program. Any sentence would be the time required to bring about rehabilitation, a period which might be a few weeks or a lifetime.

The treatment model's judicious blend of humanitarian, practical welfare, and scientific ancestry was nicely illustrated sixty years ago by the Elmira Reformatory's Zebulon R. Brockway:

> The common notion of a moral responsibility based on freedom should no longer be made a foundation principle for criminal laws, court procedure, and prison treatment. The claim of such responsibility need neither be denied nor affirmed, but put aside as being out of place in a system of treatment of offenders for the purpose of public protection. Together with abrogation of this responsibility goes, too, any awesome regard for individual liberty of choice and ac-

tion by imprisoned criminals. Their habitual conduct and indeed their related character must needs be directed and really determined by their legalized custodians . . .

The perfected reformatory will be the receptacle and refinery of antisocial humans who are held in custody under discretional indeterminateness for the purpose of the public protection. Legal and sentimental inhibitions of necessary coercion for the obdurate, intractable element of the institution population will be removed and freedom given for the wide use of unimpassioned useful, forceful measures. Frequent relapses to crime of prisoners discharged from these reformatories will be visited upon the management as are penalties for official malfeasance. The change will be, in short, a change from the reign of sentiment swerved by the feelings to a passionless scientific procedure pursuing welfare.[1]

As with any model, of course, its implementation has been uneven, often halting, and seldom complete. Perhaps the closest approximation to the ideal is in certain so-called sexual psychopath statutes under which an indeterminate and potentially lifelong incarceration can be ordered as a civil commitment without conviction of any crime. Judicial power is yielded grudgingly, however, and legislators cling to the notion that maximum penalties should be graded according to their ideas of relative blameworthiness, so that the result is a patchwork quilt of inconsistent rationales. Overall, however, the movement toward the individualized treatment model is unmistakable. Every state has some form of parole, which provides a core indeterminancy. Compared to the median time served, the maximum possible sentence for most crimes is so excessive that the disposition of almost any conviction utilizes the treatment process in some manner.

While opposition to "mollycoddling" prisoners still exists, the basic thrust of the model has been accepted by almost all liberals, reformers of all persuasions, the scien-

---

[1]Zebulon R. Brockway, *Fifty Years of Prison Service* (New York, 1912).

tific community, probably a majority of judges, and those of law-and-order persuasion who perceive the model's repressive potential.

How has the model united such a motley collection of supporters? Its conceptual simplicity and scientific aura appeal to the pragmatism of a society confident that American know-how can reduce any social problem to manageable proportions. Its professed repudiation of retribution adds moral uplift and an inspirational aura. At the same time, the treatment model is sufficiently vague in concept and flexible in practice to accommodate both the traditional and utilitarian objectives of criminal law administration. It claims to protect society by incapacitating the prisoner in an institution until pronounced sufficiently reformed. This prospect is unpalatable enough and sufficiently threatening in its uncertainty to provide at least as effective a deterrent to potential offenders as that of the traditional eye-for-an-eye model. Maximum flexibility is required to achieve the model's goal, that of treatment individualized to each offender's unique needs, so the system's administrators are granted broad discretionary powers. Whatever the effect on offenders, these powers have secured the support of a growing body of administrators, prosecutors, and judges, for it facilitates the discharge of their managerial duties and frees them from irksome legal controls. Even the proponents of retribution, although denied entry through the front door, soon discovered that harsh sentences could be accommodated within the treatment model as long as they are rationalized in terms of public protection or the necessity for prolonged regimes of reeducation.

The treatment model tends to be all things to all people. This partially accounts for the paradox that while the model's ideological command has become ever more secure, its implementation has tended to form rather than substance. In fact, the model has never commanded more than lip service from most of its more powerful adherents. The authority given those who manage the system, a power more absolute than that found in any other sphere of law, has concealed the practices carried on in the name of the treatment model. At every level—from prosecutor to parole-board member—the concept of individualization has been used to justify secret procedures, unreviewable decision making, and an unwillingness to formulate anything other than the most general rules or policy. Whatever else may be credited to a century of individualized-treatment reform effort, there has been a steady expansion of the scope of the criminal justice system and a consolidation of the state's absolute power over the lives of those caught in the net.

The irony of this outcome emphasizes the importance of a searching examination of the assumptions underlying the individualized treatment model. Hopefully such an analysis will illuminate efforts to delineate the proper role of criminal justice in a free and democratic society. It may also help us to understand what factors have perpetuated our present criminal judicial system decade after decade in the face of compelling evidence of its systematic malfunctioning.

Unexamined Assumptions

When one probes beneath the surface of the treatment model, one finds not only untenable factual assumptions, but also disturbing value judgments that pose serious policy questions for our society. Here are some of the more perplexing of these problems with which we will be concerned:

1. A model of criminal justice that rests on the proposition that at least in large measure *crime is a problem of individual pathology;* that is, the model assumes that crime rates can be reduced by the treatment and cure of individual criminals and that future crimes can be prevented by the incapacitation of those predicted to be dangerous until they are cured. The difficulty of identifying the characteristics of such a pathology, if indeed it exists at all, will be noted below. To the extent that it is also acknowledged that social and environmental factors, such as slums, poverty, unemployment, and parental guidance or the lack of it, also "cause" crime, a program of individualized treatment is inadequate. If social factors cannot be controlled or predicted, the relevance of indi-

vidualized treatment is decreased and may be negligible. If the social pathology assumed to encourage a criminal culture is not being changed, is there ethical justification for individualized preventive detention? A prisoner detained to prevent crimes that could be avoided by social reforms may bear a greater resemblance to a scapegoat than to either a patient or a public enemy. We do not and probably cannot know the relative contributions of individual and social pathology to criminality; to the extent that social causation is relevant, the rationale for individualization is undercut. To date, our society has largely ignored this dilemma.

2. At the level of individual pathology, treatment ideology *assumes that we know something about the individual causes of crime.* If it is to have any scientific basis, such knowledge must be based on the study of representative samples both of criminals and of control groups of noncriminals. Comparison of the two may reveal factors that distinguish the criminals from the control groups; whether such differences have any causal significance poses additional research problems which, in this context, we have no occasion to face. We have libraries full of criminological research on the etiology of crime, but most of it has been conducted without control groups and therefore tells us nothing about causation (and usually not much else, either). In all this research, moreover, the data about criminals are derived from those who have been subject to correctional regimes and therefore identified and made available for study. But only a small proportion of those who commit criminal acts are caught, convicted, and subjected to correctional treatment. The criminals who are the subjects of all our research are almost certainly not representative. Our available sample is heavily biased toward criminals from the poor and outcaste classes and away from the white middle and upper classes. Bias is also introduced by selective enforcement of criminal law. Welfare fraud or manslaughter in a ghetto barroom brawl is likely to land the perpetrator on the rolls of diagnosed criminals; business fraud or manslaughter by automobile on the freeway goes largely unprosecuted and unstudied. Therefore, even if we had a body of adequately controlled

research findings it would merely describe the kinds of persons subjected to criminal treatment in a society where race and poverty are major determinants for the application of the criminal label. Such data might afford revealing insights about the administration of criminal justice in such a society, but would hardly provide the basis for a usable science of individual criminal pathology. We think it is important to ask why treatment ideology was embraced with such enthusiasm without bothering to inquire about the validity of the science on which it depends.

3. Even if the existence, significance, and characteristics of an individual criminal pathology are unknown, one might in theory still evolve *treatment methods that turned criminals into noncriminals.* It has been a frequent occurrence in medicine to stumble upon treatments that worked despite ignorance about the cause of the disease or the reasons for the treatment's success. The minimum methodological standards for investigating this possibility as to any particular treatment are (a) comparison with control groups of similar subjects who are not treated; (b) control of other variables, such as maturation or changed environmental or social conditions, to negate the possibility that factors other than the treatment process were responsible for the outcome; and (c) reasonably reliable criteria for determining success or failure. Most research fails the first and second tests. Control groups are conspicuous by their rarity in treatment evaluation investigations. But the apparently insoluble problem of such research is the third requirement: the necessity of establishing indicators to distinguish success from failure. This is true even if one proceeds at the most superficial level, defining failure as recidivism, the commission of another crime following treatment. *We have no way of determining the real rate of recidivism because most criminals are undetected and most suspected criminals do not end up being convicted.* Recidivism rates are also subject to both deliberate manipulation and unconscious bias. Parole revocation (failure) rates can be manipulated for public relations or other purposes. Documented examples of such research falsification are known and the practice is probably not uncommon. Unconscious bias is introduced by the tendency of predic-

tive and diagnostic judgments to become self-fulfilling prophecies. For example, those released on parole from a treatment program are likely to be formally or informally classified for the purpose of parole supervision into good risks (responded favorably to treatment) and poor risks (resisted treatment). The "poor risks" are likely to be subjected to tighter surveillance; their violations are therefore much more likely to be detected; their parole is more likely to be revoked; and the resulting differences in recidivism rates emerge as a "research finding" validating the efficacy of the particular treatment program.

4. In the absence of credible scientific data on the causation or treatment of crime, *the content of the correctional treatment program rests largely on speculation or on assumptions unrelated to criminality.* Thus one finds that accepted correctional practice is dominated by indoctrination in white Anglo-Saxon middle-class values. In institutions this means learning a trade, establishing work habits through the therapy of labor, keeping clean and clean-shaven, minding your own business, and acquiring such basic or supplemental educational skills and religious training as the institution might provide and the parole board might think relevant. On probation or parole, in addition to abstaining from crime, the ingredients for success are similar: sticking at a job, staying where you belong, supporting your family, avoiding bad companionship and bad habits, and abiding by the spoken ideals of conventional sexual morality. Without debating the merits of these ingredients of the good life—those of us not being corrected are free to take them or leave them—the fact that the correlation between such Puritan virtues and crime causation is speculative or nonexistent would, one might suppose, have raised some troubling questions. If the treatment has no proven (or likely) relationship to criminal pathology, what is its purpose? In the absence of such evidence, what is the propriety of coerced cultural indoctorination?

The closest parallel we can think of in American history, which developed at the same time as the correctional treatment model in response to the same kinds of reform pressures, was the policy of compulsory assimilation of

American Indians, which the Indian Bureau attempted to carry out from 1849 through the end of the century. The deliberate discrediting of Indian cultural values, compulsory proselytizing, and the destruction of the tribal economic base were supplemented by government boarding schools, which Indian children were forced to attend throughout their formative years. The program and style of these schools bore striking resemblance to the correctional treatment model. There are other similarities as well. The correctional system also draws most of its clients from subcultures; perhaps half are from racial minorities (including some Indians on their second round of "treatment") and more than half from cultures of poverty or near-poverty. We do not suggest that the parallel is complete or that it follows that the motivation and purpose of the correctional system's treatment program is necessarily the same as the policy of the nineteenth-century Indian Bureau. But we are disturbed both by the similarities and by the absence of any probing dialogue that might explore the whole purpose and philosophy of correctional treatment.

5. Using rates of recidivism as the criterion for evaluating the success or failure of criminal justice programs poses more fundamental problems than the unreliability of the statistics. Surely it is ironic that although treatment ideology purports to look beyond the criminal's crime to the whole personality, and bases its claims to sweeping discretionary power on this rationale, *it measures its sucess against the single factor of an absence of reconviction for a criminal act.* Whether or not the subject of the treatment process has acquired greater self-understanding, a sense of purpose and power in his own destiny, or a new awareness of his relatedness to man and the universe is not subject to statistical study and so is omitted from the evaluation.

It will make a critical difference for the future of democracy whether our institutional and noninstitutional environments encourage the creation of morally autonomous, self-disciplined people who exercise independent judgment and purposefulness from their own inner strength, or whether instead they tend to stunt the human potential by training programs that, as with animals, condition their subjects to an unthinking conformity to inflexible, externally imposed rules. In studying the criminal justice system we have found few things to be thankful for, but the ineffectiveness of correctional treatment may well be one of those few. The only kind of morality the sticks-and-carrots regime of indeterminate treatment in correctional institutions can teach is the externally imposed variety. If such correctional methods really did work, it might be more success than a free society could endure.

6. *Remaking people is an educational function. What, then, of prison education?* We typically find an inadequate staff in a depressing environment with minimal facilities and equipment (no field studies here) operating an adult educational program across class, race, cultural, and status barriers for inmates whose chief motivation is to chalk up attendance marks so as to satisfy The Man on the Parole Board. From this soil we expect to reap the miracle—the maturation of a unique human being. At least that is what one would conclude from the uncritical acceptance of prison education as a "good thing" and a hallmark of society's humanity to prisoners.

7. The *discretionary power* granted to prosecutors, judges, and administrators in an individualized treatment system is unique in the legal system, awesome in scope and by its nature uncontrollable. If the theory posits that any one of many variables can be determinative of any individual decision, standards are necessarily nonexistent or so vague as to be meaningless, and review by any sort of court or appellate process is impossible. Yet it is evidently accepted without question that absolute power does not corrupt when exercised by government agents upon criminals. The chronicles of criminology and jurisprudence are filled with paeans celebrating the wise discretion of humble and contrite judges and administrative agencies. Their authors, however, would not for one moment surrender to the discretion of those same judges and agencies the assessment of their income and property taxes in accordance with the official's individualized determination of the subject's value to his country and his ability to pay. Indeed, the best antidote to being swept off one's feet by the

claims made for the necessity and importance of the discretion that permeates criminal justice administration is
to engage in a comparative examination of criminal law
and the laws governing taxation, corporations, and commercial transactions. One will speedily discover that when
it comes to matters concerning their vested interests, the
men who have the power to write the law in this country
give short shrift to discretion. They are not about to dele-
gate the determination of the size of the oil depletion allowance to the discretion of the local internal revenue
agent. If discretion is written into major law, it is because
legislators are confident from the outset that they will be
able to control its exercise.

Criminal justice is the surviving bastion of absolute
legal discretion. The last of its colleagues, of which it is
reputed to be the heir, was the Office for the Administration of Colonial Affairs.

8. In coming finally to the end of this preliminary
enumeration of problem areas, we reach the area that is
the most perplexing and the culmination of what has gone
before. We have sketched a number of problematic features of a correctional treatment model of criminal justice.
Most of the problems and defects that have been posed are
not very difficult to understand; one might even categorize
a number of them as obvious. How is one to account, then,
for the enthusiastic and uncritical acceptance by most of
the liberal and progressive elements in our society of re-
formative, indeterminate, individualized treatment as the
ideal goal of a criminal justice system?

There is something about this phenomenon akin to religious conversion, an acceptance of what appears to be true
and valuable, what we want to be true, even though it
cannot be reduced to anything more precise than vague
generalities. It seems obvious that extremely complex
forces lie behind liberal treatment ideology's mission to
control not just the crimes but the way of life of others.
Guilt about the gulf that separates our material well-being
from poverty and oppression may account for some of the
prejudice against and irrational fear of the poor and the
oppressed; or it may help to account for our eagerness to
hand over the problem to specialists as a way of relieving

our anxiety. Once you have delegated a problem to an expert, you are off the hook.

If we could make some sense out of this extraordinary willingness to believe unreasonable things about criminal justice and corrections, we might begin to have some understanding of the forces that perpetuate so unjust a system. We explore this problem further below; it is hardly necessary to state here, however, that we cannot provide a satisfactory solution to this major puzzle. We do, however, hope to promote its analysis and encourage its study. Such an inquiry seems to us to be prerequisite to effectuating basic changes in our concepts and practices of criminal justice. The most stubborn obstacles to such change are not, in our opinion, the growing problem of violent crime or the hard-line advocates of punitive law-and-order repression or the rigidity and increasingly conservative polarization of our law enforcement and correctional bureaucracies or the perversity of adverse public opinion. Serious as they are, such forces can be contained if adequate options are developed and promoted. We suspect that much of the current strength of these conservative forces derives from the fact that there is no tenable alternative model of a criminal justice system that affords accommodation of such competing values as equality, respect for individual dignity and autonomy, encouragement of cultural diversity, and the need for a reasonably orderly society. The correctional treatment model does not begin to meet this need.

Against Capital Punishment

Victor H. Evjen

In 1935 there were 199 executions in the United States, 23 in one state. In 1965, seven were escorted to their death. Since 1968 there have been no executions.

During the 1930s, the average number of executions was 167 a year compared with 72 a year in the 1950s and 27 in the first seven years of the 1960s.

This downward trend in executions is not explained by a drop in convictions for capital crimes (crimes for which the death penalty may be assessed). Rather, it indicates a general decline in the use of the death penalty by imposing, instead, life imprisonment or a definite term of years, or by commutation of a death sentence to a life term. About a fourth of those sentenced to death are actually executed. In other words, the death penalty seems to be on its way out.

Today, 13 states have abolished capital punishment (Alaska, Hawaii, Iowa, Maine, Michigan, Minnesota, New York, North Dakota, Oregon, Rhode Island, Vermont, West Virginia, Wisconsin). Of those states which have the death penalty, six have not used it in the last 10 years.

Although there are in this country 31 offenses for which the death penalty can be imposed, only seven of the offenses, since 1930, have resulted in executions.

Reprinted by permission by *Lutheran Women*, March 1968, Official Magazine of Lutheran Church Women.

The death penalty has been abolished in at least 35 countries. With the exception of France, Greece and Spain, all Western European countries have done away with the death penalty or have not used it in this century. Most Latin American countries have abolished capital punishment.

In 1963 the National Council on Crime and Delinquency voiced its opposition to the death penalty. Two years later the Department of Justice announced its position favoring abolition of capital punishment. In 1967, the American Correctional Association (an organization of prison administrators and professional personnel) recorded its opposition to capital punishment, recommending that the death sentence be eliminated from the Federal Criminal Code and commending the efforts of the abolition committees in the several states.

Myrl E. Alexander, retired Director of the Federal Bureau of Prisons says: "After 35 years in prison administration, I am fully convinced that execution of criminals is a vestige of those ancient and barbaric punishments which are grossly inconsistent with the growing knowledge of the human behavioral sciences."

Warden Clinton T. Duffy of San Quentin Prison (retired) calls capital punishment a "tragic failure."

Why Oppose the Death Penalty?

1. IT IS NOT A DETERRENT. Those who favor capital punishment say it deters others from committing similar crimes. No valid research, however, proves that the abolition of capital punishment leads to an increase in homicides nor that retaining it actually deters crime. The proclaimed deterrent effects of capital punishment are not supported by contemporary studies and systematic research.

There is no pronounced difference in the rate of murders and other crimes of violence between states which impose the death penalty and those bordering on them which do not. Many states and countries without capital punishment have an incidence of homicide below that of comparable states and countries touching their borders which have the death penalty. In the United States, only 10 persons per 1,000 who have committed first-degree murder pay the extreme penalty. This would hardly cause the penalty to serve as a deterrent.

Following its four year study of capital punishment, the British Royal Commission concluded in 1953 that "there is no clear evidence in any of the figures we have examined that the abolition of capital punishment has led to an increase in the homicide rate or that its reintroduction has led to a fall."

Professor Thorsten Sellin, one of the world's foremost criminologists, concludes that: "The death penalty has failed as a deterrent."

2. MOST PERSONS COMMIT MURDER WITHOUT PREMEDITATION. A high proportion of murders are committed impulsively, without forethought, and often in an irrational state of mind. The killings occur during quarrels when persons are so bewildered they cannot control what they say and do. A large proportion of homicides are committed by family members and friends and lovers of the victim. Most persons involved in homicides do not deliberate on the death of the victim or contemplate the consequences, and many do not intend the victim's death.

Warden Duffy states: "I have asked hundreds, yes thousands, of prisoners who have committed homicides whether or not they thought of the death penalty before the commission of the act. . . . I have to date not had one person say that he has ever thought of the death penalty prior to the commission of his crime."

3. MANY CHARGED WITH CRIMES OF VIOLENCE SUFFER FROM UNDETECTED MENTAL ILLNESS. Crimes of violence frequently are committed by persons suffering from a serious mental disorder; they are irresistably driven to their crimes. Their mental illness is not detected until violent acts occur. Some have been convicted and sentenced to death when they should have been declared incompetent to stand trial.

4. THERE ARE GROSS INEQUITIES IN APPLICATION OF THE
DEATH PENALTY.   The death penalty imposes a discrimination against those in society who are most generally the victims of bigotry and prejudice. It does not mete
out even-handed justice. Its application is uneven, unpre-
dictable, and frequently unjust. Those who receive the
death penalty are usually the disadvantaged members of
society—the friendless, the uneducated, the mentally unstable and retarded, the poor and minority groups. More
than half (53.5 percent) of those executed in the United
States since 1930 were Negroes. Since Negroes make up
far less than half of those charged with crimes punishable
by death, this is hardly equality before the law.

"In the 12 years of my wardenship," said Warden Lewis
E. Lawes of Sing Sing, "I have escorted 150 men and one
woman to the death chamber and the electric chair. In age
they ranged from 17 to 63. They came from all kinds of
homes and environment. In one respect they were all
alike. All were poor, and most of them friendless."

The poor cannot afford competent legal counsel or appeal their convictions. The affluent, the influential and
those adequately represented in court are seldom executed.
Those in organized crime seldom are brought to justice.
When they are, they escape the death penalty.

Since 1930, 160 American servicemen have been executed, including 148 during the period 1942–1950. All
were Army and Air Force personnel. The last execution in
the Navy was in 1849, more than 125 years ago. Thus, the
application of the death penalty may even be determined
by the geographical area in which one lives or the branch
of military service in which he serves. There are in the
death row of some states persons awaiting execution for
crimes identical in degree and extenuating circumstances
to those for which prisoners in other states are serving life
terms or less, but a possibility of parole.

5. THE INNOCENT HAVE BEEN PUT TO DEATH.   Human
judgment is not infallible. The death penalty poses the
terrifying possibility of putting to death an innocent man.
Criminologists and penologists refer to a number of in-

stances where innocent persons have been executed. Convictions are obtained, at times, by forced confessions or other violations of due process of law. Execution is the only penalty which makes final and irrevocable any miscarriage of justice.

6. CAPITAL PUNISHMENT OBSTRUCTS JUSTICE. Capital punishment is an obstruction to the swift and certain administration of criminal justice. Trials in capital crimes are lengthy, involved and costly. Trial and appellate courts are confronted with numerous post-trial applications, petitions and appeals which are time-consuming and expensive.

There also are delays from time of conviction to execution. In the last dozen years in California no one has been executed less than eight months after being received in death row. One man spent more than 11 years in death row and finally was put to death. In one state, two men have been in the death house for nearly 14 years awaiting execution. Society is thus carrying out a deliberate infliction of the death penalty years after the occurrence of the offense.

7. THERE IS NO BASIS TO THE SAVINGS-IN-COST ARGUMENT. Execution, it is argued, would result in sizeable savings. To the contrary, life-term prisoners in many jurisdictions more than pay for the cost of their keep through productive labor in prison industries and other occupational assignments. Even if this were not so, society should be no more alarmed by the costs for the custody and care of life-term prisoners than that for the hopelessly insane who are in institutions for the remainder of their lives.

Cost is hardly grounds for taking a human life.

8. LIFE TERMERS RARELY COMIT ANOTHER HOMICIDE. Those who favor the retention of the death penalty express concern about the recurrence of another homicide either in prison or following release to the outside community. This contention is not supported by the facts. Most of those convicted of homicide eventually return

to society as law-abiding citizens and rarely commit another homicide. Career prison wardens declare that society is amply protected by a sentence to life imprisonment.

"Prisoners serving life sentences for murder," Professor Sellin asserts, "do not constitute a special threat to safety of other prisoners or to the prison staff. They are, as a rule, among the best-behaved prisoners and if paroled, they are the least likely to violate parole by commission of a new crime. In a few cases where such a violation occurs, the crime usually is not a very serious once. A repeated homicide is almost unheard of."

A recent 10-year study of 342 persons committed in California for first-degree murder and paroled after serving a prison term averaging 12 years showed that 90 percent completed their parole without violation. Of those who did violate parole, only 2.9 percent committed acts of such seriousness that they had to be returned to prison.

9. THE DEATH PENALTY IS A CRUDE AND PRIMITIVE FORM OF RETRIBUTIVE JUSTICE.   The death penalty is more an act of hate and vengeance than it is justice. Retribution cannot be considered a legitimate goal of criminal law. Yet simple retribution is one of the most appealing arguments for the retention of the death penalty.

A responsible society wants protection, not revenge. It does not need to avenge itself, nor should it want to do so. Punishment for punishment's sake is not justice and is repugnant to modern civilized man. The death penalty is not only unnecessary and futile, but is also barbaric and brutal. It has no place in a civilized society that does not require the taking of a human life for its safety and welfare. As one of the country's leading prison administrators has said: "Capital punishment is brutal, sordid, and savage — unworthy of a civilized people."

The progress of any civilization is measured by the reverence it accords to human life. "The mood and temper of the public with regard to the treatment of crime and criminals," the late Winston Churchill has said, "is one of the most unfailing tests of the civilization of a country."

Historically, the death penalty was imposed to seek

vengeance. Vengeance and retribution were deemed sufficient reasons for taking a life. Life tends to be short and cheap in primitive societies. But a civilized country has greater respect for the worth, dignity and life of a human being and a deeper appreciation of human behavior and its motivations.

"Capital punishment is an archaic and ineffectual practice that is as evil as the crimes it is designed to punish," declares Austin H. MacCormick, America's leading penologist. "In the name of humanity and justice, civilized nations should take the forthright step of abolishing it."

In Favor of Capital Punishment

Jacques Barzun

A passing remark of mine in the *Mid-Century* magazine has brought me a number of letters and a sheaf of pamphlets against capital punishment. The letters, sad and reproachful, offer me the choice of pleading ignorance or being proved insensitive. I am asked whether I know that there exists a worldwide movement for the abolition of capital punishment which has everywhere enlisted able men of every profession, including the law. I am told that the death penalty is not only inhuman but also unscientific, for rapists and murderers are really sick people who should be cured, not killed. I am invited to use my imagination and acknowledge the unbearable horror of every form of execution.

I am indeed aware that the movement for abolition is widespread and articulate, especially in England. It is headed there by my old friend and publisher, Mr. Victor Gollancz, and it numbers such well-known writers as Arthur Koestler, C. H. Rolph, James Avery Joyce and Sir John Barry. Abroad as at home the profession of psychiatry tends to support the cure principle, and many liberal newspapers, such as the *Observer*, are committed to abolition. In the United States there are at least twenty-five state leagues working to the same end, plus a national league and several church councils, notably the Quaker and the Episcopal.

Reprinted from *The American Scholar*, Vol. 31, No. 2, Spring, 1962. Copyright © 1962 by the United Chapters of Phi Beta Kappa. By permission of the publishers.

The assemblage of so much talent and enlightened goodwill behind a single proposal must give pause to anyone who supports the other side, and in the attempt to make clear my views, which are now close to unpopular, I start out by granting that my conclusion is arguable; that is, I am still open to conviction, *provided* some fallacies and frivolities in the abolitionist argument are first disposed of and the difficulties not ignored but overcome. I should be glad to see this happen, not only because there is pleasure in the spectacle of an airtight case, but also because I am not more sanguinary than my neighbor and I should welcome the discovery of safeguards—for society *and* the criminal—other than killing. But I say it again, these safeguards must really meet, not evade or postpone, the difficulties I am about to describe. Let me add before I begin that I shall probably not answer any more letters on this arousing subject. If this printed exposition does not do justice to my cause, it is not likely that I can do better in the hurry of private correspondence.

I readily concede at the outset that present ways of dealing out capital punishment are as revolting as Mr. Koestler says in his harrowing volume, *Hanged by the Neck.* Like many of our prisons, our modes of execution should change. But this objection to barbarity does not mean that capital punishment—or rather, judicial homicide—should not go on. The illicit jump we find here, on the threshold of the inquiry, is characteristic of the abolitionist and must be disallowed at every point. Let us bear in mind the possibility of devising a painless, sudden and dignified death, and see whether its administration is justifiable.

The four main arguments advanced against the death penalty are: *1)* punishment for crime is a primitive idea rooted in revenge; *2)* capital punishment does not deter; *3)* judicial error being possible, taking life is an appalling risk; *4)* a civilized state, to deserve its name, must uphold, not violate, the sanctity of human life.

I entirely agree with the first pair of propositions, which is why, a moment ago, I replaced the term capital punishment with "judicial homicide." The uncontrollable brute whom I want put out of the way is not to be punished for his misdeeds, nor used as an example or a warning; he is to be killed for the protection of others, like the wolf that escaped not long ago in a Connecticut suburb. No anger, vindictiveness or moral conceit need preside over the removal of such dangers. But a man's inability to control his violent impulses or to imagine the fatal consequences of his acts should be a presumptive reason for his elimination from society. This generality covers drunken driving and teen-age racing on public highways, as well as incurable obsessive violence; it might be extended (as I shall suggest later) to other acts that destroy, precisely, the moral basis of civilization.

But why kill? I am ready to believe the statistics tending to show that the prospect of his own death does not stop the murderer. For one thing he is often a blind egotist, who cannot conceive the possibility of his own death. For another, detection would have to be infallible to deter the more imaginative who, although afraid, think they can escape discovery. Lastly, as Shaw long ago pointed out, hanging the wrong man will deter as effectively as hanging the right one. So, once again, why kill? If I agree that moral progress means an increasing respect for human life, how can I oppose abolition?

I do so because on this subject of human life, which is to me the heart of the controversy, I find the abolitionist inconsistent, narrow or blind. The propaganda for aboliton speaks in hushed tones of the sanctity of human life, as if the mere statement of it as an absolute should silence all opponents who have any moral sense. But most of the abolitionists belong to nations that spend half their annual income on weapons of war and that honor research to perfect means of killing. These good people vote without a qualm for the political parties that quite sensibly arm their country to the teeth. The West today does not seem to be the time or place to invoke the absolute sanctity of human life. As for the clergymen in the movement, we may be sure from the experience of two previous world wars that they will bless our arms and pray for victory when called upon, the sixth commandment notwithstanding.

"Oh, but we mean the sanctity of life *within* the nation!" Very well: is the movement then campaigning also against the principle of self-defense? Absolute sanctity means letting the cutthroat have his sweet will of you, even if you have a poker handy to bash him with, for you might kill. And again, do we hear any protest against the police firing at criminals on the street—mere bank robbers usually—and doing this, often enough, with an excited marksmanship that misses the artist and hits the by-stander? The absolute sanctity of human life is, for the abolitionist, a slogan rather than a considered proposition.

Yet, it deserves examination, for upon our acceptance or rejection of it depend such other highly civilized possibilities as euthanasia and seemly suicide. The inquiring mind also wants to know, why the sanctity of *human* life alone? My tastes do not run to household pets, but I find something less than admirable in the uses to which we put animals—in zoos, laboratories and space machines—without the excuse of the ancient law, "Eat or be eaten."

It should moreover be borne in mind that this argument about sanctity applies—or would apply—to about ten persons a year in Great Britain and to between fifty and seventy-five in the United States. These are the average numbers of those executed in recent years. The count by itself should not, of course, affect our judgment of the principle: one life spared or forfeited is as important, morally, as a hundred thousand. But it should inspire a comparative judgment: there are hundreds and indeed thousands whom, in our concern with the horrors of execution, we forget: on the one hand, the victims of violence; on the other, the prisoners in our jails.

The victims are easy to forget. Social science tends steadily to mark a preference for the troubled, the abnormal, the problem case. Whether it is poverty, mental disorder, delinquency or crime, the "patient material" monopolizes the interest of increasing groups of people among the most generous and learned. Psychiatry and moral liberalism go together; the application of law as we have known it is thus coming to be regarded as an historic prelude to social work, which may replace it entirely. Modern literature makes the most of this same outlook, caring only for the disturbed spirit, scorning as bourgeois those who pay their way and *do not* stab their friends. All the while the determinism of natural science reinforces

the assumption that society causes its own evils. A French
jurist, for example, says that in order to understand crime
we must first brush aside all ideas of Responsibility. He
means the criminal's and takes for granted that of society.
The murderer kills because reared in a broken home or,
conversely, because at an early age he witnessed his parents making love. Out of such cases, which make pathetic
reading in the literature of modern criminology, is born
the abolitionist's state of mind: we dare not kill those we
are beginning to understand so well.

If, moreover, we turn to the accounts of the crimes
committed by these unfortunates, who are the victims?
Only dull ordinary people going about their business. We
are sorry, of course, but they do not interest science on its
march. Balancing, for example, the sixty to seventy criminals executed annually in the United States, there were
the seventy to eighty housewives whom George Cvek
robbed, raped and usually killed during the months of a career devoted to proving his virility. "It is too bad." Cvek
alone seems instructive, even though one of the law officers who helped track him down quietly remarks: "As to
the extent that his villainies disturbed family relationships, or how many women are still haunted by the spec-
ter of an experience they have never disclosed to another
living soul, these questions can only lend themselves to
sterile conjecture."

The remote results are beyond our ken, but it is not idle
to speculate about those whose death by violence fills the
daily two inches at the back of respectable newspapers—
the old man sunning himself on a park bench and beaten
to death by four hoodlums, the small children abused and
strangled, the middle-aged ladies on a hike assaulted and
killed, the family terrorized by a released or escaped lunatic, the half-dozen working people massacred by the sudden maniac, the boatload of persons dispatched by the
skipper, the mindless assaults upon schoolteachers and
shopkeepers by the increasing horde of dedicated killers in
our great cities. Where does the sanctity of life begin?

It is all very well to say that many of these killers are
themselves "children," that is, minors. Doubtless a nine-
year-old mind is housed in that 150 pounds of unguided

muscle. Grant, for argument's sake, that the misdeed is "the fault of society," trot out the broken home and the slum environment. The question then is, What shall we do, not in the Utopian city of tomorrow, but here and now? The "scientific" means of cure are more than uncertain. The apparatus of detention only increases the killer's antisocial animus. Reformatories and mental hospitals are full and have an understandable bias toward discharging their inmates. Some of these are indeed "cured"—so long as they stay under a rule. The stress of the social free-for-all throws them back on their violent modes of self-expression. At that point I agree that society has failed—twice: it has twice failed the victims, whatever may be its guilt toward the killer.

As in all great questions, the moralist must choose, and choosing has a price. I happen to think that if a person of adult body has not been endowed with adequate controls against irrationally taking the life of another, that person must be judicially, painlessly, regretfully killed before that mindless body's horrible automation repeats.

I say "irrationally" taking life, because it is often possible to feel great sympathy with a murderer. Certain *crimes passionnels* can be forgiven without being condoned. Blackmailers invite direct retribution. Long provocation can be an excuse, as in that engaging case of some years ago, in which a respectable carpenter of seventy found he could no longer stand the incessant nagging of his wife. While she excoriated him from her throne in the kitchen —a daily exercise for fifty years—the husband went to his bench and came back with a hammer in each hand to settle the score. The testimony to his character, coupled with the sincerity implied by the two hammers, was enough to have him sent into quiet and brief seclusion.

But what are we to say of the type of motive disclosed in a journal published by the inmates of one of our Federal penitentiaries? The author is a bank robber who confesses that money is not his object:

My mania for power, socially, sexually, and otherwise can feel no degree of satisfaction until I feel sure I have struck the ultimate of submission and terror in the minds and bodies of my victims. . . . It's very difficult to explain all the queer fascinating sensations pounding and surging through me while I'm holding a gun on a victim, watching his body tremble and sweat. . . . This is the moment when all the rationalized hypocrisies of civilization are suddenly swept away and two men stand there facing each other morally and ethically naked, and right and wrong are the absolute commands of the man behind the gun.

This confused echo of modern literature and modern science defines the choice before us. Anything deserving the name of cure for such a man presupposes not only a laborious individual psychoanalysis, with the means to conduct and to sustain it, socially and economically, but also a re-education of the mind, so as to throw into correct perspective the garbled ideas of Freud and Nietzsche, Gide and Dostoevski, which this power-seeker and his fellows have derived from the culture and temper of our times. Ideas are tenacious and give continuity to emotion. Failing a second birth of heart and mind, we must ask: How soon will this sufferer sacrifice a bank clerk in the interests of making civilization less hypocritical? And we must certainly question the wisdom of affording him more than one chance. The abolitionists' advocacy of an unconditional "let live" is in truth part of the same cultural tendency that animates the killer. The Western peoples' revulsion from power in domestic and foreign policy has made of the state a sort of counterpart of the bank robber: both having power and neither knowing how to use it. Both waste lives because hyponotized by irrelevant ideas and crippled by contradictory emotions. If psychiatry were sure of its ground in diagnosing the individual case, a philosopher might consider whether such dangerous obsessions should not be guarded against by judicial homicide *before* the shooting starts.

I raise the question not indeed to recommend the prophylactic execution of potential murderers, but to introduce the last two perplexities that the abolitionists dwarf or obscure by their concentration on changing an isolated penalty. One of these is the scale by which to judge the offenses society wants to repress. I can for example imagine a truly democratic state in which it would be deemed a form of treason punishable by death to create a disturbance in any court or deliberative assembly. The aim would be to recognize the sanctity of orderly discourse in arriving at justice, assessing criticism and defining policy. Under such a law, a natural selection would operate to remove permanently from the scene persons who, let us say, neglect argument in favor of banging on the desk with their shoe. Similarly, a bullying minority in a diet, parliament or skupshtina would be prosecuted for treason to the most sacred institutions when fists or flying inkwells replace rhetoric. That the mere suggestion of such a law sounds ludicrous shows how remote we are from civilized institutions, and hence how gradual should be our departure from the severity of judicial homicide.

I say gradual and I do not mean standing still. For there is one form of barbarity in our law that I want to see mitigated before any other. I mean imprisonment. The enemies of capital punishment—and liberals generally —seem to be satisfied with any legal outcome so long as they themselves avoid the vicarious guilt of shedding blood. They speak of the sanctity of life, but have no concern with its quality. They give no impression of ever having read what it is certain they have read, from Wilde's *De Profundis* to the latest account of prison life by a convicted homosexual. Despite the infamy of concentration camps, despite Mr. Charles Burney's remarkable work, *Solitary Confinement*, despite riots in prisons, despite the round of escape, recapture and return in chains, the abolitionists' imagination tells them nothing about the reality of being caged. They read without a qualm, indeed they read with rejoicing, the hideous irony of "Killer Gets Life"; they sigh with relief instead of horror. They do not see and suffer the cell, the drill, the clothes, the stench, the food; they do not feel the sexual racking of young and old bodies, the hateful promiscuity, the insane monotony, the mass degradation, the impotent hatred. They do not remember from Silvio Pellico that only a strong political faith, with a hope of final victory, can steel a man to endure long detention. They forget that Joan of Arc, when offered "life" preferred burning at the stake. Quite of another mind, the abolitionists point with pride to the "model prisoners" that murderers often turn out to be. As if a model prisoner were not, first, a contradiction in terms, and second, an exemplar of what a free society should not want.

I said a moment ago that the happy advocates of the life sentence appear not to have understood what we know they have read. No more do they appear to read what they themselves write. In the preface to his useful volume of cases, *Hanged in Error*, Mr. Leslie Hale, M. P., refers to the tardy recognition of a minor miscarriage of justice—one year in jail: "The prisoner emerged to find that his wife had died and that his children and his aged parents had been removed to the workhouse. By the time a small payment had been assessed as 'compensation' the victim was incurably insane." So far we are as indignant with the law as Mr. Hale. But what comes next? He cites the famous Evans case, in which it is very probable that the wrong man was hanged, and he exclaims: "While such mistakes are possible, should society impose an irrevocable sentence?" Does Mr. Hale really ask us to believe that the sentence passed on the first man, whose wife died and who went insane, was in any sense *revocable?* Would not any man rather be Evans dead than that other wretch "emerging" with his small compensation and his reasons for living gone?"

Nothing is revocable here below, imprisonment least of all. The agony of a trial itself is punishment, and acquittal wipes out nothing. Read the heart-rending diary of William Wallace, accused quite implausibly of having murdered his wife and "saved" by the Court of Criminal Appeals—but saved for what? Brutish ostracism by everyone and a few years of solitary despair. The cases of Adolf Beck, of Oscar Slater, of the unhappy Brooklyn bank teller who vaguely resembled a forger and spent eight years in Sing Song only to "emerge" a broken, friendless, useless, "compensated" man—all these, if the dignity of the individual has any meaning, had better have been dead before the prison door ever opened for them. This is what counsel always says to the jury in the course of a murder trial and counsel is right: far better hang this man than "give him life." For my part, I would choose death without hesitation. If that option is abolished, a demand will one day be heard to claim it as a privilege in the name of human dignity. I shall believe in the abolitionist's present views only after he has emerged from twelve months in a convict cell.

The detached observer may want to interrupt here and say that the argument has now passed from reasoning to emotional preference. Whereas the objection to capital punishment *feels* that death is the greatest of evils, I *feel* that imprisonment is worse than death. A moment's thought will show that feeling is the appropriate arbiter. All reasoning about what is right, civilized and moral rests upon sentiment, like mathematics. Only, in trying to persuade others, it is important to single out the fundamental feeling, the prime intuition, and from it to reason justly. In my view, to profess respect for human life and be willing to see it spent in a penitentiary is to entertain liberal feelings frivolously. To oppose the death penalty because, unlike a prison term, it is irrevocable is to argue fallaciously.

In the propaganda for abolishing the death sentence the recital of numerous miscarriages of justice commits the same error and implies the same callousness: what is at fault in our present system is not the sentence but the fallible procedure. Capital cases being one in a thousand or more, who can be cheerful at the thought of all the "revocable" errors? What the miscarriages point to is the need for reforming the jury system, the rules of evidence, the customs of prosecution, the machinery of appeal. The failure to see that this is the great task reflects the sentimentality I spoke of earlier, that which responds chiefly to the excitement of the unusual. A writer on Death and the Supreme Court is at pains to point out that when that tribunal reviews a capital case, the judges are particularly anxious and careful. What a lefthanded compliment to the highest judicial conscience of the country! Fortunately, some of the champions of the misjudged see the issue more clearly. Many of those who are thought wrongly convicted now languish in jail because the jury was uncertain or because a doubting governor commuted the death sentence. Thus Dr. Samuel H. Sheppard, Jr., convicted of his wife's murder in the second degree, is serving a sentence that is supposed to run for the term of his natural life. The story of his numerous trials, as told by Mr. Paul Holmes, suggests that police incompetence, newspaper demagogy, public envy of affluence and the mischances of legal procedure fashioned the result. But Dr. Sheppard's vindicator is under no illusion as to the conditions that this "lucky" evader of the electric chair will face if he is granted parole after ten years: "It will carry with it no right to resume his life as a physician. His privilege to practice medicine was blotted out with his conviction. He must all his life bear the stigma of a parolee, subject to unceremonious return to confinement for life for the slightest misstep. More than this, he must live out his life as a convicted murderer."[1]

What does the moral conscience of today think it is doing? If such a man is a dangerous repeater of violent acts, what right has the state to let him loose after ten years? What is, in fact, the meaning of a "life sentence" that peters out long before life? Patroling looks suspiciously like an expression of social remorse of the pain of incarceration, coupled with a wish to avoid "unfavorable publicity" by freeing a suspect. The man is let out when the fuss has died down; which would mean that he was not under lock and key for our protection at all. He *was* being punished, just a little—for so prison seems in the abolitionist's distorted view, and in the jury's and the prosecutor's, whose "second-degree" murder suggests killing someone "just a little."[2]

If, on the other hand, execution and life imprisonment are judged too severe and the accused is expected to be harmless hereafter—punishment being ruled out as illiberal—what has society gained by wrecking his life and damaging that of his family?

---

[1]Editor's note: See Sheppard v. Maxwell, 346 F.2d 707 which reversed defendant Sheppard's conviction. Released from prison, Dr. Sheppard later succumbed following a brief illness.

[2]The British Homicide Act of 1957, Section 2, implies the same reasoning in its definition of "diminished responsibility" for certain forms of mental abnormality. The whole question of irrationality and crime is in utter confusion, on both sides of the Atlantic.

What we accept, and what the abolitionist will clamp upon us all the more firmly if he succeeds, is an incoherence which is not remedied by the belief that second-degree murder merits a kind of second-degree death; that a doubt as to the identity of a killer is resolved by commuting real death into intolerable life; and that our ignorance whether a maniac will strike again can be hedged against by measuring "good behavior" within the gates and then releasing the subject upon the public in the true spirit of experimentation.

These are some of the thoughts I find I cannot escape when I read and reflect upon this grave subject. If, as I think, they are relevant to any discussion of change and reform, resting as they do on the direct and concrete perception of what happens, then the simple meliorists who expect to breathe a purer air by abolishing the death penalty are deceiving themselves and us. The issue is for the public to judge; but I for one shall not sleep easier for knowing that in England and America and the West generally a hundred more human beings are kept alive in degrading conditions to face a hopeless future; while others—possibly less conscious, certainly less controlled —benefit from a premature freedom dangerous alike to themselves and society. In short, I derive no comfort from the illusion that in giving up one manifest protection of the law-abiding, we who might well be in any of these three roles—victim, prisoner, licensed killer—have struck a blow for the sanctity of human life.

Gregg v. Georgia (1976)

United States Supreme Court

Majority Opinion (Written by Justice Potter Stewart)

We address initially the basic contention that the punishment of death for the crime of murder is, under all circumstances, "cruel and unusual" in violation of the Eighth and Fourteenth Amendments of the Constitution.

The Court on a number of occasions has both assumed and asserted the constitutionality of capital punishments. In several cases that assumption provided a necessary foundation for the decision, as the Court was asked to decide whether a particular method of carrying out a capital sentence would be allowed to stand under the Eighth Amendment. But until Furman v. Georgia, 408 U.S. 238 (1972), the Court never confronted squarely the fundamental claim that the punishment of death always, regardless of the enormity of the offense or the procedure followed in imposing the sentence, is cruel and unusual punishment in violation of the Constitution.

Although the issue was presented and addressed in Furman, it was not resolved by the Court, Four Justices would have held that capital punishment is not constitutional per se; two Justices would have reached the opposite conclusion; and three Justices, while agreeing that the statutes then before the Court were invalid as applied, left open the question whether such punishment may ever be imposed. We now hold that the punishment of death does not invariably violate the Constitution.

It is clear from the foregoing precedents that the Eighth Amendment has not been regarded as a static concept. As Chief Justice Warren said, in an oftquoted phrase, "[the] amendment must draw its meaning from the evolving standards of decency that mark the progress of a maturing society." Thus, an assessment of contemporary values concerning the infliction of a challenged sanction is relevant to the application of the Eighth Amendment. As we develop below more fully, this assessment does not call for a subjective judgment. It requires, rather, that we look to objective indicia that reflect the public attitude toward a given sanction.

But our cases also make clear that public perceptions of standards of decency with respect to criminal sanctions are not conclusive. A penalty also must accord with "the dignity of man," which is the "basic concept underlying the Eighth Amendment." This means, at least, that the punishment not be "excessive." When a form of punishment in the abstract (in this case, whether capital punishment may ever be imposed as a sanction for murder) rather than in the particular (the propriety of death as a penalty to be applied to a specific defendant for a specific crime) is under consideration, the inquiry into "excessiveness" has two aspects. First, the punishment must not involve the unnecessary and wanton infliction of pain. Second, the punishment must not be grossly out of proportion to the severity of the crime.

Of course, the requirements of the Eighth Amendment must be applied with an awareness of the limited role to be played by the courts. This does not mean that judges have no role to play, for the Eighth Amendment is a restraint upon the exercise of legislative power.

But, while we have an obligation to insure that constitutional bounds are not overreached, we may not act as judges as we might as legislators.

Therefore, in assessing a punishment by a democratically elected legislature against the constitutional measure, we presume its validity. We may not require the legislature to select the least severe penalty possible so long as the penalty selected is not cruelly inhumane or disproportionate to the crime involved. And a heavy burden rests on those who would attack the judgment of the representatives of the people.

This is true in part because the constitutional test is intertwined with an assessment of contemporary standards and legislative judgment weights heavily in ascertaining such standards.

The deference we owe to the decisions of the state legislatures under our Federal system is enhanced where the specification of punishments is concerned, for "these are peculiarly questions of legislative policy." A decision that a given punishment is impermissible under the Eighth Amendment cannot be reversed short of a constitutional amendment. The ability of the people to express their preference through the normal democratic processes, as well as through ballot referenda, is shut off. Revisions cannot be made in the light of further experience. We now consider specifically whether the sentence of death for the crime of murder is a per se violation of the Eighth and Fourteenth Amendments to the Constitution.

We note first that history and precedent strongly support a negative answer to this question.

The imposition of the death penalty for the crime of murder has a long history of acceptance both in the United States and in England. The common-law rule imposed a mandatory death sentence on all convicted murderers. And the penalty continued to be used into the 20th century by most American states, although the breadth of the common-law rule was diminished, initially by narrowing the class of murders to be punished by death and subsequently by widespread adoption of laws expressly granting judges the discretion to recommend mercy.

It is apparent from the text of the Constitution itself that the existence of capital punishment was accepted by the framers. At the time the Eighth Amendment was ratified, capital punishment was a common sanction in every state. Indeed, the first Congress of the United States enacted legislation providing death as the penalty for specified crimes.

For nearly two centuries, this Court, repeatedly and often expressly, has recognized that capital punishment is not invalid per se.

For years ago, the petitioners in Furman and its companion cases predicated their argument primarily upon the asserted proposition that standards of decency had evolved to the point where capital punishment no longer could be tolerated. The petitioners in those cases said, in effect, that the evolutionary process had come to an end, and that standards of decency required that the Eighth Amendment be construed finally as prohibiting capital punishment for any crime regardless of its depravity and impact on society.

The petitioners in the capital cases before the Court today renew the "standards of decency" argument, but developments during the four years since Furman have undercut substantially the assumptions upon which their argument rested. Despite the continuing debate, dating back to the 19th century, over the morality and utility of capital punishment, it is now evident that a large proportion of American society continues to regard it as an appropriate and necessary sanction.

The most marked indication of society's endorsement of the death penalty for murder is the legislative response to Furman. The legislatures of at least 35 states have enacted new statutes that provide for the death penalty for at least some crimes that result in the death of another person. And the Congress of the United States, in 1974, enacted a statute providing the death penalty for aircraft piracy that results in death.

As we have seen, however, the Eighth Amendment demands more than that a challenged punishment be acceptable to contemporary society. The Court also must ask whether it comports with the basic concept of human dignity at the core of the amendment. Although we cannot "invalidate a category of penalties because we deem less severe penalties adequate to serve the ends of penology," the sanction imposed cannot be so totally without penological justification that it results in the gratuitous infliction of suffering.

The death penalty is said to serve two principal social purposes: retribution and deterrence of capital crimes by prospective offenders.

In part, capital punishment is an expression of society's moral outrage at particularly offensive conduct. This function may be unappealing to many, but it is essential in an ordered society that asks its citizens to rely on legal processes rather than self-help to vindicate their wrongs.

Statistical attempts to evaluate the worth of the death penalty as a deterrent to crimes by potential offenders have occasioned a great deal of debate. The results simply have been inconclusive.

Although some of the studies suggest that the death penalty may not function as a significantly greater deterrent than lesser penalties, there is no convincing empirical evidence either supporting or refuting this view. We may nevertheless assume safely that there are murderers, such as those who act in passion, for whom the threat of death has little or no deterrent effect. But for many others, the death penalty undoubtedly is a significant deterrent. There are carefully contemplated murders, such as murder for hire, where the possible penalty of death may well enter into the cold calculus that precedes the decision to act. And there are some categories of murder, such as murder by a life prisoner, where other sanctions may not be adequate.

In sum, we cannot say that the judgment of the Georgia Legislature that capital punishment may be necessary in some cases is clearly wrong. Considerations of federalism, as well as respect for the ability of a legislature to evaluate, in terms of its particular state the moral consensus concerning the death penalty and its social utility as a sanction, require us to conclude, in the absence of more convincing evidence, that the infliction of death as a punishment for murder is not without justification and thus is not unconstitutionally severe.

Finally, we must consider whether the punishment of death is disproportionate in relation to the crime for which it is imposed. There is no question that death as a punishment is unique in its severity and irrevocability. When a defendant's life is at stake, the Court has been particularly sensitive to insure that every safeguard is observed.

But we are concerned here only with the imposition of capital punishment for the crime of murder, and when a life has been taken deliberately by the offender, we cannot say that the punishment is invariably disproportionate to the crime. It is an extreme sanction, suitable to the most extreme of crimes.

We hold that the death penalty is not a form of punishment that may never be imposed, regardless of the circumstances of the offense, regardless of the character of the offender, and regardless of the procedure followed in reaching the decision to impose it.

We now consider whether Georgia may impose the death penalty on the petitioner in this case.

The basic concern of Furman centered on those defendants who were being condemned to death capriciously and arbitrarily. Under the procedures before the Court in that case, sentencing authorities were not directed to give attention to the nature or circumstances of the crime committed or to the character or record of the defendant. Left unguided, juries imposed the death sentence in a way that could only be called freakish. The new Georgia sentencing procedure, by contrast, focus the jury's attention on the particularized characteristics of the individual defendant. While the jury is permitted to consider any aggravating or mitigating circumstances, it must find and identify at least one statutory aggravating factor before it may impose a penalty of death. In this way the jury's discretion is channeled. No longer can a jury wantonly and freakishly impose the death sentence; it is always circumscribed by the legislative guidelines. In addition, the review function of the Supreme Court of Georgia affords additional assurance that the concerns that prompted our decision in Furman are not present to any significant degree in the Georgia procedure applied here.

For the reasons expressed in this opinion, we hold that the statutory system under which Gregg was sentenced to death does not violate the Constitution. Accordingly, the judgment of the Georgia Supreme Court is affirmed.

It is so ordered.

Mr. Justice Brennan, Dissenting

This Court inescapably has the duty, as the ultimate arbiter of the meaning of our Constitution, to say whether, when individuals condemned to death stand before our bar, "moral concepts" require us to hold that the law has progressed to the point where we should declare that the punishment of death, like punishments on the rack, the screw and the wheel, is no longer morally tolerable in our civilized society. My opinion in Furman v. Georgia concluded that our civilization and the law had progressed to this point and therefore the punishment of death, for whatever crime and under all circumstances, is "cruel and unusual" in violation of the Eighth and Fourteenth Amendments of the Constitution. I shall not again canvass the reasons that led to that conclusion. I emphasize only that foremost among the "moral concepts" recognized in our cases and inherent in the clause is the primary moral principle that the state, even as it punishes, must treat its citizens in a manner consistent with their intrisic worth as human beings—a punishment must not be so severe as to be degrading to human dignity. A judicial determination whether the punishment of death comports with human dignity is therefore not only permitted but compelled by the clause.

Death is not only an unusually severe punishment, unusual in its pain, in its finality, and in its enormity, but it serves no penal purpose more effectively than a less severe punishment; therefore the principle inherent in the clause that prohibits pointless infliction of excessive punishment when less severe punishment can adequately achieve the same purposes invalidates the punishment.

Mr. Justice Marshall, Dissenting

My sole purposes here are to consider the suggestion that my conclusion in Furman has been undercut by developments since then, and briefly to evaluate the basis for by brethren's holding that the extinction of life is a permissible form of punishment under the cruel and unusual punishments clause.

In Furman I concluded that the death penalty is constitutionally invalid for two reasons. First, the death penalty is excessive. And second, the American people, fully
informed as to the purposes of the death penalty and its
liabilities, would in my view reject it as morally unacceptable.

Since the decision in Furman, the legislatures of 35
states have enacted new statutes authorizing the imposition of the death sentence for certain crimes, and Congress
has enacted a law providing the death penalty for air piracy
resulting in death. I would be less than candid if I did not
acknowledge that these developments have a significant
bearing on a realistic assessment of the moral acceptability
of the death penalty to the American people. But if the
constitutionality of the death penalty turns, as I have
urged, on the opinion of an informed citizenry, then even
the enactment of new death statutes cannot be viewed as
conclusive. In Furman, I observed that the American
people are largely unaware of the information critical to a
judgment on the morality of the death penalty, and concluded that if they were better informed they would consider it shocking, unjust, and unacceptable.

Even assuming, however, that the post-Furman enactment of statutes authorizing the death penalty renders the
prediction of the views of an informed citizenry an uncertain basis for a constitutional decision, the enactment of
those statutes has no bearing whatsoever on the conclusion that the death penalty is unconstitutional because it
is excessive. An excessive penalty is invalid under the
cruel and unusual punishments clause "even though popular sentiment may favor" it. The inquiry here, then, is
simply whether the death penalty is necessary to accomplish the legitimate legislative purposes in punishment,
or whether a less severe penalty—life imprisonment—
would do as well.

The two purposes that sustain the death penalty as
nonexcessive in the court's view are general deterrence
and retribution.

The Solicitor General in his amicus brief in these cases
relies heavily on a study by Isaac Ehrlich, reported a year

after Furman, to support the contention that the death penalty does deter murder.

The Ehrlich study, in short, is of little, if any assistance in assessing the deterrent impact of the death penalty. The evidence I reviewed in Furman remains convincing, in my view, that "capital punishment is not necessary as a deterrent to crime in our society." The justification for the death penalty must be found elsewhere.

The other principal purpose said to be served by the death penalty is retribution. The notion that retribution can serve as a moral justification for the sanction of death finds credence in the opinion of my brothers Stewart, Powell, and Stevens, and that of my brother White in Roberts v. Louisiana. It is this notion that I find to be the most disturbing aspect of today's unfortunate decision.

The foregoing contentions—that society's expression of moral outrage through the imposition of the death penalty pre-empts the citizenry from taking the law into its own hands and reinforces moral values—are not retributive in the purest sense. They are essentially utilitarian in that they portray the death penalty as valuable because of its beneficial results. These justifications for the death penalty are inadequate because the penalty is, quite clearly I think, not necessary to the accomplishment of those results.

There remains for consideration, however, what might be termed the purely retributive justification for the death penalty—that the death penalty is appropriate, not because of its beneficial effect on society, but because the taking of the murderer's life is itself morally good. Some of the language of the plurality's opinion appears positively to embrace this notion of retribution for its own sake as a justification for capital punishment.

The mere fact that the community demands the murderer's life in return for the evil he has done cannot sustain the death penalty, for as the plurality reminds us, "the Eighth Amendment demands more than that a challenged punishment be acceptable to contemporary society." To be sustained under the Eighth Amendment, the death penalty must ["comport] with the basic concept of human dignity at the core of the amendment"; the objective in imposing it must be ["consistent] with our respect for the dignity of other men." Under these standards, the taking of life "because the wrongdoer deserves it" surely must fall, for such a punishment has as its very basis the total denial of the wrongdoer's dignity and worth.

The death penalty, unnecessary to promote the goal of deterrence or to further any legitimate notion of retribution, is an excessive penalty forbidden by the Eighth and Fourteenth Amendments. I respectfully dissent from the Court's judgment upholding the sentences of death imposed upon the petitioners in these cases.

Suggestions for Further Reading (in paperback):

Gertrude Ezorsky, ed., *Philosophical Perspectives on Punishment* (Albany, NY: State University of New York Press, 1972).

Milton Goldinger, ed., *Punishment and Human Rights* (Cambridge, MA: Schenkman, 1974).

H. L. A. Hart, *Punishment and Responsibility* (Oxford: Clarendon Press, 1968).

Hugo A. Bedau, ed., *Capital Punishment in America* (Garden City, NY: Doubleday, 1964).

Part V
War

When, if ever, is one country justified in waging war on another? The great medieval philosopher St. Thomas Aquinas held that war is justified if three conditions are satisfied: first, the war must be declared by a legitimate authority; second, it must be fought for a "just cause"; and third, it must be waged using "moderate means"—that is, the war must not be pursued by methods more savage than necessary to insure victory.

A little reflection shows that these three conditions cannot be enough; it is possible that all three are satisfied, and yet war not be justified. For example, a legitimate authority might declare war for a just cause, and pursue the war by moderate means; yet if war did not have to be declared to achieve the just cause—if it could have been achieved by normal diplomatic means—then surely the war is not justified. So clearly, Aquinas' list of conditions must be revised and expanded before there can be an acceptable theory of the "just" war. In his article "The Just War," which leads off this unit, Joseph McKenna, a Catholic moral theologian, attempts to provide a more adequate theory.

Some people would object that there cannot be an acceptable theory of the justification of war, simply because war cannot be justified. This sort of pacifism is often thought to be a noble moral ideal, even by those who personally do not accept it. However, in her article "War and Murder," G. E. M. Anscombe argues not only that pacifism is a false moral view, but that it has pernicious consequences as well. It is false because it denies that we have the right to self-defense. It is pernicious because it encourages people to believe that all killing is equally wrong; believing this, people then tend not to distinguish legitimate wartime killing from atrocities. The result is that war becomes more murderous, not less so. In his article on "Pacifism," Jan Narveson makes a different sort of charge against that doctrine; he claims that pacifism is *an internally inconsistent view, that is, that the pacifist's position is actually self-contradictory.*

G. E. M. Anscombe is a well known philosopher associated with Cambridge University in England. In "War and Murder," she discusses several topics in addition to pacifism. One of the most important issues addressed in her paper is the question of obliteration bombing. In earlier times, wars were mainly affairs between competing armies; it was possible for civilian populations to remain relatively uninvolved. The distinction between combatants and noncombatants was fairly clear, and it was generally accepted as morally wrong to attack and kill noncombatants. The introduction of aerial bombing into warfare, and the involvement of civilians in war efforts of modern industrialized states changed all that. During World War II, it became common practice on both sides to bomb enemy cities, killing innocent civilians along with whatever soldiers, support personnel, or other military targets were in the area. Indeed, in some instances cities containing no military installations, munitions factories, or defense machinery were obliterated.

Two arguments were commonly given in defense of obliteration bombing: first, the destruction of enemy cities was said to have strategic value because it harmed the enemy's morale, and weakened their "will to fight"; second, it was argued that in war between modern industrialized nations there were no truly "uninvolved" civilians. These arguments were used by politicians and generals not only during World War II, but during more recent wars such as in Vietnam. Both arguments are highly suspect. In the first place, the bombing of cities does not, in fact, seem to damage enemy morale—and why should it? If we were engaged in a war, and the enemy destroyed your friends and family with bombs, would it make you less determined to oppose that enemy, or more so? In the second place, the claim that there are no truly innocent civilians in modern warfare is simply false; think, for example, of little children.

Anscombe argues that obliteration bombing is murder and cannot be justified. (Over thirty years ago she was one of the leaders of a group that opposed Oxford University's awarding Harry Truman an honorary degree; the opposition was based on Truman's part in the obliteration bombing of Hiroshima and Nagasaki with atomic weapons.) In constructing her argument, she appeals to the venerable doctrine of "double effect," which says that it may be permissible to bring about a result as the foreseen but unintended byproduct of an action that would not be permissible to bring about as the direct and intended result of the same action. An example might make this easier to understand: suppose a military commander ordered that a city be bombed. Then the death of innocent people would be the direct and intended result of the bombing, and that bombing would not be permissible. On the other hand, suppose the commander ordered that a munitions factory be bombed but, since the bombsights are not perfect, he knows that some bombs will inevitably fall upon nearby civilian homes. In this case the deaths of the innocent people will be a foreseeable but unintended byproduct of the bombing raid against the factory, and so this bombing may be justified. The conclusion which emerges from Anscombe's discussion is that, contrary to modern military practice, the deliberate, indiscriminate bombing of enemy population centers is immoral and unjustifiable.

The use of nuclear bombs against enemy cities is a particularly dramatic instance of obliteration bombing. The possibility of nuclear warfare raises a set of moral issues different in kind from those raised by conventional war, for in a nuclear war there is the chance of such massive destruction that civilization as previously known would be altogether stopped. This fact has led many people—

378

even many nonpacifists—to oppose the development and stockpiling of nuclear weapons.

The problem of nuclear disarmament is usually seen as a special case of a decision situation known as "The Prisoner's Dilemma," which goes like this. Suppose you and another person are arrested, charged with a crime, and taken to separate interrogation rooms. You are told that you will be convicted and sent to prison regardless of whether you confess, but your sentence will depend on whether you and *the other person confess. In particular, you are told:*

(a) *If both of you confess, you will each be sentenced to three years in prison.*

(b) *If you confess, and the other person does not, then you will get one year and he will get four years in prison.*

(c) *If the other person confesses, and you do not, then you will get four years and he will get one.*

(d) *If neither of you confesses, you will each be sentenced to two years in prison.*

The other person, in the other interrogation room, is being given exactly the same deal, but you have no way of knowing what he is going to do. The problem is, given that your only concern is to minimize your own time in prison, *what should you do? Should you confess, or not confess? Which is in your* own *best interests? Before reading on, you may want to see if you can solve the problem on your own.*

The solution is reached by the following reasoning. First, suppose the other person confesses. Then, if you confess you will end up spending three years in prison; and if you don't confess, you will spend four years in prison. Therefore, if he confesses you will be better off if you confess. Second, suppose he does not confess. In that case, you will still be better off if you confess—because by confessing you will get one year, and by not confessing you will get two years. Therefore, no matter what the other person does, you will be better off confessing, so you ought to confess.

But now notice this: since the other person is being offered the same deal, if he is rational he will reach exactly the same conclusion, that he ought also to confess. So, if you are both rational, you will both confess, and you will each end up spending three years behind bars. However, it now appears that something has gone badly wrong, for if both of you had not confessed, you would each be spending only two years in prison! That is why this decision situation is called a "dilemma." By doing what is rational from a narrowly self-interested point of view, both persons end up worse off than if they had done the opposite. To resolve the dilemma, what the prisoners need (but cannot have under the terms of the problem) is a binding agreement that they both not confess. The agreement would have to be enforceable in some way, since an agreement that cannot be enforced is worthless in this situation.

The Prisoner's Dilemma has great theoretical interest because it is formally parallel to many actual decision situations. As already stated, many theorists believe that the decision to keep our nuclear weapons or disarm is parallel to the prisoner's decision whether or not to confess. The reasoning goes like this: suppose our enemies have nuclear weapons, and they choose not to disarm. Then we had better not disarm either, since this would put us at a great disadvantage. On the other hand, suppose our enemies choose to disarm. Then it is to our advantage to keep our nuclear weapons, since this gives us a big edge over them. So no matter what our enemies do, it seems in our own best interests not to disarm.

But other nuclear powers face exactly the same situation, and by the same reasoning they can be expected not to disarm, so the result is that nobody disarms. Now we get a paradoxical result similar to the prisoners who find themselves each spending more time in prison than if neither had confessed. If each side reasons from a purely self-interested point of view, the result is that nobody disarms; but it would be far better for everybody if both sides disarmed. Again, the natural conclusion is that what we need is a binding, enforceable agreement that everyone disarms. And this is exactly the goal of the nuclear disarmament negotiations (the "SALT" talks), that have been going on between the United States and the Soviet Union for several years.

The belief that the decision to disarm is parallel to the Prisoner's Dilemma is, therefore, at the heart of nuclear policy in most of the world's great powers. In his article "Ethics and Nuclear Deterrence," which concludes this unit, Douglas Lackey challenges this widely held belief. He argues that the situation with respect to nuclear disarmament is not parallel to the Prisoner's Dilemma. On the contrary, Lackey contends, we would be better off without nuclear weapons even if our enemies retained theirs. Moreover, he argues that for a host of other reasons the moral path would be for the United States to dismantle its own nuclear arsenal, even if no one else did likewise.

Lackey's view could hardly be more contrary to popular opinion but, as he says, people these days tend to underestimate the changes of nuclear holocaust, and so perhaps the risk of keeping our nuclear weapons is similarly underestimated.

The Just War

Joseph C. McKenna

I

In the opinion of Scholastics, both defensive and offensive wars can be morally justified. Supporting argumentation differs for the two types, and the offensive variety is more severely circumscribed. Although Pauline ideas are invoked in the argument, they do not seem strictly necessary; the analysis relies more heavily on reason than on revelation.

At the core of the position is the Scholastic concept of a political society. While this concept admittedly tends to a misleading hypostasization of the state, it does convey reality in terms more meaningful than the positive law fiction of corporate personality. For it relates to the intentions of morality's divine creator rather than to the artifice of human legislators. In the Scholastic view, because a civil society is a natural entity, it is divinely instituted. God, as author of man's natural needs, aptitudes and tendencies, is also author of the social structures which are built upon them. To these social structures, of which the state is one, He has attached certain objective moral characteristics.

One moral characteristic of the state is its obligation to seek the common earthly welfare of its citizens. Linked with this is a second, its right of self-defense. If the evil

Reprinted from Joseph C. McKenna, "Ethics and War: A Catholic View," *American Political Science Review*, 54 (1960), pp. 647–658, by permission of the *American Political Science Review*.

could with impunity impose their will upon the innocent, social life would be reduced to chaos; for the good of its citizens, then, a state unjustly attacked by force may resist by force.

The right of self-defense is not, however, absolute. It may be exercised only if action is urgently needed and no other remedy is at hand; only so much violence is allowed as will repel the unjust aggressor; a justified attack may not be resisted at all. On these restrictions of the right, Scholastics have long agreed. But two other points have recently attracted closer attention. In an important sense, the right of self-defense is founded on the requirements of a wider, equally natural, but less articulated community—that of mankind. The right aims at preventing international anarchy by restraints placed upon men of ill-will. Conceivably, this purpose would be better served in some circumstances by forbearance than by resistance; where this was the case, the state would be obligated to refrain from action. Secondly, the right of self-defense is founded on the interests of the particular community's own citizens. It aims at protecting their wealth, their lives, and their liberty. Conceivably, this objective, too, could be better achieved by self-abnegation than by self-assertion; and the state would again be obliged to let events take their course.

Another cardinal characteristic of the state is its moral authority. This is its divine authorization to rule, to exercise—with effects in the moral order itself—the functions traditionally identified with governing: to command, judge and execute. While Augustine and his followers here look to the Pauline concept of the public power, the Scholastic can derive this characteristic in sheerly rational terms, as a natural requirement of the community and therefore as a natural endowment bestowed by the community's divine author.

Upon the state's possession of moral authority turns its right of offensive war. The rights of a state or its citizens can be violated in ways other than by invasion: territory or prerogative owing to the nation can be withheld, or the movement and commerce of its nationals can be seriously impeded. The injustice thus inflicted would call not only for reparation but—in the interests of social order—for punishment. Within a society, the individual is not free to pursue such purposes on his own; he may only appeal to public authority. As between societies, however, there is no one to whom effective appeal can be made. The moral empowerment of the injured therefore receives a kind of extension: to pass and execute judgment on those who are normally beyond its jurisdiction. Just as the government may right wrongs and punish wrongdoers inside its boundaries, so it may act outside. If need be, it may vindicate its community's right even by violence. The injured state becomes with respect to another nation "an avenger to execute wrath on him who does evil."

The Scholastic does not, it should be noted, stigmatize legitimate war as the "lesser evil." International crises do not confront him, in this respect at least, with true "dilemmas." Common humanist and Protestant conceptions are quite different. Ernest Lefever, for example, writes unequivocally in a somewhat wider context that "choosing the lesser of two evils . . . is more responsible than an ethic of abstention." Reinhold Niebuhr, adapting classic Lutheran theology, finds man necessitated to sin, not only by the intrinsic corruption of human nature but also by the extrinsic dilemmas of the social milieu. For the Scholastic, by contrast, sin is never inevitable; an act of self-defense or an act of vindicative justice, although imposed by circumstances which are regrettable, is morally good. This conclusion might be censured as leading to an easy identification of selfish national interest with high moral purpose. Yet the doctrine may actually be more humanizing than the other, bleaker, views. It holds conscience to account, first for the reason, then for the measure, of violence—instead of giving over the moral agent to the uninhibited hopelessness which often follows from seeing sin as unavoidable.

II

The justification of war in general terms does not end the discussion. Conscience must render its account on certain qualifying factors. Unless particular conditions are fulfilled, the general justification has no application to specific cases. These qualifications can be conveniently summarized under seven headings—some of which are more, some less, relevant to the problems of contemporary diplomacy.

First, the war must be declared by legitimate public authority in the country which goes to war. This requirement pertains primarily to offensive wars, since these professedly vindicate justice and are therefore an exercise of divinely authorized judicial and executive power. Historically, the condition was invoked in order to limit the military activities of lesser feudal lords. Today, it has a somewhat analogous function even with respect to the major powers. Since, in choosing war or peace, the government of any state acts as surrogate for an unarticulated international authority, its decision must be controlled by international purposes. War must aim at a good which is universal rather than exclusive. Peace and the sacrifice even of a just claim may therefore be necessary sometimes for the welfare of the wider community.

Second, the injury which the war is intended to prevent or rectify must be real and certain. An imaginary injustice cannot legitimize vindication. Both the right which has been infringed and the alleged infringement of it must have substance. The possibly unjust taking of human life is not within the ambit of the "probabilism" utilized by many Scholastics in appraising most types of moral acts. The right which is at stake in war must therefore be certainly possessed and certainly violated. Some moralists believe, in addition, that a government going to war should know for certain the other party's *moral* culpability that it should be able to discount with complete assurance any suggestion of inadvertence or ignorance on his part. This belief again is based on the Scholastic notion of civil authority. Because authority is divine in origin and function, only a *moral* fault, as distinguished from a purely juridical, external, offense, can validate its use. As others indicate, however, human knowledge can never be sure of other men's dispositions, on which their moral guilt depends; malicious or not, the external violation of right disturbs social order and justifies its vindication. Typical injuries envisaged by the older moralists, it may be noted, included

seizure or retention of territory, breach of the communal
or private, the commercial or personal liberties of a country's nationals; and similar impositions on a third state.

Third, the seriousness of the injury must be proportioned to the damages that the war will cause. No criteria
are laid down for weighing either factor, except that the
assessment must be made in terms of moral rather than
material gains and losses. Self-defense, it is agreed, almost
always justifies resistance, and the positive vindication of
trivial rights is never adequate reason for hostilities. Between these two accepted judgments, however, there is
room for widely divergent appraisals. Some commentators
contend that no vindication of any right entitles a country
to wage war. For them the theory of legitimate offensive
action, although retaining its technical validity, has ceased
to be applicable in the modern world. They expressed this
view before World War II; they regard it as irrefutably
confirmed by subsequent military developments. Pope
Pius XII appears to have made it his own. The potential
damage of war will be totally disproportionate to any possible achievement.

Fourth—and this is closely linked with the third
condition—there must be reasonable hope of success in
the waging of the war. If defeat is certain, hostilities will
only aggravate the injustice which occasioned them and
leave a train of futile sorrow in their path. A nation defending itself against attack, however, may more readily
take its chances on fighting, as Finland did in 1939, than a
nation on the offensive. In extreme cases the moral value
of national martyrdom may compensate for the material
destruction of unsuccessful war, as with Belgium in 1914.

Commentators prophesy that the next war will have no
victor. The truth of their prediction depends upon what
victory can mean. It cannot mean now, if it ever did, the
categorical imposition of the winning side's will upon the
loser. The erosion of the victor's comparative advantage
vis-à-vis the vanquished in both World Wars demonstrates
this; even after an atomic clash, the cooperation of the defeated country will be worth bargaining for. Success can
then mean, at best, the accomplishment of limited objectives. But since such accomplishment remains possible,

calculation of success can still enter into the moral choice
of war or peace.

Fifth, only as a last resort may hostilities be initiated. A
war is clearly pointless if its ends can be attained by less
painful means. Negotiation, mediation, arbitration and
judicial settlement must be utilized first. Scholastics have
in fact demanded, as a necessary prerequisite for military
action, an ultimatum or a formal declaration of war, since
these are the last measures of persuasion short of force itself. Apart from the possibility that such devices might in
fact achieve their appropriate purpose, they can aid in assessing the morality of one's own decision. For they help
to establish with certainty any alleged injury as a matter
both of law and of fact, by at least hinting at the culpability of a party who shuns them. Moreover, if the rights and
wrongs of a situation remain doubtful—in which case war
would be immoral—these alternative courses furnish opportunity for compromising the issues.

Sixth, a war may be prosecuted legitimately only
insofar as the responsible agents have a right intention.
Even good acts are morally perverted if they are done with
immoral motives. The significance of this condition
should not be discounted simply because the extenal observer cannot pass judgment on its fulfilment. Governmental authorities are here challenged to confront continually their purposes with the unflinching appraisal of
their consciences. A war which is otherwise just becomes
immoral if it is waged out of hatred. A war of self-defense
becomes immoral if, in its course, it becomes an instrument of expansion. A war to vindicate justice becomes
immoral if, as it goes on, it becomes a means of aggrandizement. The facility with which nations rationalize
their resort to war is a commonplace of diplomatic histo-
rians. The inhibitory influence of conscience is cited less
frequently—and even then, with disparaging cynicism; yet
it has possibly prevented more wars than this world
dreams of. The requirement of right intention can, in addition, debar the rash initiation of war and can bridle the
vengeful dispositions which—as Kennan and others have
complained—make for the irrational termination of hostilities in "unconditional surrender" when something just

as valuable could be achieved faster, more cheaply; and in punitive clauses which fester instead of healing the wounds of the defeated.

Seventh, the particular measures used in conducting the war must themselves be moral. Noble ends do not sanctify ignoble means; evil may not be done that good may come of it. The ramifications of this restriction are wide. It raises questions about the taking of hostages, the handling of prisoners, the employment of deceptive strategems, the resort to espionage, and, above all else today, the utilization of nuclear weapons. It might be anticipated that no conceivable use of these armaments can be justified. But the Scholastic here makes important distinctions. Discussion of these best fits the application, below, of the seven enumerated conditions to the emerging international situation.

The final moral criterion which must be applied to the major contingencies deals with the measures or means to be used in warfare. The use of immoral means renders immoral the very pursuit of the war by the user. In question are the means sanctioned by the responsible policy-maker, not the activities in which individuals or subordinate officials may engage on their own authority; although war does produce a flood of these activities, their moral relevance is to the balance of good and evil consequences, already discussed. As far as the policy-maker's choice is concerned, the possible resort to nuclear weapons presents the chief difficulty. A rather extensive digression back to pertinent principles of Scholastic ethics will be necessary in approaching it.

The central issue in the use of nuclear weapons is the treatment of non-combatants. In a just war enemy soldiers, and civilians engaged in close logistical supporting action like the manufacture and transport of munitions, may legitimately be killed. Because these are intimately cooperating in the materially unjust activities of the opposing state, they are "guilty"—at least in the juridical sense—of serious injustice; the troops engaged against them are agents of the public authority which is trying to restrain them. Even in "total war," however, non-combatants remain very numerous; these are "innocent," and not subject to the drastic treatment accorded to their countrymen who are closer to the battle. The moral problem arises because nuclear weapons, in some of their contemplated uses, would inflict civilian casualties numbering tens of millions.

The Scholastic seeks moral judgment for this and other methods of warfare through the "principle of double effect." In essence, this principle asserts that an evil effect may be *tolerated* as an incident to a good effect *willed*. As elaborated, the principle requires the fulfillment of four conditions. First, the two effects must issue from a human act which is in the abstract morally good, or at least indifferent; it may not be intrinsically evil. Second, causally the good effect must flow as immediately from this act as the evil effect; it may certainly not be caused by evil effect. Third, the moral agent must, in his own mind, positively intend only the good effect, merely permitting the evil. And fourth, the good achieved must be proportionate to the evil which is incidental to it. In these terms, an act which damages the innocent can be moral if the damage is adventitious to the restraint and punishment of the guilty. Scholastics have usually regarded as legitimate the bombardment of, for example, a strategic fortress in which non-combatants have taken refuge, or a munitions plant in a populated area. The firing of projectiles is indifferent; significant military damage and unfortunate civilian casualties result simultaneously from the explosions; the agent, by hypothesis, intends only the military destruction; and the objective, again by hypothesis, is sufficiently important to outweigh the non-combatant deaths and injuries. Scholastics seem not, however, to lay down criteria for determining allowable proportions of evil and good; they appeal rather to what they assume is the common human appraisal.

Although the principle of double effect leaves room, then, for some actions which harm the innocent, moralists during World War II condemned at least one common practice connected with aerial bombardment—as falling outside the limits of the principle and therefore as an immoral military measure. This was the so-called "saturation bombing" of mixed industrial and residential neighborhoods. Military men thought of the technique partly as a way to compensate for the inaccuracy of their bombers, and partly as a device for undermining the enemy's civilian morale. If one could not lay bombs with pin-point precision on a war-plant, one could pour bombs lavishly on the general area in which the plant was situated. This would increase the mathematical probability of a "hit." And if the other nation's general populace brooded under the constant threat of sleepless nights, devastated homes, and death itself, their determination to struggle on could not endure. The moral critics objected that the military gain in crippling a factory bore no proportion to the damage inflicted on non-combatants; that demoralization was caused by direct attacks upon the innocent, rather than being incidental to attacks on the guilty; and that it was psychologically impossible to discriminate in one's moral intention while one was spraying lethal missiles with deliberate indiscrimination over a diversified area.

For the atomic bombing of Hiroshima, these strictures were more clearly valid. Even if the bomb had been aimed at a sharply defined military target, success in destroying such an installation or complex could not outweigh the resultant deaths of 80,000 or more civilians. The American argument was that this act shortened the war and saved lives on both sides. In moral terms, the argument was irrelevant. For if it was true, the good was still the consequence of the evil, the end still did not justify the means.

The censure of American action at Hiroshima does not, however, debar all licit use of nuclear weapons. Since 1945, atomic technology and politics have changed in at least two ways significant for the moralist. The fantastic upward development of explosive potency (and of fallout range and intensity) in the hydrogen bomb, and the unexpected harnessing of this same potency in tactical warheads have diversified the uses upon which he must pass judgment. And the growth of the "nuclear club" to include the most likely adversaries in any major war has added a new evil consequence which he must calculate into the double-effect. This is the possibility that any single atomic explosion will provoke a widening—whether gradually or rapidly—resort to nuclear weapons. The consensus which Scholastics have reached in observing these changes could probably be summarized in these propositions. If the likelihood of expanding a nuclear conflict be set aside, even a high-yield hydrogen bomb could legitimately be dropped upon an isolated military target such as a fleet at sea. Tactical weapons could be hurled at air-bases or at armies in the field. As for nuclear raids—restricted in scope—on industrial or communications centers, opinion is divided: some believe that if such an operation would be much less costly to the raider than a conventional precision attack, it would be permissible, while others insist that in the nature of the case it precludes the necessary discrimination in the raider's moral intentions.

Against this background of principle, one can turn again to likely contingencies in international affairs. By contrast with the other six criteria, the criterion of means touches the conduct of a war rather than its inception. Its relevance to entering upon a war is reflex, as an aspect of gauging proportionate good and evil consequences.

A war between neutrals, or a war initiated by Soviet satellites against a neutral or an American ally could, in an outsider's judgment, be repressed by an intervention which did not employ nuclear explosives. The generally superior arsenal of conventional American arms is capable of achieving this end. Action by Communist China may, as indicated earlier, represent an exception. True, from a military point of view, nuclear devices could be advantageous in these contingencies and, in the abstract, some of them are certainly licit. But the surest way to obviate all use of atomic weapons—and an upward spiral in their potency—is to refrain from first use.

If the Soviet Union were to initiate a war, however, the United States would almost certainly have to run the risk of "first use." The employment of atomic warheads in tactical operations against military installations or troops in the field would be permissible. This would be true, too, in the single conceivable instance of an American initiative. But in no contingency does it seem possible to justify the dispatch of high yield nuclear weapons against cities or essentially civilian areas—not even in retaliation.

War and Murder

G. E. M. Anscombe

I. The Use of Violence by Rulers

Since there are always thieves and frauds and men who commit violent attacks on their neighbours and murderers, and since without law backed by adequate force there are usually gangs of bandits; and since there are in most places laws administered by people who command violence to enforce the laws against lawbreakers; the question arises: what is a just attitude to this exercise of violent coercive power on the part of rulers and their subordinate officers?

Two attitudes are possible: one, that the world is an absolute jungle and that the exercise of coercive power by rulers is only a manifestation of this; and the other, that it is both necessary and right that there should be this exercise of power, that through it the world is much less of a jungle than it could possibly be without it, so that one should in principle be glad of the existence of such power, and only take exception to its unjust exercise.

It is so clear that the world is less of a jungle because of rulers and laws, and that the exercise of coercive power is essential to these institutions as they are now—all this is so obvious, that probably only Tennysonian conceptions of progress enable people who do not wish to separate themselves from the world to think that nevertheless such violence is objectionable, that some day, in this present dis-

From *Nuclear Weapons: A Catholic Response*, edited by Walter Stein, Copyright © 1961 by the Merlin Press Ltd., published by Sheed & Ward, Inc., New York.

pensation, we shall do without it, and that the pacifist is
the man who sees and tries to follow the ideal course,
which future civilization must one day pursue. It is an illusion, which would be fantastic if it were not so familiar.

In a peaceful and law abiding country such as England, it
may not be immediately obvious that the rulers need to
command violence to the point of fighting to the death
those that would oppose it; but brief reflection shows that
this is so. For those who oppose the force that backs law
will not always stop short of fighting to the death and
cannot always be put down short of fighting to the death.

Then only if it is in itself evil violently to coerce resis-
tant wills, can the exercise of coercive power by rulers be
bad as such. Against such a conception, if it were true, the
necessity and advantage of the exercise of such power
would indeed be a useless plea. But that conception is one
that makes no sense unless it is accompanied by a theory
of withdrawal from the world as man's only salvation; and
it is in any case a false one. We are taught that God retains
the evil will of the devil within limits by violence: we are
not given a picture of God permitting to the devil all that
he is capable of. There is current a conception of Christianity as having revealed that the defeat of evil must always be by pure love without coercion; this at least is
shown to be false by the foregoing consideration. And
without the alleged revelation there could be no reason
to believe such a thing.

To think that society's coercive authority is evil is akin
to thinking the flesh evil and family life evil. These things
belong to the present constitution of mankind; and if the
exercise of coercive power is a manifestation of evil, and
not the just means of restraining it, then human nature is
totally depraved in a manner never taught by Christianity.
For society is essential to human good; and society without coercive power is generally impossible.

The same authority which puts down internal dissen-
sion, which promulgates laws and restrains those who
break them if it can, must equally oppose external
enemies. These do not merely comprise those who attack
the borders of the people ruled by the authority; but also,
for example, pirates and desert bandits, and, generally,

those beyond the confines of the country ruled whose activities are viciously harmful to it. The Romans, once
their rule in Gaul was established, were eminently justified
in attacking Britain, where were nurtured the Druids whose
pupils infested northern Gaul and whose practices struck
the Romans themselves as "dira immanitas." Further,
there being such a thing as the common good of mankind,
and visible criminality against it, how can we doubt the
excellence of such a proceeding as that violent suppression
of the man-stealing business[1] which the British government took it into its head to engage in under Palmerston?
The present-day conception of "aggression," like so many
strongly influential conceptions, is a bad one. Why *must* it
be wrong to strike the first blow in a struggle? The only
question is, who is in the right.

Here, however, human pride, malice and cruelty are so
usual that it is true to say that wars have mostly been
mere wickedness on both sides. Just as an individual will
constantly think himself in the right, whatever he does,
and yet there is still such a thing as being in the right, so
nations will constantly wrongly think themselves to be in
the right—and yet there is still such a thing as their being
in the right. Palmerston doubtless had no doubts in pros-
ecuting the opium war against China, which was diaboli-
cal; just as he exulted in putting down the slavers. But
there is no question but that he was a monster in the one
thing, and a just man in the other.

The probability is that warfare is injustice, that a life of
military service is a bad life "militia or rather malitia," as
St. Anselm called it. This probability is greater than the
probability (which also exists) that membership of a police
force will involve malice, because of the character of warfare: the extraordinary occasions it offers for viciously unjust proceedings on the part of military commanders and
warring governments, which at the time attract praise and
not blame from their people. It is equally the case that the

[1] It is ignorance to suppose that it takes modern liberalism to hate and condemn
this. It is cursed and subject to the death penalty in the Mosiac law. Under that
code, too, runaway slaves of all nations had asylum in Israel.

life of a ruler is usually a vicious life: but that does not
show that ruling is as such a vicious activity.

  The principal wickedness which is a temptation to
those engaged in warfare is the killing of the innocent,
which may often be done with impunity and even to the
glory of those who do it. In many places and times it has
been taken for granted as a natural part of waging war: the
commander, and especially the conqueror, massacres
people by the thousand, either because this is part of his
glory, or as a terrorizing measure, or as part of his tactics.

II. Innocence and the Right to Kill Intentionally

It is necessary to dwell on the notion of non-innocence
here employed. Innocence is a legal notion; but here, the
accused is not pronounced guilty under an existing code of
law, under which he has been tried by an impartial judge,
and therefore made the target of attack. There is hardly a
possibility of this; for the administration of justice is
something that takes place under the aegis of a sovereign
authority; but in welfare—or the putting down by violence
of civil disturbance—the sovereign authority is itself engaged as a party to the dispute and is not subject to a further earthly and temporal authority which can judge the
issue and pronounce against the accused. The stabler the
society, the rarer it will be for the sovereign authority to
have to do anything but apprehend its internal enemy and
have him tried; but even in the stablest society there are
occasions when the authority has to fight its internal
enemy to the point of killing, as happens in the struggle
with external belligerent forces in international warfare;
and then the characterization of its enemy as non-innocent has not been ratified by legal process.

  This, however, does not mean that the notion of innocence fails in this situation. What is required, for the
people attacked to be non-innocent in the relevant sense,
is that they should themselves be engaged in an objectively unjust proceeding which the attacker has the right
to make his concern; or—the commonest case—should be
unjustly attacking him. Then he can attack them with a
view to stopping them; and also their supply lines and ar-

mament factories. But people whose mere existence and activity supporting existence by growing crops, making clothes, etc. constitute an impediment to him—such people are innocent and it is murderous to attack them, or make them a target for an attack which he judges will help him towards victory. For murder is the deliberate killing of the innocent whether for its own sake or as a means to some further end.

The right to attack with a view to killing is something that belongs only to rulers and those whom they command to do it. I have argued that it does belong to rulers precisely because of that threat of violent coercion exercised by those in authority which is essential to the existence of human societies. It ought not to be pretended that rulers and their subordinates do not choose[2] the killing of their enemies as a means, when it has come to fighting in which they are determined to win and their enemies resist to the point of killing: this holds even in internal disturbances.

When a private man struggles with an enemy he has no right to aim to kill him, unless in the circumstances of the attack on him he can be considered as endowed with the authority of the law and the struggle comes to that point. By a "private" man, I mean a man in a society; I am not speaking of men on their own, without government, in remote places; for such men are neither public servants nor "private." The plea of self-defence (or the defence of someone else) made by a private man who has killed someone else must in conscience—even if not in law—be a plea that the death of the other was not intended, but was a side effect of the measures taken to ward off the attack. To shoot to kill, to set lethal man-traps, or, say, to lay poison for someone from whom one's life is in danger, are forbidden. The deliberate choice of inflicting death in a struggle is the right only of ruling authorities and their subordinates.

---

[2]The idea that they may lawfully do what they do, but should not *intend* the death of those they attack, has been put forward and, when suitably expressed, may seem high-minded. But someone who can fool himself into this twist of thought will fool himself into justifying anything, however atrocious, by means of it.

In saying that a private man may not choose to kill, we are touching on the principle of "double effect." The denial of this has been the corruption of non-Catholic thought, and its abuse the corruption of Catholic thought. Both have disastrous consequences which we shall see. This principle is not accepted in English law: the law is said to allow no distinction between the foreseen and the intended consequences of an action. Thus, if I push a man over a cliff when he is menacing my life, his death is considered as intended by me, but the intention to be justifiable for the sake of self-defence. Yet the lawyers would hardly find the laying of poison tolerable as an act of self-defence, but only killing by a violent action in a moment of violence. Christian moral theologians have taught that even here one may not seek the death of the assailant, but may in default of other ways of self-defence use such violence as will in fact result in his death. The distinction is evidently a fine one in some cases: what, it may be asked, can the intention be, if it can be said to be absent in this case, except a mere wish or desire?

And yet in other cases the distinction is very clear. If I go to prison rather than perform some action, no reasonable person will call the incidental consequences of my refusal—the loss of my job, for example—intentional just because I knew they must happen. And in the case of the administration of a pain-relieving drug in mortal illness, where the doctor knows the drug may very well kill the patient if the illness does not do so first, the distinction is evident; the lack of it has led an English judge to talk nonsense about the administration of the drug's not having *really* been the cause of death in such a case, even though a post mortem shows it was. For everyone understands that it is a very different thing to administer a drug, and to administer it with the intention of killing. However, the principle of double effect has more important applications in warfare, and I shall return to it later.

III. The Influence of Pacifism

Pacifism has existed as a considerable movement in English speaking countries ever since the first world war. I take the doctrine of pacifism to be that it is *eo ipso* wrong to fight in wars, not the doctrine that it is wrong to be compelled to, or that any man, or some men, may refuse; and I think it false for the reasons that I have given. But I now want to consider the very remarkable effects it has had: for I believe its influence to have been enormous, far exceeding its influence on its own adherents.

We should note first that pacifism has as its background conscription and enforced military service for all men. Without conscription, pacifism is a private opinion that will keep those who hold it out of armies, which they are in any case not obliged to join. Now universal conscription, except for the most extraordinary reasons, i.e., as a regular habit among most nations, is such a horrid evil that the refusal of it automatically commands a certain amount of respect and sympathy.

We are not here concerned with the pacifism of some peculiar sect which in any case draws apart from the world to a certain extent, but with a pacifism of people in the world, who do not want to be withdrawn from it. For some of these, pacifism is prevented from being a merely theoretical attitude because they are liable to, and so are prepared to resist conscription; or are able directly to effect the attitude of some who are so liable.

A powerful ingredient in this pacifism is the prevailing image of Christianity. This image commands a sentimental respect among people who have no belief in Christianity, that is to say, in Christian dogmas; yet do have a certain belief in an ideal which they conceive to be part of "true Christianity." It is therefore important to understand this image of Christianity and to know how false it is. Such understanding is relevant, not merely to those who wish to believe Christianity, but to all who, without the least wish to believe, are yet profoundly influenced by this image of it.

According to this image, Christianity is an ideal and beautiful religion, impracticable except for a few rare characters. It preaches a God of love whom there is no reason to fear; it marks an escape from the conception presented in the Old Testament, of a vindictive and jealous God who will terribly punish his enemies. The "Christian" God is a *roi fainéant*, whose only triumph is in the Cross; his appeal is a goodness and unselfishness, and to follow him is to act according to the Sermon on the Mount—to turn the other cheek and to offer no resistance to evil. In this account some of the evangelical counsels are chosen as containing the whole of Christian ethics: that is, they are made into precepts. (Only some of them; it is not likely that someone who deduces the *duty* of pacifism from the Sermon on the Mount and the rebuke to Peter, will agree to take "Give to him that asks of you" equally as a universally binding precept.)

The turning of counsels into precepts results in high-sounding principles. Principles that are mistakenly high and strict are a trap; they may easily lead in the end directly or indirectly to the justification of monstrous things. Thus if the evangelical counsel about poverty were turned into a precept forbidding property owning, people would pay lip service to it as the ideal, while in practice they went in for swindling. "Absolute honesty!" it would be said: "I can respect that—but of course that means having no property; and while I respect those who follow that course, I have to compromise with the sordid world myself." If then one must "compromise with evil" by owning property and engaging in trade, then the amount of swindling one does will depend on convenience. This imaginary case is paralleled by what is so commonly said: absolute pacifism is an ideal; unable to follow that, and committed to "compromise with evil," one must go the whole hog and wage war *à outrance*.

The truth about Christianity is that it is a severe and practicable religion, not a beautifully ideal but impracticable one. Its moral precepts (except for the stricter laws about marriage that Christ enacted, abrogating some of the permissions of the Old Law) are those of the Old Testament; and its God is the God of Israel.

It is ignorance of the New Testament that hides this from people. It is characteristic of pacifism to denigrate the Old Testament and exalt the New: something quite contrary to the teaching of the New Testament itself, which always looks back to and leans upon the Old. How typical it is that the words of Christ "You have heard it said, an eye for an eye and a tooth for a tooth, but I say to you . . . " are taken as a repudiation of the ethic of the Old

Testament! People seldom look up the occurrence of this phrase in the juridical code of the Old Testament, where it belongs, and is the admirable principle of law for the punishment of certain crimes, such as procuring the wrongful punishment of another by perjury. People often enough *now* cite the phrase to justify private revenge; no doubt this was as often "heard said" when Christ spoke of it. But no justification for this exists in the personal ethic taught by the Old Testament. On the contrary. What do we find? "Seek no revenge," (Leviticus xix, 18), and "If you find your enemy's ox or ass going astray, take it back to him; if you see the ass of someone who hates you lying under his burden, and would forbear to help him: you must help him" (Exodus xxiii, 4–5). And "If your enemy is hungry, give him food, if thirsty, give him drink" (Proverbs xxv, 21).

This is only one example; given space, it would be easy to show how false is the conception of Christ's teaching as *correcting* religion of the ancient Israelites, and substituting a higher and more "spiritual" religion for theirs. Now the false picture I have described plays an important part in the pacifist ethic and in the ethic of the many people who are not pacifists but are influenced by pacifism.

To extract a pacifist doctrine—i.e., a condemnation of the use of force by the ruling authorities, and of soldiering as a profession—from the evangelical counsels and the rebuke to Peter, is to disregard what else is in the New Testament. It is to forget St. John's direction to soldiers: "do not blackmail people; be content with your pay"; and Christ's commendation of the centurion, who compared his authority over his men to Christ's. On a pacifist view, this must be much as if a madam in a brothel had said: "I know what authority is, I tell this girl to do this, and she does it . . ." and Christ had commended her faith. A centurion was the first Gentile to be baptized; there is no suggestion in the New Testament that soldiering was regarded as incompatible with Christianity. The martyrology contains many names of soldiers whose occasion of martyrdom was not any objection to soldiering, but a refusal to perform idolatrous acts.

Now, it is one of the most vehement and repeated teach-

ings of the Judaeo-Christian tradition that the shedding of
innocent blood is forbidden by the divine law. No man
may be punished except for his own crime, and those
"whose feet are swift to shed innocent blood" are always
represented as God's enemies.

For a long time the main outlines of this teaching have
seemed to be merely obvious morality: hence, for example,
I have read a passage by Ronald Knox complaining of the
"endless moralizing," interspersed in records of meaness,
cowardice, spite, cruelty, treachery and murder, which
forms so much of the Old Testament. And indeed, that it
is terrible to kill the innocent is very obvious; the morality that so stringently forbids it must make a great appeal
to mankind, especially to the poor threatened victims.
Why should it need the thunder of Sinai and the suffering
and preaching of the prophets to promulgate such a law?
But human pride and malice are everywhere so strong that
now, with the fading of Christianity from the mind of the
West, this morality once more stands out as a demand
which strikes pride- and fear-ridden people as too intransi-
gent. For Knox, it seemed so obvious as to be dull; and he
failed to recognize the bloody and beastly records that it
accompanies for the dry truthfulness about human beings
that so characterizes the Old Testament.[3]

Now pacifism teaches people to make no distinction between the shedding of innocent blood and the shedding of
any human blood. And in this way pacifism has corrupted
enormous numbers of people who will not act according to
its tenets. They become convinced that a number of things
are wicked which are not; hence, seeing no way of avoiding "wickedness," they set no limits to it. How endlessly
pacifists argue that all war must be *à outrance!* that those
who wage war must go as far as technological advance
permits in the destruction of the enemy's people. As if the
Napoleonic wars were perforce fuller of massacres than
the French war of Henry V of England. It is not true: the

---

[3]It is perhaps necessary to remark that I am not here adverting to the total ex-
termination of certain named tribes of Canaan that is said by the Old Testament
to have been commanded by God. That is something quite outside the provisions
of the Mosaic Law for dealings in war.

reverse took place. Nor is technological advance particularly relevant; it is mere squeamishness that deters people
who would consent to area bombing from the enormous
massacres *by hand* that used once to be committed.

The policy of obliterating cities was adopted by the Allies in the last war; they need not have taken that step,
and it was taken largely out of a villainous hatred, and as
corollary to the policy, now universally denigrated, of
seeking "unconditional surrender." (That policy itself was
visibly wicked, and could be and was judged so at the
time; it is not surprising that it led to disastrous consequences, even if no one was clever and detached enough to
foresee this at the time.)

Pacifism and the respect for pacifism is not the only
thing that has led to a universal forgetfulness of the law
against killing the innocent; but it has had a great share
in it.

IV. The Principle of Double Effect

Catholics, however, can hardly avoid paying at least lip-
service to that law. So we must ask: how is it that there
has been so comparatively little conscience exercised on
the subject among them? The answer is: double-think
about double effect.

The distinction between the intended, and the merely
foreseen, effects of a voluntary action is indeed absolutely
essential to Christian ethics. For Christianity forbids a
number of things as being bad in themselves. But if I am
answerable for the foreseen consequences of an action or
refusal, as much as for the action itself, then these prohibitions will break down. If someone innocent will die unless
I do a wicked thing, then on this view I am his murderer in
refusing: so all that is left to me is to weigh up evils. Here
the theologian steps in with the principle of double effect
and says: "No, you are no murderer, if the man's death
was neither your aim nor your chosen means, and if you
had to act in the way that led to it or else do something
absolutely forbidden." Without understanding of this principle, anything can be—and is wont to be—justified, and
the Christian teaching that in no circumstances may one

commit murder, adultery, apostasy (to give a few examples) goes by the board. These absolute prohibitions of Christianity by no means exhaust its ethic; there is a large area where what is just is determined partly by a prudent weighing up of consequences. But the prohibitions are bedrock, and without them the Christian ethic goes to pieces. Hence the necessity of the notion of double effect.

At the same time, the principle has been repeatedly abused from the seventeenth century up till now. The causes lie in the history of philosophy. From the seventeenth century till now what may be calle Cartesian psychology has dominated the thought of philosophers and theologians. According to this psychology, an intention was an interior act of the mind which could be produced at will. Now if intention is all important—as it is—in determining the goodness or badness of an action, then, on this theory of what intention is, a marvellous way offered itself of making any action lawful. You only had to "direct your intention" in a suitable way. In practice, this means making a little speech to yourself: "What I mean to be doing is. . . ."

This perverse doctrine has occasioned repeated condemnations by the Holy See from the seventeenth century to the present day. Some examples will suffice to show how the thing goes. Typical doctrines from the seventeenth century were that it is all right for a servant to hold the ladder for his criminous master so long as he is merely avoiding the sack by doing so; or that a man might wish for and rejoice at his parent's death so long as what he had in mind was the gain to himself; or that it is not simony to offer money, not *as a price* for the spiritual benefit, but only *as an inducement* to give it. A condemned doctrine from the present day is that the practice of *coitus reservatus* is permissible; such a doctrine could only arise in connexion with that "direction of intention" which sets everything right no matter what one does. A man makes a practice of withdrawing, telling himself that he *intends* not to ejaculate; of course (if that is his practice) he usually does so, but then the event is "accidental" and *praeter intentionem*: it is, in short, a case of "double effect."

This same doctrine is used to prevent any doubts about the obliteration bombing of a city. The devout Catholic bomber secures by a "direction of intention" that any shedding of innocent blood that occurs is "accidental." I know a Catholic boy who was puzzled at being told by his schoolmaster that it was an *accident* that the people of Hiroshima and Nagasaki were there to be killed; in fact, however absurd it seems, such thoughts are common among priests who know that they are forbidden by the divine law to justify the direct killing of the innocent.

It is nonsense to pretend that you do not intend to do what is the means you take to your chosen end. Otherwise there is absolutely no substance to the Pauline teaching that we may not do evil that good may come.

V. Some Commonly Heard Arguments

There are a number of sophistical arguments, often or sometimes used on these topics, which need answering.

Where do you draw the line? As Dr. Johnson said, the fact of twilight does not mean you cannot tell day from night. There are borderline cases, where it is difficult to distinguish, in what is done, between means and what is incidental to, yet in the circumstances inseparable from, those means. The obliteration bombing of a city is not a borderline case.

The old "conditions for a just war" are irrelevant to the conditions of modern warfare, so that must be condemned out of hand. People who say this always envisage only major wars between the Great Powers, which Powers are indeed now "in blood stepp'd insofar" that it is unimaginable for there to be a war between them which is not a set of enormous massacres of civil populations. But these are not the only wars. Why is Finland so far free? At least partly because of the "posture of military preparedness" which, considering the character of the country, would have made subjugating the Finns a difficult and unrewarding task. The offensive of the Israelis against the Egyptians in 1956 involved no plan of making civil populations the target of military attack.

In a modern war the distinction between combatants and non-combatants is meaningless, so an attack on anyone on the enemy side is justified. This is pure nonsense, even in war, a very large number of the enemy population are just engaged in maintaining the life of the country, or the sick, or aged, or children.

It must be legitimate to maintain an opinion—viz. that the destruction of cities by bombing is lawful—if this is argued by competent theologians and the Holy See has not pronounced. The argument from the silence of the Holy See has itself been condemned by the Holy See (Denzinger, 28th Edition, 1127). How could this be a sane doctrine in view of the endless twistiness of the human mind?

Whether a war is just or not is not for the private man to judge: he must obey his government. Sometimes, this may be, especially as far as concerns causes of war. But the individual who joins in destroying a city, like a Nazi massacring the inhabitants of a village, is too obviously marked out as an enemy of the human race, to shelter behind such a plea.

Finally, horrible as it is to have to notice this, we must notice that even the arguments about double effect—which at least show that a man is not willing openly to justify the killing of the innocent—are now beginning to look old-fashioned. Some Catholics are not scrupling to say that *anything* is justified in defence of the continued existence and liberty of the Church in the West. A terrible fear of communism drives people to say this sort of thing. "Our Lord told us to fear those who can destroy body and soul, not to fear the destruction of the body" was blasphemously said to a friend of mine; meaning: "so, we must fear Russian domination more than the destruction of people's bodies by obliteration bombing."

But whom did Our Lord tell us to fear, when he said: "I will tell you whom you shall fear" and "Fear not them that can destroy the body, but fear him who can destroy body and soul in hell"? He told us to fear God the Father, who can and will destroy the unrepentant disobedient, body and soul, in hell.

A Catholic who is tempted to think on the lines I have described should remember that the Church is the spiritual Israel: that is, that Catholics are what the ancient Jews were, salt for the earth and the people of God—and that what was true of some devout Jews of ancient times can equally well be true of us now: "You compass land and sea to make a convert, and when you have done so, you make him twice as much a child of hell as your-selves." Do Catholics sometimes think that they are im-mune from such a possibility? That the Pharisees—who sat in the seat of Moses and who were so zealous for the true religion—were bad in ways in which we cannot be bad if we are zealous? I believe they do. But our faith teaches no such immunity, it teaches the opposite. "We are in danger all our lives long." So we have to fear God and keep his commandments, and calculate what is for the best only within the limits of that obedience, knowing that the future is in God's power and that no one can snatch away those whom the Father has given to Christ.

It is not a vague faith in the triumph of "the spirit" over force (there is little enough warrant for that), but a definite faith in the divine promises, that makes us believe that the Church cannot fail. Those, therefore, who think they must be prepared to wage war with Russia involving the deliberate massacre of cities, must be prepared to say to God: "We had to break your law, lest your Church fail. We could not obey your commandments, for we did not be-lieve your promises." — *hope*

Pacifism:
A Philosophical Analysis

Jan Narveson

Several different doctrines have been called "pacifism," and it is impossible to say anything cogent about it without saying which of them one has in mind. I must begin by making it clear, then, that I am limiting the discussion of pacifism to a rather narrow band of doctrines, further distinctions among which will be brought out below. By "pacifism," I do *not* mean the theory that violence is evil. With appropriate restrictions, this is a view that every person with any pretensions to morality doubtless holds. Nobody thinks that we have a right to inflict pain wantonly on other people. The pacifist goes a very long step further. *His* belief is not only that violence is evil but also that it is morally wrong to use force to resist, punish, or prevent violence. This further step makes pacifism a radical moral doctrine. What I shall try to establish below is that it is in fact, more than merely radical—it is actually incoherent because self-contradictory in its fundamental intent. I shall also suggest that several moral attitudes and psychological views which have tended to be associated with pacifism as I have defined it do not have any necessary connection with that doctrine. Most proponents of pacifism, I shall argue, have tended to confuse these different things,

From *Ethics*, vol. 75 (1965). Rewritten for this volume, including the insertion of part of a subsequent article, "Is Pacifism Consistent?," from *Ethics*, vol. 78 (1968). With permission of the University of Chicago Press.

and that confusion is probably what accounts for such popularity as pacifism has had.

It is next in order to point out that the pacifistic attitude is a matter of degree, and this in two respects. In the first place, there is the question: How much violence should not be resisted, and what degree of force is one not entitled to use in resisting, punishing, or preventing it? Answers to this question will make a lot of difference. For example, everyone would agree that there are limits to the kind and degree of force with which a particular degree of violence is to be met: we do not have a right to kill someone for rapping us on the ribs, for example, and yet there is no tendency toward pacifism in this. We might go further and maintain, for example, that capital punishment, even for the crime of murder, is unjustified without doing so on pacifist grounds. Again, the pacifist should say just what sort of a reaction constitutes a forcible or violent one. If somebody attacks me this his fists and I pin his arms to his body with wrestling holds which restrict him but cause him no pain, is that all right in the pacifist's book? And again, many non-pacifists could consistently maintain that we should avoid, to the extent that it is possible, inflicting a like pain on those who attempt to inflict pain on us. It is unnecessary to be a pacifist merely in order to deny the moral soundness of the principle, "an eye for an eye and a tooth for a tooth." We need a clarification, then, from the pacifist as to just how far he is and is not willing to go. But this need should already make us pause, for surely the pacifist cannot draw these lines in a merely arbitrary manner. It is his reasons for drawing the ones he does that count, and these are what I propose to discuss below.

The second matter of degree in respect of which the pacifist must specify his doctrine concerns the question: Who ought not to resist violence with force? For example, there are pacifists who would only claim that they themselves ought not to. Others would say that only pacifists ought not to, or that all persons of a certain type, where the type is not specified in terms of belief or non-belief in pacifism, ought not to resist violence with force. And finally, there are those who hold that everyone ought not to do so. We shall see that considerations about this second variable doom some forms of pacifism to contradiction.

My general program will be to show that (1) only the doctrine that everyone ought not to resist violence with force is of philosophical interest among those doctrines known as "pacifism"; (2) that doctrine, if advanced as a moral doctrine, is logically untenable; and (3) the reasons for the popularity of pacifism rest on failure to see exactly what the doctrine is. The things which pacifism wishes to accomplish, insofar as they are worth accomplishing, can be managed on the basis of quite ordinary and conservative moral principles.

Let us begin by being precise about the kind of moral force the principle of pacifism is intended to have. One good way to do this is to consider what it is intended to deny. What would non-pacifists, which I suppose includes most people, say of a man who followed Christ's suggestion and, when unaccountably slapped, simply turned the other cheek? They might say that such a man is either a fool or a saint. Or they might say, "It's all very well for him to do that, but it's not for me"; or they might simply shrug their shoulders and say, "Well, it takes all kinds, doesn't it?" But they would *not* say that a man who did that ought to be punished in some way; they would not even say that he had done anything wrong. In fact, as I have mentioned, they would more likely than not find something admirable about it. The point, then, is this: The non-pacifist does *not* say that it is your *duty* to resist violence with force. The non-pacifist is merely saying that there's nothing wrong with doing so, that one has every right to do so if he is so inclined. Whether we wish to add that a person would be foolish or silly to do so is quite another question, one on which the non-pacifist does not *need* to take any particular position.

Consequently, a genuine pacifist cannot merely say that we may, if we wish, prefer not to resist violence with force. Nor can he merely say that there is something admirable or saintly about not doing so, for, as pointed out above, the non-pacifist could perfectly well agree with that. He must say, instead, that, for whatever class of people he thinks it applies to, there is something positively wrong about meeting violence with force. He must say that, insofar as the people to whom his principle applies resort to force, they are committing a breach of moral duty—a very serious thing to say. Just how serious, we shall ere long see.

Next, we must understand what the implications of holding pacifism as a moral principle are, and the first such implication requiring our attention concerns the matter of the size of the class of people to which it is supposed to apply. It will be of interest to discuss two of the four possibilities previously listed, I think. The first is that in which the pacifist says that only pacifists have the duty of pacifism. Let us see what this amounts to.

If we say that the principle of pacifism is the principle that all and only pacifists have a duty of not opposing violence with force, we get into a very odd situation. For suppose we ask ourselves, "Very well, which people are the pacifists then?" The answer will have to be "All those people who believe that pacifists have the duty not to meet violence with force." But surely one could believe that a certain class of people, whom we shall call "pacifists," have the duty not to meet violence with force without believing that one ought not, oneself, to meet violence with force. That is to say, the "principle" that pacifists ought to avoid meeting violence with force, is circular: It presupposes that one already knows who the pacifists are. Yet this is presicely what that statement of the principle is supposed to answer! We are supposed to be able to say that anybody who believes that principle is a pacifist; yet, as we have seen, a person could very well believe that a certain class of people called "pacifists" ought not to meet violence with force without believing that he himself ought not to meet violence with force. Thus everyone could be a "pacifist" in the sense of believing that statement and yet no one believes that he *himself* (or anyone in particular) ought to avoid meeting violence with force. Consequently, pacifism cannot be specified in that way. A pacifist must be a person who believes either that he himself (at least) ought not to meet force with force or that some larger class of persons, perhaps everyone, ought not to meet force with force. He would then be believing something definite, and we are then in a position to ask why.

Incidentally, it is worth mentioning that when people

say things such as "Only pacifists have the duty of pacifism," "Only Catholics have the duties of Catholicism,"
and, in general, "Only X-ists have the duties of X-ism"
they probably are falling into a trap which catches a good
many people. It is, namely, the mistake of supposing that
what it *is* to have a certain duty is to *believe* that you have
a certain duty. The untenability of this is parallel to the
untenability of the previously mentioned attempt to say
what pacifism is. For, if having a duty is believing that you
have a certain duty, the question arises, "*What* does such a
person believe?" The answer that must be given if we follow this analysis would then be, "He believes that he believes that he has a certain duty"; and so on, ad infinitum.

On the other hand, one might believe that having a duty
does not consist in believing that one has and yet believe
that only those people really have the duty who believe
that they have it. But in that case, we would, being conscientious, perhaps want to ask the question, "Well, *ought*
I to believe that I have that duty, or oughtn't I?" If you say
that the answer is "Yes," the reason cannot be that you
already do believe it, for you are asking whether you
should. On the other hand, the answer "No" or "It doesn't
make any difference—it's up to you," implies that there is
really no reason for doing the thing in question at all. In
short, asking whether I ought to believe that I have a duty
to do *x*, is equivalent to asking whether I should *do x.* A
person might very well believe that he ought to do *x* but
be wrong. It might be the case that he really ought *not* to
do *x*; in that case the fact that he believes he ought to do *x*,
far from being a reason why he ought to do it, is a reason
for us to point out his error. It also, of course, presupposes
that he has some reason other than his belief for thinking
it is his duty to do *x.*

Having cleared this red herring out of the way, we must
consider the view of those who believe that they themselves have a duty of pacifism and ask ourselves the question: What general kind of reason must a person have for
supposing a certain type of act to be *his* duty, in a moral
sense? Now, one answer he might give is that pacifism as
such is a duty, that is, that meeting violence with force is,
as such, wrong. In that case, however, what he thinks is

not merely that *he* has this duty, but that *everyone has this duty*.

Now he might object, "Well, but no; I don't mean that everyone has it. For instance, if a man is defending, not himself, but *other* people, such as his wife and children, then he has a right to meet violence with force." Now this, of course, would be a very important qualification to his principle and one of a kind which we will be discussing in a moment. Meanwhile, however, we may point out that he evidently still thinks that, if it weren't for certain more important duties, everyone would have a duty to avoid meeting violence with force. In other words, he then believes that, other things being equal, one ought not to meet violence with force. He believes, to put it yet another way, that if one does meet violence with force, one must have a special excuse or justification of a moral kind; then he may want to give some account of just which excuses and justifications would do. Nevertheless, he is now holding a general principle.

Suppose, however, he holds that no one *else* has this duty of pacifism, that only he himself ought not to meet force with force, although it is quite all right for others to do so. Now if this is what our man feels, we may continue to call him a "pacifist," in a somewhat attenuated sense, but he is then no longer holding pacifism as a *moral* principle or, indeed, as a principle at all.[1] For now his disinclination for violence is essentially just a matter of taste. I like pistachio ice cream, but I wouldn't dream of saying that other people have a duty to eat it; similarly, this man just doesn't *like* to meet force with force, although he wouldn't dream of insisting that others act as he does. And this is a secondary sense of "pacifism," first, because pacifism has always been advocated on moral grounds and, second, because non-pacifists can easily have this same feeling. A person might very well feel squeamish, for example, about using force, even in self-defense, or he might not be able to bring himself to use it even if he

---

[1]Compare, for example, K. Baier, *The Moral Point of View* (Ithaca: Cornell University Press, 1958), p. 191.

wants to. But none of these has anything to do with asserting pacifism to be a duty. Moreover, a mere attitude could
hardly license a man to refuse military service if it were
required of him, or to join ban-the-bomb crusades, and so
forth. (I fear, however, that such attitudes have sometimes
caused people to do those things.)

And, in turn, it is similarly impossible to claim that
your support of pacifism is a moral one if your position is
that a certain selection of people, but no one else, ought
not to meet force with force, even though you are unpre-
pared to offer any reason whatever for this selection. Suppose, for example, that you hold that only the Arapahoes,
or only the Chinese, or only people more than six feet high
have this "duty." If such were the case, and no reasons
offered at all, we could only conclude that you had a very
peculiar attitude toward the Arapahoes, or whatever, but
we would hardly want to say that you had a moral principle. Your "principle" amounts to saying that these particular individuals happen to have the duty of pacifism just
because they are the individuals they are, and this, as
Bentham would say, is the "negation of all principle." Of
course, if you meant that somehow the property of being
over six feet tall *makes* it your duty not to use violence,
then you have a principle, all right, but a very queer one
indeed unless you can give some further reasons. Again, it
would not be possible to distinguish this from a sheer attitude.

Pacifism, then, must be the principle that the use of
force to meet force is wrong *as such*, that is, that nobody
may do so unless he has a special justification.

There is another way in which one might advocate a
sort of "pacifism," however, which we must also dispose
of before getting to the main point. One might argue that
pacifism is desirable as a tactic: that, as a matter of fact,
some good end, such as the reduction of violence itself, is
to be achieved by "turning the other cheek." For example,
if it were the case that turning the other cheek caused the
offender to break down and repent, then that would be a
very good reason for behaving "pacifistically." If unilateral
disarmament causes the other side to disarm, then certainly unilateral disarmament would be a desirable policy.

But note that its desirability, if this is the argument, is due to the fact that peace is desirable, a moral position which anybody can take, pacifist or no, plus the purely contingent fact that this policy causes the other side to disarm, that is, it brings about peace.

And of course, that's the catch. If one attempts to support pacifism, because of its probable effects, then one's position depends on what the effects are. Determining what they are is a purely empirical matter, and, consequently, one could not possibly be a pacifist as a matter of pure principle if his reasons for supporting pacifism are merely tactical. One must, in this case, submit one's opinions to the governance of fact.

It is not part of my intention to discuss matters of fact, as such, but it is worthwhile to point out that the general history of the human race certainly offers no support for the supposition that turning the other cheek always produces good effects on the aggressor. Some aggressors, such as the Nazis, were apparently just "egged on" by the "pacifist" attitude of their victims. Some of the S.S. men apparently became curious to see just how much torture the victim would put up with before he began to resist. Furthermore, there is the possibility that, while pacifism might work against some people (one might cite the British, against whom pacifism in India was apparently rather succesful—but the British are comparatively nice people), it might fail against others (e.g., the Naxis).

A further point about holding pacifism to be desirable as a tactic is that this could not easily support the position that pacifism is a *duty*. The question whether we have no *right* to fight back can hardly be settled by noting that not to fight back might cause the aggressor to stop fighting. To prove that a policy is a desirable one because it works is not to prove that it is *obligatory* to follow it. We surely need considerations a good deal less tenuous than this to prove such a momentous contention as that we have no *right* to resist.

It appears, then, that to hold the pacifist position as a genuine, full-blooded moral principle is to hold that nobody has a right to fight back when attacked, that fighting back is inherently evil, as such. It means that we are all mistaken in supposing that we have a right of self-protection. And, of course, this is an extreme and extraordinary position in any case. It appears to mean, for instance, that we have no right to punish criminals, that all of our machinery of criminal justice is, in fact, unjust. Robbers, murderers, rapists, and miscellaneous delinquents ought, on this theory, to be let loose.

Now, the pacifist's first move, upon hearing this, will be to claim that he has been misrepresented. He might say that it is only one's *self* that one has no right to defend, and that one may legitimately fight in order to defend other people. This qualification cannot be made by those pacifists who qualify as conscientious objectors, of course, for the latter are refusing to defend their fellow citizens and not merely themselves. But this is comparatively trivial when we contemplate the next objection to this amended version of the theory. Let us now ask ourselves what it is about attacks on *other* people which could possibly justify *us* in defending them, while we are not justified in defending ourselves? It cannot be the mere fact that they are other people than ourselves, for, of course, everyone is a different person from everyone else, and if such a consideration could ever of itself justify anything at all it could also justify anything whatever. That mere difference of person, as such, is of no moral importance, is a presupposition of anything that can possibly pretend to be a moral theory.

Instead of such idle nonsense, then, the pacifist would have to mention some specific characteristic which every *other* person has which we lack and which justifies us in defending them. But this, alas, is impossible, for, while there may be some interesting difference between *me* on the one hand and everyone else on the other, the pacifist is not merely addressing himself to me. On the contrary, as we have seen, he has to address himself to everyone. He is claiming that each person has no right to defend himself, although he does have a right to defend other people. And, therefore, what is needed is a characteristic which distinguishes *each* person from everyone else, and not just *me* from everyone else—which is plainly self-contradictory.

Again, then, the pacifist must retreat in order to avoid talking nonsense. His next move might be to say that we have a right to defend all those who are not able to defend themselves. Big, grown-up men who are able to defend themelves ought not to do so, but they ought to defend mere helpless children who are unable to defend themselves.

This last, very queer theory could give rise to some amusing logical gymnastics. For instance, what about groups of people? If a group of people who cannot defend themselves singly can defend themselves together, then when it has grown to that size ought it to stop defending itself? If so, then every time a person *can* defend someone else, he would form with the person being defended a "defensive unit" which was able to defend itself, and thus would by this very presence debar himself from making the defense. At this rate, no one will ever get defended, it seems: The defenseless people by definition cannot defend themselves, while those who can defend them would enable the group consisting of the defenders and the defended to defend themselves, and hence they would be obliged not to do so.

Such reflections, however, are merely curious shadows of a much more fundamental and serious logical problem. This arises when we begin to ask: But why should even defenseless people be defended? If resisting violence is inherently evil, then how can it suddenly become permissible when we use it on behalf of other people? The fact that they are defenseless cannot possibly account for this, for it follows from the theory in question, that everyone ought to put himself in the position of people who are defenseless by refusing to defend himself. This type of pacifist, in short, is using the very characteristic (namely, being in a state of not defending oneself) which he wishes to encourage in others as a reason for denying it in the case of those who already have it (namely, the defenseless). This is surely inconsistent.

To attempt to be consistent, at least, the pacifist is forced to accept the characterization of him at which we tentatively arrived. He must say that no one ought ever to be defended against attack. The right of self-defense can be denied coherently only if the right of defense, in general, is denied. This in itself is an important conclusion.

It must be borne in mind, by the way, that I have not said anything to take exception to the man who simply does not wish to defend himself. So long as he does not attempt to make his pacifism into a principle, one cannot accuse him of any inconsistency, however much one might wish to say that he is foolish or eccentric. It is solely with moral principles that I am concerned here.

We now come to the last and most fundamental problem of all. If we ask ourselves what the point of pacifism is, what gets it going, so to speak, the answer is, of course, obvious enough: opposition to violence. The pacifist is generally thought of as the man who is so much opposed to violence that he will not even use it to defend himself or anyone else. And it is precisely this characterization which I wish to show is morally inconsistent.

To begin with, we may note something which at first glance may seem merely to be a matter of fact, albeit one which should worry the pacifist, in our latest characterization of him. I refer to the commonplace observation that, generally speaking, we measure a man's degree of opposition to something by the amount of effort he is willing to put forth against it. A man could hardly be said to be dead set against something if he is not willing to lift a finger to keep it from going on. A person who claims to be completely opposed to something yet does nothing to prevent it would ordinarily be said to be a hypocrite.

As facts, however, we cannot make too much of these. The pacifist could claim to be willing to go to any length, short of violence, to prevent violence. He might, for instance, stand out in the cold all day long handing out leaflets (as I have known some to do), and this would surely argue for the sincerity of his beliefs.

But would it really?

Let us ask ourselves, one final time, what we are claiming when we claim that violence is morally wrong and unjust. We are, in the first place, claiming that a person *has no right* to indulge in it, as such (meaning that he has no right to indulge in it, *unless* he has an overriding justification). But what do we mean when we say that he has no right to indulge in it? Violence, of the type we are considering, is a two-termed affair: one does violence *to* somebody, one cannot simply "do violence." It might be oneself, of course, but we are not primarily interested in those cases, for what makes it wrong to commit violence is that it harms the people to whom it is done. To say that it is wrong is to say that those to whom it is done have a right *not* to have it done to them. (This must again be qualified by pointing out that this is so only if they have done nothing to merit having that right abridged.)

Yet what could that right to their own security, which people have, possibly consist in if not a right at least to be protected from whatever violence might be offered them? But lest the reader think that this is a gratuitous assumption, note carefully the reason why having a right involves having a right to be defended from breaches of that right. It is because the prevention of infractions of that right is precisely what one has a right to when one has a right at all. A right just *is* a status justifying preventive action. To say that you have a right to X but that no one has any justification whatever for preventing people from depriving you of it, is self-contradictory. If you claim a right to X, then to describe some action as an act of depriving you of X, is logically to imply that its absence is one of the things that you have a right to.

Thus far it does not follow logically that we have a right to use force in our own or anyone's defense. What does follow logically is that one has a right to whatever may be necessary to prevent infringements of his right. One might at first suppose that the universe *could* be so constructed that it is never necessary to use force to prevent people who are bent on getting something from getting it.

Yet even this is not so, for when we speak of "force" in the sense in which pacifism is concerned with it, we do not mean merely physical "force." To call an action a use of force is not merely to make a reference to the laws of mechanics. On the contrary, it is to describe whatever is being done as being a means to the infliction on somebody of something (ordinarily physical) which he does not want done to him; and the same is true for "force" in the sense in which it applies to war, assault and battery, and the like.

The proper contrary of "force" in this connection is "rational persuasion." Naturally, one way there *might* be of getting somebody not to do something he has no right to do is to convince him he ought not to do it or that it is not in his interest to do it. But it is inconsistent, I suggest, to argue that rational persuasion is the only morally permissible method of preventing violence. A pragmatic reason for this is easy enough to point to: Violent people are too busy being violent to be reasonable. We cannot engage in rational persuasion unless the enemy is willing to sit down and talk; but what if he isn't? One cannot contend that every human being can be persuaded to sit down and talk before he strikes, for this is not something we can determine just by reasoning; it is a question of observation. But these points are not strictly relevant anyway, for our question is not the empirical question of whether there is some handy way which can always be used to get a person to sit down and discuss moral philosophy when he is about to murder you. Our question is: *If* force is the only way to prevent violence in a given case, is its use justified *in that case?* This is a purely moral question which we can discuss without any special reference to matters of fact. And, moreover, it is precisely this question which we should have to discuss with the would-be violator. The point is that if a person can be rationally persuaded that he ought not to engage in violence, then precisely what he would be rationally persuaded of if we were to succeed would be the proposition that the use of force is justifiable to prevent him from doing so. For note that if we were to argue that only rational persuasion is permissible as a means of preventing him, we would have to face the question: Do we mean *attempted* rational persuasion, or *successful* rational persuasion, that is, rational persuasion which really does succeed in preventing him from acting? Attempted rational persuasion might fail (if only because the opponent is unreasonable), and then what? To argue that we have a right to use rational persuasion which also succeeds (i.e., we have a right to its success as well as to its use) is to imply that we have a right to pre-

vent him from performing the act. But this, in turn, means
that, if attempts at rational persuasion fail, we have a right
to the use of force. Thus what we have a right to, if we
ever have a *right* to anything, is not merely the use of rational persuasion to keep people from depriving you of the
thing to which you have the right. We do indeed have a
right to that, but we also have a right to anything else that
might be necessary (other things being equal) to prevent
the deprivation from occurring. And it is a logical truth,
not merely a contingent one, that what *might* be necessary
is *force*. (If merely saying something could miraculously
deprive someone of the ability to carry through a course of
action, then those speech-acts would be called a type of
force, if a very mysterious one. And we could properly
begin to oppose their use for precisely the same reasons as
we now oppose violence.)

What this all adds up to, then, is that *if* we have any
rights at all, we have a right to use force to prevent the
deprivation of the thing to which we are said to have a
right. But the pacifist, of *all* people, is the one most concerned to insist that we do have some rights, namely, the
right not to have violence done to us. This is logically implied in asserting it to be a duty on everyone's part to
avoid violence. And this is why the pacifist's position is
self-contradictory. In saying that violence is wrong, one is
at the same time saying that people have a right to its prevention, by force if necessary. Whether and to what extent
it may be necessary is a question of fact, but, since it is a
question of fact only, the moral right to use force on some
possible occasions is established.[2]

We now have an answer to the question. How much
force does a given threat of violence justify for preventive
purposes? The answer, in a word, is "Enough." That the
answer is this simple may at first sight seem implausible.
One might suppose that some elaborate equation between
the aggressive and the preventive force is needed: the punishment be proportionate to the crime. But this is a mis-

---

[2]This basic argument may be compared with a view of Kant's, to be found in the
Rechtslehre, translated under the title *Metaphysical Elements of Justice* by J.
Ladd, Library of Liberal Arts, pp. 35–36 (Introduction, D).

understanding. In the first place, prevention and punishment are not the same, even if punishment is thought to be directed mainly toward prevention. The punishment of a particular crime logically cannot prevent *that* instance of the crime, since it presupposes that it has already been performed; and punishment need not involve the use of any violence at all, although law-enforcement officers in some places have a nasty tendency to assume the contrary. But preventive force is another matter. If a man threatens to kill me, it is desirable, of course, for me to try to prevent this by the use of the least amount of force sufficient to do the job. But I am justified even in killing him *if* necessary. This much, I suppose, is obvious to most people. But suppose his threat is much smaller: suppose that he is merely pestering me, which is a very mild form of aggression indeed. Would I be justified in killing him to prevent this, under any circumstances whatever?

Suppose that I call the police and they take out a warrant against him, and suppose that when the police come, he puts up a struggle. He pulls a knife or a gun, let us say, and the police shoot him in the ensuing battle. Has my right to the prevention of his annoying me extended to killing him? Well, not exactly, since the immediate threat in response to which he is killed is a threat to the lives of the policemen. Yet my annoyer may never have contemplated real violence. It is an unfortunate case of unpremeditated escalation. But this is precisely what makes the contention that one is justified in using enough force to do the job, whatever amount that may be, to prevent action which violates a right less alarming than at first sight it seems. For it is difficult to envisage a reason why extreme force is needed to prevent mild threats from realization except by way of escalation, and escalation automatically justifies increased use of preventive force.

The existence of laws, police, courts, and more or less civilized modes of behavior on the part of most of the populace naturally affects the answer to the question of how much force is necessary. One of the purposes of a legal system of justice is surely to make the use of force by individuals very much less necessary than it would otherwise be. If we try to think back to a "state of nature" situ-

ation, we shall have less difficulty envisaging the need for
large amounts of force to prevent small threats of violence.
Here Hobbes's contention that in such a state every man
has a right to the life of every other becomes understandable. He was, I suggest, relying on the same principle as I
have argued for here: that one has a right to use as much
force as necessary to defend one's rights, which include
the right of safety of person.

And needless to say, my arguments here do not give us
any reason to modify the obviously vital principle that if
force should be necessary, then one must use the least
amount of it compatible with maintaining the rights of
those being protected. There is, for example, no excuse for
sending armed troops against unarmed students to contain
protest marches and demonstrations.

I have said that the duty to avoid violence is only a duty,
other things being equal. We might arrive at the same conclusion as we have above by asking the question: Which
"other things" might count as being *un*equal? The answer
to this is that whatever else they may be, the purpose of
preventing violence from being done is necessarily one of
these justifying conditions. That the use of force is never
justified to prevent initial violence being done to one logically implies that there is nothing wrong with initial violence. We cannot characterize it as being wrong if preventive violence is not simultaneously being characterized as
justifiable.

We often think of pacifists as being gentle and idealistic
souls, which in its way is true enough. What I have been
concerned to show is that they are also confused. If they
attempt to formulate their position using our standard
concepts of rights, their position involves a contradiction:
Violence is wrong, *and* it is wrong to resist it. But the right
to resist is precisely what having a right of person is, if it is
anything at all.

Could the position be reformulated with a less "com-
mital" concept of rights? I do not think so. It has been
suggested[3] that the pacifist need not talk in terms of this

---

[3] I owe this suggestion to my colleague, Leslie Armour.

"kind" of rights. He can affirm, according to this suggestion, simply that neither the aggressors nor the defenders
"have" rights to what they do, that to affirm their not having them is simply to be against the use of force, without
this entailing the readiness to use force if necessary to protect the said rights. But this will not do I believe. For I
have not maintained that having a right, or believing that
one has a right, entails a *readiness* to defend that right.
One has a perfect right not to resist violence to oneself if
one is so inclined. But our question has been whether
self-defense is justifiable, and not whether one's belief that
violence is wrong entails a willingness or readiness to use
it. My contention has been that such a belief does entail
the justifiability of using it. If one came upon a community in which no sort of violence was ever resisted and it
was claimed in that community that the non-resistance
was a matter of conscience, we should have to conclude,
I think, not that this was a community of saints, but
rather that this community lacked the concept of justice
—or perhaps that their nervous systems were oddly different from ours.

No position can ever be shown to contain a contradiction if we allow its upholder to interpret his language in
any manner he chooses. Perhaps some pacifists have convinced themselves that to have a right is nothing more
than to possess a certain peculiar non-natural property. I
don't know. But what is this to the present subject? The
language which the pacifist employs is not his private
property, and his theories, if he should happen to have any,
about the proper logical analysis of that language, are not
entitled to any *special* hearing when we come to discuss
what he is saying in it. What I want to know is: Is it anything but verbal hocus-pocus to affirm that we *have rights*
but to deny that they ought ever to be defended? If a right
isn't an entitlement to protection, then is it anything at
all? This, I think, is the pacifist's dilemma. He would like
to live in a world utterly at peace. So would most of us.
But we do not, and so the question is, what to do about it?
The pacifist's way is, as it were, to make Munich the cor-
nerstone of our moral lives. We will act (or is that the right
word here?) as if there were no violence anywhere, and

then, hopefully, there will come a time when magic prevails and there is no more of it. By that time, the circle will no doubt also have been squared and infinity encompassed. But the rest of us, meanwhile, will wonder what has become of that supposed right to peace which we thought the pacifist was allowing us when we see him standing by, protesting at the top of his lungs, to be sure, but not *doing* anything about it, in the presence of violence by others.

It might be useful here to sum up the pacifist's problem, as I see it. To maintain the pacifist doctrine, I contend that one of the following three statements must be denied:

1. To will the end (as morally good) is to will the means to it (at least prima facie).
2. Other things being equal, the lesser evil is to be preferred to the greater.
3. There are no "privileged" moral persons: No person necessarily has a different status, counts for more or less than another as such, in matters of morals.

I claim, what might be denied, that all of these may be defended on purely logical or "meta-ethical" grounds and that in any case the pacifist seems to be committed to them. He is committed to (1) because his objection to violence is that it produces suffering, unwanted pain, in the recipients. As far as I know, no pacifist objects to football or Indian leg-wrestling among consenting parties. He is committed to (2) because he holds that to inflict suffering is the greatest of evils and that *this* is why the claims of non-violence take precedence to those of, say, justice (if these are really different). And he is committed to (3) by virtue of his claiming to address this doctrine to everyone, on general moral grounds. But these three principles among them imply, as far as I can see, both the commitment to force when it is necessary to prevent more violence and also the conception of a right as an entitlement to defense. And they therefore leave pacifism, as a moral doctrine, in a logically untenable position.

Ethics and Nuclear Deterrence

Douglas Lackey

The Strategic Arms Limitation Agreement signed by President Nixon in Moscow in May 1972 was universally and rightly hailed as a step toward peace. The principal clauses of the agreement limit the construction of antimissile systems, and these systems are the only devices within the scope of conceivable technology that can fend off a nuclear attack. In effect, the United States and the Soviet Union have agreed upon mutual defenselessness; each side has acknowledged, as practically a permanent condition, the ability of the other to attack and destroy it if it wishes. At the same time, this mutual guarantee of ability to attack carries with it a guarantee of the ability to *counterattack*; each side, if attacked first, can destroy the other with a counterstrike emanating from nuclear submarines surviving the initial attack.[1] Though this state of affairs is hardly

---

[1]My opinion about the ability of nuclear submarines to survive a nuclear attack may seem akin to optimism about the Maginot Line. But I leave it to the reader to construct a plan to neutralize 30 cruising missile submarines. First, they must be located, which is technologically impossible at present. Then they must be destroyed, which is at present very difficult. And all this must be accomplished *simultaneously*, since, if just *one* submarine survives, it can annihilate any nation not protected by an antimissile system. Some plans have been suggested for seeding the oceans with mines, but it is very unlikely that magnetic mines could affix themselves to the 30th submarine before they were detected on the 1st. A slightly more plausible suggestion would be to interrupt the military communications system with dummy messages luring all the opponent's submarines into traps. But the small likelihood that such a scheme would succeed, coupled with

utopian, it is a distinct improvement over the previous delicate balance of terror. If both sides are guaranteed the ability to counterattack, neither side, barring accidents and assuming the usual desire for self-preservation, will attack the other. For the first time since the introduction of intercontinental missiles in the early 1960s, the major powers have achieved stable deterrence.

Though the present strategic balance is an improvement over past uncertainties, this gives us no cause to believe that it is the best possible arrangement. For an indefinite period, to preserve this balance, the United States and the Soviet Union must spend large sums on armaments, endure the risk of nuclear accidents, face the possibility that any minor disagreement may escalate into a nuclear war, and maintain an attitude sufficiently bellicose to assure the other side that destruction will swiftly and surely follow upon attack. My purpose in this paper is to examine the extent to which we can rest content with the present strategic *détente*. There are two sorts of criticism possible: first, the utilitarian one that this policy will not produce the best consequences for the world over all the practical alternatives; second, the sterner criticism that our policy is intrinsically abhorrent and ought to be abandoned simply because of what it is. I shall take up each criticism in turn.

---

the devastating effects of its probable failure, would prevent anyone but a madman from acting upon it. No military or strategic authority today questions the ability of nuclear submarines to survive nuclear attack, and this optimism stands in striking contrast to pessimistic critics in the 1930s who noted the impotence of the Maginot Line against air attacks. (See, for example, Bertrand Russell's *Which Way to Peace*, ch. 2.)

To test the solidity of the present stalemate, consider the strategic impact of the MIRVs (multiple, independently targeted, reentry vehicles) with which our Minuteman and Poseidon missiles are presently being equipped. This device enables up to ten warheads, each targeted to a different location, to be placed on a single ballistic missile! Under normal conditions, an offensive device like this would give immediate victory to the side that first developed it. But suppose, for example, that the United States develops the MIRV first, possesses no antimissile system, and decides to launch a devastating attack on the Soviet Union. However powerful this offensive thrust, *some* Russian submarines would survive, and the United States would be defenseless against their counterattack. Without an antimissile system, the MIRV is strategically worthless; yet construction of it in this country proceeds apace, lest the Russians get it first.

I. A Utilitarian Critique

Utilitarian critiques are always future-oriented; given the world as it is *now*, with the weapons that actually exist on both sides, which policy will produce the best future results? This prevents retroactive criticism of past military decisions; and though they provide an interesting compendium of missed opportunities and mental lapses, the errors of the 1960s will not concern us here. The costs of the *present* policy (by present policy I mean the policy to maintain force levels at least as high as they now are, subject to the limitations of the SALT I agreement) have already been indicated. *First,* there is the enormous cost of maintaining and operating the present American weapons systems. (Notice that we cannot include present interest on loans taken to develop these systems; that is a critique of *past* action) *Second,* there is the enormous cost of the maintaining and operating of the corresponding arsenal in the Soviet Union. It is not unfair, I believe, to include costs of Soviet arms as part of the utilitarian cost of American policy, even though Americans do not decide whether Russia shall arm. "Cost" in a utilitarian calculation is cost to the human race, and each agent is responsible for such costs as can reasonably be predicted to follow from his policies. It is reasonable to predict, judging from what we know of the Soviet Union and its leadership, that if we maintain our present armament, the Russians will maintain theirs; and also reasonable to predict that if we acted differently as regards the level of arms, the Russians would also. Hence their expenditures should be charged against our policy. By parity of reasoning, the Russian policy must include among its costs the money that Americans, in all their rhetorical fury, can reasonably be predicted to spend in response to Russian armaments. But this would be relevant to a critique of Russian policy, and I am here concerned only with our own. *Third,* since the weapons of destruction exist and are very complex, there is a chance that systems will malfunction and some or all of the world be destroyed by accident. The malfunction may be due to mechanical failure, as is described in the book *Fail Safe*, or to human failure, as is depicted in the movie *Dr.*

Strangelove. Though the chances of such accidents are considerably less than they were, say, in October of 1960, when an American nuclear attack was almost ordered against Russia in response to radar signals that had bounced off the moon, the possibility of either sort of failure is still quite real. For reasons quite analogous to those given above as regards the financial burden of armaments, the possibility of malfunction in Russian systems must be charged against our policy, just as much as the possibility of malfunction in American systems. Even though the Russian systems are not supervised by us, they exist in response to ours and their possible malfunctions are concomitants of our policies. Russian expenses and Russian risks are hidden costs of our policies usually ignored even by liberal critics.

The financial burden of armaments is certain; accidental nuclear war is just a possibility. In estimating the value of current defence policy one must subtract some factor for the possibility of accidental war. This factor will be, estimated by the usual methods, the product of the chance of war and the disutility of this result. Though the chance of accidental war is slight, it is not negligible when Russian malfunctions are also considered; and since the disutility of nuclear war is great, the total subtraction from the value of the present policy on this ground alone should be substantial. *Fourth,* since the weapons of destruction exist, the there is always the possibility that they will be *deliberately* used, if the leaders of one nation deem some provocation sufficient. The subtraction for this factor, as with the third, is achieved by multiplying the chance that some conflict will escalate to nuclear war by the disutility of that war, which is considerable.

The "gains" that can be attributed to the present policy are said to be threefold. First, the certainty of an American counterattack deters the Russians from launching a nuclear attack on the United States in order to gain some end. To the extent that such attacks are deterred, the world gains and not just the United States. Second, the ability of the United States to launch a devastating counterattack vitiates all Russian attempts to use threats of attack as a regular instrument of policy. If the United States

could not attack, the Soviet Union could blackmail the
United States at every point, threatening destruction if
concessions be not made. Third, if the United States retains its capacity to counterattack, then it has the option,
in *extreme* situations, of threatening to attack even
though attack is suicidal. Though the Soviet leaders know
that any attack is unlikely, they cannot be *certain* that the
American leaders will *not* go to war over the issue concerned; and accordingly such threats by the United States
will not be totally without effect. President Kennedy used
such threats, successfully, to secure the removal of Russian missiles from Cuba. In short, the maintenance of our
present military capacity reduces the risk of attack and
blackmail, and occasionally can be used to secure goals of
policy.

Each of these three "gains" must be carefully analyzed.
First, it is claimed that American armaments "reduce the
threat of Russian attack." The superficial appeal of this
claim disappears when we raise the question: Reduce the
chances of attack *relative to what?* Certainly it reduces
the chances of attack relative to some anti-Communist
fantasy in which the leaders of the Soviet Union daily plot
the conquest of the United States. But such fantasies are
incredible and it is madness to praise a present policy because it is better than some imaginary evil. The fact is that
with the present policy there is a certain chance of war,
which can be calculated by combining the possibility of
accidental war with the possibility of deliberate attack;
and this is an evil of the policy which can only be justified
on the grounds that all other policies on balance do even
worse.

The same criticism applies to the second "plus" of our
deterrence policy: it prevents nuclear blackmail. Our policy can "prevent" nuclear blackmail only if there *is* nuclear blackmail to be prevented. But there is little evidence
that either side is prone to blackmail of this sort. On the
Russian side, the military tradition is either to act or not
to act: threatening to act is not a standard feature of Russian policy. The Soviets did not *threaten* to invade Hun-
gary and Czechoslovakia; they simply invaded them. They
did not threaten to attack us if we intercepted their ships

steaming toward Cuba in 1962; they merely stopped them. As for the United States, the use of nuclear threats was eschewed in the Acheson era, when there was often something worth blackmailing; and in the Dulles era, though the nuclear sabers were often rattled as a general display, they remained preternaturally still during the Hungarian invasion, the most provocative Soviet act of the 1950s. During this period the United States could have attacked Russia at any time with relative impunity, yet it did not even threaten to attack. In short, the major powers are not given to nuclear blackmail.[2] If this blackmail problem ever does arise, it will arise in the context of nuclear *terrorists*—revolutionary kamikazes with nuclear devices —against whom the threat of counterattack is useless. The true situation is that with the present policy there is not a "reduction" in the chance of nuclear blackmail but rather a set chance of blackmail given present conditions, and no argument has yet been provided that this chance is less than the chance that one would have in all other alternative policies.

The third "plus" of present policy is that if we possess strength we can negotiate from strength—gaining ends we could not attain otherwise. (The latest variant on this theme is the reiterated argument of the present administration that we must first increase armaments in order to facilitate negotiations to decrease them.) This third plus may be a plus from the perspective of those who make American policy, but it can hardly be considered a plus for humanity in general. "To negotiate from strength" is a euphemism for the making of threats; the making of threats increases the chance of nuclear war. The great disutility of this result outweighs any gains that might result from "negotiating from strength," even if (as is unlikely) the negotiations are aimed at a moral result. In summary, then, even if the present policy results in more good than

---

[2]Interestingly enough, one of the few persons who ever publicly advocated the use of nuclear blackmail was Bertrand Russell, who recommended in 1948 that the threat of nuclear attack be used to force the Russians to accept the Baruch-Lilienthal plan for the internationalization of atomic weapons. If a nuclear war ever does break out, Russell will have been proved right in his suggestion, but no one will remember it.

evil,[3] it is not demonstrated that it results in more good on balance than all alternative policies.

Of the alternative policies, the one that most clearly challenges the present policy of seeking bilateral arms reductions while maintaining the arms race is the policy of gradual unilateral disarmament. The most plausible unilateral disarmament policy at present would be this: first, to cease all nuclear testing; to declare a moratorim on armaments research; to deactivate the implementation of MIRV; to withdraw our strategic air bases from Spain, Thailand, Formosa, etc.; and to phase out all Minuteman missiles and sites. All of this would be merely Stage I, since it would leave the strategic balance completely unimpaired, so long as the Soviet Union built no ABM and the United States retained its fleet of missile submarines. Each one of these steps should be accompanied by requests that similar steps be taken by the Soviet Union, but compliance by the Soviet Union should not be considered a precondition for any of the American initiatives.

Stage II of the disarmament procedure should be as follows: the United States should announce that it will not counterattack if attacked by the Soviet Union and shall progressively deactivate its nuclear submarines, down to a point in which the ability of the United States to reply to a Russian attack would be considerably reduced.[4] At the same time, the United States should undertake extensive steps to increase Soviet-American trade, in such areas as exploit the natural specializations of the respective countries.

The consequences of this alternative policy would be, at a minimum, a reduction of the chance of accidental and escalated nuclear war, relative to the present policy, and the diversion of American capital and intellect into enter-

---

[3]Strictly speaking, "an increase in expected value."
[4]The reader may wonder why I consider it preferable to deactivate nuclear submarines rather than transfer them to an international agency. The reason I consider this undesirable is that American nuclear submarines are now ultimately responsible to civilian authority, and the tradition of military subservience to civilian authority is stronger in the United States than in most of the United Nations. Transfer of submarines to an international agency with no tradition of obedience would substantially increase chances of a nuclear *coup d'etat.*

prises more likely to increase the economic health of the nation.[5] In addition, it is highly likely that a reduction in the American level of armaments would lead to a reduction in Russian armaments, since one principal rationale for the Russian maintenance of these arms is the threat of American attack.

This leaves the question of "nuclear blackmail." If the United States enters into extensive economic arrangements with Russia, provided that these arrangements are not exploitative but based on a national specialization, the Soviet Union would have no cause to blackmail the United States, since an injury to a trading partner is an injury to oneself. Furthermore, the Soviet Union can ill-afford to alienate the United States, even if the United States lacks nuclear arms, since the United States holds the balance of power, both military and economic, between the Soviet Union and China, who are at present, enemies by geography, by history, and by ideology. In short, though the possibility of nuclear blackmail exists if the United States abandons its armaments, there is little likelihood that there would be such blackmail; and, in my opinion, the small chance of this bad result is far outweighed by the decreased chance of accidental or deliberate nuclear war.

The policy that I recommend bears some resemblance to suggested policies of national pacifism in the 1930s. Since these policies were discredited by events, it is important to see that the problems of the 1970s are significantly different from those of the 1930s. The principal tension of the 1930s was between Germany and other states, and Germany possessed the most advanced military technology. The principal tension of the 1970s and 1980s will be between the advanced countries and the underdeveloped countries, within which the population bomb will explode. In short, tension in the 1930s was between strong

---

[5]The argument that increased military expenditures are needed to preserve economic vitality is completely bogus. The world's two strongest and fastest developing economies—West Germany's and Japan's—are the economies of nations who have spent least for armaments, among major advanced nations, since 1945.

and strong; in the 1980s it will be between strong and weak. The underdeveloped countries do not stand to the world on the same military basis that Germany stood to the rest of Europe. Furthermore, in the 1930s, Germany and Italy were infected with an ideology that contained self-fulfilling prophecies of the inevitability of war. There is no force in the contemporary scene that corresponds to fascism. Neither ideology of democracy nor the ideology of capitalism preach the inevitability of war, and in the ideology of communism, though there will be inevitable war between *nations*, especially war by socialist states against capitalist states, who will be defeated not by external invasion but internal contradictions. There is no nation at present which simultaneously has the power, the desire, or the need to go to war.

Historical predictions are a risky business, and the policy of unilateral disarmament may appear unduly risky, even when its probable positive effects are considered. But if disarmament increases the risk of conquest, continued armament increases the risk of war; and of these two, the latter is the more serious, especially if the welfare of the entire world is considered and not the special national interests of the United States.

II. Prisoner's Dilemma Denied

A critic of the preceding section might argue that the whole proof hangs upon an overly generous interpretation of Russian intentions. "One can argue," a defender of armaments might retort, "that the United States has a moral obligation to disarm if the Soviet Union is also willing to disarm, since mutual disarmament benefits everyone. But if the Soviet Union does not disarm, no argument based on probabilities or expected values should compel us to disarm and open ourselves to conquest. Calculation of probabilities of historical events is mere guesswork, but no guesswork is involved in the judgment that Russian conquest of an armed United States is not possible but Russian conquest of a disarmed United States is a real possibility. The proper way to evaluate the strategic situation is to forget spurious probabilities and to use game-theoretic methods. In the strategic game, the disarming of the United States gives the Russians a move which simple logic compels them to take and which is disaster for us."

I would be willing, if pressed, to defend the probabilistic approach to deterrence theory, because I believe that the case for unilateral disarmament can be successfully made without spurious precision. In the preceding section, for example, I claimed that the chance of accidental war resulting from present policies is small but not negligible, and this degree of precision, which is not very great but all that the argument needs, can be supported by empirical evidence. But if a game-theoretic analysis is desired, I shall not shrink from providing one, since these analyses have their independent merits.

In a game-theoretic analysis of strategy, each opponent is viewed as having choices between various policies and payoffs are assigned to each opponent after all simultaneously make some choice of policy. In the deterrence situation as we now find it, in which each opponent knows that a first strike is suicidal, the main policy choices are "disarming unilaterally" or "remaining at an arms level equal to one's opponents." Symbolizing "retaining arms" as A and "disarming unilaterally" as D, the game matrix for deterrence looks like this:

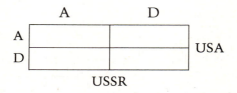

Now, if both countries disarm, neither will attack the other, neither risks accidental war, and neither wastes resources on armaments; and if both countries maintain arms at present levels, neither will deliberately attack the other, but both risk accidental war, and both pay for armaments. Obviously the payoff figures for the D–D game should be higher than the payoff figures for the A–A game, and the payoff figures should be equal for each player in each case; for example:

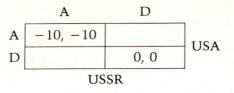

(Left-hand payoffs to USA, right-hand payoffs to USSR; scale of payoffs is arbitrary.)

This leaves us the difficulty of assigning the payoffs for the D–A games. A critic of disarmament might say that if one country is disarmed while the other remains armed, this is a tremendous advantage to the armed nation, which can do as it wills, and a tremendous disadvantage to the disarmed nation, which must suffer what it must. Accordingly, the disarmament critic sets the payoff for the armed country (against disarmed) very high, higher than the payoff for being armed (against armed); and he sets the payoff for the disarmed country (against armed) very low, lower than the payoff for being disarmed (against disarmed); for example:

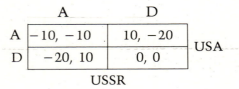

which is an instance of the game pattern known as the Prisoner's Dilemma. Having got this far, the critic of disarmament will argue: "The USSR will either arm or disarm. If the Soviet Union arms, then it is preferable (−10 to −20) for the USA to arm; and if the Soviet Union disarms, then it is preferable (10 to 0) for the USA to arm. Therefore, whatever the Soviet Union does, it is preferable for the United States to remain armed.

This is the sort of reasoning that generates arms races, and arms races are admitted on all sides to be regrettable. The difficulty is to find a flaw in this reasoning that will allow one to escape from an arms race once one is caught up in it. There have been numerous attempts, by philosophers and peace-oriented game theoreticians, to demonstrate that the policy of disarmament is rational, or moral, in the Prisoner's Dilemma situation, but all these attempts have been unconvincing. My own feeling is that the main mistake is not in the disarmament critic's reasoning once the Prisoner's Dilemma is established, but in the reasoning that assigns the payoffs so as to create the Dilemma. If one considers nuclear arms only, then it is not a tremendous advantage to be armed when your so-called opponent is disarmed. Nuclear arms are expensive; they may blow up in your face; and they cannot be used for a war of aggrandizement, since when used against an enemy they destroy the spoils. The only serviceable use of nuclear arms is to destroy an opponent who threatens you; and if your opponent is disarmed, he is no threat. In short, I deny that the Prisoner's Dilemma is the correct model to use in analysis of the present deterrence situation; the real world, I believe, looks more like this:

	A	D
A	−10, −10	−8, −2
D	−2, −8	0, 0

If *this* matrix is the correct mirror of , reality, then game-theoretic analysis shows that the strategy of disarmament is preferable whether one's "opponent" is disarmed or armed.

III. A Deontological Critique

Suppose that for some reason or lack of reason the Soviet Union launches a nuclear first strike against the United States. Even under these conditions it would be clearly immoral for the United States to retaliate in kind against the Soviet Union, since retaliation by the United States would result in the death of millions of innocent people, for no higher purpose than useless revenge. The present policy of deterrence requires preparations for such retaliation and threats and assurances by us that it will be forthcoming if the United States is attacked. Indeed, if our deterrent is to remain credible, the response of the United

States to attack should be semiautomatic. Defenders of armaments justify all the preparations on the grounds that they will prevent an attack *on us;* if retaliation is ever needed, they say, the system has already failed. Now, a Russian attack against the United States would be at least as immoral as our retaliation against the Russians. So one aspect of the moral problem of deterrence is this: Is one justified in *threatening* to do something which is immoral, if the reasoned intention behind one's threat is to prevent something immoral from occurring?

Let us consider some analogous situations.

(1) It would be immoral to kill a man in order to prevent default on a debt, even if one had no intention of killing the man at all, so long as he pays the debt. Indeed, it is immoral to threaten to kill a man in order to pay a debt, even if one has no intention of killing him under any circumstances, including nonpayment of the debt. In this case at least, threatening evil is not justified by good results or an increased chance of good results. Perhaps this lack of justification derives from the inherent wrongfulness of such threats of violence or from the bad results that would follow if everyone regularly made threats of this sort—whatever the cause, the good results that *actually* follow from the threat[6] do not justify it; even, I would say, in a state of nature containing no judicial system. (2) It might be objected that this example is unfair because the stakes in question are not high enough. Would it be equally immoral to threaten to kill Jones if the intention of the threat is to prevent Jones from doing murder himself, and if the threat will *be* carried out only when Jones actually does murder? This, perhaps, is the way deterrence theorists view the present strategic *détente.* It must be admitted that in this situation the threat to kill is not *obviously* immoral. Indeed, anyone who recommends capital punishment for convicted murderers is allowing that such threats, if tempered by due process of law, are *not* immoral.

---

[6]This includes the actual increased chance that the debt will be paid.

The difficulty with this example is that it does not truly reflect the structure of our present nuclear policy. Our policy is not to threaten a potential *murderer* with death in order to prevent him from murdering, and to execute *him* when he actually does murder, but rather to threaten *someone else* with death in order to prevent a potential murderer from attacking and to execute *someone else* when the murderer actually strikes. An American counterattack would be directed against the Russian people, and it is not the Russian people who would be ordering an attack on the American people. Similarly, if leaders in the United States ordered an attack on Russia, the Russian counterattack would fall on the American people and not on the leaders who ordered the attack.[7] In the present *détente*, the leaders of each side hold the population of the other hostage, and threaten to execute the hostages if the opposing *leaders* do not meet certain conditions. The proper moral examples, then, with which to analyze the *détente* should be examples of hostage-taking. (3) Suppose that the Hatfields and the McCoys live in an area sufficiently rural that disputes cannot be settled by appeal to a higher authority. For various reasons, the two families take a dislike to each other. Each family, let us assume, possesses hand grenades that could destroy the other family completely; and against these hand grenades there is no adequate defense. Each family, in what it considers to be a defensive move, kidnaps a child from the family of the other and holds it hostage. Each side wires its hostage to a device which will explode and kill the hostage if there is any loud noise nearby—such as the noise of a grenade attack or, what is not likely but still *possible,* the accidental explosion of the captors' own grenades or the sounding of a nearby clap of thunder. This example, I believe, fairly represents the present policies of deterrence.

---

[7] I am assuming that the Russian and American peoples cannot be held responsible for the decisions of their leaders. For the Russians, this is surely the case; for the Americans, who live in a relatively more democratic nation, the issue is more debatable. Still, whatever fraction of responsibility the American people would bear for an attack on Russia, it would hardly be sufficient to justify punishing millions of Americans with injury and death.

A defender of Hatfield foreign policy might justify himself as follows: "We have no intention of killing the McCoy child, unless, of course, we are attacked. If we are attacked, we must kill him automatically (or else lose the credibility of this deterrent); but we feel that it is very unlikely that, under these conditions, any attack will occur. True, there is some small chance that the child will die by accident, but this is only a *small* chance, and so we have good reason to believe that this will not happen. At the same time, the presence of the hostage reduces the chance that the McCoys will attack, relative to the chances of attack if we had taken no hostage. If the child dies, we cannot be blamed, since we had good reason to believe that he would not, and if he lives, we are to be commended for adopting a policy which has in fact prevented an attack."

The moral reply here is obvious: the Hatfields have no *right* to seize the McCoy child, whatever dubious advantages they gain by seizing him. True they only *threaten* to kill him, but threatening to kill him increases the chance of his being killed, and they have no right to increase these chances. The moral repulsiveness of the Hatfield policy derives from its abuse of the innocent for dubious ends. Deterring the McCoys in this manner is like deterring one's neighbors from running into you on the road by seizing their children and tying them to the front bumper of your car.[8] If everyone did this, accidents might decrease and, on balance, more lives saved then lost. Perhaps it could be predicted that the chances of a single child dying on a car bumper are slight; perhaps, by a miracle, no child would die.[9] Whatever the chances and whatever the gains, no one could claim the right to use a single child in this way. Yet it seems that the present American policy uses the entire Russian population in just this manner. In the preceding section I argued that our deterrence policy does not produce the best results when all alternative policies are considered. These examples show that even if the policy *did* produce the best results, it still ought not to be adopted.

---

[8] This example is in Paul Ramsey, *Modern War and the Christian Conscience.*
[9] This miracle, in reference to nuclear weapons, we have seen since 1945.

(4) The key step in the preceding criticism is that the Hatfields have no right to increase the chances of the McCoy child dying, and analogously the United States has no right to increase the chances of the Russian populations dying. The threat is illicit if the threat is real. This leads to the interesting possibility that the threat is licit if it is fraudulent. Suppose that the United States *says* that it will counterattack if the Soviet Union attacks and gives every indication that it will counterattack (missile silos are constructed, submarines cruise the oceans, etc.); but, in fact, unknown to anyone except the highest officials in the government, all the American warheads are disarmed and simply cannot go off. In this case the United States does not threaten, but merely *seems* to threaten to counterattack. If the chance of Russian attack is decreased, such a plan would have good results without the intrinsic repulsiveness of the present policy.

But this plan has practical and moral flaws. The practical flaw is that the bogus threat will not serve as a deterrent unless the Soviet Union *does* discover that, according to the usual analysis, the chances of war will be greatly increased. So, it is not obvious that this plan gives good results, since one must balance the decreased chance of war (if the Soviet Union respects the deterrent) against the increased chance of war (if the Soviet Union discovers that the deterrent is bogus). Furthermore, if this plan is successfully put into effect and the Soviet Union does not have a similar plan of its own, the bogus-warhead plan will result in high and wasteful Soviet expenditures and in an increased chance of accidental or deliberate attack from the Soviet side.

The chances of nuclear war have diminished considerably since the early 1960s;[10] our policies now are safer than they were then. But these improvements should not blind

---

[10]In the early 1960s, the American public overestimated the chance that nuclear war would occur. In the early 1970s, I believe that the public underestimates the chance that nuclear war will occur, and public interest in this issue is nil. But it is a good thing that this mistake is common, since lack of expectation that nuclear attacks will occur lessens the chance that nuclear accidents will be interpreted as hostile acts. In the strange world of nuclear deterrence, ignorance may bring bliss.

Part VI
Death, Suicide, and Euthanasia

Attitudes toward death and killing vary from society to society. The ancient Greeks, for example, held attitudes very different from our own. They thought it perfectly acceptable to kill newborn babies if they were deformed and, while they generally regarded suicide as a cowardly way to avoid life's problems, they thought it an honorable alternative to a lingering, painful death from incurable disease. The Romans went even further: many of the most prominent philosophers of Rome argued that suicide was an acceptable option whenever a person decided that life was no longer desirable.

The coming of Christianity caused great changes in these attitudes. The early Church was resolutely pacifist, and opposed killing in almost every circumstance. The Church fathers condemned not only infanticide, suicide, abortion, and euthanasia ("mercy killing"), but war and capital punishment as well. However, the Church's ban on participation in warfare was soon lifted, for Christianity could not become a state religion while maintaining its unqualified opposition to war. Also, as a concession to the state, the Church abandoned its early condemnation of capital punishment.

These historical developments are the source of a climate of opinion that still prevails. It is widely thought that both killing in war and capital punishment are permissible, while abortion, suicide, and euthanasia are commonly thought to be unacceptable—and almost everyone believes it is wrong to kill defective babies, even if the alternative is miserable or meaningless lives for them and continued unhappiness for their parents. In previous units we have considered the problems of abortion, war, and capital punishment; in this unit we will take up suicide and euthanasia. There is obviously a close relation between the two topics: indeed, the Greeks regarded voluntary euthanasia as nothing more than a special case of assisted suicide. If a person was dying of a painful disease and preferred death now rather than lingering on in agony, the Greeks thought it of little consequence whether he took his own life (suicide) or enlisted the aid of another to kill him (euthanasia).

Today suicide is illegal in most of the United States. (Since each state has its own laws, an action can be illegal in some states but legal in others.) Upon first thought, this may seem silly; after all, how could a person who has killed himself be punished? However, these laws do have practical consequences; because suicide is illegal, authorities can take steps to prevent people from killing themselves. For example, if you take a poison and are found before you die, your stomach can be pumped without your permission; nets can be spread below you if you hesitate before leaping from a high window. Moreover, because it is illegal, a person who attempts suicide and fails can be held liable in court.

Such laws are a reminder of the extent to which our attitudes are a product of historical Christianity. The Church has for many centuries held that suicides are condemned to Hell, and refused to grant them burial in sacred ground. In earlier times suicides were in fact buried in roadways as a special sign of scorn. The argument most often given in support of this attitude was that life is a precious gift from God; therefore, only He has the right to decide how long it will last. The suicide is guilty of "playing God," by decreeing that his life will end sooner than God intends; he is also guilty of ingratitude, for he throws the gift of life back in the face of the Creator. A very similar argument was used in opposition to euthanasia: since only God has the right to decide how long a life will last, we have no right to shorten the lives of the dying by mercy killing, even if the dying person is in agony and wants to be given a painless death.

Actually, this last argument is unsound, and must be rejected no matter what view is taken toward suicide, euthanasia, and Christianity. The fatal flaw in the argument was identified over 200 years ago by the Scottish philosopher David Hume. Hume pointed out that if only God has the right to decide how long a life will last, then we are "playing God" when we prolong lives as much as when we shorten them. Therefore we would have to stop trying to cure sick people because, since God has decreed their deaths, who are we to interfere? Medicine would have to be altogether abandoned!

In his article "The Morality and Rationality of Suicide," Richard Brandt, a distinguished American philosopher and teacher at the University of Michigan, discusses whether suicide is immoral, and whether it can ever be rational for a person to kill himself even from a person's own point of view. Brandt's article is the second selection in this unit. The first selection, "Death," by the Princeton philosopher Thomas Nagel, takes up a preliminary question, namely whether or not it is a bad thing to die.

We do, of course, commonly assume that death is a bad thing. That is why we regard murder as a heinous crime, and why we anticipate our own deaths with dismay and weep over the deaths of those we love. If killing is occasionally justified, it is the rare exception; moreover, it is difficult to justify killing even then, precisely because killing is deliberately imposing such a great evil upon the victim. However, not all thinkers have agreed with this. Epicurus (who lived three centuries BC) held that death is not an evil, and so should not be feared. Death is nothing to us, he said, because after we die we simply do not exist, and if we do not exist we cannot suffer pain or hardship or any bad thing whatsoever. Nonexistence is merely a neutral matter, neither good nor evil. This argument, and others like it, are critically discussed by Nagel, who concludes that death is an evil, but an evil of a special kind—a deprivation of the positive good of life, which is, as he says, "all that one has."

Nagel also contends that life has positive value even if a majority of one's experiences are bad. Most of us would *agree: it is better to be alive, even if we are unhappy, than to be dead. However, a person's life can become so miserable, with prospects so bleak, that life no longer seems desirable. Suppose, for example, a person has inoperable cancer, and can live in terrible pain for only a few more days or weeks. And suppose this person would prefer to die now than to live out the brief miserable remaining time. Would it be wrong to kill him, as an act of kindness, at his own request? This is the problem of euthanasia.*

Euthanasia is illegal everywhere in the United States. Anyone who would kill a person in the situation just described could be charged with first degree murder. But, legal matters aside, would it be immoral to engage in mercy killing? (We know that the law and morality do not always coincide.) This question is important for the medical profession, since it is doctors and nurses who most often have to deal with dying people, and who are most often faced with such requests. The American Medical Association has adopted an official policy on the morality of euthanasia: they hold that mercy killing is always wrong. There is, however, an important qualification— the AMA says that it can sometimes be all right to allow patients to die by withholding or ceasing the treatment necessary to keep them alive. The distinction between killing a patient, and merely allowing the patient to die, is sometimes referred to as the distinction between "active euthanasia" and "passive euthanasia."

The AMA policy, which condemns active euthanasia but endorses passive euthanasia, is consistent with a long tradition of Western thought. Even the Roman Catholic Church agrees that letting patients die can sometimes be allowed. We do not have the right to kill, says the Church, but neither do we have the obligation to prolong life indefinitely. In "Active and Passive Euthanasia," by James Rachels, the AMA policy statement is examined, and it is argued that the distinction between killing and letting die really has no moral importance. Contrary to the long tradition represented by both the AMA and the Church, it is argued that active and passive euthanasia are actually the same, from a moral point of view; therefore, if passive euthanasia is allowed, active euthanasia should be allowed also.

No arguments are given in Rachels' article to show that active euthanasia is morally acceptable. He only argues that if passive euthanasia is all right, then active euthanasia is all right too. Additional arguments are needed to establish that either form of euthanasia really is morally permissible. The most common pro-euthanasia arguments are, first, that mercy killing is justified as an act of kindness, to relieve suffering and provide dying persons with a more peaceful end; and second, that if a dying person wants to be put out of misery, it is the individual's right to make that decision, and no one else has the right to interfere or impose their values—after all, one might say, it's his life. A. D. Woozley is a well known British philosopher who has for many years taught at the University of Virginia. In his paper "Euthanasia and the Principle of Harm," Woozley provides arguments to show that euthanasia can be morally acceptable; he especially develops the idea that people's lives are their own, and that neither the state nor any other person has the right to decide what will ultimately be done with another person's life.

Death

Thomas Nagel

"The syllogism he had learnt from Kiesewetter's logic:
'Caius is a man, men are mortal, therefore Caius is mortal,'
had always seemed to him correct as applied to Caius, but
certainly not as applied to himself. . . . What did Caius
know of the smell of that striped leather ball Vanya had
been so fond of?"

Tolstoy, *The Death of Ivan Ilyich*

If, as many people believe, death is the unequivocal and
permanent end of our existence, the question arises
whether it is a bad thing to die. There is conspicuous disagreement about the matter: some people think death is
dreadful; others have no objection to death *per se*, though
they hope their own will be neither premature nor painful.

Those in the former category tend to think those in the
latter are blind to the obvious, while the latter suppose the
former to be prey to some sort of confusion. On the one
hand it can be said that life is all one has, and the loss of it
is the greatest loss one can sustain. On the other hand it
may be objected that death deprives this supposed loss of
its subject, and that if one realizes that death is not an
unimaginable condition of the persisting person, but a

This essay, in shortened form, originally appeared in volume IV, no. 1 of *Nous*, a
quarterly journal published by Wayne State University Press, Detroit, Michigan,
and is used with the publisher's permission. The shorter version was read at a
meeting of the Western Division of the American Philosophical Association in
St. Louis, May 9, 1970.

mere blank, one will see that it can have no value whatever, positive or negative.

Since I want to leave aside the question whether we are,
or might be, immortal in some form, I shall simply use the
word "death" and its cognates in this discussion to mean
permanent death, unsupplemented by any form of conscious survival. I wish to consider whether death is in itself an evil; and how great an evil, and of what kind, it
might be. This question should be of interest even to those
who believe that we do not die permanently, for one's attitude toward immortality must depend in part on one's
attitude toward death.

Clearly if death is an evil at all, it cannot be because of
its positive features, but only because of what it deprives
us of. I shall try to deal with the difficulties surrounding
the natural view that death is an evil because it brings to
an end all the goods that life contains.[1] An account of
these goods need not occupy us here, except to observe
that some of them, like perception, desire, activity, and
thought, are so general as to be constitutive of human life.
They are widely regarded as formidable benefits in themselves, despite the fact that they are conditions of misery
as well as of happiness, and that a sufficient quantity of
more particular evils can perhaps outweigh them. That is
what is meant, I think, by the allegation that it is good
simply to be alive, even if one is undergoing terrible experiences. The situation is roughly this: There are elements which, if added to one's experience, make life better; there are other elements which, if added to one's
experience, make life worse. But what remains when these
are set aside is not merely *neutral*: it is emphatically positive. Therefore life is worth living even when the bad elements of experience are plentiful, and the good ones too
meager to outweigh the bad ones on their own. The additional positive weight is supplied by experience itself,
rather than by any of its contents.

I shall not discuss the value that one person's life or
death may have for others, or its objective value, but only

---

[1]As we shall see, this does not mean that it brings to an end all the goods that a
man can possess.

the value it has for the person who is its subject. That seems to me the primary case, and the case which presents the greatest difficulties. Let me add only two observations. First, the value of life and its contents does not attach to mere organic survival: almost everyone would be indifferent (other things equal) between immediate death and immediate coma followed by death twenty years later without reawakening. And second, like most goods, this can be multiplied by time: more is better than less. The added quantities need not be temporarily continuous (though continuity has its social advantages). People are attracted to the possibility of long-term suspended animation or freezing, followed by the resumption of conscious life, because they can regard it from within simply as a *continuation* of their present life. If these techniques are ever perfected, what from outside appeared as a dormant interval of three hundred years could be experienced by the subject as nothing more than a sharp discontinuity in the character of his experiences. I do not deny, of course, that this has its own disadvantages. Family and friends may have died in the meantime; the language may have changed; the comforts of social, geographical, and cultural familiarity would be lacking. Nevertheless these inconveniences would not obliterate the basic advantage of continued, though discontinuous, existence.

If we turn from what is good about life to what is bad about death, the case is completely different. Essentially, though there may be problems about their specification, what we find desirable in life are certain states, conditions, or types of activity. It is *being* alive, *doing* certain things, having certain experiences, that we consider good. But if death is an evil, it is the *loss of life,* rather than the state of being dead, or nonexistent, or unconscious, that is objectionable.[2] This asymmetry is important. If it is good to be alive, that advantage can be attributed to a person at each point of his life. It is a good of which Bach had more than Schubert, simply because he lived longer. Death, however, is not an evil of which Shakespeare has so far received a

---

[2]It is sometimes suggested that what we really mind is the process of *dying.* But I should not really object to dying if it were not followed by death.

larger portion than Proust. If death is a disadvantage, it is not easy to say when a man suffers it.

There are two other indications that we do not object death merely because it involves long periods of nonexistence. First, as has been mentioned, most of us would not regard the *temporary* suspension of life, even for substantial intervals, as in itself a misfortune. If it develops that people can be frozen without reduction of the conscious lifespan, it will be inappropriate to pity those who are temporarily out of circulation. Second, none of us existed before we were born (or conceived), but few regard that as a misfortune. I shall have more to say about this later.

The point that death is not regarded as an unfortunate *state* enables us to refute a curious but very common suggestion about the origin of the fear of death. It is often said that those who object to death have made the mistake of trying to imagine what it is like to *be* dead. It is alleged that the failure to realize that this task is logically impossible (for the banal reason that there is nothing to imagine) leads to the conviction that death is a mysterious and therefore terrifying prospective *state*. But this diagnosis is evidently false, for it is just as impossible to imagine being totally unconscious as to imagine being dead (though it is easy enough to imagine oneself, from the outside, in either of those conditions). Yet people who are averse to death are not usually averse to unconsciousness (so long as it does not entail a substantial cut in the total duration of waking life).

If we are to make sense of the view that to die is bad, it must be on the ground that life is a good and death is the corresponding deprivation or loss, bad not because of any positive features but because of the desirability of what it removes. We must now turn to the serious difficulties which this hypothesis raises, difficulties about loss and privation in general, and about death in particular.

Essentially, there are three types of problem. First, doubt may be raised whether *anything* can be bad for a man without being positively unpleasant to him: specifically, it may be doubted that there are any evils which consist merely in the deprivation or absence of possible goods, and which do not depend on someone's *minding* that deprivation.

Second, there are special difficulties, in the case of death, about how the supposed misfortune is to be assigned to a subject at all. There is doubt both as to *who* its subject is, and as to *when* he undergoes it. So long as a person exists, he has not yet died, and once he has died, he no longer exists; so there seems to be no time when death, if it is a misfortune, can be ascribed to its unfortunate subject. The third type of difficulty concerns the asymmetry, mentioned above, between our attitudes to posthumous and prenatal nonexistence. How can the former be bad if the latter is not?

It should be recognized that if these are valid objections to counting death as an evil, they will apply to many other supposed evils as well. The first type of objection is expressed in general form by the common remark that what you don't know can't hurt you. It means that even if a man is betrayed by his friends, ridiculed behind his back, and despised by people who treat him politely to his face, none of it can be counted as a misfortune for him so long as he does not suffer as a result. It means that a man is not injured if his wishes are ignored by the executor of his will, or if, after his death, the belief becomes current that all the literary works on which his fame rests were really written by his brother, who died in Mexico at the age of 28. It seems to me worth asking what assumptions about good and evil lead to these drastic restrictions.

All the questions have something to do with time. There certainly are goods and evils of a simple kind (including some pleasures and pains) which a person possesses at a given time simply in virtue of his condition at that time. But this is not true of all the things we regard as good or bad for a man. Often we need to know his history to tell whether something is a misfortune or not; this applies to ills like deterioration, deprivation, and damage. Sometimes his experiential *state* is relatively unimportant—as in the case of a man who wastes his life in the cheerful pursuit of a method of communicating with asparagus plants. Someone who holds that all goods and evils must be temporarily assignable states of the person may of course try to bring difficult cases into line by pointing to the pleasure or pain that more complicated goods and evils cause. Loss, betrayal, deception, and ridicule are on this view bad because people suffer when they learn of them. But it should be asked how our ideas of human value would have to be constituted to accommodate these cases directly instead. One advantage of such an account might be that it would enable us to explain *why* the discovery of these misfortunes causes suffering—in a way that makes it reasonable. For the natural view is that the discovery of betrayal makes us unhappy because it is bad to be betrayed—not that betrayal is bad because its discovery makes us unhappy.

It therefore seems to me worth exploring the position that most good and ill fortune has as its subject a person identified by his history and his possibilities, rather than merely by his categorical state of the moment—and that while this subject can be exactly located in a sequence of places and times, the same is not necessarily true of the goods and ills that befall him.[3]

These ideas can be illustrated by an example of deprivation whose severity approaches that of death. Suppose an intelligent person receives a brain injury that reduces him to the mental condition of a contented infant, and that such desires as remain to him can be satisfied by a custodian, so that he is free from care. Such a development would be widely regarded as a severe misfortune, not only for his friends and relations, or for society, but also, and primarily, for the person himself. This does not mean that a contented infant is unfortunate. The intelligent adult who has been *reduced* to this condition is the subject of the misfortune. He is the one we pity, though of course he does not mind his condition—there is some doubt, in fact, whether he can be said to exist any longer.

. The view that such a man has suffered a misfortune is open to the same objections which have been raised in regard to death. He does not mind his condition. It is in fact the same condition he was in at the age of three months, except that he is bigger. If we did not pity him then, why pity him now; in any case, who is there to pity? The in-

---

[3]It is certainly not true in general of the things that can be said of him. For example, Abraham Lincoln was taller than Louis XIV. But when?

telligent adult has disappeared, and for a creature like the one before us, happiness consists in a full stomach and a dry diaper.

If these objections are invalid, it must be because they rest on a mistaken assumption about the temporal relation between the subject of a misfortune and the circumstances which constitute it. If, instead of concentrating exclusively on the oversized baby before us, we consider the person he was, and the person he *could* be now, then his reduction to this state and the cancellation of his natural adult development constitute a perfectly intelligible catastrophe.

This case should convince us that it is arbitrary to restrict the goods and evils that can befall a man to nonrelational properties ascribable to him at particular times. As it stands, that restriction excludes not only such cases of gross degeneration, but also a good deal of what is important about success and failure, and other features of life that have the character of processes. I believe we can go further, however. There are goods and evils which are irreducibly relational; they are features of the relations between a person, with spatial and temporal boundaries of the usual sort, and circumstances which may not coincide with him either in space or in time. A man's life includes much that does not take place within the boundaries of his body and his mind, and what happens to him can include much that does not take place within the boundaries of his life. These boundaries are commonly crossed by the misfortunes of being deceived, or despised, or betrayed. (If this is correct, there is a simple account of what is wrong with breaking a deathbed promise. It is an injury to the dead man. For certain purposes it is possible to regard time as just another type of distance.) The case of mental degeneration shows us an evil that depends on a contrast between the reality and the possible alternatives. A man is the subject of good and evil as much because he has hopes which may or may not be fulfilled, or possibilities which may or may not be realized, as because of his capacity to suffer and enjoy. If death is an evil, it must be accounted for in these terms, and the impossibility of locating it within life should not trouble us.

When a man dies we are left with his corpse, and while a corpse can suffer the kind of mishap that may occur to an article of furniture, it is not a suitable object for pity. The man, however, is. He has lost his life, and if he had not died, he would have continued to live it, and to possess whatever good there is in living. If we apply to death the account suggested for the case of dementia, we shall say that although the spatial and temporal locations of the individual who suffered the loss are clear enough, the misfortune itself cannot be so easily located. One must be content just to state that his life is over and there will never be any more of it. That *fact*, rather than his past or present condition, constitutes his misfortune, if it is one. Nevertheless if there is a loss, someone must suffer it, and *he* must have existence and specific spatial and temporal location even if the loss itself does not. The fact that Beethoven had no children may have been a cause of regret to him, or a sad thing for the world, but it cannot be described as a misfortune for the children that he never had. All of us, I believe, are fortunate to have been born. But unless good and ill can be assigned to an embryo, or even to an unconnected pair of gametes, it cannot be said that not to be born is a misfortune. (That is a factor to be considered in deciding whether abortion and contraception are akin to murder.)

This approach also provides a solution to the problem of temporal asymmetry, pointed out by Lucretius. He observed that no one finds it disturbing to contemplate the eternity preceding his own birth, and he took this to show that it must be irrational to fear death, since death is simply the mirror image of the prior abyss. That is not true, however, and the difference between the two explains why it is reasonable to regard them differently. It is true that both the time before a man's birth and the time after his death are times when he does not exist. But the time after his death is time of which his death deprives him. It is time in which, had he not died then, he would be alive. Therefore any death entails the loss of *some* life that its victim would have led had he not died at that or any earlier point. We know perfectly well what it would be for him to have had it instead of losing it, and there is no difficulty in identifying the loser.

But we cannot say that the time prior to a man's birth is time in which he would have lived had he been born not then but earlier. For aside from the brief margin permitted by premature labor, he *could* not have been born earlier: anyone born substantially earlier than he was would have been someone else. Therefore the time prior to his birth is not time in which his subsequent birth prevents him from living. His birth, when it occurs, does not entail the loss to him of any life whatever.

The direction of time is crucial in assigning possibilities to people or other individuals. Distinct possible lives of a single person can diverge from a common beginning, but they cannot converge to a common conclusion from diverse beginnings. (The latter would represent not a set of different possible lives of one individual, but a set of distinct possible individuals, whose lives have identical conclusions.) Given an identifiable individual, countless possibilities for his continued existence are imaginable, and we can clearly conceive of what it would be for him to go on existing indefinitely. However inevitable it is that this will not come about, its possibility is still that of the continuation of a good for him, if life is the good we take it to be.[4]

We are left, therefore, with the question whether the nonrealization of this possibility is in every case a misfor-

---

[4] I confess to being troubled by the above argument, on the ground that it is too sophisticated to explain the simple difference between our attitudes to prenatal and posthumous nonexistence. For this reason I suspect that something essential is omitted from the account of the badness of death by an analysis which treats it as a deprivation of possibilities. My suspicion is supported by the following suggestion of Robert Nozick. We could imagine discovering that people developed from individual spores that had existed indefinitely far in advance of their birth. In this fantasy, birth never occurs naturally more than 100 years before the permanent end of the spore's existence. But then we discover a way to trigger the premature hatching of these spores, and people born who have thousands of years of active life before them. Given such a situation, it would be possible to imagine *oneself* having come into existence thousands of years previously. If we put aside the question whether this would really be the same person, even given the identity of the spore, then the consequence appears to be that a person's birth at a given time *could* deprive him of many earlier years of possible life. Now while it would be cause for regret that one had been deprived of all those possible years of life by being born too late, the feeling would differ from that which many people have about death. I conclude that something about the future *prospect* of permanent nothingness is not captured by the analysis in terms of denied possibilities. If so, then Lucretius's argument still awaits an answer.

tune, or whether it depends on what can naturally be hoped for. This seems to me the most serious difficulty with the view that death is always an evil. Even if we can dispose of the objections against admitting misfortune that is not experienced, or cannot be assigned to a definite time in the person's life, we still have to set some limits on *how* possible a possibility must be for its nonrealization to be a misfortune (or good fortune, should the possibility be a bad one). The death of Keats at 24 is generally regarded as tragic; that of Tolstoy at 82 is not. Although they will both be dead forever, Keats's death deprived him of many years of life which were allowed to Tolstoy; so in a clear sense Keats's loss was greater (though not in the sense standardly employed in mathematical comparison between infinite quantities). However, this does not prove that Tolstoy's loss was insignificant. Perhaps we record an objection only to evils which are gratuitously added to the inevitable; the fact that it is worse to die at 24 than at 82 does not imply that it is not a terrible thing to die at 82, or even at 806. The question is whether we can regard as a misfortune any limitation, like mortality, that is normal to the species. Blindness or near-blindness is not a misfortune for a mole, nor would it be for a man, if that were the natural condition of the human race.

The trouble is that life familiarizes us with the goods of which death deprives us. We are already able to appreciate them, as a mole is not able to appreciate vision. If we put aside doubts about their status as goods and grant that their quantity is in part a function of their duration, the question remains whether death, no matter when it occurs, can be said to deprive its victim of what is in the relevant sense a possible continuation of life.

The situation is an ambiguous one. Observed from without, human beings obviously have a natural lifespan and cannot live much longer than a hundred years. A man's sense of his own experience, on the other hand, does not embody this idea of a natural limit. His existence defines for him an essentially open-ended possible future, containing the usual mixture of goods and evils that he has found so tolerable in the past. Having been gratuitously introduced to the world by a collection of natural,

historical, and social accidents, he finds himself the subject of a *life*, with an indeterminate and not essentially
limited future. Viewed in this way, death, no matter how
inevitable, is an abrupt cancellation of indefinitely extensive possible goods. Normality seems to have nothing to
do with it, for the fact that we will all inevitably die in a
few score years cannot by itself imply that it would not be
good to live longer. Suppose that we were all inevitably
going to die in *agony*—physical agony lasting six months.
Would inevitability make *that* prospect any less unpleasant. And why should it be different for a deprivation? If the
normal lifespan were a thousand years, death at 80 would
be a tragedy. As things are, it may just be a more widespread tragedy. If there is no limit to the amount of life
that it would be good to have, then it may be that a bad
end is in store for us all.

The Morality and Rationality of Suicide*

Richard B. Brandt

"Suicide" is conveniently defined, for our purposes, as doing something which results in one's death, either from the intention of ending one's life or the intention to bring about some other state of affairs (such as relief from pain) which one thinks it certain or highly probable can be achieved only by means of death or will produce death. It may seem odd to classify an act of heroic self-sacrifice on the part of a soldier as suicide. It is simpler, however, not to try to define "suicide" so that an act of suicide is always irrational or immoral in some way; if we adopt a neutral definition like the above we can still proceed to ask when an act of suicide in that sense is rational, morally justifiable, and so on, so that all evaluations anyone might wish to make can still be made.

The literature in anthropology makes clear that suicide has been evaluated very differently in different societies; and philosophers in the Western tradition have been nearly as divergent in their evaluative views of it. I shall not attempt to review these evaluations. What I shall do is

From Richard B. Brandt, "The Morality and Rationality of Suicide," from *A Handbook for the Study of Suicide,* edited by Seymour Perlin. Copyright © 1975 by Oxford University Press, Inc. Reprinted by permission.
*This paper was written while a Fellow at the Center for Advanced Study in the Behavioral Sciences, and also a Special Fellow in the Department of Health, Education and Welfare.

analyze the problem, and appraise some conclusions, from the point of view of contemporary philosophy. Some readers may think that to do this is merely to state another moral prejudice, but I am optimistic enough to believe that as they read on they will be convinced that this is not the case, and that contemporary philosophical thought has moved to a new level of sophistication on this issue as on many others.

I wish to discuss three questions. First, when is it rational, from the point of view of an agent's own welfare, for him to commit suicide? Second, when is it objectively right or wrong, morally, for an agent to take his own life? Third, if an agent takes his own life when it was objectively wrong for him to do so, when may we think that his action was morally blameworthy (or, if we like a theological term, sinful)? What these questions mean, and how they differ, must be explained as we go along. I shall discuss them, however, in reverse order, moving from what seems to me the least important question (listed third above) to the most important one (listed first above).

I. The Moral Blameworthiness of Suicide

In former times the question whether suicide is sinful was of great interest because the answer to it was considered relevant to how the agent would spend eternity. At present the practical issue is not great, although a normal funeral service may be denied a person judged to have committed suicide sinfully. The chief practical issue at present seems to be that persons may disapprove morally of a decedent for having committed suicide, and his friends or relatives may wish to defend his memory against moral charges. The practical issue does not seem large, but justifies some analysis of the problem.

The question whether an act of suicide was sinful or morally blameworthy is not apt to arise unless it is already believed that the agent morally ought not to have done it; this question will be examined in the following secion. But sometimes we do not believe that an agent ought morally not to have committed suicide: for instance, if he really had very poor reason for doing so, and his act foreseeably had catastrophic consequences for his wife and children. At least, let us suppose that we do so believe. In that case we might still think that the act was hardly morally blameworthy or sinful if, say, the agent was in a state of great emotional turmoil at the time. We might then say that, although what he did was wrong, his action is *excusable*, just as in the criminal law it may be decided that, although a person broke the law, he should not be punished because he was *not responsible*, e.g., was temporarily insane, did what he did inadvertently, and so on.

The foregoing remarks assume that to be morally blameworthy (or sinful) on account of an act is one thing, and for the act to be wrong is another. But, if we say this, what after all does it *mean* to say that a person is morally blameworthy on account of an action? We cannot say there is agreement among philosophers on this matter, but I suggest the following account as being safe from serious objection: "X is morally blameworthy on account of an action A" may be taken to mean "X did A, and X would not have done A had not his character been in some respect below standard; and in view of this it is fitting or justified for X to have some disapproving attitudes including remorse toward himself, and for some other persons Y to have some disapproving attitudes toward X and to express them in behavior." Traditional thought would include God as one of the "other persons" who might have and express disapproving attitudes. Another possible view would include only the justifiability of critical or disapproving attitudes toward a person on account of his action; one could then go on to say that such attitudes *are* justified if and only if the act would not have occurred but for the agent's character being below standard in some respect. I shall, however, adopt the former view.

In case the foregoing definition does not seem obviously correct, it is worthwhile pointing out that it is usually thought that an agent is not blameworthy or sinful for an action unless it is a *reflection on him*; the definition brings this fact out and makes clear why—that it would not have occurred but for a defect of character.

It may be thought that the above definition introduces terms as obscure as the one we are defining (e.g., "character" and "below standard"), and it is true these need explanation which cannot be provided here. But I think we are able to move more easily with them than with the original term; the definition is really clarifying. For instance, if someone charges that a suicide was sinful, we now properly ask, "What defect of character did it show?" Some writers have claimed that suicide is blameworthy because it is *cowardly*; and since being cowardly is generally conceded to be a defect of character, if an act of suicide is admitted to be both objectively wrong and also cowardly, the claim to blameworthiness is made out, if the above definition is correct. Of course, most people would hesitate to call taking one's own life (e.g., falling on one's sword) exactly a cowardly act; and there will certainly be controversy about which acts are cowardly and which are not. But at least we can see part of what has to be done to make a charge of blameworthiness valid.

The most interesting question is the general one: Which types of suicide in general are ones which, even if objectively wrong (in a sense to be explained below), are not sinful or blameworthy? Or, in other words, When is a suicide *morally excused* even if it is objectively wrong? We can at least identify some types of cases. (1) Suppose I *think* I am morally bound to commit suicide because I have a terminal illness and continued medical care will ruin my family financially. Suppose, however, that I am mistaken in this belief, and that suicide in such circumstances is not right. But surely I am not morally blameworthy; for I may be doing, out of a sense of duty to my family, what I would personally prefer not to do and is hard for me to do. What defect of character might my action show? Suicide from a genuine sense of duty is not blameworthy, even when the moral conviction in question is mistaken. (2) Suppose that I commit suicide when I am temporarily of unsound mind, either in the sense of the M'Naghten rule that I do not know that what I am doing is wrong, or of the Durham rule that, owing to a mental defect, I am substantially unable to do what is right. Surely any suicide in an unsound state of mind is morally excused. (3) Suppose I commit suicide when I could not be said to be temporarily of unsound mind, but simply because I am not myself. For instance, I may be in an extremely depressed mood. Now a person may be in a highly depressed mood, and commit suicide on account of being in that mood, when there is nothing the matter with his character—or, in other words, his character is not in any relevant way below standard. What are other examples of being "not myself," which might be states of a person responsible for his committing suicide, and which would or might render the suicide excusable even if wrong? Being frightened; being distraught; being in almost any highly emotional frame of mind (anger, frustration, disappointment in love); perhaps just being terribly fatigued. So there are at least three types of suicide which are morally excused even if objectively wrong.

The main point is this: Mr. X may commit suicide and it may be conceded that he ought not to have done so. But it is another step to show that he is sinful, or morally blameworthy, for having done so. To make out that further point, it must be shown that his act is attributable to some substandard trait of character. So Mrs. X after the suicide can concede that her husband ought not to have done what he did, but point out that it is no reflection on him. The distinction, unfortunately, is often overlooked, particularly by Catholic writers. St. Thomas, who recognizes the distinction in some places, seems blind to it in his discussion of suicide.

II. When Suicide Is Morally Justified, or Objectively Right

It is clear, then, that even when a suicide is objectively wrong, the person may not be reprehensible, or sinful, on account of what he did. This state of affairs is possible, of course, only because an act being objectively wrong is one thing, and a person being morally blameworthy or sinful on account of it is another.

Let us now consider our second topic: when a suicide is objectively right or morally justified.

A good many philosophers and social scientists will be sceptical whether anything helpful can be said on this topic, on the assumption, which has been popular in the past thirty years, that there can be no knowledge about such matters, and that moral statements are merely expressions of the attitudes of the speaker. (Such persons doubtless have already been feeling unhappy while reading the preceding section.) I hope, however, for better things, and expect to say something convincing on the central question.

It may be clarifying for the reader if I say at the outset that what I mean by "is objectively wrong" or "is morally unjustified" is "would be prohibited by the set of moral rules which a rational person would prefer to have current or subscribed to in the consciences of persons in the society in which he expected to live a whole life, as compared with any other set of moral rules or none at all." This definition is controversial, and nothing in the following argument will turn on it, but it may be helpful to the reader to have my cards on the table.

First, I wish to clear away some confusions which have beset discussions of our question. The distinctions I am about to make are no longer controversial, and can be accepted by sceptics on the fundamental issues as well as by anyone else.

Persons who say suicide is morally wrong must be asked which of two positions they are affirming: Are they saying that every act of suicide is wrong, *everything considered?* Or are they merely saying that there is always *some* moral obligation—doubtless of serious weight—not to commit suicide, so that very often suicide is wrong, although it is possible that there are *countervailing considerations* which in particular situations make it right or even a moral duty? It is quite evident that the first position is absurd; only the second has a chance of being defensible.

In order to get clear what is wrong with the first view, we may begin with an example. Suppose an Army pilot's single-seater plane goes out of control over a heavily populated area; he has the choice of staying in the plane and bringing it down where it will do little damage but at the cost of certain death for himself, and of bailing out and letting the plane fall where it will, very possibly killing a good many civilians. Suppose he chooses to do the former, and so, by our definition, commits suicide. Does anyone want to say that his action is morally wrong? Even Immanuel Kant, who opposed suicide in all circumstances, apparently would not wish to say that it is; he would in fact say that this act is not one of suicide, for, he says, "It is no suicide to risk one's life against one's enemies, and even to sacrifice it, in order to preserve one's duties toward oneself."[1] St. Thomas, in his discussion, may seem to say it would be wrong, for he says, "It is altogether unlawful to kill oneself," admitting as an exception only the case of being under special command of God. But in fact St. Thomas would say that the act is right because the basic intention of the pilot was to save the lives of civilians, and whether an act is right or wrong is a matter of the basic intention.[2] The charitable interpretation of St. Thomas is to assert that he recognizes that in this case there are two obligations, one to spare the lives of innocent civilians and the other not to destroy one's own life, and that of the two obligations the former is the stronger, and therefore the action is right.

-----

[1]*Lectures on Ethics*, New York, Harper Torchbook, 1963, p. 150.

[2]See St. Thomas Aquinas, *Summa Theologica*, Second Part of the Second Part, Q. 64, Art. 5. In Article 7, he says: "Nothing hinders one act from having two effects, only one of which is intended, while the other is beside the intention. Now moral acts take their species according to what is intended, and not according to what is beside the intention, since this is accidental as explained above (Q. 43, Art. 3: I–II., Q. 1, Art. 3, ad 3)."

Mr. Norman St. John Stevas, the most articulate contemporary defender of the Catholic view, writes as follows:

> Christian thought allows certain exceptions to its general condemnation of suicide. That covered by a particular divine inspiration has already been noted. Another exception arises where suicide is the method imposed by the State for the execution of a just death penalty. A third exception is *altruistic* suicide, of which the best known example is Captain Oates. Such suicides are justified by invoking the principle of double effect. The act from which death results must be good or at least morally indifferent; some other good effect must result, the death must not be directly intended or the real means to the good effect; and a grave reason must exist for adopting the course of action. (*Life, Death and the Law*, Bloomington, Ind., Indiana University Press, 1961, pp. 250–251.)

Presumably the Catholic doctrine is intended to allow suicide when this is required for meeting strong moral obligations; whether it can do so consistently depends partly on the interpretation given to "real means to the good effect." Readers interested in pursuing further the Catholic doctrine of double effect and its implications for our problem should read Philippa Foot, "The Problem of Abortion and the Doctrine of Double Effect," (*The Oxford Review*, no. 5, Trinity 1967, pp. 5–15). [Reprinted in this volume, pp. 59–70.]

In general, we have to admit that there are things there is some moral obligation to avoid which, on account of other morally relevant considerations, it is sometimes right or even morally obligatory to do. There may be some obligation to tell the truth on every occasion, but there are surely many cases in which the consequences of telling the truth would be so catastrophic that one is obligated to lie. To take simple cases: Should one always tell an author truthfully how one evaluates his book, or tell one's wife truthfully whether she looks attractive today? The same again, for promises. There seems to be some moral obligation to do what one has promised (with some exceptions); but if one can keep a trivial promise only at serious cost to another (e.g., keep an appointment only by failing to give aid to someone injured in an accident), it is surely obligatory to break the promise.

The most that the moral critic of suicide could hold, then, is that there is *some* moral obligation not to do what one knows will cause one's death; but he surely cannot say there are no circumstances in which there are obligations to do things which in fact will result in one's death—obligations so strong that it is at least right, and possibly morally obligatory, to do something which will certainly result in one's own death. Possibly those who argue that suicide is immoral do not intend to contest this point, although if so they have not expressed themselves very clearly.

If this interpretation is correct, then in principle it would be possible to argue that, in order to meet my obligation to my family, I might take my own life, as the only course of action which could avoid catastrophic hospital expenses, in a terminal illness. I suspect critics may not concede this point, but *in principle* it would seem they must admit arguments of this type; the real problem is comparing the weights of the obligation to extend my own life and of the obligation to see to the future welfare of my family.

The charitable interpretation of critics of suicide on moral grounds, then, is to attribute to them the view that there is a strong moral obligation not to take one's own life, although this obligation may be overmatched by some other obligations, say to avoid causing the death of others. Possibly the main point they would wish to make is that it is never right to take one's own life *for reasons of one's own personal welfare,* of any kind whatsoever. From here on, I shall construe the position in this way. Some of the arguments used to support the immorality of suicide, however, are so strong that if they were supportable at all, they would prove that suicide is *never* moral.

What reasons have been offered for believing that there is a strong moral obligation to avoid suicide, which cannot be overweighed by any consideration of personal welfare? I shall discuss the main arguments briefly in a common-sense way.

The first arguments may be classified as *theological.* St. Augustine and others urged that the Sixth Commandment ("Thou shalt not kill") prohibits suicide, and that we are bound to obey a divine commandment. To this reasoning one might first reply that it is arbitrary exegesis of the Sixth Commandment to assert that it was ever intended to prohibit suicide. The second reply is that if there is not some consideration which shows on the merits of the case that suicide is morally wrong, God had no business prohibiting it. Doubtless some will object to this point, and I must confess that I think that it is merely quaint to appeal to the Commandments in a serious moral discussion in the Twentieth Century. But anyone interested can find my more serious defense of this objection elsewhere.[3] A second type of theological argument with wide support was accepted by John Locke, who wrote:

> ... Men being all the workmanship of one omnipotent and infinitely wise Maker; all the servants of one sovereign Master, sent into the world by His order and about His business; they are His property, whose workmanship they are made to last during His, not one another's pleasure. ... Every one ... is bound to preserve himself, and not to quit his station wilfully. ... [4]

---

[3]R. B. Brandt, *Ethical Theory,* Englewood Cliffs, N.J., Prentice-Hall, Inc., 1959, pp. 61–82.
[4]John Locke, *Two Treatises of Government,* chap. 2.

And Kant:

> We have been placed in this world under certain conditions
> and for specific purposes. But a suicide opposes the purpose
> of his Creator; he arrives in the other world as one who has
> deserted his post; he must be looked upon as a rebel against
> God. So long as we remember the truth that it is God's
> intention to preserve life, we are bound to regulate our ac-
> tivities in conformity with it. . . . This duty is upon us
> until the time comes when God expressly commands us to
> leave this life. Human beings are sentinels on earth and
> may not leave their posts until relieved by another bene-
> ficent hand.[5]

Unfortunately, however, even if it is granted that it is the
duty of human beings to do what God commands or intends them to do, more argument is required to show that
God does *not* permit human beings to quit this life when
their own personal welfare would be maximized by so doing. How does one draw the requisite inference about the
intentions of God? The difficulties and contradictions in
arguments to reach such a conclusion are discussed at
length and perspicaciously by David Hume in his essay
"On Suicide," and in view of the unlikelihood that readers
will need to be persuaded about these, I shall merely refer
the interested to that essay.[6]

A second group of arguments may be classed as arguments *from natural law.* St. Thomas says:

> It is altogether unlawful to kill oneself, for three reasons.
> First, because everything naturally loves itself, the result
> being that everything naturally keeps itself in being, and
> resists corruptions so far as it can. Wherefore suicide is
> contrary to the inclination of nature, and to charity
> whereby every man should love himself. Hence suicide is
> always a mortal sin, as being contrary to the natural law
> and to charity.

---

[5]Immanuel Kant, *Lectures on Ethics*, Harper Torchbook, 1963, p. 154.
[6]This essay was first published in 1783, and appears in collections of Hume's
works. For an argument similar to Kant's, see also St. Thomas, *Summa
Theologica*, II, II, Q. 64, Art. 5.

Here St. Thomas ignores two obvious points. First, it is not obvious why a human being is morally bound to do what it has some inclination to do. (St. Thomas did not criticize chastity.) Second, while it is true that most human beings do feel a strong urge to live, the human being who commits suicide obviously feels a stronger inclination to do something else. The "inclination" of the deliberate suicide is not to cling to life, but to do something else instead. It is as natural for a human being to dislike, and to take steps to avoid, say, great pain, as it is to cling to life. A somewhat similar argument by Immanuel Kant may seem better. In a famous passage Kant writes: The maxim of a person who commits suicide

> . . . is "From self-love I make it my principle to shorten my life if its continuance threatens more evil that it promises pleasure." The only further question to ask is whether this principle of self-love can become a universal law of nature. It is then seen at once that a system of nature by whose law the very same feeling whose function is to stimulate the furtherance of life should actually destroy life would contradict itself and consequently could not subsist as a system of nature. Hence this maxim cannot possibly hold as a universal law of nature and is therefore entirely opposed to the supreme principle of all duty.[7]

What Kant finds contradictory is that the motive of self-love (interest in one's own long-range welfare) should sometimes lead one to struggle to preserve one's life, but at other times to end it. But where is the contradiction? One's circumstances change; and, if the argument of the following section is correct, one sometimes maximizes one's own long-range welfare by trying to stay alive, but at other times by bringing about one's demise. So, if one's consistent motive is to maximize one's long-term welfare, sometimes (usually) one will do one thing; but sometimes one may do another.

---

[7]I. Kant, *The Fundamental Principles of the Metaphysics of Morals*, translated by H. J. Paton, London, The Hutchinson Group, 1948, chap. 2. First German edition in 1785.

A third group of arguments, a form of which goes back at least to Aristotle, has a more modern and convincing ring. These are arguments to show that, in one way or another, a suicide necessarily does harm to other persons, or to society at large. Some of these arguments are far-fetched. Aristotle says that the suicide treats the *state* unjustly.[8] Partly following Aristotle, St. Thomas says: "Every man is part of the community, and so, as such, be belongs to the community. Hence by killing himself he injures the community."[9] Blackstone held that a suicide is an offense against the king "who hath an interest in the preservation of all his subjects," perhaps following Judge Brown in 1563, who argued that suicide cost the king a subject—"he being the head has lost one of his mystical members."[10] The premise of such arguments is, as Hume pointed out, obviously mistaken in many instances. It is true that Freud would perhaps have injured society had he not finished his last book (as he did), instead of committing suicide to escape the pain of throat cancer. But surely there have been many suicides whose demise was not a noticeable loss to society; an honest man could only say that in many instances society was better off without them.

It need not be denied that suicide is often injurious to other persons, especially the family of a suicide. Clearly it sometimes is. But we should notice what this fact establishes. Suppose we admit, as generally would be done, that there is some obligation not to perform any action that will probably or certainly be injurious to other people, the strength of the obligation being dependent on various factors, notably the seriousness of the expected injury. Then there is *some* obligation not to commit suicide, when that act would probably or certainly be injurious to other people—a conclusion which will probably not be disputed. But, as we have already seen, there are many cases of some obligation to do some thing, but which nevertheless are

[8]Aristotle, *Nicomachaean Ethics*, bk. 5, chap. 10, p. 1138a.
[9]Loc. cit.
[10]Blackstone, *Commentaries*, IV: 189; Brown in *Hales v. Petit*, I Plow. 253, 75 E.R: 387 (C.B. 1563). Both cited by Norman St. John-Stevas, op. cit., 235.

not cases of a duty to do that thing, *everything considered.*
So it *could* sometimes be quite justified morally to commit suicide, even if the act will do some harm to someone.
Must a man with a terminal illness undergo excruciating
pain because his death will cause his wife sorrow—when
she will be caused sorrow a month later anyway, when he
is dead of natural causes? So, to repeat, the fact that someone has some obligation not to commit suicide when that
act will probably injure other persons does not imply that,
everything considered, it is wrong for him to do it.
Moreover, the fact that there is some obligation not to
commit suicide when it will probably injure others does
not show that suicide *as such* is something there is some
obligation to avoid. It is not proved that there is an obligation to avoid suicide as such. There is an obligation to
avoid injuring others and to avoid suicide when it will
probably injure others; but this is very different from
showing that suicide *as such* is something there is some
obligation to avoid, in all instances.

Is there any way in which we could give a sound argument, convincing to the modern mind, establishing that
there is (or is not) *some moral obligation* to avoid suicide
as such, an obligation of course which might be overrriden
by other obligations in some or many cases? (Captain
Oates might have a moral obligation not to commit
suicide as such, but his obligation not to stand in the way
of his comrades getting to safety might have been so
strong that, everything considered, he was justified in leaving the polar camp and allowing himself to freeze to
death.)

To give all the argument which would make an answer
to this question convincing would take a great deal of
space. I shall therefore simply state one answer to it which
seems plausible to some contemporary philosophers and
which I suspect will seem plausible to the reader. Suppose
it could be shown that it would maximize the long-run
welfare of everybody affected if people were taught that
there is a moral obligation to avoid suicide—so that people
would be motivated to avoid suicide just because they
thought it wrong (would have anticipatory guilt feelings at

the very idea), and so that other people would be inclined to disapprove persons who commit suicide unless there were some excuse (such as those mentioned in the first section). One might ask: How could it maximize utility to mould the conceptual and motivational structure of persons in this way? To which the answer might be: Feeling in this way might make persons who are impulsively inclined to commit suicide in a bad mood, or a fit of anger or jealousy, take more time to deliberate; hence, some suicides that have bad effects generally might be prevented. In other words, it might be a good thing in its effects for people to feel about suicide in the way they feel about breach of promise or injuring others, just as it might be a good thing for people to feel a moral obligation not to smoke, or to wear seat belts. I do not say this *would* be a good thing; all I am saying is that *if* it could be made out to be welfare-maximizing for people's consciences to trouble them at the very thought of suicide (etc.), then I would think that there is some moral obligation not to commit this act. I am not at all sure, in fact, whether it *would* be welfare-maximizing for people to have negative moral feelings about suicide as such; maybe what is needed is just for them to have negative moral feelings about injuring others in some way, and perhaps negative moral feelings about failing to deliberate adequately about their own welfare, before taking any serious and irrevocable course of action. It might be that negative moral feelings about suicide as such would stand in the way of courageous action by those persons whose welfare really is best served by suicide, and whose suicide is, in fact, the best thing for everybody concerned. One piece of information highly relevant to what ought to be "taught-into" the consciences of people in this regard is why people do commit suicide and how often the general welfare (and especially their own welfare) is served by so doing. If among those people who commit suicide who are intellectually able to weigh pros and cons are usually ones who commit suicide in a depression and do not serve anybody's welfare by so doing, then that would be a point in favor of teaching people that suicide is wrong as such.

III. Whether and When Suicide Is Best or Rational for the Agent

We come now to a topic which, for better or worse, strikes me as of more considerable practical interest: whether and when suicide is the rational or best thing for a person, from the point of view of his own welfare. If I were asked for advice by someone contemplating suicide, it is to this topic, I believe, that I would be inclined primarily to address myself. Some of the writers who are most inclined to affirm that suicide is morally wrong are quite ready to believe that from the agent's own selfish point of view suicide would sometimes be the best thing for him, but they do not discuss the point in any detail. I should like to get clear when it is and when it is not. Not that we can hope to get any simple conclusions applicable to everybody. What I hope to do is produce a way of looking at the matter which will help an individual see whether suicide is the best thing for *him* from the point of view of his own welfare—or whether it is the best thing for someone being advised, from the point of view of that person's welfare.

It is reasonable to discuss this topic under the restriction of two assumptions. First, I assume we are trying to decide between a *successful* suicide attempt, and no attempt. A person might try to commit suicide and succeed only in blinding himself. I am assuming that we need not worry about this possibility, so that the alternative is between producing death and continuing life roughly as it now is. The second assumption I am making is that when a person commits suicide, he is dead; that is, we do not consider that killing himself is only a way of expediting his departure to a blissful or extremely unpleasant afterlife. I shall assume there is *no* afterlife. I believe that at the present time potential suicides deliberate on the basis of both these assumptions, so that in making them I am addressing myself to the real problem as prospective suicides see it. What I want to produce is a fresh and helpful way of looking at their problem.

The problem, I take it, is a choice between future world-courses: the world-course which includes my demise, say, an hour from now, and several possible ones which contain my demise at a later point. We cannot have precise knowledge about many features of the latter group of world-courses. One thing I can't have precise knowledge about is how or when I shall die if I do not commit suicide now. One thing is certain: it will be sometime, and it is almost certain that it will be before my one-hundredth birthday. So, to go on the rational probabilities, let us look up my life expectancy at my present age from the insurance tables, making any corrections that are called for in the light of full medical information about my present state of health. If I do not already have a terminal illness, then the choice, say, is between a world-course with my death an hour from now, and several world-courses with my death, say, twenty years from now. The problem, I take it, is to decide whether the expectable utility to me of some possible world-course in which I go on for another twenty years is greater than or less than the expectable utility to me of the one in which my life stops in an hour. One thing to be clear about is: we are not choosing between death and immortality. We are choosing between death now and death some (possibly short) finite time from now.

Why do I say the choice is between *world*-courses and not just a choice between future life-courses of the prospective suicide, the one shorter than the others? The reason is that one's suicide has some impact on the world (and one's continued life has some impact on the world), and that how the rest of the world is will often make a difference to one's evaluation of the possibilities. One *is* interested in things in the world other than just one's self and one's own happiness. For instance, one may be interested in one's children and their welfare, or in one's future reputation, or the contribution one might make to the solution of some problems, or in the publication of a book one is finishing with its possible clarifying effects on the thinking of a profession, and so on.

What is the basic problem for evaluation? It is the choice of the expectably *best* world-course. One way of looking at the evaluation, although in practice we cannot assign the specific numbers it is suggested we assign is this: We compare the suicide world-course with the continued-life-world-course (or several of them), and note the features with respect to which they differ. We then assign numbers of these features, representing their utility to us if they happen, and then multiplying this utility by a number which represents the probability that this feature will occur. (Suppose I live, and am certain that either P or Q will occur, and that it is a 50:50 chance which; then I represent this biography as containing the sum of the utility of P multipled by one-half and the utility of Q multipled by one-half.) We then sum these numbers. The sum will represent the expectable utility of that world-course to us. The world-course with the highest sum is the one that is rationally chosen. But of course it is absurd to suppose that we can assign these numbers in actual fact; what we can actually do is something in a sense simpler but less decisive.

If we look at the matter in this way, we can see that there is a close analogy between an analysis of the rationality of suicide, and a firm's analysis of the rationality of declaring bankruptcy and going out of business. In the case of the firm, the objectives may be few and simple, and indeed for some boards of directors the only relevant question is: Will the stockholders probably be better off, or worse off, financially, if we continue or if we declare insolvency? More likely the question considered will be a bit more complex, since an enlightened firm will at least wonder what will happen to its officers and employees and customers and even possibly the general public if it goes out of business, and how their utilities will be affected. There is also another difference: When the firm goes out of business, none of the people involved goes out of business (unless some officer, etc., kills himself).

Perhaps a closer analogy, if we want an analogy, to this choice between world-courses is the choice between a life-course in which I get twelve hours' sleep tonight, and one in which I do some one (the best) of the various possibilities open to me. The difference between the cases is that, to make the analogy more exact, I have to ignore the fact that I shall waken.

Since, as I have suggested, we cannot actually assign numbers in the way suggested, so as to compare expectable utilities, what then *is* the basic question we can and should answer, in order to determine which world-course is best, from the point of view of our own welfare? Certainly the question has to do with what we do or shall, or under certain circumstances would, *want* to happen, or want not to happen. But it is not just a question of what we prefer *now*, doubtless with some clarification of the other possibilities being considered. The reason for this is that we know that our preferences change, and the preferences of tomorrow (assuming we can know something about them) are just as legitimately taken into account in deciding what to do now as the preferences of today. The preferences of any future day have a right to an equal vote as to what we shall do now; there is no reason for giving special weight to today's preference, since any reason that can be given today for weighing heavily today's preference can be given tomorrow for weighing heavily tomorrow's preference. So, given this symmetry of reasons, the preferences of any time-stretch have a rational claim to an equal vote. Now the importance of that fact is this: we often know quite well that our desires, aversions, and preferences are going to be very different after a short span of time, from what they now are. When a person is in a state of despair—perhaps brought about by a rejection in love, or by discharge from a long-held position—nothing but the thing he cannot have seems desirable; everything else is turned to ashes. Yet we know quite well that the passage of time may reverse all this; after a time the grass may look green again and things in the world that are available to us will look attractive. So, if we were to go on the preferences of today, when the emotion of despair seems more than we can stand, we might find death preferable to life; but if we allow for the preferences of the weeks and years ahead, when many goals will be enjoyable and attractive, we might find life much preferable to death. So, if a choice, or what is best, is to be determined by what we want not only now but later (and later desires on an equal basis with the present)—as it should be—then what is the best or preferable world-course will often be quite different from what it would be if the choice, or what is best for one, were fixed by one's desires and preferences now. It may be hard to look to the future and see what one's attitudes are likely to be, but that is necessary if one's evaluation is to be rational.

Of course, if one commits suicide there are no future desires or aversions which may be compared with present ones, and which should be allowed an equal vote in deciding what is best. In that respect the status of the course of action which results in death is different from any other course of action we may undertake.

I do not wish to suggest the rosy possibility that it is often or always reasonable to believe that next week I shall be more interested in living than I am today, if today I take a dim view of continued existence. Quite on the contrary, when a person is seriously ill the probabilities are that he will continue to feel worse until sedations become so extensive that he is incapable of emotional reaction toward anything, one way or the other. Thus sometimes when on the basis of today's attitudes I must say that I prefer death to life, I shall find no reason to think that tomorrow the preference order will be reversed—rather, if anything, I can know that tomorrow I shall prefer death to life more strongly. When this situation obtains, I may do better by choosing the world-course which contains my own life-span as short as possible.

The argument is often used—and it may as well be introduced in this connection as any other—that one can never be *certain* what is going to happen, and hence one is never rationally justified in doing anything as drastic as taking one's life. And it is true that certainties are hard to find in this life; they do not exist even in the sciences, if we are strict about it. Unfortunately for the critic who makes use of this line of argument, it works both ways. I might say, when I am very depressed about my life, that the one thing I am certain of is that I am now very depressed and prefer death to life, and there is only some probability that tomorrow I shall feel differently; so, one might argue that if one is to go only by certainties, I had better end it now. No one would take this seriously. We always have to live by probabilities, and make our estimates as best we can. People sometimes argue that one should not commit suicide in order to escape excruciating pain because a miraculous cure for one's terminal disease might be found tomorrow. And it is true that such a cure could, as a matter of logical possibility, be found tomorrow. But if everyone had argued in that way in the past hundred years, all of them would have waited until the bitter end and suffered excruciating pain; the line of argument that ignores probabilities and demands certainty would not have paid off in the past, and there is no reason to think it will pay off much better in the future. Indeed, if the thought were taken generally that probabilities should be ignored when they are short of certainty, in practical decisions, it can be demonstrated that the policy for action *cannot* pay off. A form of much the same argument is the assertion that if you are alive tomorrow you can always decide to end it all then, if you want to; whereas if you are dead tomorrow, you cannot then decide that it is better to live. The factual point is correct, of course. But the argument has practical bearing only if there is some reason to think that tomorrow you might want to live; and sometimes it is as nearly certain as matters of this sort can be, that you will not. It is true, of course, that one can always bear another day; so why not put it off? This argument, of course, can be used for every day, with the result that one never takes action. One would think that, as soon as it is clear beyond reasonable doubt not only that death is now preferable to life, but also that it will be every day from now until the end, the rational thing is to act promptly.[11]

Let us not pursue the question whether it is rational for a person with a painful terminal illness to commit suicide; obviously it is. However, the issue seldom arises, and few patients of this sort do so. With such patients matters get

---

[11]A patient who announces such a decision to his physician may expect amazement and dismay. The patient should not forget, however, that except for the area of the physical sciences his physician is likely to be almost a totally ignorant man, whose education has not proceeded beyond high school. The physician is not a reliable source of information about anything but the body.

Physicians are also given to rosy prognoses about the absence of pain in a terminal illness. The writer once had some bone surgery, and after a night of misery listened to a morning radio program entitled "The Conquest of Pain," in which hearers were assured that the medical profession had solved the problem of pain and that they need not give a second thought to this little source of anxiety.

worse only slowly so that no particular time seems the one calling for action; they are so heavily sedated that it is impossible for the mental processes of decision leading to action to occur; or else they are incapacitated in a hospital and the very physical possibility of ending their lives is not available. Let us leave this gruesome topic and turn to the practically more important problem: whether it is rational for persons to commit suicide for some other reason than painful terminal physical illness. Most persons who commit suicide do so, apparently, because they face some nonphysical problem which depresses them beyond their ability to bear. It is to them that the above point, about the rational necessity of taking into account attitudes one will have next week, is primarily addressed.

If we look over a list of the problems that bother people, and some of which various writers have regarded as good and sufficient reasons for ending life, one finds (in addition to serious illness) things like the following: some event which has made one feel ashamed or has cost one loss of prestige and status; reduction to poverty as compared with former affluence; the loss of a limb or of physical beauty; the loss of sexual capacity; some event which makes it seem impossible that one will achieve things by which one sets store; loss of a loved one; disappointment in love; the infirmities of increasing age. It is not to be denied that such things can be serious blows to one's prospects of happiness.

In deciding whether, everything considered, one prefers a world-course containing one's early demise as compared with one in which this is postponed to its natural terminus, there are various plain errors to be avoided—errors to which a person is especially prone when he is depressed. Let us forget for a moment the relevance to the decision of preferences that we may have tomorrow, and concentrate on some errors which may infect our preference as of today, and for which correction or allowance must be made.

In the first place, depression, like any severe emotional experience, tends to primitivize one's intellectual processes. It restricts the range of one's survey of the possibilities. One thing that a rational person will do is compare the world-course containing his suicide with his *best* alternative. But his best alternative is precisely a possibility he may overlook if, in a depressed mood, he thinks only of how badly off he is and does not contemplate plans of action which he has not at all considered. If a person is disappointed in love, it is possible to adopt a vigorous plan of action which carries a good chance of acquainting him with someone he likes at least as well; and if old age prevents one from continuing the tennis games with one' favorite partner, it is possible to learn some other game which provides the joys of competition without the physical demands.

There is another insidious influence of a state of depression, on one's planning. Depression seriously affects ones judgment about probabilities. A person disappointed in love is very likely to take a dim view of himself, his prospects, and his attractiveness; he thinks that, because he has been rejected by one person, he will probably be rejected by anyone who looks desirable to him. In a less gloomy frame of mind he would make, quite correctly, different estimates. Part of the reason for such gloomy probability estimates is that depression tends to repress one's memory evidence which supports a non-gloomy prediction. Thus a rejected lover tends to forget all the cases in which he has elicited enthusiastic response from ladies in relation to whom he has been the one who has done the rejecting. Thus his pessimistic self-image is based upon a highly selected, and pessimistically selected, set of data. Even when he is reminded of the data, however, he is apt to resist an optimistic inference. Even if he knows enough about the logic of inductive inference to know that the rational thing to do is project the frequency of past experiences into the future, basing one's estimate of the probability of a future event on the frequency of that event in the past, he is apt, doubtless sometimes with some reason, to reject the conclusion, for instance, on the ground that past experiences are unrepresentative and cannot be relied upon for a prognosis of the future. Obviously, however, there is such a thing as a reasonable and correct prognosis on the basis of an accurate account of past experience, and it is the height of irrationality not to estimate the future on that basis.

Another kind of distortion of the look of future prospects is not a result of depression, but is quite normal. Events distant in the future feel small, just as objects distant in space look small. The prospect of them does not have the effect on motivational processes that it would have if it were of an event in the immediate future. Rat-psychologists call essentially this fact the "goal-gradient" phenomenon; a rat, for instance, will run faster toward a food-box when he is close enough so that he can actually see it, and does not do as well when he can only represent it in some nonperceptual way, as presumably he does in the early stages of a maze. Similarly, a professor will accept an invitation to give a lecture or read a paper a year ahead, which he would not dream of accepting only a month ahead; the vision of the work involved somehow does not seem as repellent at the greater distance. Everyone finds it hard to do something disagreeable now, even for the sake of something more seriously important at a future date; the disagreeable event now tends to be postponed, unless one makes one's self attend to the importance of the event which is thereby jeopardized. In the case of a person who has suffered some misfortune, and whose situation now is an unpleasant one, this phenomenon of the reduction of the motivational size of events more distant in time has the effect that present unpleasant states are compared with probable future pleasant ones, as it were by looking at the future ones through the wrong end of binoculars. The future does not elicit motivation, desire, or preference in relation to its true size. So, at the time of choice, future good things are apt to play less of a role than is their due. A rational person will, of course, make himself see the future in its proper size and compensate for this feature of human psychology.

Another serious source of error in estimating the potential value to us of possible future outcomes of various courses of action is the very method we sometimes must use, and naturally tend to use, in determining how much we do or will want them or like them when they occur. It is true that sometimes we can and do rely on memory; we can recall, with something less than perfect reliability, how much we enjoyed certain situations in the past (but sometimes we must correct projections from these recollections by information about how we have changed as persons with the effect that we may be able to meet these situations better or worse—say, a night's camping out—and enjoy them more or less, in future). But most frequently what we do, and sometimes the only thing we can do, is simply imagine as vividly as we can what a certain situation would be like, and notice whether it now seems attractive, whether we are now drawn toward it and enthusiastic about it, or not. Unfortunately the reliability of this subjective test, as an indicator of how much we shall want or enjoy a certain kind of thing tomorrow is seriously affected by the frame of mind in which we make it. Something which in fact we should much like in the future may utterly fail to stir us or even repel us, in a depressed or disappointed frame of mind; its favorable features either escape attention or simply fail to set the motivational machinery into motion which would make it seem attractive. Just as the sight of a good steak leaves us cold when we have just finished a hearty meal (presumably because chemical processes in the hypothalamus desensitize the relevant nervous channels or at any rate block the stimuli from having their ordinarily arousing effects), so the percept of a charming woman and *a fortiori* the mere thought of her will not elicit enthusiastic response from the rejected lover. Sorrow or depression simply shuts off or turns down the motivational machinery on which we customarily rely for deciding whether we will want, or enjoy having, certain things. Except, of course, the thing about which we are depressed; with it, the process is reversed. If there is something we have lost, or are debarred from getting, those of its features which normally strike us as unpleasant or unfavorable are excluded from attention or at any rate lose their repulsive force; whereas a halo is cast upon the features of the object which have been liked or wanted, rather as if the good features were now seen under a microscope and appear much larger than in real life. Why this should be so is not obvious. But even rats, it has been shown, will run harder for something which they have been frustrated in getting, than they run in ordinary circumstances. There is something about being frustrated in getting something which makes it look much better than it ordinarily does.

It is obvious that if we are trying to determine whether we now prefer, or shall later prefer, the outcomes in one world-course to the outcomes of another (and this is leaving aside the question of the weight of the votes of preferences at a later date), we have to take into account these infirmities of our "sensing" machinery. To say this does not tell us what to do about it, since to know that the machinery is out of order is not to tell us what results it would give us if it were working. One maxim of many wise people is to refrain from making important decisions in a stressful frame of mind; and one of the "important" decisions one might make is surely suicide. But, if decisions have to be made, at least one can make one's self recall, as far as possible, how one reacted to outcomes like the ones now to be assessed, on occasions in the past when one was in a normal frame of mind. Such reactions, however rough and defective in reliability, are at least better than the feeble pulses of sensing machinery which is temporarily out of order.

Most suicides which are irrational seem to be suicides of a moment of despair. What should be clear from the above is that a moment of despair should be, if one is seriously contemplating suicide, a moment of reassessment of one's goals and values, a reassessment which the individual must realize is very difficult to make objectively, because of the very quality of his depressed frame of mind. Let us consider in an example what form such a reassessment might take, based on a consideration of the "errors" we have been considering.

Suppose the president of a company is ousted in a reorganization and, to make matters as bad as possible, let us suppose he has made unwise investments so that his income from investments is small and, to cap it off, his wife has eloped with another man. His children are already grown, and he is too old to hope for election to a comparable position in another business. So his career and his home life are gone. Here we have the makings of a suicide. Let us suppose his pessimistic estimates are right: that there is no comparable future open to him in business, and that his wife is really gone. The prospect is one of uninteresting employment, if any; loneliness and no affection from a wife; moving from a luxurious home into a modest apartment; inability to entertain his friends in the manner to which he has been accustomed; and so on. Is all this bearable?

Obviously the man has to find a new mode of life. If he is an interesting man he can count on finding a woman with whom he can be close and who can mean as much to him as his wife actually did; or he may even find that he can become close to several persons of real interest, possibly resulting in an experience enriched beyond his imagination, as compared with the confines of traditional married life. The matter of career is more serious. Even Kant, who condemned suicide in all cases, says (inconsistently, I think) that a man unjustly convicted of a crime, who was offered a choice between death and penal servitude, would certainly, if honorable, "choose death" rather than "the galleys. A man of inner worth does not shrink from death; he would die rather than live as an object of contempt, a member of a gang of scoundrels in the galleys." Kant may have been right about what it is rational to do, in this extreme instance. Would death be better for the ex-president of a company, than accepting a job, let us say, as a shoe salesman? There are some compensations in the latter. An intelligent man might find himself interested in engaging in conversation a variety of customers from all walks of life. He can try out his psychological knowledge by devices to play on the vanity of women as a motivation for buying expensive shoes. The prospect might seem unattractive. But, if he wants to be rational, he will not fail to get a full view of the various things about the job which he might enjoy—or which he might enjoy, after a time, when he had got over contrasting them with a past career which is no longer open to him. He will hopefully not forget that as a shoe salesman he will not require sleeping pills because of company problems which he cannot get off his mind. If he understands human nature and his own, he may be able to see that while this job is not as desirable as the post he lost, after a time he can enjoy it and be happy in it and find life worth living. Other reflections which this man may have,

relevant to his initial impulse to end it all, will come to
mind—applications of the distinctions made above.

At this point David Hume was not his usual perspicuous self—nor was Plato before him.[12] For Hume speaks of
the propriety of suicide for one who leads a hated life,
"loaded with pain and sickness, with *shame and poverty.*"[13] Pain and sickness are one thing; they cannot be
enjoyed and cannot be escaped. But shame and poverty are
another matter. For some situations Hume might be right.
But Hume, accustomed as he was to the good things of
life, was too short with shame and poverty; a life which he
would classify as one of shame and poverty might be a
happy life, inferior to Hume's life style, but still preferable
to nothing.

A decision to commit suicide may in certain circumstances be a rational one. But a person who wants to
act rationally must take into account at least the various
possible "errors" mentioned above, and make appropriate
rectifications in his initial evaluations.

IV. The Role of Other Persons

We have not been concerned with the law, or its justifiability, on the matter of suicide; but we may note in passing that for a long time in the Western world suicide was
a felony, and in many states attempted suicide is still a
crime. It is also a crime to aid or encourage a suicide in
many states; one who makes a lethal device available for a
suicidal attempt may be subject to a prison sentence—
including physicians, if they provide a lethal does of seda-
tives.[14]

The last-mentioned class of statutes raises a question
worth our consideration: what are the moral obligations of
other persons toward those who are contemplating
suicide? I ignore questions of their moral blameworthiness, and of what it is rational for them to do from the

---

[12]*The Laws*, Bk. IX.
[13]Loc. cit.
[14]For a proposal for American law on this point see the *Model Penal Code*, Proposed Official Draft, The American Law Institute, 1962, pp. 127–128; also Tentative Draft No. 9, p. 56.

point of view of personal welfare, as being of secondary concern. I have no doubt that the question of personal interest is important particularly to physicians who may not wish to risk running afoul of the law; but this risk is, after all, something which partly determines what is their moral obligation, since moral obligation to do something may be reduced by the fact that it is personally dangerous to do it.[15]

The moral obligation of other persons toward one who is contemplating suicide is an instance of a general obligation to render aid to those in serious distress, at least when this can be done at no great cost to one's self. I do not think this general principle is seriously questioned by anyone, whatever his moral theory; so I feel free to assume it as a premise. Obviously the person contemplating suicide is in great distress of some sort; if he were not, he would not be considering seriously terminating his life.

How great a person's obligation is to one in distress depends on a number of factors. Obviously a person's wife, daughter, and close friend have special obligations to devote time to helping this sort of person—to going over his problem with him, to think it through with him, etc.—which others do not have. But that anyone in this kind of distress has a moral claim on the time of anyone who knows the situation (unless there are others more responsible who are already doing what should be done) is obvious.

What is there an obligation to do? It depends, of course, on the situation, and how much the second person knows about the situation. If the individual has decided to terminate his life if he can, and it is clear that he is right in this decision, then, if he needs help in executing the decision, there is a moral obligation to give him help. If it is sleeping pills he needs, then they should be obtained for him. On this matter a patient's physician has a special obliga-

---

[15]The law can be changed, and one of the ways in which it gets changed is by responsible people refusing to obey it and pointing out how objectionable it is on moral grounds. Some physicians have shown leadership in this respect, e.g., on the matter of dispensing birth control information and abortion laws. One wishes there were more of this.

tion, from which all his antiquated talk about the Hippo-
cratic oath does not absolve him. It is true that there are
some damages one cannot be expected to absorb, and some
risks which one cannot be expected to take, on account of
the obligation to render aid. But the cowardice and lack of
social responsibility of some physicians can be excused
only by conviction of a charge of ignorance.

On the other hand, if it is clear that the individual
should not commit suicide, from the point of view of his
own welfare, or if there is a presumption that he should
not (when the only evidence is that a person is discovered
unconscious, with the gas turned on), it would seem to be
the individual's obligation to intervene, and prevent the
successful execution of the decision, see to the availability
of competent psychiatric advice and temporary hospitali-
zation, if necessary. Whether one has a right to take such
steps when a clearly sane person, after careful reflection
over a period of time, comes to the conclusion that an end
to his life is what is best for him and what he wants, is
very doubtful, even when one thinks his conclusion a mistaken one; it would seem that a man's own considered decision about whether he wants to live must command
respect, although one must concede that this could be
debated.

The more interesting role in which a person may be
cast, however, is that of adviser. It is often important to
one who is contemplating suicide to go over his thinking
with another, and to feel that a conclusion, one way or the
other, has the support of a respected mind. One thing one
can obviously do, in rendering the service of advice, is to
discuss with the person the various types of issue discussed above, made more specific by the concrete circumstances of his case, and help him find whether, in
view, say, of the damage his suicide would do to others, he
has a moral obligation to refrain, and whether it is rational
or best for him, from the point of view of his own welfare,
to take this step or adopt some other plan instead.

To get a person to see what is the rational thing to do is
no small job. Even to get a person, in a frame of mind
when he is seriously contemplating (or perhaps has already
unsuccessfully attempted) suicide, to recognize a plain

truth of fact may be a major operation. If a man insists, "I am a complete failure," when it is obvious that by any reasonable standard he is far from that, it may be tremendously difficult to get him to see the fact. The relaxing quiet of a hospital room may be a prerequisite of ability to think clearly and weigh facts with some perspective.

But there is another job beyond that of getting a person to see what is the rational thing to do; that is to help him *act* rationally, or *be* rational, when he has conceded what would be the rational thing.

How either of these tasks may be accomplished effectively may be discussed more competently by an experienced psychiatrist than by a philosopher. But it may not be inappropriate to point out that sometimes an adviser can *cure* a man's problem, in the course, or instead, of giving advice what to do about it. Loneliness and the absence of human affection (especially from the opposite sex) are states which exacerbate any other problems; disappointment, reduction to poverty, etc., seem less impossible to bear in the presence of the affection of another. Hence simply to be a friend, or to find someone a friend, may be the largest contribution one can make either to helping a person be rational or see clearly what is rational for him to do; this service may make one who was contemplating suicide feel that there is no longer a future for him which it is impossible to face.

Active and Passive Euthanasia

James Rachels

The distinction between active and passive euthanasia is thought to be crucial for medical ethics. The idea is that it is permissible, at least in some cases, to withhold treatment and allow a patient to die, but it is never permissible to take any direct action designed to kill the patient. This doctrine seems to be accepted by most doctors, and it is endorsed in a statement adopted by the House of Delegates of the American Medical Association on December 4, 1973:

> The intentional termination of the life of one human being by another—mercy killing—is contrary to that for which the medical profession stands and is contrary to the policy of the American Medical Association.
> The cessation of the employment of extraordinary means to prolong the life of the body when there is irrefutable evidence that biological death is imminent is the decision of the patient and/or his immediate family. The advice and judgment of the physician should be freely available to the patient and/or his immediate family.

However, a strong case can be made against this doctrine. In what follows I will set out some of the relevant arguments, and urge doctors to reconsider their views on this matter.

From *The New England Journal of Medicine*, vol. 292 (1975).

To begin with a familiar type of situation, a patient who is dying of incurable cancer of the throat is in terrible pain, which can no longer be satisfactorily alleviated. He is certain to die within a few days, even if present treatment is continued, but he does not want to go on living for those days since the pain is unbearable. So he asks the doctor for an end to it, and his family joins in the request.

Suppose the doctor agrees to withhold treatment, as the conventional doctrine says he may. The justification for his doing so is that the patient is in terrible agony, and since he is going to die anyway, it would be wrong to prolong his suffering needlessly. But now notice this. If one simply withholds treatment, it may take the patient longer to die, and so he may suffer more than he would if more direct action were taken and a lethal injection given. This fact provides strong reason for thinking that, once the initial decision not to prolong his agony has been made, active euthanasia is actually preferable to passive euthanasia, rather than the reverse. To say otherwise is to endorse the option that leads to more suffering rather than less, and is contrary to the humanitarian impulse that prompts the decision not to prolong his life in the first place.

Part of my point is that the process of being "allowed to die" can be relatively slow and painful, whereas being given a lethal injection is relatively quick and painless. Let me give a different sort of example. In the United States about one in 600 babies is born with Down's syndrome. Most of these babies are otherwise healthy—that is, with only the usual pediatric care, they will proceed to an otherwise normal infancy. Some, however, are born with congenital defects such as intestinal obstructions that require operations if they are to live. Sometimes, the parents and the doctor will decide not to operate, and let the infant die. Anthony Shaw describes what happens then:

When surgery is denied [the doctor] must try to keep the infant from suffering while natural forces sap the baby's life away. As a surgeon whose natural inclination is to use the scalpel to fight off death, standing by and watching a salvageable baby die is the most emotionally exhausting experience I know. It is easy at a conference, in a theoretical discussion to decide that such infants should be allowed to die. It is altogether different to stand by in the nursery and watch as dehydration and infection wither a tiny being over hours and days. This is a terrible ordeal for me and the hospital staff—much more so than for the parents who never set foot in the nursery.[*]

I can understand why some people are opposed to all euthanasia, and insist that such infants must be allowed to live. I think I can also understand why other people favor destroying these babies quickly and painlessly. But why should anyone favor letting "dehydration and infection wither a tiny being over hours and days"? The doctrine that says that a baby may be allowed to dehydrate and wither, but may not be given an injection that would end its life without suffering, seems so patently cruel as to require no further refutation. The strong language is not intended to offend, but only to put the point in the clearest possible way.

My second argument is that the conventional doctrine leads to decisions concerning life and death made on irrelevant grounds.

Consider again the case of the infants with Down's syndrome who need operations for congenital defects unrelated to the syndrome to live. Sometimes, there is no operation, and the baby dies, but when there is no such defect, the baby lives on. Now, an operation such as that to remove an intestinal obstruction is not prohibitively difficult. The reason why such operations are not performed in these cases is, clearly, that the child has Down's syndrome and the parents and the doctor judge that because of that fact it is better for the child to die.

But notice that this situation is absurd, no matter what view one takes of the lives and potentials of such babies. If the life of such an infant is worth preserving what does it matter if it needs a simple operation? Or, if one thinks it better that such a baby should not live on, what difference

---

[*]Shaw, Anthony, "Doctor, Do We Have a Choice?" *The New York Times Magazine*, January 30, 1972, p. 54.

does it make that it happens to have an unobstructed intestinal tract? In either case, the matter of life and death is being decided on irrelevant grounds. It is the Down's syndrome, and not the intestines, that is the issue. The matter should be decided, if at all, on that basis, and not be allowed to depend on the essentially irrelevant question of whether the intestional tract is blocked.

What makes this situation possible, of course, is the idea that when there is an intestinal blockage, one can "let the baby die," but when there is no such defect there is nothing that can be done, for one must not "kill" it. The fact that this idea leads to such results as deciding life or death on irrelevant grounds is another good reason why the doctrine would be rejected.

One reason why so many people think that there is an important moral difference between active and passive euthanasia is that they think killing someone is morally worse than letting someone die. But is it? Is killing, in itself, worse than letting die? To investigate this issue, two cases may be considered that are exactly alike except that one involves killing whereas the other involves letting someone die. Then, it can be asked whether this difference makes any difference to the moral assessments. It is important that the cases be exactly alike, except for this one difference, since otherwise one cannot be confident that it is this difference and not some other that accounts for any variation in the assessments of the two cases. So, let us consider this pair of cases:

In the first, Smith stands to gain a large inheritance if anything should happen to his six-year old cousin. One evening while the child is taking his bath, Smith sneaks into the bathroom and drowns the child, and then arranges things so that it will look like an accident.

In the second, Jones also stands to gain if anything should happen to his six-year-old cousin. Like Smith, Jones sneaks in planning to drown the child in his bath. However, just as he enters the bathroom Jones sees the child slip and hit his head, and fall face down in the water. Jones is delighted; he stands by, ready to push the child's head back under if it is necessary, but it is not necessary. With only a little thrashing about, the child drowns all by himself, "accidentally," as Jones watches and does nothing.

Now Smith killed the child, whereas Jones "merely" let the child die. That is the only difference between them. Did either man behave better, from a moral point of view? If the difference between killing and letting die were in itself a morally important matter, one should say that Jones's behavior was less reprehensible than Smith's. But does one really want to say that? I think not. In the first place, both men acted from the same motive, personal gain, and both had exactly the same end in view when they acted. It may be inferred from Smith's conduct that he is a bad man, although that judgment may be withdrawn or modified if certain further facts are learned about him—for example, that he is mentally deranged. But would not the very same thing be inferred about Jones from his conduct? And would not the same further considerations also be relevant to any modification of this judgment? Moreover, suppose Jones pleaded, in his own defense, "After all, I didn't do anything except just stand there and watch the child drown. I didn't kill him; I only let him die." Again, if letting die were in itself less bad than killing, this defense should have at least some weight. But it does not. Such a "defense" can only be regarded as a grotesque perversion of moral reasoning. Morally speaking, it is no defense at all.

Now, it may be pointed out, quite properly, that the cases of euthanasia with which doctors are concerned are not like this at all. They do not involve personal gain or the destruction of normal healthy children. Doctors are concerned only with cases in which the patient's life is of no further use to him, or in which the patient's life has become or will soon become a terrible burden. However, the point is the same in these cases: the bare difference between killing and letting die does not, in itself, make a moral difference. If a doctor lets a patient die, for humane reasons, he is in the same moral position as if he had given the patient a lethal injection for humane reasons. If his decision was wrong—if, for example, the patient's illness was in fact curable—the decision would be equally regrettable no matter which method was used to carry it out.

And if the doctor's decision was the right one, the method used is not in itself important.

The AMA policy statement isolates the crucial issue very well; the crucial issue is "the intentional termination of the life of one human being by another." But after identifying this issue, and forbidding "mercy killing," the statement goes on to deny that the cessation of treatment is the intentional termination of a life. This is where the mistake comes in, for what is the cessation of treatment, in these circumstances, if it is not "the intentional termination of the life of one human being by another?" Of course it is exactly that, and if it were not, there would be no point to it.

Many people will find this judgment hard to accept. One reason, I think, is that it is very easy to conflate the question of whether killing is, in itself, worse than letting die, with the very different question of whether most actual cases of killing are more reprehensible than most actual cases of letting die. Most actual cases of killing are clearly terrible (think, for example, of all the murders reported in the newspapers), and one hears of such cases every day. On the other hand, one hardly ever hears of a case of letting die, except for the actions of doctors who are motivated by humanitarian reasons. So one learns to think of killing in a much worse light than of letting die. But this does not mean that there is something about killing that makes it in itself worse than letting die, for it is not the bare difference between killing and letting die that makes the difference in these cases. Rather, the other factors—the murderer's motive of personal gain, for example, contrasted with the doctor's humanitarian motivation—account for different reactions to the different cases.

I have argued that killing is not in itself any worse than letting die; if my contention is right, it follows that active euthanasia is not any worse than passive euthanasia. What arguments can be given on the other side? The most common, I believe, is the following:

The important difference between active and passive euthanasia is that, in passive euthanasia, the doctor does not do anything to bring about the patient's death. The doctor does nothing, and the patient dies of whatever ills already afflict him. In active euthanasia, however, the doctor does something to bring about the patient's death: he kills him. The doctor who gives the patient with cancer a lethal injection has himself caused his patient's death; whereas if he merely ceases treatment, the cancer is the cause of the death.

A number of points need to be made here. The first is that it is not exactly correct to say that in passive euthanasia the doctor does nothing, for he does do one thing that is very important: he lets the patient die. "Letting someone die" is certainly different, in some respects, from other types of action—mainly in that it is a kind of action that one may perform by way of not performing certain other actions. For example, one may let a patient die by way of not giving medication, just as one may insult someone by way of not shaking his hand. But for any purpose of moral assessment, it is a type of action nonetheless. The decision to let a patient die is subject to moral appraisal in the same way that a decision to kill him would be subject to moral appraisal: it may be assessed as wise or unwise, compassionate or sadistic, right or wrong. If a doctor deliberately let a patient die who was suffering from a routinely curable illness, the doctor would certainly be to blame for what he had done, just as he would be to blame if he had needlessly killed the patient. Charges against him would then be appropriate. If so, it would be no defense at all for him to insist that he didn't "do anything." He would have done something very serious indeed, for he let his patient die.

Fixing the cause of death may be very important from a legal point of view, for it may determine whether criminal charges are brought against the doctor. But I do not think that this notion can be used to show a moral difference between active and passive euthanasia. The reason why it is considered bad to be the cause of someone's death is that death is regarded as a great evil—and so it is. However, if it has been decided that euthanasia—even passive euthanasia—is desirable in a given case, it has also been decided that in this instance death is no greater an evil than the patient's continued existence. And if this is true, the usual reason for not wanting to be the cause of someone's death simply does not apply.

Finally, doctors may think that all of this is only of academic interest—the sort of thing that philosophers may worry about but that has no practical bearing on their own work. After all, doctors must be concerned about the legal consequences of what they do, and active euthanasia is clearly forbidden by the law. But even so, doctors should also be concerned with the fact that the law is forcing upon them a moral doctrine that may be indefensible, and has a considerable effect on their practices. Of course, most doctors are not now in the position of being coerced in this matter, for they do not regard themselves as merely going along with what the law requires. Rather, in statements such as the AMA policy statement that I have quoted, they are endorsing this doctrine as a central point of medical ethics. In that statement, active euthanasia is condemned not merely as illegal but as "contrary to that for which the medical profession stands," whereas passive euthanasia is approved. However, the preceding considerations suggest that there is really no moral difference between the two, considered in themselves (there may be important moral differences in some cases in their *consequences*, but, as I pointed out, these differences may make active euthanasia, and not passive euthanasia, the morally preferable option). So, whereas doctors may have to discriminate between active and passive euthanasia to satisfy the law, they should not do any more than that. In particular, they should not give the distinction any added authority and weight by writing it into official statements of medical ethics.

Euthanasia and the Principle of Harm

A. D. Woozley

A function, some would say *the* function, of the criminal law is to proscribe conduct by which people cause harm to people. The prohibition needs to be stated in that form, "causing harm to people," rather than in the form in which it is commonly stated, "causing harm to *other* people," which confuses a factor's being common with its being essential. It is true that most of the harm which people can do to people, and which the law has an interest in their not doing, is harm to other people (e.g., murder, rape, mugging, etc.), but the law can legitimately be concerned with the harm which a person may do to himself. The issues of paternalism, for example, are not to be settled by the crude doctrine that what harm a person chooses to do to himself, as long as he thereby harms nobody else, is none of the law's business. It is, instead, a matter of assessing and weighing against each other, in each particular case or kind of case, the harm which a person will do, or risks doing, to himself if the law takes no action and the value of his being free to decide for himself without interference from the law; there is no *a priori* reason why the first of these factors, or why the second, should always outweigh the other.

The need to emphasize the range of this "person-neutrality" is well illustrated by the case of self-defence, which is popularly supposed to be a special case in which killing an assailant is legally acceptable, if that is the only way, or reasonably appears to be the only way, of preventing him from killing you. But there is nothing special about *self*-defence: if the only way A can prevent B from killing C (who may be incapable of self-defence) is by killing B, then the killing of B by A would be either excusable or justifiable exactly as it would have been had it been performed by C.

So, about an action one does to somebody (himself or another) there are two questions to ask: (a) Will it harm him? If not, there is no objection to the action on this score. (b) Will it be done with his consent? (By "consent" throughout is meant the consent which is uncoerced, understanding and rational.) If so, there is no violation of his autonomy, and no objection to the action on this score. If no harm is done to anybody, or if the harm is considered to be of less importance than the value of the agent being left free to choose for himself, we may have what is sometimes called a "victimless crime," such as gambling or prostitution, which in some jurisdictions are illegal although there is no victim, while in others they are not illegal because there is no victim.

The two questions to be asked about the action have a consequence for law, that, if there are killings (or allowings to die),[1] which are not harmful to the person concerned and which are performed with the person's consent, they ought not to be made illegal, as in fact they are. Can there be such killings? And are there any workable criteria for distinguishing genuine from non-genuine cases? The latter would be a practical question of the first importance for law, because we could not accept a straight murder (which is both harmful to the victim and almost always also performed without his consent) to be successfully disguised as a killing that was both non-harmful and consented to. The medical profession understandably has a close interest in the provision of a clear answer to this question.

---

[1] It will be shown below that the distinction which is commonly drawn, when euthanasia is under discussion, between killing and allowing to die is completely unreal, and is merely a euphemistic device to avoid facing the issue squarely.

We might be tempted to foreclose discussion by maintaining that all killing of a human being is harmful to the person killed, and therefore that no such killings should be allowed by law. But that answer will not serve, especially in the USA, for at least two reasons. First, it is inconsistent with the present state of law, which allows killings in some circumstances and prescribes it in others, e.g., killing in defense of life, in preventing escapes by persons trying to avoid arrest, in judicially pronounced capital executions, etc. That is, the view is already taken, and perhaps always has been taken, by law that, even if all killing is harmful, that can be overridden by other considerations. Secondly, the thesis that killing is harmful has a gap in it, just where the person concerned has no interest in continuing to live. Attempts made to plug the gap, e.g., in the case of suicide, are not conspicuously successful. The thesis that, even if life has no more to offer a person than pain, misery or distress, it would still be wrong for him to take his own life because he would thereby be harming his soul or jeopardizing its prospects for the afterlife is a widely held religious doctrine, and is symbolized by the old Christian refusal to bury suicides in consecrated ground. Similarly, the argument that it is not for a man to end his own life because it belongs not to him but to God, from whom he holds it in trust is an orthodox Christian argument, and long preChristian too; Plato, for example, has Socrates propound it in the *Phaedo.* Being religious arguments does not make them bad arguments, but it does make them unavailable to U. S. law, given the constitutional separation of state and church.

If we take suicide, bar the religious arguments against it, and exclude cases which although they are never *called* suicides, indeed are so (such as one person knowingly giving up his own life to save those of others), we are left with a wide range of suicides, some of which are most implausibly represented as harmful to the person concerned (whatever they may be to others, such as his family); this is reflected in the fact that fewer and fewer jurisdictions keep suicide as a crime. It is possible for a person to be in a situation where continued life would be an intolerable burden to him for a variety of reasons, incurable and painful sickness being only one—and really *be* in it; and it is possible for him comprehendingly and rationally to choose to end his life. Although courts have not uniformly acknowledged the right of a competent person in certain circumstances to decline or to terminate medical treatment, where that will lead to his death, the declaration of that right was one of the main features of the New Jersey Supreme Court's judgment in the case of Karen Quinlan.[2] The force of the declaration is not weakened by the court's irrational belief that "the ensuing death would not be homicide but rather expiration from natural causes."

If ending one's own life can be non-harmful, then ending another's life can be non-harmful, viz., in just those circumstances where ending the other's life by that other person would be non-harmful. The only difference—and it is, of course, a great difference—that bringing another person into the story makes it that the person who has to end the life (or not) is *one* person while the person who has to consent (or not) to the ending of his life is *another* person. It therefore becomes critically important that the consent really is given (not just seems to be given) and that it really is free, informed, etc.

The present state of the law is unsatisfactory because, while it has almost everywhere removed suicide from the category of crime, it has not correspondingly decriminalised at least that case of ending someone else's life where the person consented and has no reason for continuing to live. It is at this stage that lawyers are liable to remind us that law is not a matter of logic; indeed it is not, but it is hard to understand why they should be so proud of that. It would not do to pretend that the case for law reform does not present grave problems, but problems are for solving, not for keeping hidden under the rug. Fifty years ago an English judge, in summing up for the jury a case in which a father was charged with murder for having drowned his incurably ill child because he could no longer bear to see her suffering, pointed out that "It is a matter which gives food for thought when one comes to consider

---

[2]*In the Matter of Karen Quinlan*, 355 A. 2d 647, 669–70 (New Jersey, 1976).

that, had this poor child been an animal instead of a human being, so far from there being anything blameworthy in the man's action in putting an end to its suffering, he would actually have been liable to punishment if he had not done so."[3]

The problems center round the issue of consent. If we take for illustration the most common and most often cited type of case, that of incurable patients who either are minimally and only biologically alive or are suffering extreme pain, then some (of the latter) may be capable of giving consent themselves, but many (including all of the former) will not: they may be too far gone as geriatric patients, or too eaten up with pain (or drugged against it), or they may be coma patients suffering from irreversible brain damage. If the law is to be asked to recognize consent in their cases, it will have to be either consent given *by* them in the past while they were still competent, i.e., had the capacity for judgment (as in the "living will" proposals), or consent given *for* them in the present by somebody granted legal authority to do so. It is likely that, with the very exceptions of patients who both had executed a living will and now had no surviving family, the first alternative would in practice come down to the second; for it is doubtful that many physicians would be willing to act on the authority of a living will without also obtaining the agreement of the patient's next of kin or family, who would consequently have the responsibility of consenting (or not) for the patient. The Quinlan judgment, appointing her father her legal guardian for the express purpose of exercising that responsibility on her behalf, may be followed by other courts in other states, but its legal authority does not extend beyond New Jersey. We may ask how such consent differs in principle (clearly it differs in degree and extent of gravity) from that which hospitals at present require to be given for a patient to have, say, surgery, when the patient is unable to give that consent himself. Such consent is required by the hospital, in case something should go wrong and the hospital be afterwards accused of

---

[3]Glanville Williams, *The Sanctity of Life and the Criminal Law* (New York: Knopf, 1957), p. 328.

having acted without authority (which needs to be distinguished from having acted with authority but shown negligence in the action). By the vicarious consent (if the person giving it is legally recognized as having authority to do so) the hospital has the protection of law against that charge. It is also important that the hospital, by requiring consent, is implying its recognition that the patient has at least a moral right to refuse treatment, even if such refusal will result in his death.

So, the principle that, if A is incapable of giving or withholding consent, there can be a B who has the authority to give or withhold it on his behalf is already well known and accepted in law. That is how the New Jersey Supreme Court argued in its Quinlan judgment, and it was clearly right about *that* (some other features of the judgment were more dubitable, or at least unfortuantely fuzzy). Its line of argument was that, if the outcome to which consent is being given is not a harmful one (or, more strongly, is the ending of a present irreversibly harmful one), and if the consent is being given by someone with the right to consent, then the law should allow that action consented to to be performed, i.e., not make criminal the performance of it. At least, that was the argument in one section of the judgment. In another section a further condition was inserted, that the circumstances be such that the individual's right of consent be not overriden by the state's interest in the protection of life.[4] This brought the case into some relation of resemblance to the U.S. Supreme Court's 1973 decision on abortion,[5] but did nothing to improve clarity in doing so. There was a certain looseness too in the court's reasoning for appointing Karen's father her legal guardian for the express purpose of asserting her right to privacy.[6] The argument was: (1) she should not have her right of privacy (here the right to choose discontinu-

---

[4]355 A. 2d at 663–4.

[5]*Roe v. Wade.* 410 U.S. 113, 153 (1973).

[6]This right, which may be characterized as the right against "judicial intrusion into many aspects of personal decision," appears to have been canonized as a constitutional right in 1965, when the Connecticut law against contraception was struck down by the U.S. Supreme Court, *Grisworld v. Connecticut*, 381 U.S. 479 (1965).

ance of artificial life-support) destroyed by her own inability to exercise it herself; (2) the only way "to prevent destruction of the right is to permit the guardian and family ... to render their best judgment [subject to certain later qualifications] as to whether she should exercise it in these circumstances."[7] Therefore, (3) her father was to be appointed her guardian for the purpose. The implication clearly was that Mr. Quinlan was to make the decision which, in his best judgment, his daughter would have made if only she had been conscious, lucid and (with the prognosis unaltered) able to make if for herself. While, in that particular instance, the failure to distinguish between the wishes and the interest of the patient did not matter, for they would surely have been coincident, in other cases the distinction could be important. A guardian's concern is the interest, not the wishes, of his ward; and it needs to be made clear whether his authority to exercise the right of choice on the ward's behalf is to be restricted by the requirement that his choice must be the same as, to the best of his judgment, his ward's would have been, if only the ward had been capable of choosing. Being competent to make a choice is not identical with having one's wishes conform with his interest.

If patients, or those legally authorized to act as legal guardians for them, are to have the right to have life support removed, what of the physicians who are to terminate, or to give the order to terminate support? Clearly, they should not be required to terminate it, if that is contrary to their best professional and moral judgment. (Equally clearly, the patient or guardian, if the physicians refuse, should be allowed to appoint other physicians in their place; this too was provided for in the Quinlan judgment). But, if in the physicians' judgment termination would be best, and if in their judgment the person consenting to termination has authority to do so and really appreciates the alternatives between which he is choosing, then they should terminate. This is not uncommon practice in Britain (and probably, although less openly, in the

---

[7]355 A. 2d at 664.

USA too) in the case of seriously malformed babies, where the malady makes the prospect for a mental, as well as a physical, life dismal; *spina bifida* is such a condition.

As a matter of social tactics it might be prudent to begin legal reform by allowing first, in appropriate cases, the withholding or suspension of what is necessary to maintain the patient's life, and then, as a later change, to allow action, such as a lethal injection, which is sufficient to end the life. But we should recognize that it would be simply a tactical concession to social taboos, and to the pretence that there really is a difference in this area between killing and allowing to die. When addressing itself to the question of criminal liability, the Quinlan court gave the opinion that if, in the case before it, the patient were taken off the respirator "the ensuing death would not be homicide but rather expiration from existing natural causes."[8] It is hard to credit that the court really believed that. If a mother living alone with her baby dies, and if her death is undiscovered, then sooner or later the baby will die from existing natural causes, but, there will have been no homicide. If the mother does not die, but for whatever reason fails to feed her baby, then sooner or later it will die from exactly the same existing natural causes as in the first example; but now there will have been a homicide. Omissions (not putting a patient on a respirator, when he will die without it) and commissions (taking a patient off a respirator, when he will die without it) are as much putting an end to the patient's life as is giving him a lethal injection. The important moral and legal question is not how the ending of life is to be described, whether it is to be called "allowing nature to take its course" or not, but whether there was someone responsible for the ending of it, i.e., whether, if he had acted (by commission or omission) differently from what he did, the ending would have been postponed; and, if so, whether he is to be held morally and/or legally culpable.

Fortunately, the court recovered itself at the next step with its opinion that, even if the death resulting from ter-

---

[8]355 A. 2d at 670.

mination of treatment "were to be regarded as homicide it would not be unlawful." The argument was simple: (1) the state's power to punish the taking of human life does not reach to individuals terminating their medical treatment by exercising their right of privacy; and (2) that constitutional protection extends to third parties whose action is necessary for the exercise of the right. Thus, where the individual would not himself be liable to criminal prosecution for an act pursuant to his right of privacy, another party whose cooperation was necessary for the achievement of the end would not be liable to the same criminal prosecution nor to the charge of being accessory to a crime.[9]

If that step taken by the court is followed by other courts, and by official prosecutors in deciding whether to bring criminal charges, a major change will have been achieved. Legislators are slow to make reforms on issues where reforms can lose votes but will not gain votes: the lingering force of taboo is too strong for them. As a practical matter, reform by courts is less difficult to achieve. And the declaration of the Quinlan court that no party participating in the termination of treatment for the patient, leading to her death, "whether guardian, physician, hospital or others" would carry "any civil or criminal liability therefore" must have made many doctors feel that their position was much clearer. It is not quite as clear a declaration as it might have been. First, while the court emphasised the *right* of the patient in such a case to have treatment discontinued, it did not impose on any party the correlative duty of discontinuing treatment, or of seeing to it that treatment was discontinued; what it did was, provided that certain other duties were discharged, to give *permission* for treatment to be withdrawn. Secondly, one of the two conditions which had to be fulfilled before treatment could be withdrawn without incurring civil or criminal liability was somewhat odd. The first condition was that, with the concurrence of the guardian, the attending physicians should conclude that there was no reasonable possibility of the patient's "ever emerging from her

---

9355A. 2d at 670.

present comatose condition to a cognitive, sapient state"
(a *factual* conclusion) and that "the life-support apparatus
. . . should be discontinued" (an *ethical* conclusion). If that
condition was met, i.e., if the physicians arrived at those
two conclusions, then they were required to consult with
the hospital's Ethics Committee "or other like body." And
the second condition to be fulfilled was that that body
should agree that there was no reasonable possibility of
the patient's "ever emerging from her present comatose
condition to a cognitive, sapient state." If that condition
too were met, then "the present life-support system may
be withdrawn."[10] Why a hospital's *Ethics* Committee
should be required to confirm their physicians' technical
and professional conclusion on a question of fact or of professional judgment is puzzling. And why a hospital's
Ethics Committee should not be required to confirm their
physicians' conclusion on a matter of ethical judgment is
still more puzzling. There is plenty of clearing up for later
opinions and judgments to do. But at least a start has been
made in the direction of legal recognition not merely that
there are circumstances in which an individual may
legitimately end his life, but also, and of more practical
significance, that in such circumstances he may legitimately have others end it for him, if he cannot do it himself.

Suggestions for Further Reading (in paperback):

Tom L. Beauchamp and Seymour Perlin, eds., *Ethical Issues in Death
    and Dying* (Englewood Cliffs, NJ: Prentice-Hall, 1978).

A. Alvarez, *The Savage God: A Study of Suicide* (New York: Bantam
    Books, 1971).

Marvin Kohl, ed., *Beneficent Euthanasia* (Buffalo, NY: Prometheus
    Books, 1975).

A. B. Downing, ed., *Euthanasia and the Right to Death* (Los Angeles:
    Nash, 1969).

---

[10]355 A. 2d at 671.